Slavery on Trial

New Perspectives on the History of the South

UNIVERSITY PRESS OF FLORIDA

Florida A&M University, Tallahassee
Florida Atlantic University, Boca Raton
Florida Gulf Coast University, Ft. Myers
Florida International University, Miami
Florida State University, Tallahassee
New College of Florida, Sarasota
University of Central Florida, Orlando
University of Florida, Gainesville
University of North Florida, Jacksonville
University of South Florida, Tampa
University of West Florida, Pensacola

Slavery on Trial

Race, Class, and Criminal Justice
in Antebellum Richmond, Virginia

James M. Campbell

University Press of Florida
Gainesville/Tallahassee/Tampa/Boca Raton
Pensacola/Orlando/Miami/Jacksonville/Ft. Myers/Sarasota

Copyright 2007 by James M. Campbell
Printed in the United States of America on acid-free paper
All rights reserved

First cloth printing, 2007
First paperback printing, 2011

Library of Congress Cataloging-in-Publication Data
Campbell, James M.
Slavery on trial : race, class, and criminal justice in Antebellum
Richmond, Virginia / James M. Campbell
p. cm. — (New perspectives on the history of the South)
Includes bibliographical references and index.
ISBN: 978-0-8130-3091-3 (alk. paper)
ISBN: 978-0-8130-3566-6 (pbk.)
1. Discrimination in criminal justice administration—Virginia—
Richmond—History—19th century. 2. Slaves—Virginia—Richmond—
Social conditions—19th century. 3. Freedmen—Virginia—Richmond—
Social conditions—19th century. 4. Richmond (Va.)—Race
relations—History—19th century. I. Title.
HV9955.V8C36 2007
364.9755'45109034—dc22   2007013477

The University Press of Florida is the scholarly publishing agency
for the State University System of Florida, comprising Florida
A&M University, Florida Atlantic University, Florida Gulf Coast
University, Florida International University, Florida State University,
New College of Florida, University of Central Florida, University of
Florida, University of North Florida, University of South Florida, and
University of West Florida.

University Press of Florida
15 Northwest 15th Street
Gainesville, FL 32611-2079
http://www.upf.com

For Mum and Dad

Contents

List of Illustrations ix

Preface xi

Introduction 1

1. Abandoned to "causes of corruption": Slave Life and Policing in the City 10

2. "An evil which demands a speedy remedy": White Criminality in an Urban Slave Society 41

3. "The victim of prejudice and hasty consideration": Slave Trials, Clemency, and Punishment 76

4. "With these *poor* rogues their *judge* had never dined": Honor, Law, and the Trial and Punishment of White Criminals 108

5. The "stigma, of the deepest degradation, was fixed upon the whole race": Free African Americans and the Criminal Justice System 146

Epilogue 186

Appendixes 193

Notes 199

Bibliography 237

Index 255

Illustrations

Figures

1. Map of central Richmond, ca. 1854   13
2. Richmond City Hall   24
3. Mayor Joseph Mayo   28
4. Governor John Buchanan Floyd   44
5. Richmond Almshouse   74
6. Front view of Virginia State Capitol   78
7. Governor's Mansion   105
8. Virginia State Penitentiary   117
9. Governor John Letcher   129
10. Governor Henry A. Wise   131
11. Governor William Smith   147
12. First African Church   179
13. Group of Freedmen by canal   190

Tables

1.1. Richmond slaves charged with felonies, 1830–1860   21
1.2. Richmond Mayor's Court cases: Female defendants   22
1.3. Arrests in Richmond, 1855–1860   23
1.4. Richmond Mayor's Court cases: Stealing   26
1.5. Richmond Mayor's Court cases: Assault   27
1.6. Richmond Mayor's Court cases per capita, 1838–1860   29
2.1. Prosecutions of white defendants for property crimes and violent crimes in Richmond Hustings Court, 1830–1860   45
2.2. Richmond Mayor's Court cases: White defendants   56
2.3. Female victims in white-on-white assault cases: Richmond Mayor's Court   60
3.1. Slave felony prosecutions in southern criminal courts   80
3.2. Slave defendants in Richmond Oyer and Terminer Courts, 1830–1860   84

3.3. Change over time in slave conviction rates for capital and noncapital felonies   87
4.1. Richmond Hustings Court felony examinations, 1830–1860   113
4.2. White Richmond Hustings Court defendants by gender (misdemeanors and felonies), 1830–1860   119
4.3. Change over time in Richmond Hustings Court conviction rates, misdemeanor trials   127
5.1. Free black defendants in Richmond Oyer and Terminer Courts, 1833–1860   151

Preface

In antebellum Virginia, more so than anywhere else in the United States, the criminal law was fundamentally bifurcated by race. While white defendants were treated in accordance with established rules of Anglo-American common law due process, African Americans engaged with a judicial system based on force and violence that paid scant regard to abstract notions of justice. Black men and women in Virginia were subject to more wide-ranging and severe state laws and city ordinances than those that governed whites; as defendants they were denied procedural rights that were commonplace for whites, and as convicts they were sentenced to punishments that diverged widely in form from those imposed on whites. When convicted of the most serious crimes, whites commonly suffered penitentiary imprisonment and rarely faced the death penalty. By contrast, African Americans were typically punished at the whipping post, on the auction block, and on the gallows. Invariably, slaves fared worse in Virginia's courts of justice than free black Americans, but during the antebellum period free blacks were increasingly made subject to the same modes of trial and similar punishments as slaves, and it was always race, rather than free or slave status, that was the primary determinant of an individual's legal experiences.[1]

The aim of the racial divide in Virginia criminal law was to keep separate and distinct the legal experiences of blacks and whites in order to enhance control of the African American population, strengthen the racial ideology of white supremacy, and perpetuate the slaveholders' rule. However, statute laws never operated in practice entirely as the elite white men who conceived and enacted them expected. Criminal laws that discriminated against the enslaved and free African Americans often had unintended outcomes that, at the local level, affected all aspects of slavery and race relations in complex and often contradictory ways that could compromise slave discipline and white racial ideals as often as they served their intended purposes. This was evident not only in the trial and punishment of African Americans but also in cases involving white defendants, and it was a profound weakness of the slaveholders' legal system that in regulating criminal activity the law was constrained by the unique dynamics of social relations between classes of whites in the context of a racially based slave society.

This book is about the way in which Virginia's race-based criminal justice system functioned in a single jurisdiction, the city of Richmond, in the late antebellum period. Based on analysis of more than seven thousand criminal cases that came to the attention of the city authorities between 1830 and 1860, *Slavery on Trial* examines how race infused every aspect of the judicial system in both theory and practice and delineates the implications for urban slave society that criminal trials and punishments had outside of the courtroom and prison cell and away from the whipping post and the gallows. More than simply telling the story of Richmond's antebellum criminal justice system, *Slavery on Trial* is a cultural, political, and social history of the city as viewed through the documentary record of its police, courts, and penal institutions. As an industrial city in which slavery thrived, Richmond was a unique location in the Old South, and the purpose of this book is to trace how the distinctive features of an urban-industrial slave society both impacted, and at the same time were shaped by, the manner in which the law was enforced, subverted, and resisted by both blacks and whites. More specifically, the book demonstrates that tensions and inconsistencies in Virginia's race-based judicial system were manifested in a particularly stark and politically significant manner in Richmond because of the city's economic, social, demographic, and cultural peculiarities.

As a Brit researching U.S. history, I've been dependent at all stages of my research for *Slavery on Trial* on the goodwill and generosity of American hosts and archivists. Most of the research for this book was conducted at the Library of Virginia, where Gregg Kimball, Chris Kolbe, Pat Watkinson, Minor Weisiger, and many others provided invaluable advice and the benefit of their great knowledge of the library's collections. I am also indebted to the Virginia Historical Society, the Valentine Richmond History Center, the Alderman Library at the University of Virginia, and the Huntington Library in San Marino, California. Staff at all of these locations were always accommodating and made my research a pleasure.

Several organizations have provided financial support for this book. The Arts and Humanities Research Board (now the AHRC) funded a nine-month research trip in Virginia. I also received a travel scholarship from the British Academy to present a paper based on aspects of chapter 2 at a conference in Edgefield, South Carolina, in 2005. The Centre for European and International Studies Research at the University of Portsmouth has also generously funded several trips to the British Newspaper Library, as well as a reduced teaching load in the spring of 2006 that helped me finally to bring the manuscript to completion. In altered form, parts of *Slavery on Trial* have previously been published as: "'The victim of prejudice and hasty consideration': Urban Slavery Society and the Slave Trial System in Richmond, Virginia, 1830–1861," *Slavery and Abolition*, 26, no. 1 (2005): 71–92; "A Murderer of 'a somewhat dark complexion'?: Criminal Justice and Constructions of Race in Antebellum Virginia," *American Nineteenth Century History*, 5, no. 3 (2004): 28–49; "African American Victims and Responses to Crime in Antebellum Richmond, Virginia," *U.S. Studies Online* 3 (Spring 2003). I thank the editors of all three publications for permission to reproduce sections of each article here.

I first researched and wrote about antebellum crime and punishment while a student at the University of Warwick. I am grateful for the advice and help I received at that time from Tim Lockley and Gad Heuman, whose special subject first interested me in the topic of race and slavery in the Americas. More recently, at the University of Nottingham John Ashworth provided invaluable guidance on all aspects of the research and writing process, as well as posing challenging questions that helped me to formulate the central arguments of the book. Martin Crawford and Richard King also provided insightful suggestions on the manuscript, while several friends, including Celeste-Marie Bernier, Sasha Handley, Christer Petley, and Monica Riera took the time to read and comment on early versions of various chapters. Finally, Gregg Kimball and a second, anonymous reader offered feedback that improved the manuscript beyond all recognition, while the staff at the University Press of Florida have made the publication process as easy as I could have hoped. Above all, Kate Dossett has read countless drafts, made numerous suggestions, and always been the most extraordinary friend from the start to the end of the project.

I consider myself very lucky that in writing *Slavery on Trial* I've been led to places where Zoë Hilton's encouragement, cajoling, and love have been able both to temper my obsession with the project and make it worth finishing.

This book is dedicated to my Mum and Dad, whose endless support and unwavering confidence in me always has and always will mean the world.

Introduction

Antebellum Richmond was the political capital of Virginia and by the 1850s the leading industrial city in the Upper South. Between the Revolution and the Civil War, Richmond grew from a small trading post that was home to just six hundred people, into a thriving center of iron, flour, and tobacco production with a population of nearly forty thousand. The city's ready access via the James River and Kanawha Canal to the agricultural and mineral wealth of the interior; hundreds of stores, dwellings, and manufactories rising in every direction; and trading connections with all the principal markets in the United States, Europe, and Latin America led the editor of an 1845 business directory to declare confidently that there was nothing to prevent Richmond becoming "the successful rival of the largest emporiums in this country."[1] Richmond never lived up to this hype, and in comparison to northern cities its economic potential was far from extraordinary. Even so, within the overwhelmingly agricultural landscape of the slave states, Richmond's urban-industrial society stood out as a stark anomaly.[2]

A diverse population provided the labor force that undergirded Richmond's antebellum expansion. An influx of white workers from the rural South, the free labor states of the North, as well as many parts of western Europe, notably Ireland and Germany, caused Richmond's white population to increase more than threefold between 1830 and 1860 to 23,635. Richmond's black population also increased substantially throughout the late antebellum decades, albeit not at a rate to keep pace with the growth of the white community. Large numbers of slaves and free African Americans were employed in tobacco factories, ironworks, and flour mills, as well as in domestic service, such that on the eve of the Civil War nearly 12,000 slaves and over 2,500 free African Americans constituted almost 40 percent of all Richmonders.[3] In this regard, Richmond was distinct from other urban centers in the South. In cities such as Baltimore, New Orleans, St. Louis, and Charleston, where the economy was based on commerce rather than industry, the slave population declined precipitously during the mid-nineteenth century, and slave ownership was of decreasing social and cultural significance.

Even as Richmond's industrial-slave society flourished in the 1850s, economic success was accompanied by social, cultural, and political changes that fueled tensions between disparate groups of residents. Richmond was not unique in this respect. Social dislocation, cultural diversity, and the breakdown of traditional hierarchical and paternalistic structures of authority that ordered rural society were features of the market revolution and urbanization across nineteenth-century America.[4] However, in the slave South these developments assumed a distinctive character and significance. Most notably, urban slavery was dependent on a variety of slave-hiring practices and independent living arrangements that profoundly altered the relationship between slaveholder and slave, introducing a distance and anonymity that was less common in rural communities. This contrast between city and countryside was particularly notable in a state such as Virginia. In contrast to the vast plantations of the Deep South, Virginian slaveholdings were typically small, and relatively few slaves lived and worked in large groups. On the contrary, slaves in rural Virginia often worked on farms alongside their owners and overseers, while slaveholder absenteeism was less widespread than on the plantations of the Cotton Belt.[5]

It was not only bonds between masters and slaves that assumed distinctive characteristics in southern cities; relations between classes of whites also evolved in different ways from rural regions. White poverty and class stratification were not unique to the urban context, but impoverished white men and women assumed greater political prominence in Richmond on account of their large numbers and visibility in the public sphere, as well as the breakdown of informal community and kinship networks that in less diversified societies bound whites together and fostered cross-class support for the slave regime.[6] Even in Richmond, white supremacy and solidarity never threatened to collapse beneath the weight of class pressures. Most of the city's middling-sort, who comprised tradesmen, merchants, and manufacturers, associated with the ideals of the southern planter class whether or not they themselves owned slaves. However, urban social and economic conditions meant that slaveholders could not take for granted that the city's emergent bourgeoisie, still less the white poor, would continue to support slavery unquestioningly.[7]

Still less could Richmond slaveholders depend on free African Americans to endorse the peculiar institution. Freedom and blackness were deemed by whites to be a combustible and undesirable combination throughout Virginia, but especially so in cities like Richmond where the most extensive, autonomous, and well-resourced free African American communities developed.

As traditional ties of kinship and hierarchy in Richmond were challenged by urban-industrial growth, institutional judicial mechanisms assumed a central role in the regulation of crime and the maintenance of social order.[8] During the antebellum years, Richmond expanded its police provisions, strengthened its municipal ordinances, and established new criminal courts in order to cope with a marked increase in the number of criminal prosecutions. In all societies, most crime goes unrecorded, and the increase in prosecutions in Richmond might have resulted from more efficient policing or changing attitudes toward lawlessness rather than from a real rise in the number of crimes committed.[9] Certainly it was, at least in part, a response to growing white fear of criminal activity, and especially African American criminality, the regulation of which was made more imperative than ever before by the emergence of immediate abolitionism and the heightened sectional tensions of the 1850s.

The criminal law in Virginia and other slave societies had always reflected the overwhelming white concern with slave crime. Based on a clear race divide that discriminated against enslaved and free African Americans, and written and administered by slaveholders and other white men sympathetic to elite interests, Virginia's statute laws and judicial processes served two distinct purposes. They were intended in the first place to facilitate strict regulation of the slave population, but, of equal importance, they also aimed to support notions of white egalitarianism and herrenvolk democracy.[10] In Richmond, as elsewhere in Virginia, therefore, the judicial system was not only central to crime control; it also had a profound social, cultural, and political significance through its impact on race, class, and gender relations in the city. Black defendants were afforded only limited due process rights, and this made the law an efficient and powerful tool that supported slaveholders' domination of the slave population. At the same time, the superior legal rights that all white men and women were afforded irrespective of their wealth or social status served, in David Roediger's term, as one of the "wages of whiteness" that compensated "for alienating and exploitative class relationships" within white communities brought about by early nineteenth-century urban-industrial development.[11] This was undoubtedly to the great benefit of Richmond slaveholders, for the viability of urban slavery depended not only on restricting slaves' opportunities for resistance but also on securing the support of nonslaveholding whites for the peculiar institution of slavery through the continual reaffirmation in everyday practice of the primacy of the race divide in southern society.

When Richmonders participated in criminal cases as defendants, victims, witnesses, judges, jurors, and attorneys, they scarcely considered the broader implications for slave society of their actions in court. Instead, they acted on the basis of their personal experiences and ideals and in pursuit of private ends that usually were limited in scope, relating only to the particular circumstances and outcome of a specific case. Among white Richmonders, these private ends were sometimes consistent with the more broadly based ambitions of the city's slaveholders, but this was rarely as a result of overt calculation. Indeed, it is a central argument of this book that even if slaveholders had been fully sentient of their interests as a class, they would have struggled to reconcile those interests consistently with the day-to-day activities of Richmond's criminal courts. As is demonstrated in the chapters that follow, this was due to the way in which the law worked, the agency of participants other than slaveholders in the judicial process, the characteristics of the urban environment, and the sectional tensions of the antebellum era.

Scholarship on criminal justice in the pre–Civil War South has given limited consideration to the significance for southern society of events in the region's courtrooms. In particular, historians have failed to examine the workings of justices of the peace and trial courts at the local level and the relationship between judicial processes and social and economic change in the slave states.[12] Historians seeking to understand the relationship between criminal justice and mid-nineteenth-century southern society have typically depicted the region as all but bereft of law and more dominated by lynch mobs and duelers than by judges and jurors. In an influential article published in 1940, Charles Sydnor argued that

> ruralness, slavery, the plantation system, and the existence of a strong unwritten code operated in the plantation areas of the Old South to restrict the power of ordinary law and to enlarge the area of life in which man acts without reference to legal guidance.[13]

Later historians, including Eugene Genovese, Bertram Wyatt-Brown, and Michael Hindus broadly accepted Sydnor's interpretation. All claimed that the rule of law was marginalized in the Old South; that crime was typically dealt with informally according to notions of honor and mastery; and that even within the courtroom there was widespread disregard for legal formalism. In sum, southern "justice" was based more on community consensus than abstract notions of law except on rare occasions when adherence to due process was of benefit to the slaveholding class.[14]

However, to argue that events in southern courtrooms were significant only for their scarcity or for their failure to abide by established rules of due process is to misinterpret the relationship between law and society and underestimate the importance of criminal justice in the slave states. The law may have been marginalized in certain southern contexts, yet local studies by Edward Ayers and Christopher Waldrep have shown that the judicial system could act as an autonomous force in southern society, particularly in heavily populated areas.[15] Moreover, while slaveholders may have had considerable influence over the role that formal crime-control mechanisms played in southern society—and they certainly took a leading role in determining what was written on southern statute books—they never controlled completely what would transpire when the law was applied in practice. Nor could slaveholders dictate what would be the wider ramifications of events in the courtroom. As critical legal scholars have demonstrated, "the law is not simply an armed receptacle for values and priorities determined elsewhere; it is part of a complex social totality in which it constitutes as well as is constituted, shapes as well as is shaped."[16] This was undoubtedly the case in the antebellum South. In Laura F. Edwards's depiction, southern law was "an unwieldy, imperfect tool," which "proved difficult for any single group to control completely." Rather than perceiving law as a hegemonic force that supported the slaveholders' rule unproblematically, Edwards has argued that the law's "logic and universalizing principles . . . could alter and impede as well as facilitate the interests of those who tried to use it."[17]

Examining the intersection of law, race, class, and gender at the local level, other scholars have suggested that events in southern courtrooms could subvert the social and racial order. Work by Sharon Block, Stephanie Cole, Walter Johnson, Christopher Waldrep, and Ariela Gross has demonstrated that slaveholders could not always control legal processes, and that subordinate individuals including slaves, free African Americans, and white women could at times exercise agency in legal arenas in an attempt to shape judicial outcomes to their own ends.[18]

Building on this scholarship, *Slavery on Trial* reveals the complexity and significance of judicial processes in an urban slave context. In Richmond, social and economic conditions dictated that law could not readily be set to one side, as it might be in plantation regions. On the contrary, an extensive judicial system was imperative to the functioning and profitability of slavery in the city. By the 1850s, thousands of arrests were made in the city every year, and hundreds of defendants, black and white, were put on trial. In the overwhelming majority of these cases, subordinate groups were unable to exercise legal agency in ways that directly and immediately were to their benefit as individuals. Nevertheless, the actions in Richmond courtrooms of slaves, free African Americans, and poor whites had broader significance for they highlighted inconsistencies and complexities in the relationship between the law and slave society and between the law in theory and practice, which could compromise both crime control and the ideological basis of the slaveholders' rule. This is not to deny that the law invariably supported the slaveholders' interests or to suggest that slavery was unworkable in an industrial city. However, analysis of crime and punishment in antebellum Richmond does reveal very clearly that the city's social order was riven with class and race tensions and that slaveholders were engaged in a constant struggle to make the law work for them at the local level.

The way in which the criminal justice system functioned in Richmond never threatened to destroy slavery, but at times it could reveal its weaknesses and could threaten, at least momentarily, the slaveholders' dominance. At the very least, judicial processes often had consequences that were unintended by any of the parties that shaped events in the courtroom. Though southern law was constructed and administered in the explicit interests of the slaveholding class, in practice criminal cases were shaped by and impacted slavery and the racial order in ways that lawmakers could neither predict, nor control, nor always even recognize. This was true as often in cases involving white defendants, as when slaves and free blacks stood accused of criminal acts. It is in this sense that whenever Richmond's criminal courts were in session, it was not only individual defendants but also urban slave society itself that was on trial.

Slavery on Trial is structured thematically around the interactions of slaves, whites, and free African Americans with Richmond's criminal courts. Chapter 1 establishes the significance of criminal justice in regulating routine aspects of urban slave conduct that in rural areas were commonly the preserve of individual slaveholders. Responsibility for policing slave conduct fell on the municipal government, and ordinances were passed to control every aspect of slaves' daily activities. Particularly in the 1850s, under the direction of Mayor Joseph Mayo, these ordinances were strictly enforced. Nonetheless, there were inherent problems with the reliance on judicial apparatus to police everyday slave conduct. Slaveholders often disagreed with the mayor's treatment of their slaves, especially when his decisions deprived them of their property's labor. Events in the courtroom could also demonstrate to the slaves themselves a degree of conflict within the ruling class. Furthermore, routine reliance on municipal justice to police slaves' day-to-day conduct was at odds with proslavery claims for the positive good that derived from the personal relationship between master and slave.

In the antebellum period, the policing of slaves in Richmond was entangled with the regulation of white society and, in particular, the burgeoning poor white population. Chapter 2 examines the growing regulation of white petty crime and public order offenses in Richmond during the antebellum era and considers the tensions in white society that judicial processes revealed and aggravated. Although integral to the maintenance of social order, reliance on institutionalized law enforcement to police urban white society could exacerbate divisions within the white community along lines of class and ethnicity. Not only did the police and lower criminal courts tend to collapse the distinction between crime and poverty by imprisoning drunkards and paupers along with petty criminals in the city jail, but a litigious culture developed among the Richmond poor, who regularly turned to the mayor's court for protection from crime and in search of order in their daily lives. By the 1850s, the very act of reporting a petty offense, such as an insult or threatened violence, had become in itself an indication of lower-class status that distinguished, in particular, poor white women from their slaveholding sisters. Furthermore, white social dislocation had become so extensive in Richmond that the city council established a chain gang on which white paupers labored alongside free African Americans and convicted criminals. There could be little clearer evidence of how the intersection of class and race in matters of crime and punishment could compromise notions of white supremacy than the sight of black and white men shackled together and performing menial labor on the public streets.

Chapters 3 and 4 examine the contrasting systems of trial and punishment for enslaved and white defendants in Richmond. Chapter 3 looks at the summary courts of oyer and terminer in which slaves charged with felonies were examined, judged, and sentenced by a panel of magistrates and without a jury. With no requirement to abide by common-law standards of due process, oyer and terminer judgments were highly responsive to the slaveholders' interests as property holders. This was significant given the central role of judicial mechanisms in maintaining slave discipline in the city, yet even slave trials sometimes had resolutions that highlighted divisions among classes of whites over slavery. The lack of due process concerned some contemporaries, notably attorneys, and by the late 1850s the punishment of slave felons provoked growing controversy among competing white interest groups.

While statute law limited procedural regulations in slave trials, chapter 4 argues that, even in cases involving white defendants, the criminal trial process was shaped by diverse extralegal factors including the type of crime allegedly committed, and the race, class, and gender of the defendant and victim. Judicial discretion enabled some defendants to escape conviction contrary to the evidence, for example when the accused was a well-known local figure, was charged with a violent crime committed in defense of honor, or was a woman, in which case an acquittal was consistent with southern gender conventions of female purity and passivity. However, most white defendants were poor males who were often transient members of the community and who were more commonly accused of crimes against property than against person. These factors discouraged judicial discretion in favor of the accused, yet justices could not violate common-law due process and rules of evidence to secure convictions in these cases, for to do so would compromise the ideology of white supremacy that helped bind the interests of even the poorest whites to the slave regime.

The division between the legal rights of whites and the nonrights of African Americans was the basis of southern slavery, yet in the realm of the criminal law in practice it had anomalous implications. In Richmond, the law prohibiting black testimony against white defendants hindered attempts to control crimes committed by whites against and in association with slaves, notably violent slave abuse, receiving stolen goods, and aiding slaves to escape. This prompted calls to permit black testimony against whites in certain circumstances, but this was politically infeasible. Vigilantism provided an alternative means of policing interracial conduct in many parts of the South, but in Richmond lynch law was often attacked as antithetical to urban business interests and on the grounds that it provided fuel for northern antislavery sentiment.

The final chapter looks at the relationship between free African Americans and the criminal law in Richmond. Throughout the antebellum period, Virginia's free black laws were revised in ways that made the legal status of free African Americans increasingly similar to that of slaves. By reducing the influence of free status in the trial and punishment of free blacks, Virginia's justice system reaffirmed the primacy of the racial divide in southern society. Even so, free African Americans continued to subvert the equation of race and status that infused the criminal code. Although many free African Americans across the South fled to free labor states in the North rather than submit to the South's draconian penal laws, in Richmond many others challenged legislative attempts to extend the ideal of slave passivity and powerlessness before the law to the free black population. Free black women appeared in court regularly as complainants and occasionally obtained favorable verdicts, although only rarely against whites. Others decided instead to report crimes to the African Baptist church courts, where they encountered very different notions of justice that were invariably more favorable to their interests.

Structural inconsistencies deriving from the necessarily incomplete racial division of the criminal law also undermined judicial efforts to regulate free African American crime. From the 1830s, free African Americans charged with felonies were tried in the same oyer and terminer courts as slaves, except when accused of offenses that carried the death penalty. This made the conviction and punishment of free black felons more efficient, yet it also highlighted lawmakers' lack of faith in the verdicts of oyer and terminer courts upon which they were unwilling to base the execution of a free African American. Furthermore, the growth of an interracial, diverse, and transient lower-class population in Richmond made determining racial categories in the courtroom increasingly problematic. Defendants, witnesses, and victims challenged the legal definitions of their racial status, sometimes initiating complex legal arguments that enabled the accused to evade conviction, and that in one exceptional case resulted in persons previously classified by the courts as free blacks being redefined as white. As the courts struggled to determine who was black and who was white, their ability to uphold a criminal law that was increasingly based on a racial divide was severely compromised.

The stereotype of a lawless Old South where crime was controlled by informal mechanisms ranging from lynch mobs to slave patrols does not fit antebellum Richmond. The criminal justice system was an integral and inescapable part of everyday life, and although extralegal factors influenced every stage of the prosecution process, this did not make the police and the courts an unproblematic extension of the slaveholders' authority. Irrespective of the extent to which events in Virginia's courtrooms were conducted in accordance with legal due process and rules of evidence, and notwithstanding whether the defendant was black or white, slave or free, criminal trials embodied contests over understandings of race, slavery, crime, and justice. These contests derived from contradictions at the heart of Virginia's race-based criminal law, which required courts at the local level to reconcile aims that often were mutually exclusive: controlling crime, supporting white supremacy, and protecting the investment of individual slaveholders in human property. In a complex, urban social milieu such as existed in Richmond, these diverse aims could not always be pursued through the judicial system in ways that were unambiguously advantageous to the slaveholding class.

1

Abandoned to "causes of corruption"

Slave Life and Policing in the City

On the morning of July 19, 1852, the citizens of Richmond awoke to news of a vicious and frenzied attack on the esteemed and respectable merchant Joseph P. Winston and his young family.[1] A large crowd soon gathered at the site of the crime, the Winston family home at the northern extremity of Seventh Street close to the city spring. A gruesome scene awaited police captain Burwell Jinkins, his officers, and the members of the coroner's jury who, in the following hours, entered the house and ascended the flight of stairs to the master bedroom. There they found the bodies of Joseph Winston, his wife, Virginia, and their infant child lying motionless in their beds, "weltering in their blood and butchered in the most horrible manner."[2] Joseph and Virginia had both been repeatedly stabbed about the head and face with a blunt instrument, and the child, Virginia Bell Winston, "seemed to have been smothered, or choked to death or dashed against the wall—the throat and breast exhibiting severe bruising."[3] Joseph Winston recovered from his injuries, but it would be several days before he was deemed capable of receiving the news that his wife and daughter were dead.

Within hours of the killings, police had arrested six slaves belonging to Joseph Winston. The prisoners included Jane Williams and her husband, John, and when a blood stained hatchet was found in the couples' bedroom they became the prime suspects in the investigation. Two days later, the coroner's jury formally concluded "that Mrs. V B Winston and daughter came to their death from blows inflicted by John and Jane Williams."[4] Subsequently, the two accused were brought before the mayor and remanded to jail to await a full examination as soon as Joseph Winston was sufficiently recovered from his injuries to testify in court. The mayor's office was even more crowded with spectators than usual for this brief appearance of the already notorious slaves. One week later, after initially denying all charges against her, Jane Williams confessed to Reverend Robert Ryland, the white pastor of Richmond's First African Baptist Church, that she had committed the murders. Jane also maintained that, although her husband had been aware of her felonious intentions, she had acted alone and that John Williams had taken no part in the commission of the crimes.[5]

Judicial authorities and the Richmond press alike were dismissive of Jane Williams's claim that she was solely responsible for the murders. Antebellum gender conventions of female innocence and passivity could apply to slaves as well as white women, and the *Richmond Daily Dispatch* claimed that, "it will not be credited, that the whole act, and the pillaging of the house, was the work of one woman."[6] Though there was little overt evidence to cast suspicion upon John Williams, circumstantial details emerged as the investigation proceeded that supported white suspicions that John was somehow implicated in the killings. Anna, one of the Winston's domestic slaves, claimed that John had never liked Mr. Winston because he had threatened to whip him. More significantly, the tobacco merchant John Enders testified to the coroner's jury that "his father sold John Williams some years since, because of threatening to kill a Mr. Rock."[7] Letters found in his bedroom suggested that John might also have had a more politicized motive to commit murder than simple dissatisfaction with the treatment he received from Joseph Winston. In a letter addressed to Zacharia Miller in Liberia, care of Rev. Mr. Roberts, and dated "Richmond, July 3d," John expressed his intention to "use every *prudent* exertion to see you all again." James Lyons, the prosecuting attorney in John Williams's murder trial, explained that the letters illustrated "the determination of John to transfer himself to Liberia, there to live with some of his friends."[8]

Jane Williams appeared before a court of oyer and terminer on August 9, 1852. She formally entered a plea of guilty to the murder of Virginia Winston and was sentenced to death. One month later, some days after his wife's execution, John Williams was also brought before the court, tried, and convicted of murder. Within weeks, John, too, was dead. He was hanged by the neck, like his wife, in front of an "immense multitude, comprising upwards of six thousand persons of all sexes, colors, and ages."[9]

The execution of slaves in antebellum Richmond was rare; Jane and John Williams were two of only five slaves hanged in the city between 1830 and 1860. However, their experiences of urban slavery were far from uncommon. Slaves in the city had opportunities to move about independently, work for a variety of owners, learn to read and write, sustain transatlantic acquaintances, worship as part of an all-black congregation, and escape to freedom via road, rail, and sea. Some of these activities were carried out clandestinely, and others had the explicit consent of the slaveholding class, but all were facilitated by the expansion of Richmond's industrial economy and the distinctive forms of urban social relations that it encouraged. Foremost among these developments were the labor demands of city manufacturers, the distant relationships that routinely and necessarily evolved in the city between slaveholders and their slaves, and the growth of a strong and multifaceted black community.[10]

Slaveholders, hirers, and other white men and women routinely punished slaves who took advantage of the opportunities for resistance that the city environment provided. Whippings could be as bloody and sadistic in the city as anywhere else in the slave states, and the threat of being sold thousands of miles away from the city to a new life in the Deep South in consequence of recalcitrant conduct hung over urban slaves as much as it did those who lived on farms and plantations. However, the frequency with which Richmond slaves lived and worked beyond their owners' control meant that, unlike in rural parts of the South, informal mechanisms of surveillance and punishment provided inadequate regulation of slave resistance and crime. Consequently, slaveholders in Richmond depended to a far greater extent than their counterparts elsewhere in the South on institutional mechanisms of slave control. Not only to police serious slave criminality but also to regulate everyday forms of slave conduct and petty offenses such as drunkenness, gambling, theft, fighting, and assault, Richmond's city council appointed police officers and night watchmen and enacted black codes that limited slaves' freedom of movement and association in the city. These codes, along with state criminal laws, were enforced by the mayor of Richmond, who examined slaves at his daily court session and passed sentence on all he judged guilty, with the exception of those charged with felonies, whom he instead remanded for a further examination. Jane and John Williams fell into this latter category of slave defendants, and therefore, while their experiences of city slave life were highly representative, their dealings with the justice system were less so. Richmond slaves were most often arrested for minor misdemeanors rather than sensational murders, and they commonly engaged with the criminal law not in trial courtrooms or on the gallows but rather in encounters with judicial officers on the streets, in the city jail and watch houses, and within the walls of city hall, where the mayor's court convened.[11]

On a day-to-day basis, the slave experience of municipal justice in Richmond was characterized by high rates of arrest, summary convictions in the mayor's court, and violent punishments inflicted at the public whipping post. The system functioned explicitly to protect the interests of the slaveholding class, and was as unconcerned with the administration of justice as

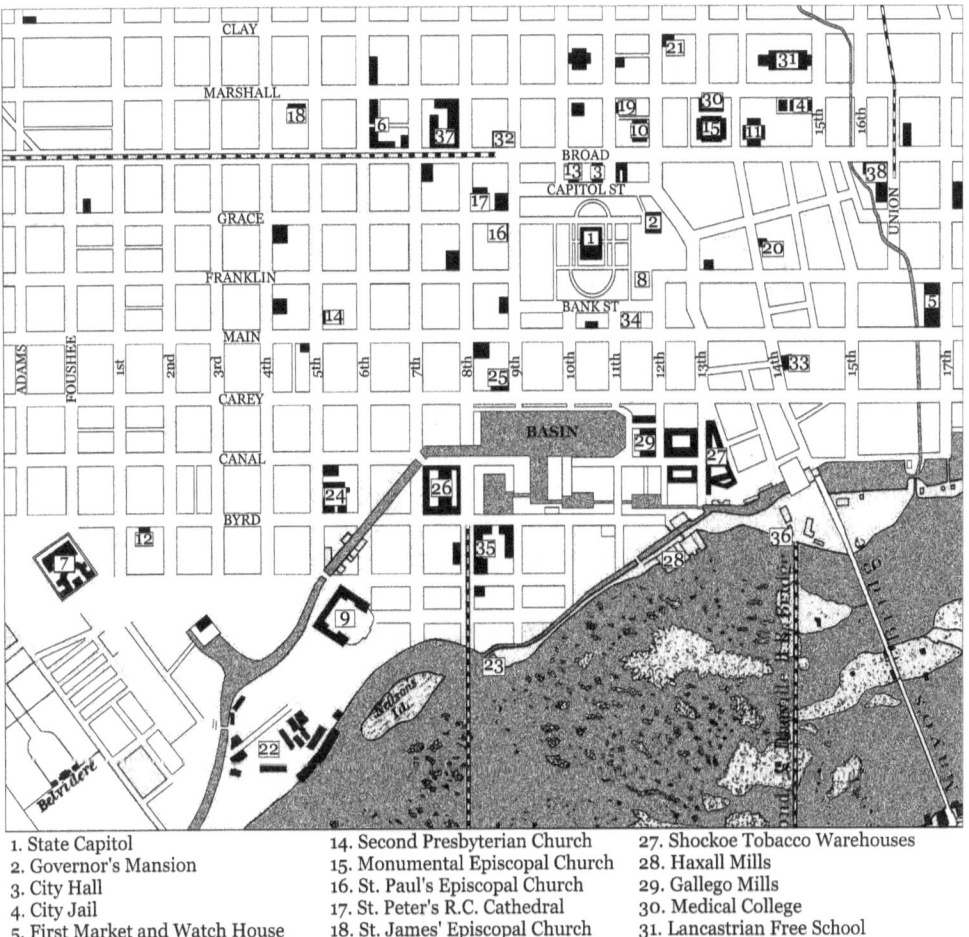

1. State Capitol	14. Second Presbyterian Church	27. Shockoe Tobacco Warehouses
2. Governor's Mansion	15. Monumental Episcopal Church	28. Haxall Mills
3. City Hall	16. St. Paul's Episcopal Church	29. Gallego Mills
4. City Jail	17. St. Peter's R.C. Cathedral	30. Medical College
5. First Market and Watch House	18. St. James' Episcopal Church	31. Lancastrian Free School
6. Second Market and Watch House	19. Sycamore Church (Disciples)	32. Broad Street Hotel
7. State Penitentiary	20. First Hebrew Synagogue	33. Exchange Hotel
8. State Court House	21. Second Hebrew Synagogue	34. Exchange Bank of Virginia
9. State Armory and Iron Works	22. Tredegar Iron Works	35. Richmond and Petersburg Railroad
10. First Baptist Church	23. Virginia Steel and Iron Works	36. Richmond and Danville Railroad
11. First African Baptist Church	24. Samson & Pae's Foundry	37. Richmond, Fredericksburg & Potomac Railroad
12. Second African Baptist Church	25. Bower's Foundry	
13. First Presbyterian Church	26. Public Tobacco Warehouses	38. Virginia Central Railroad

Fig. 1. Map of central Richmond, ca. 1854. By author. Based on "Map of the city of Richmond, Virginia." Library of Congress online. <http://hdl.loc.gov/loc.gmd/g3884r.cw0645700>

were slaveholders who whipped their human property in the privacy of their own homes. However, the efforts of the mayor, police officers, and night watchmen to arrest and punish slaves did not provide an unproblematic alternative to slaveholders' personal authority and discipline. Analysis of the fragmentary records of arrests and mayor's court proceedings in Richmond that survive from the late 1830s and 1850s indicates that the complexities of urban slavery ran much deeper than this.[12] Notwithstanding that slaveholding interests dominated the municipal justice system, the power of the mayor provided a profoundly different form of control from that exercised by slave owners and overseers. Slaves were arrested, examined, and punished with sufficient frequency that slavery remained profitable and relatively stable in Richmond throughout the antebellum years. However, the confrontations that were played out in the mayor's court between slaves and city legal authorities, and in which the interests of myriad members of the wider community were inevitably entangled, could never entirely replicate or compensate for the breakdown of the master-slave relationship. On the contrary, they routinely exposed underlying tensions in urban slave society that were symptomatic of a system of slave control that, while shrouded in the cloak of law, was based almost entirely on force alone. In this light, it was a telling indictment of slave policing in Richmond that it was only when Virginia Winston was murdered that officers became aware of the less sensational subversive activities that Jane and John Williams had committed over the years.

In the immediate aftermath of the Winston murders, Richmond was shaken by the brutality of the crimes, but in the ensuing weeks politicians and newspaper editors became more concerned with the broader implications of the killings as evidence of the endemic problems of slave control in an urban-industrial society. In July 1852, two sermons were preached that contemplated the causes and implications of the murders and provide a commentary on aspects of slavery and crime in the antebellum city. At the First Presbyterian Church, Reverend T. V. Moore, presiding over the funerals of Virginia Winston and her infant child, delivered a discourse that considered at length some of the general causes of the killings. Moore's sermon was a sweeping condemnation of the condition of Richmond's slave population that railed against the extensive freedoms enjoyed by slaves in the city and "the abandonment of them during part of their time to causes of corruption that are at work." Grogshops and eating houses, illicit trading, parties, and excursions were just some of the activities in which slaves indulged in their free time that drew the scorn of Reverend Moore.[13]

Just four blocks to the east of the Presbyterian Church stood the First African Baptist Church, and it was here that Reverend Ryland, the church's long-serving white pastor, preached a sermon to Richmond's largest black congregation entitled "In Reference to the Murder of the Winston Family." As Richmond citizens made their way to their respective places of worship, the murders doubtless dominated the talk of both the black Baptists and the white Presbyterians, yet the concerns represented in the conversations held by the African American congregants were very different from those expressed by the whites who mourned the passing of Virginia Winston. The greatest fear of the black community was that white authorities would respond to the murders by placing tighter restrictions on the ways in which they conducted their daily lives. Ryland's sermon reflected these fears, lamenting that Jane Williams had been a member of the church and warning the congregation that the murders "will excite strong prejudices against this church, and tend to endanger your religious privileges." Indeed, Ryland believed that civic regulation of all aspects of black life in Richmond would be augmented as a consequence of the murders. Not least on account of Ryland's white skin, the members of his congregation probably greeted with some skepticism his advice that both slaves and free African Americans would need "to be more obedient and submissive for the future than you have ever been heretofore." Even so, many doubtless still concurred with the veracity of these sentiments with knowing resignation.[14]

The rhythms of city life provided innumerable opportunities for slaves to enjoy the simple pleasures that Moore believed to be at the root of slave criminality in Richmond and that Ryland thought would soon be curtailed. Industrial growth made slavery a very different institution in Virginia's capital city from any other locality in the South, urban or rural. Although the slave population declined in many southern cities in the late antebellum years, the number of slaves in Richmond increased, albeit by the 1850s at a slower rate than the free white population. As late as 1860, slaves accounted for almost one-third of Richmond's population and one-half of the adult male workforce.[15] In contrast to most southern cities, which were primarily commercial centers and where most slaves worked as domestic servants, in Richmond thousands of slaves toiled in industrial enterprises. Slaves in Richmond were employed in the manufacture of iron, cotton, flour, and, most important, tobacco.

Richmond's tobacco industry expanded throughout the late antebellum years. In 1840, around 1,000 slaves worked for approximately twenty different firms, but just ten years later more than forty-three tobacco factories employed over 2,500 slaves. By 1860, at least 3,000 slaves were involved in the production of tobacco, but equally important as this rise in numbers by the 1850s was that the relationship between enslaved workers and the tobacco manufacturers had undergone a profound change. As late as 1840, most tobacco manufacturers owned the slaves who worked for them, but after this date they increasingly turned to hired slaves to fulfill their labor needs.[16]

The practice of slave hiring, whether arranged directly by the slave's owner and employer, by a third-party slave broker, or, as was increasingly, controversially, and illegally the case, by slaves themselves, meant that by the 1850s more than half of the slaves employed in Richmond's tobacco industry worked beyond the direct control of their owners.[17] Often tobacco factory slaves experienced harsh working conditions and strict discipline imposed by a factory overseer, yet their hired status nevertheless enabled many to live their daily lives with a degree of personal autonomy that was unthinkable in the plantation South and that to many white minds was incompatible with the maintenance of slave discipline and white supremacy.

As well as working away from their owners, many slaves also made their own living arrangements. Tobacco manufacturers in particular often did not provide housing for their enslaved workers but instead paid them a small allowance to obtain their own food and lodgings.[18] Many whites criticized this practice as giving slaves excessive independence and also on the grounds that it shattered the proslavery ideal of paternalistic relations between master and slave and encouraged slaves to form connections with free blacks and nonslaveholding whites. In 1852, however, a committee of tobacco manufacturers defended their bondsmen's independent living arrangements. In response to a proposal to obligate owners and hirers to provide housing for their slaves, the manufacturers claimed that often there was insufficient space near the factories to house slave workers, and that even if space were available, it would compromise the safety and well-being of the community for so many slaves to live together in the center of the city. Furthermore, the tobacco manufacturers protested that far from encouraging criminality, in contrast to other African Americans in Richmond, "the factory slaves are not as immoral and debased as represented, but on the contrary are a well-behaved and orderly class."[19] Charles Montague concurred. When his aunt, Frances Hughes, expressed her fear that life in the city would corrupt the morals of her slave Anthony, Montague advised that she should, "hire him [Anthony] in the factory where he will have least opportunities for knowing vice because under the constant superintendence of an overseer."[20]

In reality, living out, along with other aspects of industrial slavery, such as the payment of bonuses to slaves who worked extra hours during busy periods, had by the 1850s become integral to the maintenance of work discipline among factory slaves and was crucial to the continued profitability of tobacco manufacturing.[21] This was vividly illustrated during the economic crisis of 1857 that forced a number of tobacco factories to cease production and that, according to Richmond's most popular newspaper, the *Daily Dispatch*, resulted in "thousands of unemployed negroes turned loose to do as they will until the hiring time of the new year begins." The *Dispatch* warned that, "having had no opportunity for accumulating money by overwork in the tobacco factories for several months," many of the idle slaves "will resort to all sorts of thefts to get the 'needful' for their Christmas frolics."[22] Though the implication was that the slaves were not lacking basic necessities but only the luxuries that they demanded during the festive period, the *Dispatch*'s commentary demonstrated that industrial slaves were subject to the whims of the market as well as the authority of the slaveholding class. As Richmond's economy struggled to cope with four recessions between 1837 and 1857, the influence of national and international economic currents on urban slave discipline heightened concerns about slave control in the city.[23]

Bowing to the tobacco manufacturers' opposition, Richmond's Common Council rejected the proposed 1852 ordinance against slaves' independent living arrangements, but calls for greater regulation of living out and slave self-hire persisted throughout the 1850s. Self-hire had been prohibited in Virginia since 1801, but it was only amidst the sectional, social, and racial tensions of the final years of the antebellum period that a concerted movement to enforce the law was undertaken in Richmond. The number of cases in which white defendants were accused of permitting slave self-hire increased from just thirty-seven between 1830 and 1849 to fifty-nine in the next eleven years.[24] Moreover, in 1857 and 1858 the council finally introduced municipal ordinances to reinforce the state legislation against self-hire and to regulate slave living arrangements.

For some white Virginians, the importance of enforcing rigorously the laws against slave hiring could scarcely be overstated. In a message to the Virginia General Assembly in the aftermath of John Brown's raid at Harper's Ferry in 1859, Governor Henry A. Wise proposed a list of measures to protect Virginia from similar abolitionist attacks in the future. Among his recommendations, Wise demanded that steps be taken to "correct the evils and mischiefs which arise out of the manner in which negroes are hired, boarded and lodged and paid for extra work in the various factories, particularly of Richmond." Evidently Wise did not consider sufficient, or was unaware of, the increase in prosecutions for crimes related to slave hiring that had occurred in Richmond during the 1850s. Despite the many other causal factors of John Brown's raid, Wise claimed that the living conditions of urban factory slaves "ought to be specially inquired into."[25] While Wise did not explain how he thought the law should be changed, he may have considered that part of the problem lay with the punishments that were imposed for illegal slave hiring. Although four out of every five slaveholders charged in Richmond in the 1850s with permitting slave self-hire were convicted, the fine for the offense was just ten dollars. This provided little disincentive for slaveholders to abandon such a lucrative and time-saving practice, and it actually represented a decline in the severity of the punishment in comparison with the 1830s and 1840s, when fines for permitting slave self-hire were sometimes as high as fifty dollars.[26] As much as there was growing concern about slave control in 1850s Richmond, it is apparent that there was also ambivalence at the local level toward legal attempts to restrict slaveholders' right to determine how best to profit from their slaves' labor.

Industry and manufacturing dominated Richmond's economy, but throughout the antebellum period a majority of slaves in the city worked as domestic servants within white households.[27] The profits to be gained from employing slave men in factories meant that domestic service was mostly the preserve of female slaves. There were approximately 4,500 slave women working as domestics in 1860, and in consequence of working and living in the same households as their owners and employers, these slaves tended to be subject to more direct white control than those who toiled in industry and manufacturing. However, by 1860 as many as 1,500 female domestic slaves were hired out, and even those who worked for their owners sometimes found themselves without immediate white supervision, as they were required to move about the city running errands and buying and selling goods.[28] More important—and in contrast to rural domestics who labored in relatively isolated plantation houses—urban servants needed only to step outside of their owner's residence to enter a thriving lower-class community where they could develop associations across lines of race and status.[29] At the four black Baptist churches established in pre–Civil War Richmond, as well as in the city's markets, members of the black community could interact with a degree of legitimacy. In addition, grogshops, eating houses, alleyways, and street corners were all sites of impromptu and illegal gatherings of slaves, free blacks, and poor whites.

When black Richmonders met together either in public or private, they posed a serious threat to slave discipline. In Richmond's diverse urban society, the distinction between hired slaves, those on the streets without their owners permission, and free blacks could become very easily blurred. Protected by the anonymity of urban life and the structures of the black community, slaves had opportunities to run away, pass as free people, engage in criminal activities, or, more commonly, simply avoid detection by their owners for short periods of time during which they could visit friends and family in other parts of the city.[30] On the night that the Winstons were bludgeoned in their beds, for example, one of their hired slaves, Anna, was sleeping with a white man at Branch's tobacco factory on Byrd Street. The previous night she had stayed at the home of a white woman on nearby Cary Street, and it was to this residence that she returned on the Monday morning that news of the killings broke.[31] Anna was described in the press as a runaway, but it is probable that like many other slaves she had every intention of returning to her master's service, particularly as Joseph Winston's grocery store was located just five blocks from the Branch factory.[32] Irrespective of individual slaves' motives, however, memories of the rebellions in Richmond in 1800, Charleston in 1822, and Southampton County, Virginia, in 1831 were testament to the fact that slaves like Anna could exploit even limited opportunities to act independently of their owners' authority to form connections and pursue ends that could pose a very serious threat to white security.[33]

Slaveholders' fears of the events that transpired when slaves were absent from direct white control or when they gathered in secluded parts of the city prompted Richmond's council to criminalize a range of slave behavior that in rural areas was punished at the discretion of individual slaveholders. According to an ordinance passed in 1831, slaves were subject to a public whipping for offenses including "setting a boat afloat in the Basin or Canal," "neglecting to place sufficient barriers to warn foot passengers against passing under a roof, wall or chimney undergoing repairs," "rolling a hogshead down the Basin bank or through any street, square, lane or alley," "flying kites, playing at ball, bandy or quoits, or throwing stones or other missiles," "firing a gun, pistol, fowling-piece or fire-arm or making any other unusual noise that might alarm the citizens," and selling "oysters, cakes, pies, fruits or other eatables."[34]

The restrictions that municipal ordinances imposed on Richmond slaves increased in the 1850s. The Black Code of 1859 was the most comprehensive and systematic attempt to regulate slave conduct in the city. The code stated that slaves had to carry a pass from their master or hirer at all times and were prohibited from smoking tobacco, carrying a cane at night or firearms at any time, and from using insolent or menacing language to a white person. Neither could slaves form secret societies or enter places designated as "city grounds," including city hall and Capitol Square. Finally, no more than five blacks were permitted to assemble together in public.

Although violations of the municipal slave codes were apparently trivial in themselves, slaveholders perceived them as contrary to their interests as property holders and masters, for they were symptomatic of slaves' more general discontent with their condition and were often connected to more serious crimes. Drunkenness, for example, had a direct impact on the value and productivity of slave labor such that the *Dispatch* claimed that, "if the law of the State against selling liquor to slaves could be rigidly enforced, that class of property in Virginia would be worth double as much as it now is."[35] Unlawful assemblies of slaves, meanwhile, could be used to plan acts of resistance or strategies for escaping to the free states, while profits gained from trading in stolen goods could be used to buy passage on a ship bound for the North.

In November 1841, the hustings court grand jury claimed that the board money given to tobacco factory slaves was often spent in dram shops and led to riots and violations of the slave laws.[36] Dr. George Watson complained of "the precarious tenure by which you hold a hireling & the want of that absolute and lasting control which is necessary to keep the proper degree of authority."[37] Similarly, Reverend Moore noted a lack "of adequate moral instruction" and a "growing relaxation of that system of firm restraint" necessary for the control of the urban slave population as factors that had contributed to a long-term increase in violent crime in Richmond.[38] Had Moore wished to illustrate his point, the life of John Williams would have provided a perfect example of the seemingly injurious effects of the city on the slave population. In the year preceding the murder of Virginia Winston, Williams was hired to at least two different employers, the lumber merchants T. J. Glenn & Co. and the stonemason James Green. Both employers were dissatisfied with Williams's conduct. Green found him "turbulent and refractory" and was afraid to punish him for fear "of having his house burned by him," while James Wortham of T. J. Glenn & Co. complained that Williams had arrived late for work on many occasions. Wortham also claimed that he feared for his safety "all the time he [Williams] was at the factory."[39]

Nor was Williams alone. Between 1850 and 1860, forty-seven slaves were tried in Richmond for serious violent crimes, an increase of 68 percent on the previous decade.[40] Over the same period, the number of slaves charged with property crimes classed as felonies increased from 102 to 142, and although this rise was not inconsistent with the growth in Richmond's slave population, most whites believed slave crime to be on the increase. This perception was no doubt fueled by the emergence of newspapers like the *Dispatch* (first published in 1852), which peppered its columns with crime

Table 1.1. Richmond slaves charged with felonies, 1830–1860

	Number of cases			Annual cases per 1,000 of population		
	Property crime	Violent crime	Total[a]	Property crime	Violent crime	Total
1830–34	29	9	38	0.9	0.3	1.2
1835–39	43	9	53	1.2	0.3	1.5
1840–44	60	14	74	1.5	0.4	1.9
1845–49	42	14	60	0.9	0.3	1.3
1850–54	63	24	88	1.2	0.5	1.7
1855–59	79	23	104	1.4	0.4	1.9
1860	15	12	27	1.3	1.0	2.3
Total	331	105	444	—	—	—

Source: Richmond Hustings Court Minutes, 1830–60.
Note: Calculations involving population figures assume consistent population increase between decennial census figures.
[a]Totals include 8 cases that do not fall into the categories of violent or property crime.

stories and court reports and ensured that slave trials assumed a prominence in the public sphere that they would rarely have held in earlier times.[41]

There is further evidence that the slave hiring system was instrumental in many of the most serious crimes committed by slaves in Richmond. Court records show that between 1830 and 1850, hired slaves, along with those whose owners lived outside Richmond and who may or may not have been hired out, accounted for 19 of the 45 slaves examined for violent felonies and 86 of the 163 slaves charged with property crimes.[42] Although some slaves stole from their owners, many more targeted businesses and boardinghouses where they were not known and therefore were less likely to be suspected once the stolen goods had been discovered missing. Hired slaves were well placed to target businesses because of the relative freedom with which they were often able to move about the city, and there is evidence that this made it extremely difficult for the prosecution to find witnesses whose testimony could secure a conviction. Between 1830 and 1848, when the clerk of the court systematically recorded whether slaves were hired out, just 43 percent of hired slaves who appeared in courts of oyer and terminer charged with stealing were found guilty compared to 75 percent of slaves who lived and worked with their owners.[43]

In the case of less serious crimes, as well, the judicial system was disproportionately involved in the control of hired, industrial slaves. This is evident from the stark disparity in the number of male and female slaves who appeared as defendants in mayor's court cases. In three sample years (1838, 1852, and 1860), enslaved women—who were mostly domestics and

Table 1.2. Richmond Mayor's Court cases: Female defendants

	Number of female defendants				Women as a percentage of all defendants			
	Slaves	Whites	Free African Americans	Total	Slaves	Whites	Free African Americans	Total
1838	11	29	39	79	5.7	9.5	32.2	12.8
1852	56	70	83	209	12.5	12.7	31.1	15.0
1860	21	164	81	266	8.9	17.7	36.7	19.2

Sources: Richmond Mayor Court Docket Book, 1838; *Richmond Daily Dispatch*, 14 Feb. 1852–13 Feb. 1853, and 1860.

less likely than men to be hired out—accounted on average for less than 10 percent of all slaves who appeared for examination in the Richmond Mayor's Court. This was less even than the proportion of white defendants who were women, although the figures should not be interpreted as evidence that official attitudes toward female criminality transcended racial lines for in the case of free African Americans, women comprised one-third of mayor's court defendants. Seemingly, therefore, even though female domestic slaves lived and worked with some independence in the city, most enslaved women in Richmond had either limited opportunities or inclination to engage in the types of conduct that would have attracted the attention of the police and courts.

On average, by the late 1850s more than nine hundred slaves—or almost one in ten of the slave population—were arrested annually in Richmond. By comparison, whites were taken into custody at less than half this rate, although free blacks were almost twice as likely as slaves to be arrested. The rate of free black arrests supported southern whites' conviction that only slavery could temper what they interpreted as African Americans' inherent criminal tendencies, yet these figures more accurately reflect that free black people were subject to racially discriminatory statutes and law enforcement, and that slaveholders and hirers frequently punished slave criminality themselves without involving the law, even in the city. Although free African Americans in Richmond were also subjected to informal chastisement by whites, the courts were the primary means of regulating free black conduct and crime.[44]

The vast majority of slaves arrested in Richmond were accused of relatively minor offenses, such as drunkenness, disorderly conduct, unlawful assembly, and violation of the pass laws.[45] In such cases, the decision as to whether the slave would be punished or discharged without sanction rested with the mayor or, in his absence, the city recorder or an alderman. Particularly after Joseph Mayo became mayor in 1853, many slaves accused of the

Table 1.3. Arrests in Richmond, 1855–1860

	Whites		Slaves		Free blacks	
	Number	Per 1,000 population	Number	Per 1,000 population	Number	Per 1,000 population
1855	499	25.7	699	64.7	233	94.2
1856	657	32.4	1,051	95.6	402	161.1
1857	646	30.6	874	78.3	380	151.0
1858	805	36.7	1,070	95.2	497	195.9
1859	866	38.0	815	70.7	380	148.6
1860	1,101	46.6	949	81.1	353	137.0

Sources: Richmond Daily Dispatch, 3 Jan. 1856; 2 Jan., 6 Feb., 6 Apr., 4 May, 2 Jul., 3 Aug., 2 Nov., 3 Dec. 1857; 2 Jan., 2 Feb., 3 Mar., 5 Apr., 2 Jun., 9 Jul., 2 Aug., 2 Sept., 4 Oct. 1858; 3 Jan., 2 Feb., 2 Mar., 2 Apr., 4 Jun., 7 Jul., 1 Aug., 3 Oct., 2 Nov. 1859; 2 Jan., 2 Feb., 2 May, 5 Jun., 2 Jul., 4 Aug., 3 Sept., 1 Oct. 1860. Arrest figures are missing for two months in 1858 and 1859 and three months in 1860. It was assumed that arrests in these months equaled the average for other months in the year. Population figures are calculated on the assumption of a constant increase between the decennial censuses of 1850 and 1860.

most trivial offenses were examined with minimal ceremony or formality at the watch houses located in Richmond's two marketplaces where slaves were held when first taken into custody.[46] In more serious cases, however, as well as when a formal warrant had been issued prior to the slave's arrest, the examination was postponed until later in the day when the mayor's court convened in city hall.

Specific details of the events that transpired during the watch house examinations were not recorded in any of the extant sources, but press reports from the 1850s indicate that Mayor Joseph Mayo generally conducted a cursory examination and then either discharged the slaves or ordered that they should be whipped before being returned to their owners. This form of justice met with the approval of the *Dispatch*, which commended Mayo on the "prompt and efficient manner" in which he handled cases of "Negro delinquency and drunkenness," at what became known as his "sunrise courts."[47]

A small number of slaves arrested for drunkenness and disorderly conduct were remanded for examination in the mayor's court, but the reasons why Mayo afforded some slaves this more formal and public examination are rarely evident in the records.[48] On one morning in July 1853, four out of five slaves arrested for unlawful assembly were punished with five lashes at the cage, but the fifth "was brought to Court because he undertook to elude arrest, and said no watchman should take him."[49] Perhaps Mayor Mayo hoped to impress the recalcitrant slave with a more formal style of justice than

Fig. 2. "Richmond, Va. City Hall; Sycamore Church beyond [Capitol Street]." 1865. The heart of judicial activity in Richmond, city hall was the site of the daily mayor's court, monthly hustings court sessions, as well as oyer and terminer trials. It also housed council chambers and the offices of several local and federal clerks of court. Courtesy of Library of Congress, Prints and Photographs online, Selected Civil War Photographs, 1861–1865. <http://hdl.loc.gov/loc.pnp/cwpb.00447>

could be dispensed at the cage, or maybe it was necessary to conduct a full hearing before he could impose the more severe sentence that was doubtless deemed appropriate for slave insubordination toward an officer of the law.

Compared with the scant records of watch house examinations, far more evidence survives of slave cases that were heard at the daily mayor's court sessions held in city hall. From the perspective of enslaved defendants, the nature of justice in the two venues was likely very similar. Throughout the antebellum period, all of Richmond's mayors adjudged a majority of slave defendants guilty and sentenced them to corporal punishment that was administered at the whipping post located in clear public view in the First Market. There was little that was exceptional about the fate of slave defendants in the Richmond Mayor's Court; similar proceedings were conducted in cities throughout the South.[50] Although slave examinations occasionally involved a considerable number of witnesses, indicating a degree of judicial concern to establish the facts of the case, more commonly black defendants were treated in a manner that showed scant regard for procedural regularities.[51] Archy Page received twenty lashes for transporting stolen goods on the basis of evidence "amounting almost to proof" and his having "always borne a doubtful character," while Reuben received ten lashes simply for being in possession of "a piece of leather not accounted for and supposed to be stolen." Similarly, Ralph was sentenced to twenty lashes as he was unable to account for the tobacco found in his possession. Daniel Batley, arrested with a piece of bacon that was supposed to be stolen, was ordered twenty-five lashes after "failing to prove his innocence of the charge."[52] The burden of proof in these cases rested with the enslaved defendant, who could not legally own property, rather than with the prosecutor.

The general neglect of due process in the examination of slave defendants in the mayor's court was evident in the lack of regulations governing the court proceedings. To take one example, unlike in felony trials there was no statutory provision or procedural precedent for dealing with slaves suspected of perjury in the mayor's court. In October 1837, a female slave named Tamer Smith appeared as a witness against Winney, an elderly slave accused of receiving stolen goods. Commenting on the case, Mayor Joseph Tate noted: "Tamer Smith has perjured herself in the course of her testimony in these cases—swearing at one time one way and at another directly contrary. This she admitted in the course of her examination this day. Query— How is a slave to be proceeded ag[ain]st. for perjury?"[53] Tate made a further note to himself to draw the attention of the Commonwealth's attorney to the matter, but there is no record that an answer was ever forthcoming, and it is evident from Tate's docket book that neither Tamer Smith nor any other slave was ever prosecuted for lying under oath.

Controlling crime among Richmond's African American population was the most important function of the Richmond Mayor's Court, but it was never of such importance as to undermine entirely proper consideration of the evidence. On one occasion when a white witness testified that a slave named Robert had stolen a jug of molasses, the case was dismissed on the grounds that the evidence "was not sufficiently connected and positive to warrant punishment."[54] Likewise, when Edward was accused of stealing a pig belonging to Harriet Jacobs, a free black woman, he was discharged as the evidence left unclear "which of several committed the offence." Francis, a hired slave arraigned for the theft of a pocketbook and caught stealing many times before, was also discharged due to lack of evidence.[55] Mayor Tate did recommend, however, that Francis be returned to his owner and sold out

Table 1.4. Richmond Mayor's Court cases: Stealing

	Slaves			Whites			Free blacks		
	Cases (N)	Guilty (N)	Percent	Cases (N)	Guilty (N)	Percent	Cases (N)	Guilty (N)	Percent
1838	106	83	78.3	20	12	60.0	28	19	67.9
1852	107	86	80.4	49	34	69.4	34	23	67.6
1860	102	95	93.1	67	38	56.7	40	35	87.5

Sources: Richmond Mayor's Court Docket Book, 1838; *Richmond Daily Dispatch*, 14 Feb. 1852–13 Feb. 1853, and 1860.

of Virginia. This ruling suggests the mayor believed Francis may have been guilty but was unwilling to impose a judicial sanction due to inadequate evidence. In another case, the slave James Owen was discharged despite being caught in the act of stealing by his hirer, Mr. A. S. Lee. As Owen confessed to the crime while being thrashed by Lee, Mayor Mayo ruled that the confession had been illegally obtained and dismissed the case. It is significant that the court did not return Owen to Lee, who might have inflicted further punishment, but instead turned him over to an agent of his owner.[56] The decisions of the court may have been designed to control black crime, but this was not always to be achieved through the indiscriminate punishment of slaves for crimes that the evidence suggested they did not commit or when procedural regulations had been entirely ignored.

The summary nature of examinations in the Richmond Mayor's Court resulted in the conviction of most enslaved defendants. In contrast to the historian Arthur Howington's finding that rates of acquittal in the Memphis Recorder Court were similarly low for all defendants irrespective of race and slave status, in Richmond slaves were far more likely to be found guilty than either whites or free African Americans.[57] In 1838, 106 of the 193 slave defendants in mayor's court cases were charged with stealing, and almost 80 percent were adjudged guilty and ordered to be whipped or, in the most serious cases, sent for trial before a court of oyer and terminer. By comparison, in the same year only 60 percent of the 20 whites accused of stealing were found guilty and these fourteen out of twenty-two defendants were not sentenced, but instead sent on to the hustings court for further examination and trials, at which several were ultimately acquitted. By the eve of the Civil War, the disparity in the treatment of slaves and whites charged with stealing had increased substantially. In 1860, more than 90 percent of slaves, but just 57 percent of whites charged with stealing were adjudged guilty by the mayor. Conviction rates for other crimes, notably assault, followed a similar pattern.[58]

Table 1.5. Richmond Mayor's Court cases: Assault

	Slaves			Whites			Free blacks		
	Cases (N)	Guilty (N)	Percent	Cases (N)	Guilty (N)	Percent	Cases (N)	Guilty (N)	Percent
1838	26	22	84.6	98	71	72.4	27	22	81.5
1852	29	25	86.2	114	91	79.8	50	40	80.0
1860	24	19	79.2	254	155	61.0	23	20	87.0

Sources: Richmond Mayor Court Docket Book, 1838; *Richmond Daily Dispatch*, 14 Feb. 1852–13 Feb. 1853, and 1860.

Not only were slaves more regularly convicted in the mayor's court at the end of the antebellum period than previously, they were also subject to more brutal punishments. Between the late 1830s and early 1850s, the proportion of slaves convicted of nonfelonious stealing who were sentenced to the maximum penalty of thirty-nine lashes increased from just 15 percent to more than 75 percent. Similarly, while none of the slaves convicted of assault in 1838 were sentenced to more than thirty lashes, 50 percent received thirty-nine lashes in 1852.[59]

As well as more severe punishments of slaves for petty thefts and acts of violence, the 1850s also witnessed more rigorous enforcement of the municipal ordinances. In 1852, for example, when white Richmonders were put on edge by the Winston murders and a series of other violent attacks by slaves on their masters and overseers, Mayor William Lambert examined more than 140 slaves for violations of the pass ordinances. Fourteen years earlier, in a less racially sensitive atmosphere, only eight slaves came before Mayor Tate for similar offenses.[60]

With the election of Joseph Mayo as mayor in early 1853, following the death of William Lambert, police control of all aspects of slave conduct in Richmond intensified further. A staunch Democrat, in the antebellum era Joseph Mayo was among the most prominent figures in Richmond politics and government. Born in Powhatan County, Virginia, in 1795, Mayo briefly studied medicine in Philadelphia before embarking on a legal career in 1815. Mayo was appointed Commonwealth's attorney seven years later and held this position for the next thirty years until his election as mayor. During this time, Mayo also pursued a political career. He sat on the city council from 1832 to 1845, and in 1846 he was elected to a four-year term in the state legislature. Evidently the Richmond electorate held Mayo in high esteem by the early 1850s, and they gave a clear endorsement to his actions as mayor by returning him to office for thirteen consecutive years until the end of the Civil War and then again for a further two years from 1866 to 1868.[61]

Fig. 3. Joseph Mayo, Commonwealth's attorney, 1822–52, and mayor of Richmond, 1853–65. Reprinted by permission of Cook Collection, Valentine Richmond History Center.

As Commonwealth's attorney, Mayo had been responsible for prosecuting cases in all of Richmond's criminal courts, including the mayor's court. He knew better than anyone how the Richmond justice system handled slaves, and this knowledge, coupled with his identity as a slaveholder and astute politician, shaped his decision to erode even the limited procedural protections that slaves had in the mayor's court. On taking office, Mayo announced his determination "to make all negroes and mulattoes know their places and obey the laws," and throughout his thirteen-year tenure African Americans were arrested and sentenced to corporal punishment in large numbers for even trivial offenses such as drunkenness and curfew violations. In one of his first acts as mayor, Mayo announced that he would determine the fate of slaves arrested for all minor offenses not at his main midmorning court session in city hall, but at the watch houses.[62] This extended the existing practice of "sunrise" watch house examinations to cover a wider variety of slave offenses, including unlawful assembly and pass violations. While there are no comparable figures for earlier years, in April 1860, a month in

Table 1.6. Richmond Mayor's Court cases per capita, 1838–1860

	Whites		Slaves		Free blacks	
	Number	Per 1,000 population	Number	Per 1,000 population	Number	Per 1,000 population
1838	305	30.1	193	26.5	121	62.7
1852	553	32.6	449	43.8	267	110.7
1860	928	39.3	236	20.1	221	85.8

Sources: Richmond Mayor Court Docket Book, 1838; *Richmond Daily Dispatch*, 14 Feb. 1852–13 Feb. 1853, and 1 Jan.–31 Dec. 1860.

which 178 prisoners were arrested in Richmond, a total of 108 examinations were conducted at the watch houses.[63] It is probable that in most of these cases the accused was an African American and, invariably, a slave. This is suggested by the fact that even though the number of slave arrests in the 1850s relative to population was far higher than the number of white arrests, in contrast to earlier decades slaves were much *less* likely than whites to appear for examination in the mayor's court. Whereas a large majority of whites who were taken into custody were examined in the mayor's court, by the mid-1850s this was true for perhaps as few as 25 percent of arrested slaves. In 1860, for example, 1,101 whites were arrested in Richmond, and 928 were examined in the mayor's court. By contrast, slave arrests in the same year numbered 949, but only 236 were brought before the mayor.[64] Notably, although the *Dispatch* regularly commented that drunkenness was the main cause of slave arrests in the city, in 1860 only six slaves appeared in the Mayor Court charged with this offense, suggesting that hundreds were punished and discharged at the watch houses.

Slaves therefore found themselves under closer police surveillance in the 1850s than ever before and were ever less likely to be permitted even the minimal procedural rights that were afforded by a mayor's court examination. However, while strict enforcement of the black codes supplemented the slaveholders' control, it did not entirely compensate for the distinctive features of urban slavery that undermined the master-slave relationship. In the first place, the enforcement of the law sometimes met with resistance from slaveholders who disagreed with the mayor's verdicts and resented the intrusion of an external authority into their slaveholding affairs. On occasions when slaveholders entered the courtroom and found their interpretation of slave conduct at odds with that of the law, the very meaning of slavery and mastery was brought into question. Second, Richmond's police provisions could not keep pace with the increasing opportunities for resistance that were a product of continuing urban expansion. Third, slaves resented police crackdowns on aspects of their daily lives into which the law had not previously intruded. Slaves were under no illusion that the mayor's verdicts were unjust and intended to maintain white dominance rather than to serve the ends of justice. As such, the increasing brutality of the mayor's sentences encouraged slave resistance and undermined the efficiency of the urban economy.

Slaveholders' attitudes toward the police control of slaves in Richmond reflected their concerns as the owners and employers of individual slaves and as members of the dominant white race. Urban slaveholders depended on the municipal justice system to control the African American population, and they rarely complained about the largely indiscriminate treatment of enslaved defendants.[65] However, individual slaveholders sometimes took steps to protect their slaves from judicial punishment and on occasion expressed outright opposition to the mayor's authority. When James Breeden paid a fine in order to save his slave, named German, from a whipping for violating the ordinance against depositing rubbish on the public streets, he explained to the court that German was a good slave and this was his first offense.[66] In a similar case, the mayor agreed not to punish the slaves Henry and Lewis for straining horses after their master testified to their good character and expressed himself eager to redeem them from the whipping post.[67] When the slave Robert was charged with being out without a pass and carrying an unlawful weapon, meanwhile, he was punished only for the latter offense after his owner, a Mr. Slater, testified that he had allowed Robert to go out without a pass, "he having retired at the time the request for it was made."[68] Other slaveholders who believed that a slave was innocent argued more forcefully that punishment was unjust. When Mr. Dill's slave Abram was sentenced to ten lashes for fighting, Dill opposed the sentence "most violently" and said "that he would rather pay $100 than it should be executed." Mayor Lambert recorded that when he refused to discharge Abram, Dill replied with "a good deal of foolish talk" that was "wholly subversive of order touching the slave population, as far as concerns its proper subjection and discipline."[69]

As well as criticizing the mayor's rulings, Richmond slaveholders also complained that the police arrested slaves without justification. After Thomas Massie's slave Billy had been arrested for being without a pass, resisting arrest, and creating a disturbance in the street, "Massie said he would sooner believe his man, than the watchmen, who were a set of worthless lazy fellows, who would take up occasionally inoffensive servants, merely to show they did something."[70] On another occasion, Isaac Goddin was so incensed when night watchmen Daniel Boaz and Thomas Granger woke him at eleven o'clock at night to complain about the behavior of his slaves that he made a complaint against them for trespassing. Granger claimed that Goddin's slaves had been impertinent and used abusive language toward him, and he threatened to shoot any slaves who repeated the offense. However, Goddin claimed that Granger was motivated by a "personal pique" against him that was the result of a recent property dispute, and that he had previously arrested one of his slaves, William, "at ten minutes of 10 o'clock, when he had a pass to be out until 10 o'clock."[71] Isaac Goddin did not press his official complaint, but because of the seriousness of the matter, Mayor Mayo chose to conduct a public inquiry and advised the watchmen that although they could enter a house when chasing a known felon, in cases of "trifling misdemeanors . . . [they] had no right, in the night time, to enter any person's property in any way."[72]

Surveillance of the slave population was at times compromised by such regulations. Many urban slaves lived in attics, kitchens, outhouses, and elsewhere in white-owned properties that the police could not always enter freely. Even in the most serious cases, such as when the police suspected free blacks of assisting runaway slaves, their investigations were sometimes hampered by the need to obtain search warrants before entering a property. In 1837, Mayor Tate issued a warrant to search the house of Maria Bellentine, a free black woman, for a runaway slave named Ann, the property of John C. Brockenham. The following year, a warrant was issued to search the house of Harrison Swan, also a free black, for Mary, another runaway who was owned by a man in Hanover County. The mayor noted that Burwell Jinkins, the captain of the night watch, was to aid in this search, again indicating a potentially significant delay before the police could enter the property.[73]

There is some evidence that even obtaining a search warrant could be problematic without some evidence on which to base suspicions. Although the mayor, the police, and the *Dispatch* were certain that Clinton James, a free black shopkeeper, was an agent of the Underground Railroad and in regular contact with abolitionists in Boston, they were unable to bring charges against him as the only evidence they had was in the form of letters sent from slaves who had successfully escaped to Canada, and this was inadmissible in court. The police kept a constant watch on James's house in the hope of proving his involvement with runaways, but they seemingly chose not to enter his property, and charges were never brought against him.[74] These cases indicate that slaveholders and judicial officers could not enter private property without legal authority, although it is unlikely they would have faced any sanctions had they done so and successfully retrieved a runaway slave.[75]

Some slaveholders were so convinced of a slave's innocence that they hired attorneys to argue the case before the mayor. Defense attorneys routinely represented slaves in capital cases, a practice that historians have explained as having been necessary to protect the property rights of slaveholders and the financial interests of the state, which had to compensate the owners of executed slaves.[76] However, this explanation cannot account for the presence of defense attorneys in noncapital cases. Slave defendants who benefited from legal counsel in the mayor's court were usually accused of relatively trivial offenses that were commonly dealt with in a summary, speedy fashion with little concern for proper legal procedure. Most slaves faced corporal punishment if convicted by the mayor, and one of the main benefits for slaveholders of slaves being whipped rather than suffering an alternative sanction such as a prison term or fine was that the slaves could be quickly returned to work. Although the *Dispatch* urged public officials to use a "cobbing board or strap" rather than a cowhide to punish slaves, as this "would not scar and disfigure the property of an individual, thus deprecating its value," the property interests of slaveholders were not nearly as seriously threatened in the majority of mayor's court cases as they were in capital trials. As such, permitting defense lawyers to represent slaves in mayor's court examinations can be interpreted as a concession on the part of the mayor to slaveholders' demand that slaves should not suffer arbitrary punishment and perhaps also to the desire of attorneys to profit from slave cases.[77]

Proslavery advocates such as Georgia's Thomas Cobb hailed the legal requirement that trial courts were required to appoint lawyers to represent slaves facing capital charges, but the practices of lawyers who defended black clients before the mayor drew the scorn of white contemporaries.[78] Commenting on a case in which four lawyers had defended a slave named Albert Anderson, the *Dispatch* noted with annoyance that the attorneys "delivered themselves of four unfathomable arguments, and kept up a cross-examination of 30 minutes duration." Although lawyers had been employed in cases involving slave defendants in the mayor's court throughout the antebellum period, they had rarely performed their task with such diligence and had not relied on the technical legal arguments and cross-examinations that became more common in the 1850s. Instead, they had, in the estimation of the *Dispatch*, "confined themselves within the appropriate bounds."[79] In Richmond's slave society, it was highly problematic that slaves could escape punishment on the basis of complex legal arguments for minor offenses for which the evidence suggested they were guilty. Affording legal rights to slave defendants in trivial cases appeared to white contemporaries to be quite unnecessary and even unseemly. It wasted court time, gave slaves a degree of legal protection that equated them with white defendants, and undermined the crime-control functions of the court. Protecting the rights of slaves in high-profile capital trials may have been acceptable; extending such protection to a lower tribunal, the primary function of which was to keep order among the slave population on a daily basis, was not.

Slaveholders who disputed the mayor's verdicts against their slaves could appeal to the hustings court. The appeal process required that security be given for the defendant's appearance before the hustings court or that the accused slave be jailed until the case was heard. In practice, few slaveholders were willing to be deprived of the labor of a slave imprisoned while waiting for an appeal to come to court or to risk having to pay costs if the appeal was unsuccessful. The attitude of J. W. Ditrell was probably typical. In December 1837, Ditrell was adjudged to have permitted his slave Billy to hire himself out contrary to law. In consequence, Ditrell was fined ten dollars, a ruling that he disputed with "considerable temper." When Mayor Tate offered to commit Billy to jail so that the hustings court might decide the case, however, Ditrell relented, as "he wished the case finally disposed of."[80] Some white men, however, were willing to venture the expense of an appeal on behalf of a slave. James Brown paid the costs of an unsuccessful appeal by his slave Henry Mathews, and James G. Chenery financed a similarly vain protest against a punishment of twenty-five lashes imposed by the mayor on the slave James Robinson. Chenery's involvement in the case is intriguing for the court did not record his relationship to the defendant, and although he may have owned or hired Robinson, it is also possible that he was simply a white acquaintance who was willing to protest what he perceived to be an unjust punishment.[81]

Slaveholders such as Ditrell who challenged the legal regulation of their slaves were concerned not only by injustice but also by the law's impact on their economic investment in slave property. Restrictions on slave hiring, for example, though potentially beneficial to slaveholders as a class, were at odds with the right of individuals to employ and support their slaves as they saw fit. When Fleming James was fined for permitting a slave to hire himself out, he declared the fine "quite unwarrantable," as he was unaware of the law and had intended "to do an act of pure benevolence to a worthy negro."[82] The sporadic enforcement of the laws against slave self-hire also prompted consternation among slaveholders, including Edward Van Lew, who, after being fined two dollars for permitting his slave to go at large, was "much displeased at being singled out."[83]

As well as economic self-interest, slaveholders who defended their slaves against accusations of criminality also acted to protect their reputation as masters capable of rearing disciplined slaves. Such considerations were evident in the actions of Colonel John M. Trevilian, who directed the *Dispatch* to report "that the Negro who was before the Mayor on Saturday, for an assault, and who stated that he belonged to him, was guilty of a falsehood. He owns no such Negro."[84] Trevilian was clearly anxious that his reputation should not be tarnished by association with the criminal actions of someone else's slave.

In March 1859, a similarly concerned slaveholder wrote to the *Dispatch* to refute allegations that one of his slaves was responsible for a series of robberies. The available evidence indicates that the slave was never charged, but the *Dispatch* nevertheless recommended that the slave should be sold away from the city, arguing that no one who knew him could feel safe while he remained in Richmond. Were he employed in "the country," by contrast, the *Dispatch* believed it would "quiet the minds of those who doubt his reformation." The slave's owner rejected this suggestion. He claimed that his slave was now entirely honest, and offered to give one hundred dollars to any person "who could connect his man with any of the robberies."[85] Like Trevilian, this slaveholder could not leave unchallenged allegations that compromised his reputation as a master, or his right to determine when and where to sell his enslaved property.

As the historian Suzanne Schnittman has argued, when public institutions disciplined a slave, the authority of the slave's owner was compromised along with "his stature as a master in the eyes of overseers, slaves, and traditional slaveholders like planters."[86] Furthermore, any punishment imposed on a slave in the mayor's court that the slave's owner believed to be too harsh or entirely erroneous challenged the sanctity of the master-slave relationship. For such reasons, slaveholders were reluctant to permit external authorities to discipline their slaves. As the South Carolinian planter Louis Manigault explained, "the *Master* when on his place is *the one* to examine into his own property & When not there himself *then* his Overseer who has his confidence." Manigault went further and claimed that in the interests of slave discipline, he would not permit even patrollers onto his plantation or allow the imposition of any other "new regulations" on his slaves.[87] The dangers inherent in permitting a third party to assume responsibility for controlling and punishing a slave were clearly articulated by North Carolina chief justice Thomas Ruffin in his famous pronouncement in *State v. Mann* that the courts "must recognize the full dominion of the owner over the slave.... The slave, to remain a slave, must be made sensible that there is no appeal from his master; that his power is in no instance usurped."[88]

To the extent that judicial procedures were loaded against the enslaved, they mimicked an element of the informal discipline routinely imposed by slaveholders on plantations where the law was a distant presence in the lives of all but the most recalcitrant slaves. Slave discipline in rural areas was less based on institutionalized mechanisms of control than on direct personal relationships. According to proslavery arguments, the personal bond between master and slave was the basis of a paternalistic system of mutual dependence in which, "benevolent patriarchs . . . cared for, protected, and cherished their slaves," who, in return, were grateful and loyal and "labored happily and diligently."[89] The reality of slave life on farms and plantations across the South was far from this ideal. Few slaves internalized slaveholders' values and beliefs, and most were owned by slaveholders who did not conform to the benevolent, compassionate expectations of paternalistic ideology. Indeed, on many plantations, the master-slave relationship was as distant as in the city, due to planter absenteeism and the routine delegation of responsibility to overseers. Yet this form of private, personal discipline was nevertheless very different from the public proceedings of Richmond's courtrooms, however unjust they might have been.[90]

Contrary to Chief Justice Ruffin's warning, in Richmond the mayor and his officers routinely usurped the slaveholders' power. What is more, they did so out of necessity. Urban slaveholders were *forced* to rely on the courts to control their slaves, even though legal processes could expose the limitations that the city placed on their personal authority and were in conflict with proslavery ideals.[91] Every time that a slaveholder unsuccessfully challenged a slave's conviction, his mastery was compromised, and even when owners concurred with the mayor's judgments, the very fact that cases came to court at all served as a public affirmation of slaveholders' inability to fulfill their responsibilities as paternalists, patriarchs, and masters, while at the same time pursuing their best financial interests by employing slaves in the city. If performing mastery over slaves was a means by which white southerners could conform to the dictates of southern notions of honor, then owners of urban slaves were disadvantaged in comparison to their rural counterparts. The arrest, examination, and punishment of slaves by municipal authorities, and, equally important, the public record of mayor's court proceedings published in newspapers like the *Dispatch*, stood testament to those distinctive features of urban slavery that were contrary to broader currents in southern slaveholding culture and ideology.

The extant documentary record indicates that the potential for overt conflict between the sources of authority embodied in the person of the mayor and the slaveholder rarely materialized in practice. Certainly any conflict was not often of benefit to enslaved defendants themselves, who always had to submit to the decisions of their masters and hirers in relation to legal matters. Lawyers were appointed or dispensed with at the instigation of the owners of enslaved defendants, and an appeal could not take place without the slaveholder's consent. Furthermore, most slaves received little support from their owners in the face of criminal charges, and, most significant, all were potentially subject to punishment by their owners and employers as well as on the orders of the mayor. Even those who were acquitted by the mayor could face chastisement from their owners on returning home from the courtroom. For example, when the slave Alexander was charged with stealing, the mayor could not hear the case on the assigned day because of the absence of a material witness. The *Dispatch* reported that if the witness did not appear the following morning, Alexander would "be delivered up to his master," who could inflict punishment himself.[92] When another slave, Susan, was charged with assaulting her master and threatening to poison his child, the case again could not be clearly proved. However, when Susan was discharged from custody, it was noted that she "was turned over to her master to be dealt with as to him might seem right and proper."[93] So long as suspected slave criminals were punished by someone, Richmond whites were rarely concerned with who cracked the whip.

The number of slaves who suffered punishment both on the orders of the mayor and at the hands of their owners cannot be known. However, there is evidence that some slaveholders chastised slaves they suspected of committing crimes and then turned them over to the mayor for further punishment, although it is also apparent that Richmond mayors sometimes reduced a slave's sentence if there was evidence that the slave's owner had already inflicted punishment for the offense. When the slave Anderson was convicted of stealing a pair of shoes from a Mr. Crew, the mayor initially sentenced him to receive twenty-five lashes, but he reduced this to fifteen lashes after Anderson claimed that Crew had already whipped him. Although Crew admitted that he had punished Anderson, he claimed that it was for lying, not for stealing the shoes.[94] Fifteen lashes was not an inconsiderable punishment, and Crew may have administered a further whipping outside the courtroom, but even so Anderson had won a minor victory in convincing the mayor to accept, at least partially, his interpretation of the whipping he had earlier received, rather than that of Crew.

Unfortunately, the nature of the relationship between Crew and Anderson is not known, and Crew did not elucidate why he decided not to inflict additional punishment on Anderson for stealing and instead turned him over to the mayor. It is possible, however, that Crew hired Anderson and was conscious of the negative view that Anderson's owner might take of too severe a punishment that could have left lasting injuries and diminished

Anderson's market value. Similar concerns may have motivated other white men and women who hired slaves to report slave crimes to the court so that punishment would be sanctioned by the mayor.[95] In the course of the examination of Jim, a slave charged with threatening to strike his hirer, the shoemaker Jesse Franklin, "it appeared that Franklin had inflicted Forty lashes on the back of Jim before he bro[ugh]t him before me [Mayor Tate]—to have him dealt with according to Law!"[96] Tate reprimanded Franklin in the strongest terms and discharged Jim, but he did not inquire as to Franklin's reasons for prosecuting in the first place. Franklin may have feared that Jim's owner would hold him accountable for damaging his slave property if he inflicted any further punishment himself, and this might have gained him a reputation for cruelty that would have made it difficult for him to hire slaves in the future.[97] Alternatively, Franklin may have believed that the solemnities of the courtroom processes would have a salutary influence on Jim's future behavior, and, possibly, that a formal conviction by the mayor would confer a greater semblance of legitimacy on the punishment that he had himself inflicted. Doubtless, other slaveholders and hirers who prosecuted their slaves in court after inflicting their own punishments outside of the judicial sphere went undetected by the mayor, and when the parties left court there was, of course, little to prevent men such as Franklin beating their slaves as and when they chose, irrespective of the mayor's ruling.

As the police and the mayor cracked down on slave freedoms in the 1850s, some slaves undoubtedly submitted to the violence and power of the law and accepted new constraints on their conduct. However, there is little indication that such a response was common; police surveillance was never so complete as entirely to prevent slaves from congregating illegally and drinking and gambling in Richmond's alleys, factories, and grogshops. At times slaves violated the black codes with impunity and showed little fear of arrest. A resident in Jefferson Ward complained that on the Sabbath, "you may see from 20 to 30 negroes on the walk-ways, at, or around grog shops or tipling houses, intoxicated, between the Old Market House and the Court House of the County, at any time during the day, and it is with difficulty a lady, accompanied by a gentleman, can pass the street, without her ears being saluted with language that is a degradation even to uncivilized man!"[98]

As slaves continued to violate the municipal ordinances, even the strict enforcement of the law could prove disadvantageous to slave discipline, as it increased discontent within the black community and resulted in acts of resistance against the slaveholders' authority. When Charles Colcock Jones's slave Lucy was found not guilty of theft by a jury in Liberty County, Georgia, his son commented that the verdict would have a beneficial impact on the other slaves on the family plantation and impress on them "a new element of mercy and forbearance."[99] However, reports in the *Dispatch* in the 1850s suggest that Mayor Mayo's attack on slave freedoms in Richmond did not have this affect on the city's slave population. The paternalistic ideal was for slaves to identify with and internalize their masters' values and beliefs, but as slaveholders typically played no role in the mayor's court proceedings, the punishments imposed by the mayor could not serve paternalistic ends even in theory. Rather, because the relationship between slaves and the mayor was not one of mutual obligation, the policing of slaves in Richmond had the entirely contrary result of enhancing slaves' understanding of the chasm that separated the proslavery ideal of slaves and owners bound by mutual interests from the reality of slavery in the city. Speaking to a northern reporter in the mid-1850s, a free black storekeeper explained that discontent among Richmond's African American community had "increased a hundred times, especially within the last eight years," due to the introduction of new municipal ordinances restricting black freedoms. The storekeeper went on to explain the changes in black attitudes to city life that had occurred since his childhood:

> When I was a boy, the colored people didn't think much about freedom, because they were allowed a great deal of liberty; but now it seems as if the laws were becoming worse and worse for us every day; we can't enjoy anything now; we can't have the social meetings as we used to have; and now I tell you, Sir, the colored people do think about it a good deal. They run away every good chance they can get. I know about a hundred that's gone North since last New Year; most of them got away altogether, and plenty's ready to follow them.[100]

After the Civil War, ex-slaves in Richmond still remembered the injustice and brutality of the mayor's court verdicts, and when Joseph Mayo died in 1872, a popular poem encapsulated their attitudes toward the nature of their treatment at his hands:

> Here lies old Joe Mayo in his grave dead
> Often he whipped us till we bled.
> He will send us no more to the whipping post,
> For he has gone to join the silent host.
> To Judgment seat he must come
> To give account for the deeds he has done.[101]

"Proper precaution on the part of owners," wrote the *Dispatch* in 1856, "will save the health of their slaves, and keep them from engaging in vices that may lead them into trouble."[102] This conclusion probably overstated the ability of even the most diligent slaveholders to regulate the activities of their slaves in any setting, but as a prescription for ameliorating the problem of slave control in Richmond it was an entirely unrealistic proposition. The essence of slavery in the urban-industrial environment was that slaveholders were all too rarely in a position to keep their slaves from engaging in vice and crime. Industrialists and manufacturers required a highly flexible slave labor force, and hiring out, living out, and the use of incentives such as cash payments to increase productivity were necessary innovations in the city even though they compromised slave discipline.

Incapable of regulating all aspects of slave conduct themselves, slaveholders in Richmond depended on the municipal justice system to supplement their authority. Throughout the antebellum period, and particularly in the 1850s, slaves were routinely arrested, examined by the mayor, and brutally punished for all manner of offenses. Richmond slaveholders largely endorsed the manner in which the mayor's authority was exercised on the city's slaves, yet the system of institutionalized slave control was far from unproblematic. For example, the strict enforcement of the municipal ordinances in the 1850s encouraged slave discontent, conflicted with the economic interests of slave hirers, particularly tobacco manufacturers, and undermined the claims to mastery of individual slaveholders who disputed the mayor's interpretation of their slaves' conduct.

At the same time, slave arrests and punishments stood as very public testimony to the fallacy of paternalistic ideologies that depicted slaves as fundamentally content with their condition and slavery as a positive good on account of the personal bond of mutual dependence between owner and slave. This ideal was far from reality anywhere in the South, but only in the cities was it violated so openly and with slaveholders' acquiescence. When Jane and John Williams attacked the Winston family and murdered their mistress and her daughter, the crime could not be explained in terms of failed paternalism or as an aberration in what was fundamentally a secure system of control, as may have been the case elsewhere in the South. Rather, the Williamses' crimes seemed to derive from the very conditions of slave life on which the city's economic viability depended. In this context of slaveholders murdered by their human property, as well as more general white fears of abolitionist influences and growing sectional tensions, it was a profoundly unsettling prospect for white society to confront in the daily press the records of arrested slaves confined in the city watch houses and examined in the mayor's court, for these records were evidence that the conditions of, in particular, John Williams's life were far from exceptional. The punishments that the mayor imposed on slaves did nothing to alter this situation; nor could they, for conditions that facilitated slave resistance and crime were integral to the profitability of the urban economy. All the mayor could do was discourage slaves from exploiting the freedoms that the city allowed them through ever more liberal use of the whip.

Despite its limitations, the system of slave policing overseen by the mayor of Richmond functioned effectively enough throughout the antebellum era for slavery in the city to remain profitable and for crimes such as those committed by John and Jane Williams to remain rare. However, in the years immediately preceding the Civil War, Richmond slaveholders could not maintain their rule through policing the slave population alone, no matter how effectively the mayor's court performed this task. By the 1850s, limiting slave criminality depended also on increased regulation of Richmond's diverse and impoverished white community.

2

"An evil which demands a speedy remedy"

White Criminality in an Urban Slave Society

On 14 August 1856, Charles Cook, an impoverished white man arrested for drunkenness, and Samuel Vandervall, a free African American, became the first convicts sentenced by Joseph Mayo, the mayor of Richmond, to labor on the city's new chain gang. It was a further two weeks before the chain gang made its first appearance on Richmond's streets, but when it did Cook and Vandervall were accompanied by two other free black men. In accordance with the hopes of the *Richmond Daily Dispatch*, drunkards and "wife-whippers" were soon toiling on the chain gang, and within a month the hustings court magistrates had also sentenced white men convicted of theft to be shackled to a ball and chain and forced to labor on the public streets. The symbolism of these events was unmistakable. The very existence of white criminals and paupers in the South compromised the arguments of men such as James Henry Hammond and John Townsend that slavery benefited all whites. However, the sight of poor and intemperate white men laboring together in public and in chains along with convicted criminals, both black and white, left an even more indelible impression on the thousands of poor white citizens in Richmond who had reason to sympathize with the prisoners' plight or to fear that they too might one day be reduced to a similar condition because of their susceptibility to alcoholic overindulgence, poverty, petty criminal activities, or even judicial error and malpractice.[1]

White men and women in Richmond appeared as defendants in the mayor's court with growing frequency during the antebellum period. Invariably they were accused of relatively minor offenses, such as drunkenness, disorderly conduct, and assault; crimes that Bertram Wyatt-Brown has described as "misdeeds of anonymity and insignificance" that upheld the social order by demonstrating "the wilfulness and disorderliness of the lower ranks" and helping "to separate the worthy from the demeaned." Yet in Richmond, the specter of white criminality concerned the slaveholding elite for at least two reasons. First, white crime and disorder could compromise slave discipline, most notably when whites and slaves engaged in joint criminal activities and when whites facilitated slaves' efforts to violate municipal codes by permitting unlawful gatherings of African Americans and selling liquor to slaves. Second, in southern slave cities the culture of violence, vice, and criminality that developed among the white laboring poor contributed to growing divisions among whites along lines of class and ethnicity that were fueled also by immigration, industrialization, urbanization, and the rising costs of slave ownership that limited social mobility.[2]

White crime could not be ignored, therefore, yet neither was controlling it a straightforward process. The urban context required a response to white crime and disorder that was qualitatively distinct from forms of social control outside of the city. In rural southern societies, the maintenance of the public peace was overwhelmingly the concern of individual citizens, and the forms and ends of crime control were determined as much by popular notions of honor, shame, and patriarchy as by law. Extralegal whippings, beatings, and maimings were common responses to perceived criminal activity, and more ritualistic forms of violence such as duels and lynchings were also used to uphold a community's notions of right and wrong. The law was not entirely absent from rural southern society; magistrates were usually prominent local figures, and court dockets were often crowded. Yet, until the early twentieth century, rural policing was limited, and even when criminal investigations and trials were held, community sentiment exerted considerable influence over courtroom proceedings and judicial decision making.[3]

The characteristics of rural law enforcement were not entirely absent from urban Virginia, but in the antebellum years the growing complexity of Richmond's social relations demanded an increasingly pervasive role in everyday life for state institutions, including the police, poorhouse, courts, and prisons.[4] In particular, Richmond slaveholders perceived a need for more rigorous law enforcement mechanisms to regulate the conduct of the white poor, immigrants, and other community outsiders. These groups seemed to threaten the stability of southern slave society not only through criminal conduct, but also because they lived on the economic margins of society and many were not reared in southern social, cultural, and racial mores.

As Charles Cook discovered, the introduction of the chain gang was one way in which Richmond authorities sought to exert greater control over the lives of the white poor in their midst. However, the chain gang was not an exception, but rather part of a broader trend that also included greater discretionary judicial decision making by the police and in the mayor's court, as well as more rigorous regulation of public order offenses, such as drunkenness, prostitution, and vagrancy, when committed by the lower classes. These developments occurred at the same time that efforts to clamp down on slave crime were intensifying, yet the significance of police activities for the wider community was very different when the individuals in the dock were white. James Oakes has argued that any actions or events that divided the southern white community were "ominous portents of disunity in the face of a rising antislavery threat."[5] Certain forms of white criminality were, in themselves, evidence of such disunity, but by the 1850s whites' experiences of the law could also reflect and sharpen class divisions. Charles Cook's time on the chain gang, for example, was a consequence not simply of intemperance but also of his inability to raise sufficient funds to pay the peace bond that would have led to his discharge from custody on bail. In this sense, Cook's punishment institutionalized his poverty, set him apart from wealthier white residents, and helped to define a distinctive lower-class sensibility in the city.

Class was not only important in the way that law was imposed on white criminals; it also influenced how white victims of crime, especially women, engaged with the police and the courts. By the 1830s, poor white Richmonders turned to the courts as a matter of routine to impose order in their daily lives, and their right to do so helped solidify white solidarity across class and ethnic lines.[6] However, the urban culture of legal redress also enabled subordinate groups to contest established hierarchies. Notably, poor white women brought cases that challenged patriarchal authority, and in entering the public sphere of the courtroom they contested notions of female domesticity.[7] In the context of growing sectional tensions in the 1850s, these developments were of no little significance, for they tended to place constraints primarily on the conduct of poor whites, the very people who benefited least from slavery in terms of their economic and social status. Although the racial divide in Virginia's statute laws reinforced notions of white solidarity, the way in which poor whites encountered the law in practice in Richmond had more ambiguous implications for their relationship to southern slavery and racial ideology.

In his annual report of 1851, Governor John Buchanan Floyd hailed Virginia as a bastion of tranquility and order and, by way of contrast, condemned the crime and poverty that he claimed plagued the northern states. "We have no riots, mobs, arson and wholesale murder to mourn over, to punish or to countenance," Floyd wrote. "We have no work-houses crowded with famishing and unprovided wretchedness, [and] no swarms of beggars infesting our

Fig. 4. "Hon. John B. Floyd." Ca. 1855–1865. John Buchanan Floyd was governor of Virginia, 1848–52. Courtesy of Library of Congress, Prints and Photographs online, Brady-Handy Photograph Collection. <http://hdl.loc.gov/loc.pnp/cwpbh.01730>

cities. . . . All is peace, quiet and order. From one extremity of the land to the other, there is felt in every ramification of society, perfect and absolute personal security."[8]

Governor Floyd's comments were not unusual in the context of the late antebellum debate on the nature of free labor and slave societies, yet they were at odds with the reality of increasing crime and poverty that characterized Richmond in the antebellum period.[9] Between the early 1830s and late 1850s, the number of white men and women charged in Richmond's hustings court with crimes against person and property increased by 600 percent, from 16.6 to 98.8 per year. Throughout the period, a majority of these cases involved property crimes, predominantly stealing, forgery, and receiving stolen goods, although in the 1850s the most substantial increase was in cases of violent crime, which in comparison to the 1840s doubled in number relative to the size of Richmond's white population.

Table 2.1: Prosecutions of white defendants for property crimes and violent crimes in Richmond Hustings Court, 1830–1860

	Number of cases			Annual cases per 1000 of population		
Years	Property crimes	Violent crimes	Total	Property crimes	Violent crimes	Total
1830–34	56	27	83	1.3	0.6	2.0
1835–39	109	46	155	2.2	0.9	3.1
1840–44	102	72	174	1.7	1.2	2.9
1845–49	132	61	193	1.9	0.9	2.7
1850–54	207	150	357	2.4	1.7	4.1
1855–59	276	218	494	2.6	2.0	4.6
1860	48	80	128	2.0	3.4	5.4
Total	930	654	1,584	—	—	—

Source: Richmond Hustings Court Minutes, 1830–60.

Less serious forms of white criminal activity that did not reach the trial courts also increased in the antebellum era. The number of white men and women examined in the mayor's court rose from a rate of 31 per thousand of population in 1852 to 39 per thousand in 1860, with the greatest increases in cases of assault and drunk and disorderly conduct.[10] Of greater concern to the slaveholding class, there was a particularly substantial rise in prosecutions of whites for violating laws intended to control the slave population. For example, between 1830 and 1850 just four whites were charged in the hustings court with permitting or participating in unlawful assemblies of slaves, but over the next ten years forty-three cases were heard. There was also an increase in indictments for keeping a disorderly house, an offense associated with prostitution and interracial sexual relationships. It is significant that these increases occurred at the same time as prosecutions for other offenses related to moral conduct declined. Between 1830 and 1850, there were 1,164 indictments in Richmond for gambling offenses, but in the 1850s there were only 42. Prosecutions for retailing ardent spirits without a license did not decline so sharply, but, they, too, became less prevalent toward the end of the antebellum era. These trends perhaps reflect declining support in the South for moral reform movements after the 1830s due to their association with northern abolitionism.[11] However, they also indicate that Richmond's criminal courts were increasingly preoccupied by crimes against person and property and offenses that involved relations across the color line and that compromised slave discipline.[12]

Patterns of criminal prosecutions of white defendants evolved in mid-nineteenth century Richmond in ways different from other cities in the South. The ratio of violence to property crime provides the most useful comparison of prosecutions in different jurisdictions, and the available figures show that Richmond was unique among southern cities in charging a greater number of white defendants with property offenses than violence. Between 1830 and 1860, 930 indictments were issued against white defendants in Richmond for property crimes but only 654 for violent crimes. By contrast, the Superior Court of Chatham County, Georgia, which had jurisdiction over the city of Savannah, dealt with twice as many violent crimes as property offenses during the 1850s, while the Circuit Court of Warren County, Mississippi, which included the city of Vicksburg, heard 623 cases of crime against persons and only 355 property crime cases between 1822 and 1859. The pattern in Charleston, South Carolina, was similar, with violent crimes accounting for 58.3 percent of criminal prosecutions between 1800 and 1860, more than four times the rate of property crime prosecutions. In two counties containing sizable towns in mid-Georgia, 31 percent of indictments were for crimes against person and only 17 percent for property offenses. Violent crime was also pervasive on court dockets in rural parts of the South. In the Central Piedmont of North Carolina, assault and battery and fighting accounted for at least half of the crimes prosecuted, while between 1820 and 1860 violence was also the most common type of crime experienced in two very different Virginia counties, Shenandoah, located in the Blue Ridge Mountains, and Louisa, a plantation county.[13]

Prosecution patterns in Richmond were more similar to those in northern than southern cities. In Massachusetts between 1833 and 1858, almost twice as many property crimes were prosecuted as violent crimes against persons.[14] In Philadelphia, meanwhile, the proportion of property crime cases prosecuted at the court of quarter sessions increased from 27 percent of the total between 1800 and 1838, to 42 percent between 1844 and 1855. During the same two periods, violent crime prosecutions declined from 45 percent to 35 percent of all cases.[15]

A number of factors might account for Richmond's distinctive pattern of criminal prosecutions relative to the rest of the South. The high proportion of property crimes in Richmond may have been a consequence of the growth of industry and manufacturing that distinguished the city from others in the slave states that were primarily commercial centers. In the light industries and workshops of commercial cities such as Charleston and Savannah, there was an intimacy between employers and white workers that resulted in less social stratification than was common in industrial cities and that discouraged property offenses.[16] Furthermore, the decline of Virginia's plantation economy and its location in the Border South may have meant that Richmond was more heavily influenced by bourgeois northern cultural mores than other slave cities, particularly those in more recently settled western states like Alabama and Mississippi. The diversification of Virginia's economy and an influx of northern people, goods, and ideas into Richmond may have undermined factors that have been used to explain high rates of violence characteristic of the antebellum South as a whole. These include the frontier character of southern life, the region's slave-based social hierarchy, the influence of Celtic settlers in the colonial era, and a code of honor that demanded that personal disputes be resolved by the individuals directly concerned rather than legal arbitration.[17]

Crime patterns in Richmond were undoubtedly different from elsewhere in the South, but despite the unusually high proportion of property crime prosecutions, it is notable that the city did not experience a corresponding decline in white violence. On the contrary, the number of cases of violent crime prosecuted in the city more than doubled between the 1830s and the 1850s. In this regard, antebellum Richmonders had the worst of two worlds; while the social, economic, and demographic impact of industrialization brought about increased levels of property crime, it did not inculcate a cultural change based on the ideals of self-control, discipline, and personal dignity that developed and discouraged violence in the northeastern states.[18] In the antebellum era, Richmond's industrial development remained at an early stage and its population for the most part retained rural values. Even by the outbreak of the Civil War, a large part of the immigrant population had not been resident in the city for sufficient time to develop the industrial discipline and "secondary relationships" that contributed to declining levels of interpersonal violence in later stages of industrialization.[19] Moreover, the persistence of slavery meant that ideals of rationality, dignity, and self-control that were developed in free labor societies, but that were contrary to the authoritarian prerogatives of the slaveholding class, could never entirely take hold in Richmond.

Sensitive to any evidence of divisions within the native white community, Richmond elites tended to downplay the significance of white crime and instead highlighted the criminal tendencies of slaves and free African Americans. When white crime was addressed, it was invariably northern and immigrant workers or transient visitors to the city who were cited as the root of the problem.[20] However, as the introduction of the chain gang indicates, although crime and poverty were by no means synonymous in antebellum Richmond, politicians, local commentators, and visitors to the city also considered rising crime rates in the context of class divisions within the white community.

Had white society in Richmond conformed to the ideal of a herrenvolk democracy in which all whites had a direct and clearly identifiable stake in the slave regime and in which the racial divide was secure, the administration of criminal justice in cases involving white criminals would have had limited ramifications for slavery in the city.[21] As it was, Richmond's antebellum white community was marked by social stratification. The city elite consisted primarily of Virginia-born industrialists, manufacturers, and professionals who had extensive property holdings in local counties and in most cases owned large numbers of slaves. These men promoted internal improvements and capitalist advancement and were tied to Virginia's planter class through family and commercial connections.[22]

Property holding was relatively widespread among Richmond whites outside of the elite. In the 1850s, 25 percent of white male householders owned their own house, and more than 50 percent owned at least one slave.[23] Yet beyond this middle class, and despite the rhetoric of southern boosters and proslavery intellectuals, the condition of the urban poor in antebellum Richmond was little better than that of the impoverished classes in northern cities.[24] One particularly infamous alley in Rocketts—a notorious riverside area situated in the east of the city—was described in 1860 as "little better than the Five Points of New York, in its darkest days. Families occupy pens eight by ten feet, men and women get drunk and fight and scratch like so many cats; and to mend the matter, dances are given on Sunday nights, to the annoyance of the neighborhood."[25]

The cramped living conditions of the Richmond poor attracted the attention of Charles Dickens, who, in characteristic fashion, commented on the "deplorable tenements, fences unrepaired, walls crumbling into ruinous heaps" that he found in Richmond in the early 1840s.[26] White poverty in Richmond became particularly acute in the 1850s as a result of increased immigration and a series of economic downturns that culminated in the depression of 1857. To Samuel Mordecai, a white Richmonder writing in the harsh winter of 1855, there seemed to be a strange reversal of the racial order inherent in the condition of the city's poor, for while "slaves are provided with food, fuel, and clothing . . . our poor-houses and other receptacles for the destitute and dissipated whites, are crowded to overflowing, chiefly with foreign paupers."[27]

Another famous visitor to antebellum Richmond, Frederick Law Olmsted, was of the opinion that "there was at least as much vice and what we call rowdyism in Richmond as in any northern town of its size."[28] The laboring class of whites included many "ruffianly looking fellows," whose demeanor Olmsted compared unfavorably with the decent civility of the

African Americans he encountered. The canal boatmen in particular seemed to Olmsted "to be quite as rude, insolent and riotous a class as those of New York," while he expressed himself shocked by the plight of the "very dirty German Jews," many of whom were storekeepers in "the narrowest and meanest streets, which seem to be otherwise inhabited mainly by negroes."[29]

The German Jews whom Olmstead encountered were part of Richmond's rapidly growing immigrant population. In 1850, there were 2,101 immigrants in the city, but by 1860 this figure had risen to almost 5,000, and immigrants made up 20 percent of all Richmond whites. More significantly, 39 percent of adult free workingmen in the city were foreign born, the same proportion of whites as were natives of the slave states, and this made immigrants a potentially powerful and subversive force in city politics.[30]

The Irish were the largest immigrant group in Richmond, and, as in other American cities, they were entrenched in the lowest-paid, least reputable, and least secure occupations. In contrast to British and German immigrants, many of whom worked in skilled trades, including the iron industry, shoemaking, stonecutting, house building, and printing, Irishmen were overwhelmingly employed as unskilled laborers. Young Irish women, meanwhile, accounted for almost all of the growing number of white domestic workers in 1850s Richmond.[31] To a far greater extent than other immigrants, therefore, the Irish found themselves in competition for employment with free blacks and slaves. Unable to afford the rent payments demanded in white suburbs, many Irish residents also lived in predominantly black neighborhoods, and they continually balanced precariously on the edge of social acceptability as well as impoverishment.[32]

Immigrant poverty increased the fears of many native-born white Richmonders that the foreign-born threatened the city's racial stability. Unfamiliar with the culture and conventions of slave society and usually with little prospect of becoming slaveholders themselves, most immigrants, like other white workers, did not derive great economic benefits from slavery.[33] Furthermore, as many white workers in Richmond labored alongside blacks, sympathetic relationships could develop across racial lines, although on other occasions interracial associations were discouraged by the traditional southern notion that wage labor was "degrading rather than ennobling" because of its association with slavery.[34] Reflecting this latter sensibility, a number of strikes launched by white workers in the late 1840s and 1850s challenged the employment of slaves. White workers attacked the employment of African Americans in cities throughout the nation. However, it was only in the South that working-class racism so starkly embodied confrontation with the ruling elite, as slaveholders resisted attempts to limit their right to employ their slaves in any way they saw fit.[35]

The attitudes of immigrants and other white workers toward slavery were diverse. The historian Werner Steger has interpreted the resistance of white workers toward employment alongside slaves and free blacks to indicate that most immigrants in Richmond "supported slavery and the racial caste system and integrated themselves into the political and economic community of the city."[36] In contrast to immigrants who settled in the North, those who made their homes south of the Mason-Dixon Line did not have to "negotiate their whiteness" but were automatically afforded all the privileges of their race. According to this analysis, clear lines of demarcation in the social and legal sphere made fraternization between the African American and immigrant populations of little threat to the racial order of the city.[37] This argument is reinforced by evidence of increasing racial segregation in industrial employment in the 1840s and 1850s and the growth of predominantly white residential districts on the outskirts of the city, away from Richmond's major black communities that remained concentrated in Shockoe Creek near the docks, factories, and railroad depots where most African American workers were employed.[38]

In spite of developments in residential and employment patterns, however, the spatial separation of the races was never so complete in Richmond as to undermine entirely the well-established lower-class cultural ties that bound poor whites and blacks together.[39] An interracial subculture had formed in Richmond as early as the 1780s, but it assumed a particularly threatening form in the mid-nineteenth century in the context of immediate abolitionism and the augmentation of the southern-born white working class by large numbers of young and unattached male immigrants with little stake in the slave regime.[40] This was particularly true after the 1850 Virginia Constitutional Convention, which extended the suffrage to all white adult males, thereby imbuing the actions and beliefs of even the poorest whites with a new political significance that appeared to confirm the fears of some conservative slaveholders "that they would lose control of the Commonwealth to those with little interest in the peculiar institution."[41] The widespread working-class support for the Richmond politician John Minor Botts, who throughout the 1850s attacked slaveholders' dominance of Virginia politics, made the city elite especially sensitive to the attitudes of nonslaveholding whites.[42]

Many immigrants readily adapted to the racial mores of slave society, and significant numbers became slaveholders themselves, but still native southerners in Richmond expressed concern about the influence of foreign immigrants on slavery in the city.[43] The chief engineer of the James River and Kanawha Canal Company complained that immigrant workers "war against our institutions, and refuse to work with our slaves." The *Richmond Republican*, however, was more concerned about the disreputable neighborhoods on the banks of the James where "large numbers of strangers from all quarters of the world . . . settled together with our extensive negro population."[44] As connections and mutual sympathies were forged between slaves, free blacks, and poor whites in Richmond's crowded downtown streets, back alley grogshops, and places of work, they raised "the possibility that at least some white workers blamed the system of slavery and not the slave for their condition."[45]

While most nonslaveholding whites knew better than to publicly denounce slavery, when the northern reporter James Redpath visited Richmond in 1854, he interviewed a free black storekeeper who claimed that many whites had told him that they opposed slavery, "but they never talk about it to white people: *they're afraid to do so!*"[46] Herrmann Schuricht expressed similar sentiments when he took over as editor of the German-language edition of the *Richmond Enquirer* on the condition "that he should not be obliged to write in favor of slavery."[47] Doubtless many poorer immigrants who were excluded from slave ownership could not but be skeptical of proslavery claims that racial slavery secured republican citizenship and independence for white men. As was true in other southern cities, nonelite whites in Richmond adopted a flexible and pragmatic approach to race relations, such that even those who supported slavery as an institution were not averse to acting in ways that compromised southern racial ideology and violated laws and ordinances intended to maintain slave discipline.[48]

In this context of white class divisions and ethnic tensions over slavery and labor relations, native Richmonders did not hesitate to blame increasing rates of white crime on foreign and northern influences. The attorney John Coles Rutherford believed that European immigrants corrupted American society. He claimed that the majority of Europeans who crossed the Atlantic "must be an inferior class. . . . Men in easy circumstances and good repute in their own country are not likely to abandon it. Crime, poverty and mania are the causes which bring so many thousands across the ocean to our American shores."[49] Had Rutherford visited Richmond's city jail, his suspicions about immigrant criminality would have been reaffirmed. One police officer estimated in the 1850s that "at least eight out of every ten white persons committed to the cages are foreigners or non-residents of this State." This was an exaggeration, but the city jail was increasingly filled with foreign-born inmates.[50] The 1850 census recorded just two non-Virginians among the prisoners, one of whom was from Maryland and the other an Irishman named Patrick Donahoe, who was charged with larceny. When the census takers returned in 1860, however, fifteen of the jail's forty-nine white inmates were of European extraction, and a further eleven were Americans from outside Virginia.[51]

White poverty, immigration, and growing divisions between rich and poor whites meant that slaveholders in Richmond could not take for granted the white racial solidarity on which their rule depended. At the same time, however, institutions were formed in the city that helped to sustain the race divide and give value to whiteness: benevolent associations tempered the suffering of the white poor; militias symbolically represented the fundamental equality of all whites irrespective of wealth and status; mechanics' associations asserted the dignity of wage labor; schools offered free education to all white children; and municipal ordinances restricted employment opportunities for free blacks, thereby protecting and elevating the jobs of poor whites.[52]

At the same time as white crime was increasing in Richmond, therefore, slaveholders sought to contain tensions between the interests of whites as a race and the poor as a class by reinforcing social and economic divisions between blacks and whites. The administration of criminal justice contributed to this process by affording whites legal rights that were denied to African Americans. However, white crime presented the municipal authorities with a complex dilemma for judicial efforts to control white conduct could also appear contrary to ideals of republican independence and freedom. This is not to say that lower-class whites resented the enforcement of laws that protected their person and property or that they were in fundamental disagreement with lawmakers over statutes that regulated moral conduct. On the contrary, poor whites frequently reported crimes and used the judicial system to manage aspects of their everyday lives and personal relationships.[53] Nonetheless, particularly as the mayor and his subordinates acted to regulate relatively minor offenses such as drunkenness, vagrancy, the illegal liquor trade, petty theft, and assault, the fact that their efforts were invariably directed against nonslaveholding whites was a potential source of division within white society.

In terms of financial investment and institutional development, the response of Richmond's civic leaders to rising white crime and disorder was limited. Although the chain gang was introduced in 1856, proposals for the establishment of a workhouse, a facility for incarcerating juveniles, new watch houses in the suburbs, and the expansion of the city jail did not come to fruition in the pre–Civil War years, and a new poorhouse was completed only as Virginia went to war in early 1861 and was soon taken over for military purposes. Similarly, although the number of police officers and night watchmen in Richmond increased between 1830 and 1860, calls for more fundamental reform of the police elicited little support. In all cases, financial considerations constrained the council's investment in law enforcement. However, it is also apparent that, even with the substantial increase in white criminal activity in the 1850s, many slaveholders remained of the opinion that there was no need to expand the police force except to maintain order among the enslaved. When the Common Council passed an ordinance in 1859 providing for four additional day policemen, for example, even the supporters of the plan claimed that additional officers were not required to combat the criminal element in Richmond's rapidly growing population and across its geographically scattered environs, but rather to prevent the escape of slaves from the city.[54]

Although many American cities, including New York, New Orleans, Boston, and Savannah, established professional, uniformed police forces that operated under an integrated chain of command in the mid-nineteenth century, Richmond retained its traditional division between the day police and night watch throughout the antebellum period. As late as 1860, the municipal government employed only eight day police officers and forty night watchmen.[55] In addition, a public guard of ninety men policed federal buildings in Richmond and protected the city against slave rebellions. The public guard was formed after Gabriel's Rebellion in 1800, and as Richmond's slave population remained substantial throughout the antebellum era, it retained widespread support among Richmonders, particularly as it was funded at state expense. By contrast, in other southern cities where the slave population was in decline, the presence of a paramilitary force began to appear as an antirepublican threat to white liberty, and this may explain why Richmond lagged in terms of police reform.[56]

There is no evidence that the public guard ever contributed to policing the white population—not even in the 1850s when the day police and night watch struggled to respond to increasing white crime and disorder in Richmond's growing suburban areas.[57] In 1859, a "friend connected with the Night Police" indicated that the most dangerous neighborhoods in the city were located in "out-of-the-way places." These areas included "Sugar Bottom," at the southern end of Ninth Street, "Ram Cat Alley," situated off Brooke Avenue in the northwest of the city, and also nearby "Ruinsville." The friend of the night watch suggested that, although these localities occupied a great deal of police time, the overall police presence was insufficient to maintain order, and he warned that unless the mayor and the grand jury took action "to renovate these foul places . . . respectable residents will be compelled to remove their quarters."[58] Policing provisions were particularly inadequate in those suburbs that spilled outside the corporation limits into neighboring Henrico County, where there were no police patrols and law enforcement was dependent on the efforts of district constables. Screamersville, in particular, was renowned as "the stamping ground of many rowdies, who assemble there to carouse and fight" safe from the interference of the city watchmen. It was believed that thieves and burglars targeted properties in Church Hill and Union Hill for the same reasons, as well as seeking refuge there after perpetrating crimes in the city itself.[59]

The authority of the mayor of Richmond extended for one mile beyond the corporation line, and in the 1850s Mayor Joseph Mayo did take some steps to extend police surveillance beyond the city's central areas.[60] In 1855, for example, he ordered two officers to patrol on horseback, enabling them to do "more real service . . . than five times their number could have done in double the time." Moreover, when a riot broke out in Screamersville in 1859, Mayo exercised his authority "to arrest and punish the disorderly."[61] Without a radical overhaul in police methods and numbers, however, it remained impossible for Richmond law officers to systematically police outlying districts, and in 1860 Mayo announced that he would no longer interfere with events in the suburbs but would instead "let the county officers take care of their citizens, so that his own aids may devote all their time to city matters."[62]

The difficulties faced by watchmen in outlying areas were compounded by the location of the city's two watch houses within five blocks of the Capitol at a substantial distance from many of Richmond's most disorderly neighborhoods.[63] Transporting prisoners from the point of arrest to the watch house could be a hazardous task. All arrests involved some degree of physical coercion and, although watchmen were provided with rattles to summon assistance if required, many were injured by prisoners who put up fierce resistance as they were carried to the watch house.[64] In 1860, after at least three night watchmen had been violently beaten in the streets and two others stabbed, the *Dispatch* envisaged that it would soon be necessary to arm Richmond's police officers for their own protection, as "the Courts and juries seem but little disposed to punish such outrages as they deserve."[65] As well as fear of attack, the time involved in transporting persons from outlying areas to the watch houses may have discouraged watchmen from making arrests, particularly for petty offenses and when it seemed unlikely that a prosecution would ensue.

Even in Richmond's central areas, police surveillance did not improve significantly in the 1850s. The number of night watchmen did increase from thirty to forty men over the course of the decade, but this rise did not keep pace with the growth of the city's population. In 1854, the *Dispatch* criticized the organization of the night watch, noting that one district that was patrolled by just two watchmen extended for more than one mile from Seventeenth Street to the East Corporation line and for three blocks south of Main Street to the James River.[66] Given that watchmen walked repetitive beats around their districts, the *Dispatch* complained that potential thieves and burglars "have only to secrete themselves till the watchmen pass by on their rounds, and they will then have an hour or two to do their work and get away before that point is again passed."[67]

In spite of the limited numbers and unreformed organization of the Richmond police, the relationship between the police and the public in the city was fundamentally distinct from surrounding rural areas. The police may have done little to prevent crime, but their presence on the streets shaped responses to criminal activity. These responses involved both the enforcement of the criminal laws and municipal ordinances by the officers and watchmen as they walked their beats and also the reporting of crimes by victims and witnesses. Victims sometimes called for a watchman in the immediate aftermath of a crime, but they could also report incidents to the mayor or one of the twelve city aldermen who were empowered as justices of the peace to issue peace warrants, arrest warrants, and search warrants.[68] Usually warrants were handed to one of the day police officers who endeavored to make an arrest and ensure the prompt appearance of a suspect in the mayor's court.

As with slaves, the mayor's court was the fulcrum of white interaction with the law in Richmond. The mayor's authority over white men and women was defined by the state legislature in 1819. "An Act, extending the Jurisdiction of the Magistrates of the City of Richmond, and for other purposes" authorized the mayor to pass judgment on "all breaches of the peace committed within the jurisdiction of the City, and . . . all infractions of the City Ordinances, and his judgments touching the same shall be final."[69] The mayor also examined and passed sentence on white men and women charged with misdemeanors punishable by a fine of twenty dollars or less.[70] In all other criminal cases involving white defendants, whether misdemeanors or felonies, the mayor inquired into the probable guilt of the accused and, if the evidence tended to establish culpability, bound the offender to a recognizance to answer an indictment for the offense at the next grand jury term of the hustings court.

In contrast to Richmond's two trial courts, where white defendants were most commonly charged with offenses against property, mayor's court cases

Table 2.2. Richmond Mayor's Court cases: White defendants

Type of crime	1838	1852	1860
CRIMES AGAINST PERSON			
Assault	98	114	254
Fighting	8	22	62
Other violent crimes	4	13	30
Total	110	149	346
CRIMES AGAINST PROPERTY			
Stealing	20	49	67
Receiving stolen goods	5	14	15
Injuring property	1	9	9
Other property crimes	5	6	25
Total	31	78	116
PUBLIC ORDER AND OTHER OFFENSES			
Drunkenness	131	166	226
Threatening violence	12	48	76
Abusive language	1	8	32
Disorderly conduct	7	35	15
Offenses related to slavery	3	5	14
Trespassing	2	8	18
Vagrancy	2	11	26
Ill-fame/prostitution	1	3	28
Unknown	4	6	0
Other	1	36	31
Total	164	326	466
Grand total	305	553	928

Sources: Richmond Mayor's Court Docket Book, 1838; *Richmond Daily Dispatch*, 14 Jan. 1852–13 Jan. 1853, and 1 Jan.–31 Dec. 1860.

were more often concerned with violent crimes and drunkenness. Most acts of violence that the mayor investigated were assaults and fights that were little more than breaches of the peace. In the vast majority of such cases, the mayor ordered the accused to enter into a recognizance to be of good behavior, and if the bond was not paid, the defendant faced up to twelve months in jail. In order for the mayor to issue a peace bond, it was not necessary for the complainant to prove that a crime had been committed but only to convince the mayor that the accused posed a threat to the public peace.

The mayor could also hold white men and women to a recognizance for the loosely defined offense of "not being of '*good fame*.'" John B. Minor, professor of law at the University of Virginia in the 1850s, defined this term to mean, "being guilty of scandalous behavior, contrary to good manners and morals, [such] as keeping, frequenting, or maintaining bawdy-houses, prostitution, drunkenness, gaming, cheating, keeping suspicious company, &c."[71]

Offenses of this type, as well as the use of threatening, insulting, or abusive language, accounted for between 50 and 60 percent of the thousands of accusations made against whites in the mayor's court during the antebellum era, and the manner in which they were resolved depended a great deal on the individual magistrate hearing the case.

Despite the guidelines laid down by men such as John Minor, the mayor of Richmond exercised considerable discretion over the fate of the white men and women who appeared before him, as he did in slave cases. In practice, it was the prerogative of the mayor, rather than the law, to determine whether complainants were right to fear for their personal safety and when an assault was sufficiently serious to be classed as a misdemeanor. The mayor could also define precisely what constituted "scandalous behavior," "good morals," and "suspicious company." The anthropologist Barbara Yngvesson has outlined the complexities of such discretionary decision-making processes. She claims that the decisions of examining courts are not determined in a vacuum but rather within the context of an "ambiguous legal/social world." Within this world, Yngvesson explains that a

> "threat to commit a crime is a crime and it isn't a crime," depending on the clerk's [or, in antebellum Richmond, the mayor's] interpretations of whether specific actions constitute "threat." This, in turn, is dependent on his understanding of local lifeways, his connections to those who live them, and his sense of whether a finding of probable cause makes political and moral sense in the context of local politics and local moralities.[72]

The rulings of the mayor of Richmond not only reflected but also contributed to the construction of local moralities. To this end, mayor's court judgments served an overt social-control, as well as a crime-control function, as they determined certain forms of conduct to be illegal and, through their dissemination in the press and other public forums, helped to define local conceptions of criminality. However, magistrates' interpretations of "local lifeways" rarely reflect the uncritical acceptance of dominant cultural ideals but rather are the product of courtroom processes in which these ideals are contested and potentially transformed. It is central to an understanding of the role of law in Richmond, therefore, to recognize that as the mayor's court assumed a more important and pervasive influence in the regulation of Richmond's white population, it also inevitably provided marginal groups with opportunities to contest aspects of the social order.[73]

As with all other aspects of the Richmond justice system, mayor's court cases involving white defendants had political and social ramifications that could not be divorced from questions of urban slavery. In cities such as Baltimore, where slavery declined precipitously during the antebellum period, elites confronted an uncertain social and economic order and attempted "to fortify the allegiance of working-class whites" in part by supporting an "egalitarian legal process" that was accessible to all classes of whites.[74] At least in terms of the number of slaves and the profitability of their labor, slavery was more stable in Richmond than in Baltimore, yet given the social tensions that abounded within the white community, the elite was similarly obliged to uphold an egalitarian legal process for whites. Not only was this important to the maintenance of the racial order within Richmond, but also the denial to southern whites of any legal rights that were held by whites in the North was incompatible with a defense of slavery based on race and, therefore, with the broader interests of the slaveholding elite.[75]

The events that transpired in the mayor's court were not only important to controlling white crime, therefore; they also had an abiding cultural and political significance.[76] Although a majority of the cases resolved by the mayor were of a trivial nature, the verdicts and sentences, as well as the commentary on illegal conduct provided by the mayor and reported and interpreted in the press, codified and shaped popular understandings of white criminality. Most notably, the poor and marginal groups frequently appeared before the mayor as defendants, complainants, and witnesses, and disorderly conduct and criminality became firmly associated with lower-class status and foreign birth. Not only was the very act of reporting violence and disorderly conduct defined as a sign of lower-class status and, therefore, a contributing factor to class divisions in white society, but to the extent that they relied on institutional justice to order their daily lives, poor whites violated southern ideals of independence, honor, and patriarchal governance. Illustrative is an analysis of the experiences of white women who appeared in the mayor's court.

In southern cities, the judicial system was an alternative source of authority to the governance of white male household heads. This was significant, as in the Old South the defense of slavery was strengthened by the notion that white men ruled over all household dependents, not only slaves themselves but also white women, children, and servants. Southern patriarchy bolstered nonslaveholding support for the existing social order, as it transcended class inequalities and gave poor white men "common cause with planters in maintaining and policing the class, gender, and racial boundaries of citizenship in the slave republic."[77] Stephanie McCurry has argued that proslavery writers viewed the relationship of a wife to her husband as comparable to that of a slave to her master. Both wives and slaves assumed a subordinate role in proslavery rhetoric, while husbands and masters were imbued with a power that needed no regulation due to their "natural" benevolence.[78] In this understanding of the marriage compact, even if a white husband did not own any slaves, he was, at the very least, master of his wife within his own home.

The presence of women in the mayor's court as complainants can be interpreted as evidence of a breakdown in the system of male household governance, as well as an indication of women's determination to use the law to regulate their daily lives. Women in this latter category often had poor or disreputable backgrounds, and many were described in highly derogatory terms by Richmond's mayors and the press. When Patsy and Jane Jackson were charged with taking Mary Sullivan from her father and keeping her in their house for "improper purposes," they were dismissed from prosecution because "Mary Sullivan was known to the Mayor as one of the vilest pieces of her age in the city." Similarly, the charge of using abusive and provoking language made against Maria Willis, a free black woman, was thrown out in part because the complainant, Nancy Traiman, was "an abandoned woman of the lowest order."[79] The *Dispatch* was also critical of the actions of Amelia J. Baker, a woman living in Rocketts who took out a complaint against four men for "entering her house and using violent and insulting language to herself and the other inmates." Implying that the inmates at Baker's house were involved in less than respectable occupations, the *Dispatch* deemed it "bad policy" for women who "keep open doors for all who may choose to enter ... to be running to courts with trivial complaints."[80]

Despite such criticism, white women appealed frequently to the mayor for protection and redress in the wake of threatened or actual violence. In the sample years of 1838, 1852, and 1860, women were the victims or complainants in one-third of the 411 cases of white-on-white assault that were examined in the mayor's court. Moreover, 37 percent of these women (55 out of 149) were assaulted by their husbands. This indicates the importance of the mayor's court as a forum for responding to domestic abuse, and it also suggests that in the antebellum era the judicial system facilitated challenges to traditional sources of white male authority.[81]

As the gulf separating rich and poor whites was particularly wide in Richmond, so it was in the city that ideals of mastery and patriarchy could have served an especially important function in unifying white men of diverse backgrounds. However, it was precisely in the urban context that opportunities for household dependents to shape domestic power relations were greatest. This was not only due to the pervasiveness of the law in urban life but also because of the nature of white women's social and cultural experiences in the city. Lower-class women in Richmond were more likely to be

Table 2.3. Female victims in white-on-white assault cases: Richmond Mayor's Court

	Total white victims	Total female white victims	Female white victims married to defendant
1838	76	35	13
1852	107	34	15
1860	228	80	27
Total	411	149	55

Sources: Richmond Mayor's Court Docket Book, 1836–39; *Richmond Daily Dispatch*, 14 Jan. 1852–13 Jan. 1853, and 1 Jan. 1860–31 Dec. 1860.

employed outside of their own homes than in rural areas and were able to develop friendships and acquaintances that could prove a valuable source of support against an abusive husband. The connections that women formed in the city could provide them with a place of refuge from violent husbands and also with witnesses who could testify to violent incidents in court. When Lavinia Childrey reported that her husband, Thomas, had threatened to assault her, for example, the mayor initially proposed to discharge him on the payment of a $500 bond, but friends of the couple thought it best that Thomas should remain in jail "until he is completely sobered up and in his right mind."[82]

Abused women in Richmond were also assisted in their recourse to legal protection by urban spatial dynamics. In contrast to plantation areas where private homes existed in relative isolation, in the more crowded environment of the city neighbors, passersby, and officers of the law were readily alerted to the sound or appearance of disorder. In May 1858, for example, Officer Seal, responding to "the shrieks of females," entered a house in Rocketts through the window and arrested William Sullivan, who was beating his wife. On another occasion, in 1860, it was discovered when neighbors complained about his drunken and noisy behavior that Merriweather Roach had assaulted his wife, Emily.[83]

In Richmond, most cases of domestic abuse that came to the attention of the mayor involved lower-class couples. None of the thirteen men charged with violence against their spouse in 1838 paid any personal property tax in either 1835 or 1840, while only seven of the seventeen defendants in 1852 had residences that were listed in the Richmond City Directory for that year. It cannot be known whether these figures reflect that elite women suffered domestic abuse less often than lower-class women. Irrespective of how frequently they were assaulted by their husbands, however, upper-class white women had several reasons for choosing not to seek judicial protection. For some, considerations of political economy may have been paramount; charging a slave-owning husband with domestic violence would have compromised the very gender conventions on which elite women's class privileges were based. However, more important in dissuading abused white wives from seeking redress in the courts were social and cultural factors.[84] A remarkable set of letters written by Charlotte Cullen to the Richmond attorneys Samuel Taylor and James Lyons in the mid-1840s illustrates the constraints that elite women's social experience placed on their use of the law and the alternative means of responding to patriarchal violence that were available to them.

Charlotte Cullen's story as recounted in her letters to Taylor and Lyons was a traumatic tale of abuse at the hands of her husband, Dr. John Cullen, the son of a Dublin tanner. Charlotte claimed that John had pursued a "brutal course of conduct" toward her and that he believed "that he could treat me as he liked." John's actions left Charlotte in a "deranged state," and she invoked various strategies of resistance to his abuse. Charlotte tried to take her own life on a number of occasions, "but was prevented by an all wise and over ruling providence." On a more routine basis, she "endeavored to pacify and reconcile" her husband by "my unbounded submission and patience," but to no avail. It was only after eight years of suffering, by which time Charlotte knew "of no proper course to take except that of the law," that she reluctantly decided to appeal to the courts for protection. Charlotte had considered this course of action before, but had been dissuaded from pursuing legal redress by her husband, who had warned her that she "had no friends, no standing in society and that I would find the law yielded to influence, money, and standing and he beg me never to make myself a fool by applying to the law for I would find no relief from it."[85]

In mid-nineteenth-century America, however, John Cullen's threats were increasingly at odds with judicial decisions made in both civil and criminal courts that brought the private sphere of the home under increasing legal and public scrutiny. At the state level, the Virginia General Assembly expanded the admissible grounds for divorce to include "just cause of bodily fear," while locally in Richmond the mayor jailed abusive husbands more frequently than in the past, and the press highlighted and condemned cases of domestic violence.[86] Charlotte Cullen therefore had different options as to how to proceed against her husband, and it was thus significant that she elected to seek a divorce rather than to prosecute her husband in the mayor's court for breach of the peace or threatening and abusive language.[87] Although Charlotte's reasons for acting in this manner are not revealed in her correspondence, it is probable that her high social status and her unfamiliarity with the machinery of criminal justice were important factors. In contrast to many Richmond women who relied on police intervention and peace warrants to restrain an abusive spouse, Charlotte Cullen's social standing enabled her to appeal to Samuel Taylor, an esteemed attorney, to argue her case in a civil court. In a letter to Taylor, Charlotte claimed that her husband was "not my equal in Birth or family," for her ancestors included General Elliot, a great-uncle, "who gained the siege at the rock of Gibraltar," and George W. Howard, her father, who had also fought and been wounded in battle.

A more important consequence of Charlotte's social position than her personal connections may have been its impact on her daily life and routine. Charlotte Cullen's everyday experiences as presented in her correspondence were more restrictive than those of many lower-class women whose work provided them with opportunities to engage in social relationships outside of the domestic sphere and who were more likely to be aware that city magistrates would issue peace warrants against their violent husbands. Given her husband's profession and slaveholding status, not only is it unlikely that Charlotte ever worked, but it appears from her letters that she was prevented from leaving the house for any reason. Furthermore, like many respectable women in Richmond, Charlotte might also have found repellent the idea of having to testify against her husband in a criminal courtroom where she would have encountered thieves, vagrants, drunkards, and slaves.[88]

The Cullen family's economic security may also have influenced Charlotte's response to her husband's violence. Even if Charlotte had desired to take out a peace warrant against John, she would have been aware that he could easily have paid any recognizance to which he might have been held and she might have feared that this sanction would therefore have had little long-term impact on his violent conduct. Peace warrants held more appeal for lower-class women who usually could not countenance divorce, as they relied on their husband's income for their daily sustenance and would be entirely without support if they dissolved their marriage. This was particularly true for four women of European origin who sought protection from their husbands in the Richmond Mayor's Court in 1852. As immigrants, it is unlikely that these women could have turned to their families for support in the same manner as Charlotte Cullen and other elite native-born women such as the young Mrs. Thomas, who simply returned to her father in 1842 after she had "separated forever" from her husband because of his "brutal conduct" toward her.[89]

In the mayor's court, the treatment of abusive husbands was not determined only by law but was a product of negotiations between the mayor, the female victim, and the defendant. In the 1830s, Mayor Tate usually attempted to instigate an out-of-court settlement before imprisoning an abusive husband. When Virginia Pritchard charged her husband, James, with assault, Tate dismissed the case and advised the couple "to try and settle the matter at home."[90] Similarly, even though Lockley Pitt had long endured cruel treatment at the hands of her husband, James, when she reported one violent incident, Tate "advised her to consider of it", noting that "[s]he said she would let me know in the morning her determination." The following day, Lockley "withdrew her application for the present."[91] Other women dropped their complaints even before the case came before the mayor. In some instances, this was probably in response to further threats of violence from abusive husbands. However, some women who took out peace warrants as a means of controlling male aggression withdrew their complaints only after their husbands had spent a few days in jail.

The case of Rebecca and Emanuel Lyons demonstrates how white women negotiated their domestic relations in the antebellum courtroom. On January 8, 1838, Rebecca reported to the mayor that Emanuel had beaten her. A peace warrant was issued against Emanuel, and as he could not provide the required security, he was jailed until Rebecca dropped the complaint two days later. Relations in the Lyons household remained fractious, however, and on January 14 Rebecca again sought the protection of the law, only for Mayor Tate to dismiss the complaint and advise her to try to "manage" Emanuel herself. Only if she did not succeed did the mayor invite Rebecca "to call again." One week later, the Lyons were back in court following evidently futile attempts by Rebecca to control her husband's aggression. Emanuel was again sent to jail after failing to raise the required $100 bond, but within a week he was free once more, Rebecca having again dropped her complaint. Unlike Charlotte Cullen and Mrs. Taylor, Rebecca was possibly dependent on Emanuel's income and could not long sustain herself while he languished in jail. Nevertheless, like many other victims, Rebecca Lyons used the forum of the mayor's court to express her own conception of justice and not only seized control of the decision to prosecute but also engaged in a process of negotiation with the mayor that determined the length of her husband's incarceration.[92] In so doing, Rebecca and other poor women in southern cities used their access to the law to set limits on their husbands' authority.

In the 1850s, amidst increasing expression in the Richmond press of repugnance at wife beating and following the General Assembly's transfer of jurisdiction over divorce cases to local superior courts of chancery, the mayor exercised less discretion in his response to domestic violence. Although women could still secure their husbands' release after a few days in jail, it was rare that the mayor dismissed allegations of domestic assault altogether. In 1852, William Lambert demanded bail of at least $100 from sixteen of the seventeen men charged with assaulting their spouse, and in the course of the 1850s five men were sent on to the hustings court for assaulting their wives. In the previous twenty years, only one white man had stood trial for domestic violence.[93] These cases demonstrated to critics of the South that the region's criminal courts would not tolerate husbands who abused their patriarchal authority.[94] At the same time, however, as most domestic assault prosecutions involved poor white couples, they intervened in the domestic relations of the very men whose support for the southern social order was probably most conditional on their power over dependents within their own households.

The fate of abusive husbands in the mayor's court was symptomatic of a more general shift in the handling of assault complaints in the 1850s. Urban sensibilities had become more sensitive to violence, and incidents that had previously seemed innocuous were now considered a serious threat to the public peace and indicative of a general and threatening disorder. This was evidenced by a dramatic rise in the number of white defendants accused of assault who were remanded to the hustings court for trial in the course of the final antebellum decade. In 1838 and 1852, just 9 out of a combined total of 166 white defendants judged guilty of assault in the mayor's court were sent on for trial, while the remainder were held to sureties to keep the peace. By contrast, in 1860, 47 out of 130 white assault defendants whom the mayor deemed guilty were remanded for an appearance in the hustings court where, if convicted, they were subject to fines and imprisonment, far more serious sanctions than the mayor himself could impose.[95]

In part, the rise in hustings court assault prosecutions reflected the rigorous approach that Joseph Mayo brought to many aspects of urban law enforcement following his election as mayor in 1853. Although Richmond's police force remained small in number and unreformed in organization in the 1850s, under Mayo's direction, and in response to evolving urban bourgeois sentiments, the interests of industrialists, and the growing abolitionist threat, the criminal law assumed a greater role in the regulation of the white community, and especially in disciplining the urban poor. This was evident not only in prosecutions for assault, which increased three-fold during Mayo's first year in office, but also in the changing ways that the police and the mayor handled cases of prostitution, public drunkenness, and disorderly conduct.[96]

As in other U.S. cities, popular and judicial attitudes toward prostitution in Richmond underwent a major shift in the mid-nineteenth century. In the 1830s, Richmond's legal authorities sought to control prostitution and restrict it to the less reputable parts of the city. This policy reflected the prevailing cultural view that prostitution was not a great social problem and that the women involved in the illicit-sex trade did not require special legal protection. By the 1850s, however, attitudes had changed, and Mayor Mayo introduced a more proactive approach to policing prostitution. Numerous white women and men appeared in the mayor's court charged with keeping a disorderly house or house of ill-fame, and in the course of the decade, twenty-one of these cases reached the hustings court, a substantial increase from the twelve cases that had been prosecuted in the previous twenty years.[97] This rise in prosecutions was symptomatic of the concern with all kinds of disorderly conduct in mid-nineteenth-century Richmond that accompanied immigration and population growth. However, it was also a product of white fears of interracial sexual relationships. Whether in theaters, brothels, or on the street, prostitution in Richmond had always encompassed interracial sexual encounters, and amidst the heightened sectional sensitivities of the pre–Civil War years, this made it a particularly troublesome vice.[98]

Although prosecutions for keeping a disorderly house increased in the 1850s, there remained limits to the regulation of vice in Richmond. Prostitution itself was not illegal in Virginia, and although many women appeared in the mayor's court as a consequence of their involvement in the sex trade, most were required only to pay a bond for their future good conduct, and few were sent on for trial in the hustings court. Indeed, although in the 1850s prosecutions for keeping a disorderly house occurred with greater frequency than previously, it was actually in the late 1830s that the courts imposed the most severe penalties on the proprietors of Richmond's largest brothels. In the summer of 1837, six women were convicted in the hustings court of keeping a disorderly house and sentenced to fines of up to $2,000 and, in four cases, to jail terms of between thirty days and three months.[99] In the stricter racial and sexual climate of the 1850s, however, the five women who were convicted of keeping a house of ill-fame and keeping a disorderly house were fined between ten and thirty-four dollars, and in only one case did the court impose a prison sentence.[100]

Despite the increase in hustings court prosecutions, therefore, Joseph Mayo's antiprostitution drive in the 1850s was evidently based more on police vigilance and his own judgments as mayor rather than on the formal trial and punishment processes of the hustings court. Women suspected of prostitution and charged with disorderly conduct or keeping a disorderly house were, like other white defendants convicted in the mayor's court, usually held to a peace warrant. Women who were unable to pay the peace bond could be jailed for up to twelve months, and for the many who were driven into prostitution by poverty in the 1850s, imprisonment became an almost inevitable consequence of arrest. The resolution of cases in the mayor's court could therefore bring about a more swift, certain, and severe form of punishment than could be imposed in the hustings court, where procedural regulations and the time between court sessions gave women the chance to construct a defense that might lead to the prosecution being dropped or enable them to leave the city before their case came to court.[101]

Julia Dye, a twenty-six-year-old woman from Georgia, was one brothel keeper who left Richmond at a time when she was involved in criminal proceedings. Dye's establishment attained notoriety in 1851, when Harriet Hooper and Elizabeth Mitchell, two women who lived and worked in the brothel, were involved in a dispute that culminated in Hooper stabbing Mitchell and subsequently being convicted and imprisoned for attempted murder. By the time of Hooper's trial, Dye had moved to Lynchburg, and it is probable that she had done so to escape the attention of the legal authorities.[102] Yet this reveals only one aspect of Julia Dye's complex relationship with the law. Just months prior to the altercation between Mitchell and Hooper, Dye had worked in tandem with Thomas White, a Richmond police officer, to arrest John Fisher, whom she suspected of using a counterfeit fifty-dollar bill to pay for the services of one of her girls. At Fisher's trial, Officer White recounted the events immediately preceding the arrest:

> On Saturday, the 2nd March, I heard he [Fisher] was down in the neighbourhood of Saddler's. I advised Miss. Dye to disguise herself in male attire and go with me; she saw the prisoner near a lamp, stepped up to him, and raising her cap, asked him if he knew her and recollected passing a $50 note upon her.[103]

Fisher replied that he did remember the note and, despite his protest that he was unaware that it was counterfeit, he was arrested and taken to the mayor's court for examination. Although remanded for trial in the circuit court, Fisher was ultimately acquitted by a jury. The trial record suggests that the revelation that Dye ran a brothel may have undermined her testimony, yet her brothel stayed in business, and Dye neither faced criminal proceedings herself nor felt the need to leave Richmond at this time. Perhaps it was significant that Dye owned two slaves and paid personal property tax, indicating that she held a more elevated status than most prostitutes in the city. In any case, it seemingly was only when the Hooper-Mitchell conflict marked Dye's brothel as particularly disorderly that her position became untenable and led her to relocate to Lynchburg.[104]

Incidents of drunkenness and disorderly conduct, which provided the mayor with a continual stream of business throughout the antebellum era, were, like assault and prostitution, taken much more seriously in Richmond as the Civil War approached. Mayor Tate convicted all but one of the 151 white men and women who appeared before him on drunk and disorderly charges in 1838, but in 80 percent of cases the only sanction that he imposed was a fine of just eighty-three cents, and in nine out of ten instances this went unpaid.[105] By the 1850s, however, peace bonds were the standard punishment for defendants convicted of drunkenness in the mayor's court. A majority of the men and women found guilty in these cases were unable to make bail and were imprisoned in the city jail for a period of between twenty days and twelve months, set by the mayor, or until such time as the bail money could be raised.

At the same time as punishments for drunk and disorderly conduct became more severe in Richmond, greater discretion was exercised in the handling of drunkenness cases. In the 1850s, the *Dispatch* claimed that as many as nine-tenths of whites held in Richmond's two watch houses were committed for drunkenness, yet there was a significant decline in the proportion of white defendants in mayor's court cases who were accused of drunkenness from 43 percent in the late 1830s to 30 percent in 1852 and 24 percent in 1860.[106] In 1854, the *Dispatch* estimated that "not more than one fourth the persons arrested and locked up at night for drunken and disorderly conduct in the streets, are brought to the police court to be disposed of by the Mayor," implying that the majority were examined and discharged, along with many slaves, earlier in the morning when the mayor visited the watch houses and when his discretionary judgment was almost entirely unchecked by law.[107]

The discretionary influence of the mayor in drunkenness cases was also evident in the examination of those defendants who did appear at the main midmorning session of the mayor's court. While almost all of the defendants charged with drunk and disorderly conduct in the late 1830s were convicted, in 40 percent of the cases recorded in the *Dispatch* in 1852 and 1860, the defendant was discharged. There is little evidence to suggest what factors influenced the mayor's decisions in these cases. Justice for white defendants in the mayor's court was usually dispensed in a swift and summary manner, as it was for slaves, and this was especially true in relatively trivial cases such as drunkenness. Given the mayor's increasing caseload in the 1850s, it is unlikely that the examination process became more rigorous or that more complex legal arguments accounted for the decline in convictions.[108] Rather, the combination of more acquittals and harsher punishments for the convicted may have been a response to the widening gap between Richmond's white rich and poor. Specifically, there was an imperative for the courts to punish severely those drunkards who were poor or foreign because they themselves, as well as their disorderly conduct, were symptomatic of the growing instability of urban southern society.[109] Moreover, the increasing importance of time discipline and productive efficiency among industrial workers also made prosecutions for drunk and disorderly conduct particularly important as a means of regulating Richmond's lower-class workforce.[110]

This bilateral approach to drunkenness is one example of the extent to which, by the 1850s, regulation of the white poor had become a primary aim of policing in Richmond. The association between poverty and crime, which was implicit in Mayor Mayo's approach to domestic violence, prostitution, and drunkenness, was made explicit in the debate on the introduction of a chain gang and workhouse. These institutions were intended less as punishments for white criminals than as a means to discourage foreign vagrants from settling in Richmond and living at public expense. The *Dispatch*, for example, claimed that the building of a workhouse was demanded by

> the most urgent considerations of public policy.... The swarms of lazy, loafing and dishonest free negroes, and a greater number of idle, dissolute, and vagabond whites, constantly filling our jail yards and eating, fiddling, and dancing at the public expense, at the cost of the honest and working portion of the community, is an evil which demands a speedy remedy.[111]

Such arguments marked a clear shift in attitudes toward the punishment of white defendants charged with disorderly conduct. In the 1830s, vagrants, impoverished drunkards, and other disorderly characters who were arrested in Richmond and were unable to provide security for their future good conduct were often spared imprisonment if they agreed to leave the city. John Andrews, for example, was ordered to leave Richmond for New York, "whence he stated he came," following his arrest for drunkenness.[112] Such stipulations were always informal, and there was no guarantee that they would be adhered to. In late August 1836, Martha Bullifin was remanded to jail in default of security for an assault but was released when she promised to move to Petersburg. Whether Bullifin ever reached Petersburg is unclear, but two months later she was back in Richmond and arrested for drunk and disorderly conduct. On this occasion, Bullifin spent almost eight weeks in jail before being released when her daughter promised to remove her from the city. Mayor Tate was not discouraged from releasing Bullifin on this condition, despite her previous failure to leave Richmond.[113] The uppermost concern of the mayor in such cases was less to punish the offender than to ensure that the local community was rid of the presence of a disreputable influence.

Even as Mayor Tate encouraged petty criminals to leave the city in order to avoid punishment, however, he recognized problems with this policy. Explaining in a letter to Virginia governor Windham Robinson his decision to jail six mariners from northern states who had rioted and assaulted the liquor store proprietor William Castigan, Tate claimed that he had acted leniently in the case. "Had they been residents," Tate wrote, "They would have been presented to a Grand Jury for exemplary punishment." As the men were outsiders and transients who were unknown in the local community, however, exemplary punishment would have served little purpose, and this prompted Governor Robinson to suggest to Tate that this was a case in which "it might be as well to let them go," as they would immediately leave Richmond for other ports. In rejecting this suggestion, Tate was influenced by the more general concern of keeping order in the city and maintaining police morale. Tate argued, "If these men would leave the Com[monweal]th, it might be as well to let them go," as far as they are concerned but, in my opinion it would be extremely injurious to the operations of the Police of this City."[114]

The views that Tate expressed to Governor Robinson assumed greater prominence as vagrancy and disorder increased and simply removing disreputable persons from Richmond became an inexpedient and unrealistic policy. The overseers of the poor claimed as early as 1840 that the establishment of a workhouse "would do more to rid the City of pauperism generally, than any other means or mode that we can devise," but it was not until 1855 that Richmond's Common Council appointed a committee to inquire into the feasibility of the project.[115] The committee proposed that the city jail should be converted into a jail and workhouse and that the municipal authorities should be authorized "to cause the male convicts to be daily taken from the jail and Workhouse under the charge of Overseers and kept at hard labor upon the streets, the City Quarries or at such other work as the City Council may deem expedient." It was also recommended that provisions be made for female prisoners to labor away from public view and the *Dispatch* recommended that women should be employed in picking oakum, a task that could be performed "within doors."[116] Richmond's male elites evidently could not countenance the sight of impoverished women working in chains on the public streets, for this image would have shattered their ideals of patriarchy and female domesticity.[117]

The gender dynamics of the chain-gang proposals were less significant than their overt basis in class considerations. The most significant part of the committee's recommendations was the provision that vagrants in the poorhouse would be employed at hard labor alongside prisoners convicted of criminal offenses. This policy was intended to discourage vagrants from seeking refuge in Richmond by transferring "the largest class" of poorhouse inmates to the workhouse. The new policy toward crime and poverty was also designed to distinguish between the virtuous poor, who would continue to receive public assistance, and those vagrants who were capable of working and were deemed to be undeserving of charity.

The workhouse committee believed that the majority of adult vagrants were beyond moral reform, could not be returned "to a life of sobriety industry and honesty," and should no longer be provided for at public expense. It was also claimed that the establishment of a workhouse and chain gang would not only prove fiscally prudent but would elevate the poorhouse into "a House of Refuge for the unfortunate but virtuous poor."[118] However, the poorhouse census returns for 1850 and 1860 suggest that attempts to distinguish the worthy poor from those who were beyond moral reform were not so straightforward as the poorhouse committee suggested. Rather, they were entangled with matters of ethnicity. Indeed, the debate on the establishment of the chain gang and the mayor's handling of cases of petty crime and disorder involving white defendants can be considered primarily as a response to the changing ethnic composition of the Richmond poor. Echoing concurrent developments in the city jail population, between 1850 and 1860 the proportion of white poorhouse residents born in Virginia decreased from more than 80 percent to less than 40 percent, and the number of Irish paupers increased from less than one in ten to more than one-half. It was far more palatable for southern politicians to propose establishing a chain gang for white paupers when the majority of those who would eventually labor on the city streets were foreign-born.[119]

An act allowing for the establishment of a workhouse and chain gang in Richmond was passed by the Virginia General Assembly in February 1856, and six months later the first sentences of chain-gang labor were imposed by the mayor.[120] The *Dispatch* welcomed the chain gang, and within a few months an attorney proclaimed it a successful initiative that was "preventing the assemblage here of vagrants from all parts of the world."[121] Soon the hustings court also started sentencing convicts in the city jail to labor on the chain gang during their term of imprisonment. In September 1856, William Vest, who had served four jail terms of between thirty days and six months since 1843, was sentenced to three months on the chain gang. Thereafter such sentences became commonplace for white men convicted of theft, although Vest himself never worked on the chain gang, as that element of his punishment was revoked by the governor of Virginia following a petition by his attorney, Jonathan Shook. Vest was an "ignorant fellow," according to Shook, yet he was a veteran of the Mexican-American War, "industrious," "hard working," and, so it was claimed, very possibly the victim of a miscarriage of justice. In such circumstances, Shook considered it would be the "height of degradation" if Vest were forced to work on the chain gang, a punishment that was "a *barbarous* torture to body and mind which would better suit Dartmouth or the Bastille than any of our prison walls." Shook claimed that even in despotic countries, the chain gang was punishment for only the most serious crimes and not "trivial" offenses such as petty theft. Surely Virginia whites could not be made to suffer such indignities?[122]

There is no record that anyone who was sentenced to the chain gang in Richmond other than William Vest was spared by executive intervention during the antebellum era. Between 1856 and 1860, fourteen white men convicted of stealing were ordered to labor on the public works during their time in jail, and in September 1859 the punishment was imposed for the first time on a prisoner convicted of a violent misdemeanor. In the following twelve months, a total of five men found guilty of assault were remanded to the chain gang. Significantly, however, all but one of these men also received the maximum jail sentence of twelve months. Such a long period of incarceration was rare in assault cases and suggests that the chain gang was reserved for only the most serious cases of violent misdemeanor. By contrast, although not all property-crime convicts worked on the chain gang, sentences sometimes included the provision of labor on the public works even when the jail term was as short as sixty days. Unlike violent criminals, it was widely believed that immigrants and northerners were responsible for most thefts and burglaries committed in Richmond, and this perhaps made the sentencing of these convicts to the chain gang a less politically sensitive issue than if more southern-born whites had been similarly treated.[123]

The introduction of the chain gang was a response to rising crime rates and their impact on the municipal finances, but it also reflected changing attitudes toward white criminality in late antebellum Richmond that were a product of social and demographic developments. The growth and diversification of Richmond's white population in the 1850s had resulted in a greater awareness and classification of a lower class that was distinct from the reputable majority of the community. The chain gang reflected this development and collapsed further the distinction between poverty and criminality by providing for vagrants to labor alongside convicted criminals. This was a distinction that Jonathan Shook, the attorney, had been keen to maintain. When he petitioned on behalf of William Vest, Shook emphasized that although his client was poor he was "not a vagrant by any means."[124]

By sentencing both blacks and whites to labor on the chain gang, Richmond's courts acknowledged the limitations on the ideal of white racial egalitarianism in the urban context and the extent to which urban social dislocation was a problem rooted in issues of class rather than race. This situation contrasted with other aspects of penal change at the local and state level. Specifically, the establishment of the chain gang as a punishment for both blacks and whites contrasted with attempts to reinforce the racial basis of Virginia's penal laws through ending the practice of sentencing white convicts to corporal punishment and, in 1860, the introduction of sale into slavery for free black felony convicts in place of penitentiary imprisonment. The operation of the chain gang also distinguished Richmond from other southern cities that were reluctant to subject blacks and whites to common forms of punishment. In Charleston, for example, the recommendation of the poorhouse commissioners in 1838 that paupers should be forced to grind corn on a treadmill was rejected, "because the long established connection of such an establishment with the Work House has rendered it one of the modes of punishment for slaves and other colored persons."[125]

Richmond had not always been so anomalous in its treatment of white criminals as it was in the mid-1850s. In the 1840s, even before the Virginia General Assembly outlawed the public whipping of whites, the hustings court magistrates in Richmond took a lead on the issue and sentenced convicts to fewer lashes than had been common in earlier decades. After 1835, it was unusual for a defendant to receive more than five lashes, and on the rare occasions that a white convict was sentenced to more than twenty lashes, the court usually ordered that the punishment should not be inflicted at once, but spread over a number of days or even months.[126] While African Americans regularly received thirty-nine lashes on a single day, when Edward Pepper, a white man, was sentenced to three months in jail and thirty lashes for stealing a blanket worth just one dollar, the court ordered that he should receive ten lashes on the first day of each of the three months he spent in jail.[127]

Like other white southerners, white Richmonders viewed whipping as a punishment suitable only for African Americans.[128] The disgrace of being subjected to the lash assumed special connotations in the southern states, where the whip was a symbol of slavery and the scars that cut across the back of chastised slaves were daily read as evidence of a criminal and insubordinate character on plantations and in slave markets.[129] To whip a white person was not only to inflict pain and public humiliation; more significantly, it was to blur the racial divide by equating the white criminal with the black slave.

The degradation that attended corporal punishment was made evident in clemency petitions submitted during the 1830s and early 1840s by white convicts facing public whippings. When John Wade was sentenced to the lash, he pleaded "to be saved from the ignominy of so disgraceful a punishment" that would remain with him always, "no matter how upright a life he may live."[130] Martha Folkes made an equally impassioned appeal on behalf of her son, William McDowell, "on account of the degradation" he would feel should his corporal sentence be carried out. Elizabeth Bovan claimed that if she were whipped, "her friends, and her three infant children would be also included in that disgrace."[131] Virginia governors were consistently receptive to such pleas, and in the 1830s and 1840s extended clemency to sixteen out of the seventeen white men and women in Richmond who sought relief from corporal punishment.

As a form of forced labor, the chain gang had degrading associations with slavery similar to those of the whipping post and the lash. The convicts and vagrants on the chain gang had a ball and chain attached to their leg to prevent their escape, and on at least one occasion the overseer of the chain gang, John D. Perrin, whipped a recalcitrant white convict, prompting outrage in the press. Although the mayor condemned this incident and claimed that no officer had the right to apply the lash to a white man, Perrin was never prosecuted for an assault. Furthermore, despite the public furor, it was not clearly established whether or not the overseer had the right to employ the lash in self-defense, as Perrin claimed to have done.[132]

In an urban context where many slaves were able to move around the city with considerable independence, the sight of white men laboring in irons and threatened with the lash was a stark and dangerous reversal of the southern racial order. Any success that the chain gang had in limiting the number of vagrants settling in Richmond and combating disorderly conduct was achieved only at the considerable expense of acknowledging the limitations on white racial supremacy in the city. What is more, within a few years the problem of white vagrancy seemed to require yet further regulation and elicited new measures that would deny the independence and compromise the freedom of white men. When Richmond's new poorhouse was constructed in 1860, its grounds were enclosed by a brick wall eighteen feet in height,

Fig. 5. "Richmond, Virginia. Almshouse." 1865. Courtesy of Library of Congress, Prints and Photographs online, Civil War glass negative collection. <http://hdl.loc.gov/loc.pnp/cwpb.00400>

and a substantial iron railing was erected in front of the main building to counter the problem of "straggling paupers" who were able to leave the old poorhouse "at pleasure" and to the annoyance of the public.[133] Meanwhile, after a spate of suspicious fires in 1860, the *Dispatch* wondered, "Has not the Mayor the power to arrest suspicious idlers found lurking about the streets, and require them to give some account of their mode of living, or hold them to bail?"[134] Free black Richmonders who were required to carry at all times a register attesting to their liberty might have noted to their white acquaintances that they had long lived under such conditions.

Crime and disorder plagued American cities on either side of the Mason-Dixon Line in the antebellum period. In the context of southern slavery, however, the disorderly conduct of the white lower classes posed a distinct threat to social stability. Like white poverty, petty crime challenged proslavery arguments about the benefits of slavery to all classes of whites, while in the manner in which it was regulated it could appear at odds with republican ideals. Moreover, a great deal of white crime threatened to undermine the control of slaves, and for this reason more than any other, Richmond's municipal authorities had little choice but to enforce the criminal law ever more rigorously against whites as well as African Americans by expanding police provisions, introducing new punishments, and resolving a growing proportion of cases in the lowest municipal court, the mayor's court, where justice was most swift and there was greatest judicial discretion over the outcome of cases.

Even as southern politicians at the national level made arguments in support of slavery that rested on the egalitarian nature of white society in the slave states, responses to social dislocation and disorder at the local level in Richmond recognized and reaffirmed distinctions between different white class and ethnic groups. Police surveillance disproportionately targeted marginal groups such as the poor and immigrants, and, along with the discretionary judgments of the mayor and the great propensity with which poor whites made use of the courts as complainants, this led to the association of certain forms of behavior, notably public drunkenness, disorderly conduct, and domestic violence, with the lower classes.

Punishments for such routine offenses invariably took the form of fines and peace bonds, sanctions that were particularly burdensome when visited on the poor, who, when unable to raise the requisite bail, were imprisoned in the city jail or the poorhouse or forced to labor on the chain gang. These penalties distinguished lower-class white judicial experiences and contrasted with the racial divide that was enshrined in the criminal law at the state level. The chain gang in particular collapsed distinctions between poverty and crime and between black and white by punishing diverse groups of white men, including vagrants, paupers, drunkards, and convicted criminals, alongside free African Americans.

For the thousands of impoverished white men and women in Richmond whose interest in the slaveholding regime depended primarily on the status that slavery afforded them on account of their race, the growing municipal interference in their everyday activities and the declining distinction between their experiences of the law and those of free African Americans must have carried at the very least a latent threat to their identity as independent white citizens. The attorney Jonathan Shook equated criminal punishments for whites in Virginia with those found in despotic regimes, and, notwithstanding proslavery rhetoric, white men and women who found themselves laboring on the chain gang or locked behind the bars of the city jail or the imposing walls of the new poorhouse, sometimes in close proximity with slaves and free blacks, were unlikely to appreciate the benefits of their whiteness. More worrying for the southern elite, some may have been caused by their experience of local law enforcement to question their support for slavery itself.

3

"The victim of prejudice and hasty consideration"

Slave Trials, Clemency, and Punishment

Standing in the dock of the Richmond Hustings Court in the summer of 1840, charged with burglary, Robert was conspicuous by the color of his skin. The black slave of William Allison, Robert was surrounded by some of the wealthiest and most powerful white men in Virginia. The prosecution case was laid out by the Commonwealth's attorney and future mayor of Richmond, Joseph Mayo, and rebutted by the counsel for the defense, Gustavus A. Myers. On the dais at the front of the courtroom sat six magistrates who would decide Robert's fate. Like Mayo and Myers, all six of the magistrates were slaveholders.[1] The evidence presented to the court was limited. Samuel F. Adie, the white victim of the crime, deposed that money had gone missing from his store on several occasions since the loss of a key some twelve months previously. Suspecting that Robert was responsible for the thefts, Adie claimed that he had sat watch one evening and caught Robert red-handed in possession of stolen banknotes. On the basis of this testimony, Robert was convicted of burglary and sentenced to the mandatory penalty of death by hanging, although like most slaves found guilty of burglary in antebellum Virginia, executive clemency eventually saved him from the gallows.[2]

Robert's experience of the Virginia justice system was unexceptional. In stark contrast to the trial of slaves in most southern states and the trial of white defendants throughout the United States in the antebellum period, the trial and punishment of slaves charged with felonies in Virginia was swift, severe, and fundamentally at odds with common-law precedent. Unlike most southern states, where slaves were tried for felonies in the same courts as whites, in Virginia there was an entirely separate trial system for slaves. This system was subject to few legal regulations, and, as a result, the outcome of all cases was heavily influenced by judicial discretion. Slaves were convicted or acquitted on the basis of numerous factors in addition to their guilt or innocence such that, invariably, the decisions of the court reflected the interests of the slaveholding elite. The nature of the crime, the race, gender, and class of the victim, the severity of the punishment prescribed under Virginia law, and the social and economic context of the time all influenced the verdicts and punishments handed down in Virginia slave trials. Most important of all, the courts based their decisions on the fact that the defendants before them were both persons and property. This meant that most of the courts' verdicts and sentences were compatible with slaveholders' concerns as property holders, as well as the demand of the white community as a whole for rigorous control of slave criminality. However, in antebellum Richmond, there was not always agreement within the white community over the fate of enslaved defendants. By the 1850s, the influence that slaveholders' interests exerted over slave trials and punishments provoked antagonism among nonslaveholders in the city, while the limited due process protections for slave defendants drew criticism from Virginia attorneys and northern abolitionists.

In 1692, the Virginia House of Burgesses passed "an act for the more speedy prosecution of slaves committing capital offenses." This act established an entirely separate trial process for slaves and denied them rights that were at the core of the Anglo-American legal system. In place of trial by jury, a panel of at least five justices of the peace, who sat as what was known as a court of oyer and terminer, was summoned to examine, judge, and pass sentence on slave defendants. In contrast to the regular, biannual sessions of the circuit court at which white defendants were tried, courts of oyer and terminer sat on an impromptu basis within five to ten days of any slave being indicted by the mayor for a serious crime and for the sole purpose of trying and sentencing the specific slave named in the indictment. Furthermore, though white prisoners could appeal a guilty verdict to a higher court, the decisions of oyer and terminer courts were final and incontestable.[3]

Regulations that were refined and clarified during the colonial and early national periods governed the conduct of oyer and terminer tribunals: magistrates had to be unanimous in their verdict to secure a conviction; at least four justices, comprising a majority of the court, had to be in agreement to condemn a slave to death, and all slave defendants were assigned legal counsel by the court.[4] Other procedural rules were less specific, and the rules of evidence were especially vague. An act of 1792 stated, "the Court may take for evidence the confession of the offender, the oath of one or more credible witnesses, or such testimony of negroes or mulattoes, bond or free . . . as to

Fig. 6. "Richmond, Va. Front view of Capitol." 1865. Courtesy of Library of Congress, Prints and Photographs online, Selected Civil War Photographs, 1861–1865. <http://hdl.loc.gov/loc.pnp/cwpb.02891>

them shall seem convincing."[5] With no requirement to adhere to common-law precedent, this act gave local magistrates almost unlimited license to interpret the evidence before them in any way they saw fit.

An important development in the administration of slave justice in Virginia occurred in 1801, when the governor was empowered to reprieve slaves condemned to death for sale and transportation out of the United States.[6] By the nineteenth century, slaves in Virginia were subject to capital punishment for seventy-three different offenses, yet with the introduction of gubernatorial review and sale and transportation lawmakers sought to reconcile these extreme penal laws with slaveholder property interests, humanitarian concerns, and Enlightenment penal philosophies that denied that the widespread use of the death penalty deterred criminal activity.[7] The rules governing slave trials were sufficient to convince Virginia slaveholders that the system was a just means for judging black defendants, yet in practice the procedural laws governing oyer and terminer courts in Virginia provided defendants with scant protection and left them subject to the whims of local racial prejudices and the recurrent errors of justices of the peace who were often ill trained in the law.[8]

The legal protections afforded slave defendants in Virginia were not only minimal in comparison to those enjoyed by white defendants, they were also less than those granted to slaves in most other southern states. With the exception of South Carolina and Louisiana, where panels of magistrates and slaveholders sat in judgment on slave defendants in capital cases during most of the antebellum period, Virginia was unique in denying trial by jury to slaves charged with felonies.[9] In the rest of the southern states in the nineteenth century, there was a movement toward greater formalism and increased adherence to common-law due process in slave trials. Georgia's slave trial system was originally based on the South Carolina model of examination by a panel of justices and freeholders acting without a jury, but in 1811 jurisdiction over slave felony cases was transferred to county inferior courts and in the 1850s to superior courts. Similar developments occurred in North Carolina, which in 1816 granted jurisdiction in slave felony cases to county courts. In most of the newer slave states, trial by jury and other due process rights for slaves were enshrined in constitutions.[10]

Although Virginians were inheritors of the same Anglo-American legal heritage as other states where slaves were tried by jury, oyer and terminer tribunals did not deal even in the rhetoric of egalitarianism. In part, this reflected the early establishment of Virginia's slave codes in the late seventeenth century at a time when there was little concern with due process even for white defendants and particularly indentured servants. By contrast, many other southern states established slave laws more than a century later in a context of Enlightenment humanitarianism, evangelical fervor, and penal reform. But the lack of due process protections for slaves was also a sign of the weakness of slavery in Virginia in comparison with the expanding slave markets to the west. The slave rebellions that struck Virginia in 1800 and 1831 and the increasing sectional tensions of the first half of the nineteenth century, which were felt particularly strongly in the Border South states, dampened any latent enthusiasm for a revision of the laws that may have compromised the ability of the legal system to maintain control over the African American population.[11] At the same time, the falling demand for slaves in the Upper South also made Virginia slaveholders less concerned with legal protections for slave defendants.[12]

The evidence from Richmond shows that the characteristics of Virginia's oyer and terminer system had a very direct and significant impact on the

Table 3.1: Slave felony prosecutions in southern criminal courts

	Years	Slave defendants	Total defendants	Slaves as % total defendants
Richmond Hustings Court	1830–60	444	1,355	33
Chatham County Inferior and Superior Courts (Savannah)	1833–64	59a	659	9
Spartanburg District, S.C.	1830–60	321	1,537	21
Warren County, Mississippi (Vicksburg)	1841–59	47a	588	8

Sources: Richmond Hustings Court Minutes, 1830–60; Byrne, "Slave Crime in Savannah, Georgia," 357–59; Hindus, Black Justice under White Law, 582; Waldrep, *Roots of Disorder*, 32.

administration of slave justice at the local level. In the first place, slaves in the city appeared before the criminal courts far more regularly than in other jurisdictions in the South where slaves were tried by jury.[13] Slaves accounted for about one-third of the 1,355 defendants, black and white, who were prosecuted for felonies in Richmond between 1830 and 1860, and this figure was broadly commensurate with the proportion of slaves in the city's total population. However, in both Savannah and Vicksburg, where slaves comprised a similar percentage of the population as in Richmond, they made up respectively just 9 percent and 3 percent of all defendants.[14]

Slaves not only came before the criminal courts more frequently in Richmond than in urban areas outside Virginia but were also far more likely to be convicted. In the thirty-one-year period from 1830 to 1860, 444 slaves were tried for felonies in Richmond, and 65 percent were found guilty. In Savannah felony trials, by contrast, just nine out of fifty-nine enslaved defendants were convicted between 1833 and 1864.[15] Similarly, Tennessee circuit court juries convicted just 29 percent of slaves charged with capital crimes. The comparable capital crime conviction rate in Richmond was more than 50 percent.[16] In Greene County, Georgia, meanwhile, slaves were convicted at exactly the same rate as whites, but in Richmond slaves remanded for trial by the mayor on charges of violent felony were 60 percent more likely to be found guilty than whites charged with the same crimes.[17]

Slaves were also prosecuted more speedily in courts of oyer and terminer than in common-law jurisdictions. It was not necessary in Virginia to wait for the next sitting of a regular court session for a slave trial to commence, and, once under way, the trial process itself was much more efficient than under the common law, as lawyers were not "positively required" to argue from case precedent. As such, in 97 percent of Richmond slave cases the court reached its final verdict within three weeks of the commission of the alleged crime.[18] While oyer and terminer magistrates could readily ignore matters of law, judges' rulings were more constrained in common-law slave trials because if they overlooked legal technicalities, they would set dangerous precedents that could be applied to cases involving white defendants.[19] Finally, with defendants denied the right of appeal, punishment was inflicted swiftly in Richmond, and this meant that in many cases the owners of slave defendants were deprived of their slaves' labor for only a relatively short time.[20]

The difference between rates of prosecution and conviction for slaves in Richmond and other southern cities was so large that it is improbable that the number of prosecutions simply derived from different crime rates. Instead, they reflected the impact of different trial systems on white attitudes toward slave law. In comparison to the rest of the South, the centrality of slaves' status as property in oyer and terminer trials meant that the potential antagonism between the aims of the justice system and slaveholders' interests as masters and property holders was minimized.[21] Where slave trials were conducted in accordance with the common law, slaveholders were reluctant for their slaves to appear before the courts because they recognized that "law carried to the zenith of its logic would have undermined slavery as often as it protected slave property."[22] By contrast, as the oyer and terminer system was unconstrained by rules of evidence and due process, Virginia slaveholders could shape events in the courtroom almost as they pleased and consequently acquiesced more readily in the role of the state in the punishment of serious slave crime.[23]

To a greater extent than elsewhere in the South, slave criminal law in Virginia served explicitly as an extension of the slaveholders' power rather than as a system of justice, and this was reflected in slave conviction rates and trial processes in Richmond. Slaves were more likely to be judged guilty of a criminal offense in Richmond than in other cities for which data are available, and even a cursory analysis of Richmond slave trial records reveals numerous instances when slaves were convicted on the basis of disputable testimony and coerced confessions.[24] However, the high overall conviction rates for slave defendants mask significant variations in the outcome of Richmond slave trials according to the seriousness of the alleged crime and also the race, gender, and class of the victim. Extant court records reveal that these factors infused the magistrates' decision-making process insofar as they were consistent with the interests of slaveholders as individuals and as a class. In particular, magistrates treated the prosecution evidence more skeptically and acted with greater discretion on account of the race of the victim and the gender of the accused in capital cases than when slaves were indicted for less serious offenses.

The tension between protecting slaveholder property interests and enforcing a strict, swift, and summary form of slave justice was most evident in slave murder trials. Although slaves in Virginia could be hanged for a wider range of offenses than in any other southern state, in practice in Richmond only slaves convicted of murder ever went to the gallows. Richmond courts also sentenced slaves to hang for burglary, stealing, arson, and assaulting a white person, but all slaves convicted of these crimes after 1830 were pardoned or had their sentence commuted by the governor. Indeed, in the whole of Virginia between 1800 and 1865, only thirty slaves were put to death for any form of crime against property, and only eight of these executions occurred after 1832.[25] It was by no means certain even that slaves convicted of murder would be executed, and the governor in fact spared five of the nine slaves convicted of murder in antebellum Richmond.[26] Nonetheless, the possibility that the decision of the court might lead to the defendant's death had a profound impact on the conduct and outcome of slave murder trials.

Although murder was the most serious crime that a slave could commit, the prospect that the defendant might be executed upon conviction meant that the magistrates employed far stricter standards of evidence in slave murder trials than in any other cases. As such, the thirty-one slaves examined for murder in courts of oyer and terminer in late antebellum Richmond were less likely to be convicted than defendants accused of any other offense. While only nine slaves indicted for murder were found guilty as charged, seven others were convicted of murder in the second degree or manslaughter. These slaves were sentenced to sale and transportation and, in one case, thirty-nine lashes at the public whipping post, punishments that did not compromise slaveholders' interests as property holders to the same degree as the death penalty.

Women accounted for a higher proportion of slave defendants charged with murder than were accused of any other crime, and their gender, as well as the nature of their crimes, had an especially significant impact on the outcome of their trials. Eleven of the thirteen enslaved women murder defendants in Richmond were accused of killing an infant, and in seven cases the victim was their own child. Irrespective of the race of the victim and the relationship of the child to the defendant, however, slave women were far less likely to be convicted than male murder defendants. Two of the three cases in which the infant victim was white ended with the accused being discharged, while the other resulted in a verdict of manslaughter. In the only two cases when a female slave was found guilty of first-degree murder, the victim was her own child, but even in these two instances the court demonstrated some sympathy for the plight of the condemned defendants by recommending them to the mercy of the executive.[27]

Male slaves were far more likely to be convicted of murder than were slave women. Twelve of eighteen male slave murder defendants were found guilty as charged or convicted of a lesser offense between 1830 and 1860, and, in contrast to cases in which the defendant was female, the race and status of the victim had a significant bearing on these verdicts. Specifically, male slaves were least likely to be convicted of murder when their victim was also enslaved. Four of the six men found not guilty of murder had been accused of killing a slave, as had four of the five murder defendants found guilty on a lesser charge of manslaughter or murder in the second degree. By contrast, only two of the seven slave men convicted of murder and sentenced to death had killed a slave, and both eventually had their sentences commuted to sale and transportation. Four of the five slaves who were eventually executed for murder had killed a white person, and one, Moses Henry, had murdered his free black wife.[28] It is apparent, therefore, that while the gender of the defendant heavily influenced the verdict in slave murder trials, the race of the victim was an equally important consideration at the sentencing stage.

The high conviction rate and frequent capital sentences that were passed on male murder defendants in oyer and terminer courts reflected wider distinctions in the social meaning of slave gender than were immediately apparent in the courtroom. Murder seemed to pose a more serious threat to the social stability of both the black and white communities when committed by male slaves, as it was an indictment of the extensive independence that slave men often enjoyed in the city when hired out or living away from their owners. The murder of a slave owner or overseer by a male slave appeared symptomatic of a dangerous rebelliousness in the slave population that was not so immediately apparent when a female slave, who was often a domestic servant and less likely than a male slave to be hired out, committed infanticide. Nevertheless, women who murdered their slave children may have been more consciously rebelling against their slave status by deliberately destroying their owner's slave property than male murderers who were often provoked to violence in the momentary heat of passion.[29] Even Jordan Hatcher, a factory hand who murdered his white overseer and became one of the most notorious slave felons in the Old South when the governor commuted his death sentence, had committed his crime while being punished for the poor quality of his work.[30] Although the killing was undoubtedly a

Table 3.2: Slave defendants in Richmond Oyer and Terminer Courts, 1830–1860

	Defendants	Convicted	Convicted of a lesser crime	Pleaded guilty	Total sentenced (%)
VIOLENT CRIMES					
Murder	31	9	7	1	54.8
Assault	22	11	1	0	54.5
Poisoning	6	2	0	0	33.3
Rape	1	0	0	0	0.0
Robbery	2	0	1	0	50.0
Shooting with intent to kill	2	1	0	0	50.0
Stabbing with intent to kill	41	33	2	0	85.4
Total	105	56	11	1	64.8
PROPERTY CRIMES					
Arson	34	8	1	0	26.5
Burglary	107	50	25	0	70.1
Forgery, fraud, counterfeiting	5	1	0	0	20.0
Receiving stolen goods	10	6	0	0	60.0
Stealing	175	107	2	15	70.9
Total	331	172	28	15	65.0
OTHER					
Aiding a slave to abscond	4	4	0	0	100.0
Conspiracy to murder	1	0	0	0	0.0
Inciting slaves to steal	3	1	0	0	33.3
Total	8	5	0	0	62.5
Grand total	444	234	39	16	65.1

Source: Richmond Hustings Court Minutes, 1830–60.

product of tensions inherent in a slaveholding society, it represented a very different type of attack on the institution than the premeditated murder of a white master or an infant slave.

All of the slave women charged with murder in Richmond had engaged in explicit acts of resistance against slavery, either committing infanticide or murdering their owners. By contrast, evidence in the trials of male slaves charged with violent attacks against other African Americans suggests that although the violence of slave men was shaped by issues of race and slavery, it was often not an overt and conscious act of resistance but was instead motivated by all the vagaries of human emotions and associations that also were at the root of white violence. The slave Perry fatally stabbed Abram because he "had been interfering between him and his wife," while Scott supposedly murdered Priscilla, with whom he had lived as husband and wife until just a few weeks before the crime, following "a quarrel between prisoner and deceased about prisoner's clothes, which deceased had to wash, and refused to give up until prisoner paid her for the washing."[31] Similarly, Emanuel killed Isaac, "a quarrelsome, drunken vicious Negro," after Isaac had insulted him with "language of the most savage character" and threatened to set him up with the police for a crime he had not committed.[32] In all of these cases, valuable slaves had been killed, but white society had not been overtly threatened, and magistrates therefore had no intention of compounding the loss of human property by sentencing the murderer to death. To Richmond slaveholders, there seemed no need to destroy valuable slave property unless a white person had been killed. In cases when both the victim and defendant were enslaved, the more important function of the trial was not to punish the perpetrator but to provide a narrative for the crime that reassured the white community that it was not indicative of any general discontent with slavery among the black community.

The crime for which slaves were most frequently sentenced to death in antebellum Richmond was burglary. In contrast to murder cases, the governor reprieved all slaves sentenced to hang for property crimes in Richmond after 1830, but the oyer and terminer magistrates still demonstrated a marked reluctance to convict slaves of burglary. In the 1830s and 1840s, only thirty-two out of fifty-seven slaves charged with burglary were found guilty, and after the revision of Virginia's Criminal Code in 1849, when the statutory punishment for slaves convicted of burglary was changed to sale and transportation, only eighteen out of fifty were convicted. This represented a surprising fall in the conviction rate from 56 percent to 36 percent. This decline might reflect the increasing difficulty of obtaining evidence on which to base a conviction in the urban environment, but it is also indicative of the growing demand for slave labor within Virginia that discouraged the removal of slaves from the state and suggests that some magistrates considered even sale and transportation too severe a penalty for a crime against property. Similar factors might also explain magistrates' decisions to convict 23 percent of slaves charged with burglary of the lesser crimes of petty and grand larceny.[33] As the punishment for both forms of larceny was a public whipping, slaves could be punished and returned to work within a matter of days and without waiting for the governor to commute the sentence.

The influence that slaves' property status had on verdicts in burglary cases is evident from a comparison with the fate of free African Americans charged with the same crime. At a time when the death penalty was being reserved as a punishment for murder in the first degree in every state in the Union, the execution of a slave for burglary not only represented the unnecessary destruction of valuable property but was also an inhumane act at odds with prevailing moral values. When committed by free blacks, however, burglary was not a capital offense in Virginia, and consequently both financial and humanitarian considerations were absent from the magistrates' deliberations. As a result, free African American burglary defendants were 57 percent more likely than slaves to be convicted as charged, and just two out of nineteen free black burglary defendants were found guilty of a less serious crime between 1830 and 1860.[34] Justices evidently had few qualms about convicting free blacks of burglary even though punishments ranged from three to eighteen years in the penitentiary and, from 1860, sale into absolute slavery.[35]

In comparison to slaves charged with homicide and burglary, those accused of noncapital crimes against person and property were more likely to be convicted and less likely to benefit from judicial discretion or mercy when sentenced. As slaves could not be executed for crimes such as stabbing, assault with intent to kill, and stealing, the fate of defendants accused of these offenses was less influenced by slaveholders' property interests or the fiscal concerns of the state than was the case in murder trials. The significance of their status as property in guaranteeing enslaved defendants a degree of protection from arbitrary verdicts in capital cases is made apparent in the high conviction rates for noncapital felonies. Whereas less than 30 percent of murder defendants were found guilty as charged, more than 80 percent of the forty-one slaves accused of stabbing with intent to kill were convicted, and only two were adjudged guilty of the less serious crime of "unlawful but not malicious stabbing." Similarly, 61 percent of the 175 slaves charged with stealing were found guilty as charged in comparison to only 47 percent of the 107 slaves charged with burglary. The less serious punishments in noncapital cases also meant that the race of the victim had a less overt influence on the magistrates' verdict than in capital trials. In cases of stabbing with intent to kill, for example, convicted slaves were sentenced to be whipped irrespective of the race of their victim and for this reason were no more likely to be convicted when the victim was white than if they were charged with attacking a slave or free African American.[36]

The outcome of slave examinations for noncapital crimes was far more responsive to social and political developments and evolving racial tensions than when a conviction might result in a death sentence. In the course of the antebellum period, the conviction rate for burglary and murder declined markedly, suggesting that trial processes became increasingly rigorous.[37] However, amidst sectional tensions between North and South and growing social dislocation in Richmond, slave conviction rates for noncapital crimes rose sharply in the 1850s. From 1850 to 1860, 23 out of 25 slaves charged with stabbing with intent to kill were found guilty, as were 8 out of 9 slaves

Table 3.3: Change over time in slave conviction rates for capital and noncapital felonies

Type of crime	1830–49		1850–60		
	Cases[a]	Convicted as charged (%)	Cases	Convicted as charged (%)	Change in conviction rate (%)
CAPITAL CRIMES					
Burglary	57	56.1	50	36.0	-64.2
Murder	14	28.6	16	25.0	-12.6
Total	71	50.7	66	33.3	-34.3
NONCAPITAL CRIMES					
Assault	13	38.5	9	88.8	+130.6
Stabbing	16	62.5	25	92.0	+47.2
Stealing	84	54.8	76	80.3	+46.5
Total	113	54.0	110	83.6	+54.8

Source: Richmond Hustings Court Minutes, 1830–60.
[a]Cases in which the defendant pleaded guilty are excluded from this table.

prosecuted for assault and 61 out of 76 accused of stealing. In comparison with the previous twenty-year period, these figures represent an overall increase in conviction rates of 55 percent.

A comparison with conviction rates for free African Americans, indicates that the stark change in the outcome of slave trials was linked specifically to white fears of slave disorder in the city rather than to more general racial tensions. In the years before the Civil War, free African American conviction rates in Richmond oyer and terminer trials remained stable, even though there was a greater rise in the rate of free black prosecutions than slave prosecutions, and despite the routine claims of politicians in Virginia that free blacks were the most criminally inclined class in the state. Although free black defendants were tried in the same courts as slaves and were subject to the same summary legal procedures, their cases were seemingly handled with a greater degree of consistency throughout the antebellum era.

The rapid increase in conviction rates for noncapital crimes in the 1850s indicates that magistrates were least concerned with due process and the justice of their verdicts in cases in which slaves were accused of relatively trivial crimes. In states where slaves were tried according to common-law due process, the distinction in the treatment of slave defendants according to the severity of the charge was institutionalized: for the most serious crimes, slaves were tried by a jury; and for noncapital offenses, they were summarily examined and punished outside of the judicial system, usually by their owner.[38] In Richmond, there was a similar dividing line, though it was less clear-cut, as the summary nature of the oyer and terminer examination allowed greater scope for variations in the treatment of defendants within the judicial system. This was far less feasible in jury trials when common-law precedent placed greater constraints on the court proceedings.

The decision of oyer and terminer magistrates to convict or acquit a slave defendant was not made arbitrarily depending on the type of crime committed but rather was the product of a trial process that was itself shaped by whether the slave was charged with a capital or noncapital offense. Magistrates consistently considered the evidence far more critically when a defendant faced the death penalty than in noncapital cases. As such, in many, though by no means all, capital trials the prosecution went to greater lengths to prove its case, and defense attorneys made more strenuous efforts on behalf of the accused than in less serious cases. The relatively low proportion of slaves found guilty of murder, burglary, and arson reflected this more rigorous trial process. By contrast, the high conviction rates for stealing and assault with intent to kill were indicative of the low standards of evidence that were applied in the vast majority of oyer and terminer trials.

In most cases of stabbing, assault, and stealing, convicted slave defendants were sentenced to a public whipping and immediately returned to their owner or employer. This being the case, there was little onus on magistrates to consider slaveholder property interests in their deliberations, and convictions were consequently often based on the uncorroborated testimony of whites or on evidence from slaves and free African Americans. Indeed, the summary nature of oyer and terminer proceedings meant that even in some capital cases slave defendants might be convicted upon depositions that did little more than raise the suspicion of guilt. Charles Davis's slave George, for example, was convicted of burglary even though the testimony presented at his trial proved nothing more than that stolen goods were found in his possession some time after the alleged crime was committed. The testimony upon which Nancy was convicted of arson was equally weak, consisting only of her own confession—made while she was tied up—and the fact that she had been seen chopping wood just before the fire started. No witnesses could place Nancy at the scene of the crime or produce any noncircumstantial evidence of her guilt. Similarly, Lewis was sentenced to death for burning a house belonging to Mr. Perry even though the evidence produced in court proved only that Lewis had threatened "to drag the third part of Hell" out of Perry's lot.[39] Again, no witnesses provided any details about the commission of the crime itself. These cases show that guilty verdicts could be secured in oyer and terminer courts without conclusive proof even in capital cases.

Slave convictions were not always based on such insubstantial evidence as was presented against Nancy and Lewis. While it was not unusual for suspects to be convicted on the testimony of just one or two witnesses, the prosecution often had to go to much greater lengths to convince the court that a defendant was guilty and sometimes had difficulty in obtaining sufficient evidence to secure a conviction.[40] When the slaves John Simms, Jasper, and Nelson were acquitted of burglary in 1853, for example, the *Richmond Dispatch* reported that only one member of the court was in favor of their discharge, and that there was strong circumstantial evidence against them. Another illustrative case was the trial of Robert G. Scott's slave Daniel, who in 1830 was accused of murdering James Drummond, a white man. The case commenced on June 8, and it took four days for the court to hear all of the evidence from a total of twenty-seven witnesses. This was much longer than almost any other slave trial heard in antebellum Richmond. The prosecution's main preoccupation was proving that Daniel had fired the shot that killed Drummond, and, to this end, medical experts were called to testify as to the nature of the injuries sustained by the deceased. Dr. William Tazewell testified that the bullet must have entered Drummond's skull from an elevated position, and this was shown to be consistent with evidence that Daniel had been on horseback at the time of the killing. Such detailed evidence was rare in slave trials and illustrates the extra concern that characterized proceedings in capital cases. Similarly, the large number of witnesses who testified at Daniel's trial stood in stark contrast to a sample of forty-three nonmurder slave trials in which an average of fewer than three witnesses were summoned to give evidence.[41]

Daniel's defense counsel, James Lyons, went to equally great lengths as the prosecution in an attempt to win the case. There is little extant defense testimony from Richmond slave trials, and although this in part reflects the legal requirement that only the evidence of the Commonwealth's witnesses had to be recorded by the court, the fact that the defense testimony that has survived is drawn from murder trials suggests that many slaves charged with lesser crimes may have been convicted without any defense witnesses being called before the court. It is all the more remarkable, then, that Lyons called a total of sixteen witnesses to refute the charges against Daniel and constructed an alternative narrative of Daniel's actions on the night of the murder than that which was proposed by the prosecution.

One of the key defense witnesses was another of Robert Scott's slaves Lucy, who told the court that she had seen Daniel lying asleep in the dining room of Scott's house just two or three minutes after she had heard the fatal shot being fired. Lucy admitted that she was the sister of the prisoner, but despite this family bond claimed that she "would say no more for him than for another, for her soul would be in danger." To lend credibility to this statement,

Lyons introduced three white character witnesses. Wilson Bryan had known Lucy for many years and considered her "a servant of most exemplary deportment" whose word on oath he "would not at all doubt." Dr. Tazewell, a close friend of Robert Scott, had also known Lucy for a number of years and deposed that he "would believe her on oath as soon as any servant he knows whatever—Her character is among the very best of colored persons." Finally, Scott himself declared that he had never known Lucy to tell a lie.[42] That Scott was willing to allow Lucy to testify and to endorse her words suggests that he supported James Lyons's efforts on behalf of Daniel and did not wish to see him go to the gallows. As Scott was a lawyer himself and in 1830 defended three of the six slaves charged with felonies in Richmond, he was undoubtedly well acquainted with the workings of oyer and terminer courts and their potential for erroneous verdicts. It was possibly for this reason, as well as out of concern for his property investment, that he demanded that his slave should be rigorously defended.

Circumstantial evidence alone was rarely sufficient to convict a slave of murder. When Mary was charged with killing her master's six-week-old child in 1845, the prosecution presented extensive circumstantial evidence to the court. Witnesses established that Mary had borrowed a full phial of laudanum from a neighbor on the instructions of her mistress, Mrs. Powell, and returned it with a third of its contents missing the day after the child's death. Dr. Albert Snead and Dr. James Beale both testified that food that had been prepared by Mary and given to the child had a strong smell of laudanum, and when Dr. Beale carried out a postmortem he concluded that the child had "died of some narcotic poison." Mrs. Lee, who had been nursing Mrs. Powell at the time of the child's death, told the court that Mary had suggested giving the child some laudanum when he was restless, and Mr. Powell testified that the day before the child died he had told Mary that she would have to attend the child and stay in the house that night. Mary was not pleased by this and responded that "she did not like to nurse white children."[43] However, despite the seriousness of the alleged crime and the strong suspicions raised against Mary by the prosecution testimony, the court would not condemn her to death without more concrete evidence.

The cases of the slaves Mary and Daniel indicate that the low conviction rate in slave murder trials was not a product of arbitrary verdicts returned by magistrates determined to protect the property interests of defendants' owners, but rather the outcome of unusually rigorous trial processes. Nevertheless, although magistrates who sat in oyer and terminer courts were sporadically concerned with standards of evidence and legal rules, many slaves were convicted on evidence that would have been inadmissible against whites.

For example, despite African Americans being prohibited from testifying against white defendants on the grounds that the veracity of a black witness could not be relied upon, the Pennsylvania jurist George M. Stroud noted that "the slaveholding states, have nevertheless, directed the testimony of the slave, without oath or solemn affirmation, to be received for or *against* a fellow slave."[44]

In antebellum Richmond, black testimony was not only admitted against slaves, but sometimes formed the very basis of the prosecution case. This had not always been common practice. In 1692, a law was passed in Virginia excluding all testimony not given under oath, which effectively prohibited all slaves from appearing as witnesses. In 1705, the racial restrictions on testimony were made more explicit, and all "negroes, mulattoes and Indian servants, and others, not being Christians . . . [were] . . . deemed and taken to be persons incapable in law, to be witnesses in any case whatsoever." In 1723, however, the legislature, noting the difficulty of securing convictions in slave conspiracy cases, permitted nonwhites to testify in capital slave trials. This law was clarified and expanded in 1792 by an act stating that "the Court may take for evidence the confession of the offender, the oath of one or more credible witnesses, or such testimony of negroes or mulattoes, bond or free, with pregnant circumstances, as to them shall seem convincing."[45] Accordingly, magistrates could not convict a defendant on the basis of slave testimony alone, but only if they had good reason to trust the slave's word.

In practice, "pregnant circumstances" most often took the form of evidence from whites who swore to the good character and previous good conduct of the slave witness. These white witnesses were almost always male and usually owned or hired the slaves whose words they endorsed. This system of verifying slave testimony therefore gave slaveholders further control over the oyer and terminer trial process. Indeed, making the validity of courtroom testimony dependent on a white man's assessment of a black person's character enabled white slaveholders to maintain the fiction that they were capable of determining the truthfulness of statements made by black slaves. Even so, this was also one of the rare occasions that slaves themselves could influence the trial process, and, as Ariela Gross has argued in relation to civil cases, the difficulty that whites faced in "reading" slaves' character could also bring into question the character and honor of the white parties in the courtroom, especially if they disagreed in their interpretations of slave evidence.[46]

Pregnant circumstances were not always necessary to secure a conviction on the basis of black testimony. The slaves Moses Campbell and Frederick Banks, for example, were convicted of burglary largely on the evidence of a single free African American witness, George Cook. Cook deposed that, on the night of July 22, 1845, between two o'clock in the morning and daybreak, he saw the defendants remove a number of barrels of flour from the lumber house of Warwick & Barksdale. Cook claimed to know the prisoners well, and, although he was in his own house some forty yards from the scene when the crime was committed, he was able to identify them because "the moon was shining very brightly during the whole time."[47] Following the arraignment of Banks and Campbell before the mayor, warrants had been issued for the appearance of four other witnesses on behalf of the Commonwealth. The official transcript of the evidence in the case, however, records the deposition of only one other witness besides Cook. Burwell Jinkins, the longtime captain of the night watch, testified that he had "heard the statement of George Cook given two or three times before, and he thinks that his statement on each occasion has been remarkably similar."[48]

Jinkins's testimony provided the only corroboration necessary to convict Banks and Campbell and condemn both men to death, and it raised more questions than it answered about the case. When were the other occasions that Jinkins might have heard Cook's statement? One was probably during the mayor's court examination, and the other may well have been at the time of the defendants' arrest when Cook, due to the proximity of his house to the scene of the crime, may have been interrogated by a police officer or by Warwick and Barksdale as they inquired into the theft of their property.[49] Alternatively, Cook himself may have reported the crime and given his account independently before the defendants were arrested, in which case further questions arise about his motives. Cook testified that he knew the prisoners well, yet no evidence was presented regarding the nature of his relationship with the two slaves. Were the three men friends? Had anything occurred between them that may have prompted Cook to testify against Banks and Campbell? Was Cook coerced into testifying? Cook deposed that he "first noticed the men [Banks and Campbell] about two o'clock in the morning; and he continued to observe them until about day break." It seems strange that although he watched the movements of the defendants throughout the night, at no point did Cook attempt to alert a watchman or a neighbor to the crime being committed or endeavor to prevent the burglary himself. It is even possible that Cook may have colluded with Banks and Campbell before striking a deal with the Commonwealth's attorney agreeing to testify against the prisoners in return for immunity from prosecution.

There is no evidence from the oyer and terminer trial transcripts that slave defendants ever gave evidence at their own trials. This was in keeping with the practice in most white trials for which records survive, and although accused felons were not legally prohibited from testifying, attorneys doubtless realized that the stigma associated with being an accused felon would have rendered the testimony of a black defendant entirely untrustworthy in the eyes of the bench.[50] As such, the only instances in which the thoughts of the accused were heard by the magistrates occurred when witnesses testified that the defendant had confessed to the alleged crime.

Contemporary legal authorities agreed that it was necessary to handle slave confessions with care when presented as legal evidence. The proslavery legal scholar Thomas Cobb wrote that slave confessions

> should be received with great caution, and allowed but little weight, especially when made to the jailor or arresting officers, for the habit of obedience in the slave compels him to answer all questions of the idlest curiosity, while his mendacious disposition will always involve even the most innocent in the most contradictory inconsistencies.[51]

Despite such concerns, in Richmond it was far from uncommon for a slave's confession to be introduced through the deposition of a prosecution witness. Richmond magistrates heard, for example, that a slave named George Mercer called Burwell Jinkins, the captain of the night watch, into his cell and made a full confession that he was guilty of burglary. Similarly, the slave Perry did not hesitate to answer in the affirmative when asked if he was the man who had murdered Joseph Anstread's slave Abram.[52] Both of these defendants were convicted, and their confessions may have carried particular weight with the court due to their ostensibly voluntary nature. In Mercer's case, it is probable that the justices adhered to similar logic as was advanced by the Virginia Court of Appeals in an 1858 ruling on the question of the admissibility of declarations of guilt by white defendants. The court of appeals deemed it a "fair presumption" that any confession brought about by the questioning of an officer of the law was "given either under the fear of punishment or the hope of leniency or reward." However, if the prisoner "voluntarily makes a statement to an officer who has asked him no questions, or held out any inducements to him, then the confession is a proper one to be given to the jury."[53]

Not all slave confessions were handled with such care. In 1818, Richmond's Common Council confirmed that a finger screw had been used to obtain confessions from slaves, and although this practice was criticized, more subtle tactics were employed with the acquiescence of white authorities.[54] When Robert Ford's slave Mathew was arrested on suspicion of burglary, William Brown, the victim of the crime, confronted him in his cell. Brown's purpose in questioning Mathew was to secure the return of his stolen property, but Mathew at first refused to reveal its whereabouts, taunting Brown and claiming that if he "did not get his watch and money, until he got it from him, witness [Brown] would have to wait a long time." Frustrated in his objective, Brown warned the slave "that he had proof of his guilt, and that prisoner had better make a clean confession, if he did, it might go better with him." Apparently fearing the consequences, Mathew made a full confession before the mayor the very next morning.[55] There is no evidence that the magistrates questioned the circumstances under which Mathew's confession was made, and there was no possibility that their decision to convict him could have been challenged on the basis of illegal evidence, as might have been the case for a white defendant with the right of appeal. As such, Mathew's confession was just one of the more overt ways in which court procedures in Richmond recreated in the judicial sphere the dynamics of the master-slave relationship.[56]

Attorneys represented all slave defendants charged with felonies in Richmond. In contrast to magistrates, who were representatives of the city government charged with maintaining order in the community, attorneys could not help but be aware of the conflict between their legal training and the handling of cases of black prisoners they represented. Unlike the aldermen who sat as magistrates in oyer and terminer trials without any requirement of an education in law, men such as Thomas P. August and Robert G. Scott, who between them represented almost one-quarter of all slaves tried in Richmond between 1830 and 1860, were among the most prominent and experienced attorneys in Virginia, appeared frequently before the Virginia Supreme Court, and were schooled in common-law principles that influenced their defense of slaves.[57] August was renowned as "an ingenious and effective pleader ... [who] never failed to win at the least the kind feeling of the jury," while Scott appeared in more criminal supreme court cases in pre–Civil War Virginia than any other lawyer except Benjamin Watkins Leigh.[58]

The efforts of attorneys on behalf of their slave clients doubtless varied considerably, yet in all cases the lack of an avenue of appeal from the decisions of the court meant that attorneys' ability to affect the court's rulings was severely constrained. Nonetheless, legal representation for slave defendants was not an insignificant factor in slave trials. For example, it was perhaps on account of attorneys' support that between 1830 and 1860 only sixteen slaves (3.5 percent) pleaded guilty in Richmond oyer and terminer trials. By forcing the court to conduct a trial, enslaved defendants who pleaded innocent at the very least postponed their punishment and instigated a confrontation in which the court was required to reconcile competing white interests, most often those of the slave's owner and the victim.[59] Especially if the victim was a nonslaveholder, this could generate tensions between whites, as the victim's demand for severe punishment was potentially at odds with the interests of the defendant's owner.

In their efforts to secure the acquittal of enslaved defendants, attorneys often challenged specific court rulings on technical grounds and in so doing contested the aim of the oyer and terminer process to dispense swift and efficient justice in the interests of controlling slave crime. Richmond magistrates did, on rare occasions, dismiss charges against slave defendants for errors on the face of the indictment, suggesting at least a nominal concern with procedural regularity in oyer and terminer examinations. For example, the warrant charging William Lipscomb's slave Elick with burglary was quashed in January 1831 because it did not fix a trial date.[60] When John Morris's slave Fanny was convicted of arson in 1849, meanwhile, the court upheld a motion for a new trial even before passing sentence. The reason for the court's decision may well have related to the "purely circumstantial evidence" against Fanny, although it seems unlikely that further evidence would have come to light in the mere two days before Fanny's second trial. At that trial, the magistrates once again found her guilty, and on this occasion they did not hesitate to pass sentence of death.[61] Even as Fanny's case suggests a concern with standards of evidence, the speed with which a second oyer and terminer hearing was arranged reiterates the efficiency of Virginia's slave trial system, for it was in stark contrast to similar events in the circuit court, where white defendants had to wait at least six months until the next court session for a new trial. Such a delay in the administration of slave justice would have been unacceptable to the owners of slave defendants, as it would have deprived them of valuable labor for a prolonged period of time.

The cases of Elick and Fanny were unusual, and magistrates more commonly rejected attempts to extend due process protections to slaves. For example, in a final attempt to save Daniel from the hangman's noose in 1830, James Lyons moved that judgment should not be given against the prisoner on the grounds that the mayor's warrant fixed the date for the trial contrary to law, "and because the court is, by the warrant, constituted and convened as an examining court, for the examining of the fact not for the trial." Similar arguments sometimes led the hustings court magistrates to quash indictments against white defendants in felony examinations, but sitting as an oyer and terminer court the same men did not hesitate to overrule Lyon's motion.[62] Nonetheless, although specifically legal arguments rarely determined the outcome of an oyer and terminer case, even by making such arguments attorneys demonstrated that the mode of slave trial in Virginia could not be entirely divorced from Anglo-American legal culture.

Attorneys' criticisms of decisions taken in the course of oyer and terminer trials were more successfully voiced in clemency appeals to the governor. James Seddon repeatedly expressed concern about standards of justice in slave trials. In 1841, Seddon represented Henry Blakey's slave John Watkins, who was charged with burglary. After Watkins had been convicted and sentenced to death, Seddon argued: "The principle of evidence . . . on which the court acted in convicting of burglary is very unsatisfactory in reason and of doubtful propriety in law. There was no direct testimony of the commission of the burglary by him (the slave) and the only evidence was his possession of the stolen goods."[63] The following year, Seddon and H. A. Claiborne criticized the trial of their client Emanuel, who was sentenced to hang for the murder of a slave named Isaac. In a clemency petition, Seddon and Claiborne contrasted Emanuel's experience in court with ideals derived from common-law precedent. In particular, they referred to evidence, not included in the record of the trial, that showed that Emanuel had been continually provoked and threatened by Isaac. Tellingly, Seddon and Claiborne concluded, "We are confident that the prisoner would have been acquitted had the affray occurred between white men," an opinion that implicitly suggested that Emanuel deserved the same legal protections as white defendants, which, in this case, may have resulted in a noncapital conviction such as manslaughter or second-degree murder.[64]

Thomas J. Evans, counsel for Scott, sentenced to hang for murder in 1859, also argued that the court had erred in sentencing his client to death. Evans claimed, successfully, that the proper punishment according to the revised Virginia Penal Code of 1849, was sale and transportation, as there was little evidence that the crime was premeditated, and it was therefore "not such an offense as might have been punished with death if a white person had been charged with it." The slave John Rawlings was more direct in highlighting the deficiencies of the oyer and terminer system and disputed the testimony introduced by a slave named Ann that "he had no means either of excluding . . . [or] of bringing discredit upon" in the course of the trial. After the sentence had been read, however, "several circumstances and some statements of fact which could not have been brought out in the trial made it very doubtful to the minds of several members of the Court and of the Attorney for the Commonwealth whether the aforesaid Ann had spoken the truth."[65]

Within six days of his conviction, John Rawlings was granted a full pardon, a decision that reflected the appellate function of executive clemency in oyer and terminer cases. Although slaves were often reprieved from execution, they were rarely granted full pardons, but the Rawlings case shows that Virginia governors did, on rare occasions, agree with attorneys that the decision of an oyer and terminer court was erroneous because of legal technicalities. Further evidence of this is provided by the case of a slave named Armistead, who was sentenced to death for burglary and subsequently pardoned in 1842. This executive ruling was not based on evidence that Armistead was not guilty but instead on "the uncertainty of the judgment fixing the day of Execution." The court had wrongly specified that Armistead would be hanged on Friday, February 17, 1842, when in actual fact the Friday in question was February 18.

Armistead's pardon was an extraordinary decision that illustrates the tension between the legal culture of due process protections and the disregard for these protections embodied in the oyer and terminer system.[66] Although defense motions to overturn court verdicts rarely proved successful, the fact that they were entered at all is evidence of a conception of the rights of black defendants on the part of Richmond's legal professionals that was distinct from that laid down in law. Even so, by acceding to attorneys' complaints about the oyer and terminer process in individual cases, it is also possible that Virginia's governors succeeded in tempering more stringent criticisms of the slave trial system as a whole.

The appellate function that the governor served in the cases of John Rawlings and Armistead was incidental to the main purposes of the executive clemency process, which was to convert death sentences to sale and transportation. In fulfilling this ameliorative role, the governor acted according to similar considerations as the courts of oyer and terminer, yet with one important difference. While the court magistrates had to maintain at least a façade of justice, the executive based most of his decisions on factors related explicitly to the property status of the slave convict. As well as providing a means to challenge the decisions of the court on the basis of law and evidence, the executive review of all cases in which an enslaved defendant was sentenced to death enabled the owners of condemned slaves to influence the case to a greater extent than was possible in the courtroom and ensured that the state would not have to meet the costs of recompensing the owners of executed slaves.

The salient fact about the decision to commute a slave death sentence to sale and transportation was that it shifted the burden of compensating slaveholders for the loss of their property from the state treasury to a private slave trader. The clearest evidence of this is that although just five of the forty-three slaves who were sentenced to death by a court of oyer and terminer in Richmond between 1830 and 1860 were ultimately executed, only three received a full pardon. The remaining thirty-five had their sentences commuted to sale and transportation, labor on the public works for life, or, in the case of three slaves who were due to be emancipated when they reached a certain age, penitentiary imprisonment.[67] On average, in every instance that a slave condemned to death by a Richmond court was reprieved and sold out of Virginia after 1830, the state treasury saved more than $600.[68] Nonetheless, an analysis of appeals for clemency made on behalf of condemned slaves in Richmond demonstrates that more complex dynamics also shaped the pardoning process and mediated discourses of clemency, slavery, and the market in accordance with a spectrum of slaveholder concerns ranging from alleged paternalistic sympathy for the fate of a favored servant to economic self-interest.

Although the oyer and terminer trial system was itself highly responsive to slaveholder concerns, the clemency process enabled the owners of slave defendants to influence still further the fate of their human property. More specifically, it provided a means for slaveholders to convert their human property into its cash value in a way highly compatible with their paternalistic pretensions. As historians of the domestic slave trade have argued, the slaveholders' image of themselves as benign patriarchs concerned with the well-being of their slaves was undermined when they voluntarily initiated slave sales and especially when they broke up slave families. However, when a slave was sold by mandate of a court, the pecuniary interest of the slave's owner in the sale was masked.[69]

The appeals for clemency made on behalf of condemned slaves in Richmond were infused with financial considerations expressed in the language of paternalism. However, slaveholders who wrote petitions expressing humanitarian concern for the fate of a condemned slave, did so in the knowledge that a full pardon was unlikely to be granted and, even if the death sentence was commuted to sale and transportation, they were still assured of financial compensation for the loss of their property. This is not to suggest that slaveholders who wrote clemency petitions feigned interest in the fate of their slaves, but it is to acknowledge the limits and complexities of a paternalism that spared the life of a condemned slave in order that that life might then be sold in a property transaction.[70]

White petitioners often sought clemency for slaves with whom they had a close personal relationship even when the culpability of the condemned was not in question.[71] When "a faithful and much esteemed nurse" in the Ellis family asked Thomas H. Ellis to request executive clemency for her grandson, the condemned slave George Mercer, Ellis responded in a manner that implied that his personal paternalistic concerns outweighed his interest in the proper ends of justice. Ellis freely admitted in a letter to the governor that the mother of the condemned man had begged him to use his influence to seek clemency and that he would "fair do any thing I could, properly, to gratify my old 'mammy.'" Although Ellis claimed that as a matter of principle he "would not interfere with the execution of a sentence at law justly passed," and further explained that he had no proper grounds upon which to base an appeal for executive intervention, he asked the governor to inform him of any measures he could take to secure clemency for Mercer and he would "gladly adopt them."[72] John W. Morris, owner of the slave Fanny, who was sentenced to death for arson in February 1849, was equally aware of his paternalistic responsibilities and explained in a petition that "Holding the relation he does, to this unfortunate convict, he feels it a duty which he owes not only to her but to himself to appeal on her behalf to the clemency of your Excellency."[73] In contrast to Ellis's limited knowledge of the facts in the Mercer case, Morris believed firmly in Fanny's innocence and questioned the evidence against her, yet it was clearly a concern for his duty as a slaveholder as much as reservations about the vicissitude of the court verdict that prompted him to bring the matter to the attention of the governor.

In a more complex and unusual case, the response of the Govan family to the impending execution of their slave Virginia, who had been convicted of arson, highlights the tension between the public demand for swift and harsh punishment of slave criminals and the private interests of individual whites whose slaves were the subject of criminal prosecutions. Lucy Govan was deeply distressed by the prospect of Virginia's execution. Although Lucy did not doubt Virginia's guilt and wrote her father that "there was everything to prove her guilty even without her confession," she vehemently opposed the death penalty in the case and appealed to the governor to pardon Virginia as she believed that Virginia had not intended to "consummate the crime" but had acted only to arouse suspicion so that she would be sent away from the employment of William B. Ruschmer, to whom she was hired at the time. Implicit in Lucy's comments was the belief that Virginia would not have committed the crime had she remained in the Govan household, and in this regard the appeal for a pardon was an attempt to absolve the Govans of responsibility for Virginia's criminal conduct.[74] Prompted by similar concerns of paternalism, benevolence, and his reputation as a slaveholder, Archibald Govan, Lucy's husband, sent a petition to the governor requesting a pardon for Virginia on the condition that he "pledges himself to detain the said slave in custody until a favorable opportunity shall offer for sending her beyond the limits of this Commonwealth."[75] In this event, Govan promised that he would "try and get her a master some where in North Carolina and not let her be sent off so far from her parents."[76]

On March 26, 1843, having been informed that Virginia had been granted a full pardon on the condition that she would be kept in close confinement as long as she remained in the Commonwealth, Archibald Govan immediately removed her from the city jail and deposited her in Bacon Tait's slave jail, "a place of private confinement, where her comfort was better consulted." Govan instructed Tait to sell Virginia at the earliest opportunity to a "purchaser to obligate himself to remove her beyond the limits of the State," but more than two months later no sale had been made. On the very day that she had been placed in Tait's custody, Virginia "was seized with Epileptick [sic] fits" that continued at regular intervals until early June. It was the opinion of Dr. George Minor, who treated Virginia, that "the nature of her malady is such as to be likely to be incurable while she is confined in a jail," and it was further represented by Bacon Tait that "the girl can not be sold even at a nominal price as long as she may labor under the present malady." Dr. Minor advised that the only hope of curing Virginia was "restoration to her liberty, change of scene, and regular intercourse with the other sex," and upon this recommendation and after consulting with the governor, Govan took Virginia home, where he hoped "to repair her shattered mental and physical energies."[77]

Archibald Govan had never before felt himself "in a position where there was so much difficulty in reconciling a sense of duty, with the dictates of common humanity," and he knew not "how to avoid public censure & at the same time keep clear of what I fear infinitely more, self condemnation." For Govan, the issues at stake were moral; they concerned his reputation as a slaveholder, his relationships with his slaves, and his obligations as a white southerner. What he did not acknowledge was the extent to which his efforts to seek clemency for Virginia also reflected his interests as a property holder and how those interests constrained and defined his paternalism. Though Govan's petition was couched in paternalistic language, the consequence of the executive pardon was to reassert the primacy of the master-slave relationship and to reestablish Govan's property interest in Virginia over the claims of the state.

In presenting his concern for Virginia's well-being to the executive, Archibald Govan sought to deny the significance of Virginia's dual status as person and property. As a paternalist, Govan focused on the human aspects of Virginia's circumstances—her illness—to explain his failure to act in accordance with the terms of the pardon and sell Virginia out of the state. The illness, Govan maintained, raised doubts as to whether Virginia could even survive the long journey to the North Carolina border. At the same time, however, Virginia's malady undermined her value as property, and it is a clear illustration of the underlying paradox of slaveholder paternalism that, by taking steps to repair Virginia's "shattered mental and physical energies," Govan was effectively preparing her for market. The problem that Govan faced was not only that he was unable to sell Virginia out of state, but also that he could not do so without sacrificing his financial investment in her person. It is probable that Virginia was aware of her economic value to Govan and she may even have perceived her illness in a positive light and possibly feigned her epileptic fits in order to postpone her sale and remain with her family in Richmond.[78]

Not all slaveholders were as burdened by the conflicting claims of humanity and property interests as Archibald Govan. Henry Blakey, for example, organized a petition on behalf of his slave John Watkins that was openly motivated by pecuniary self-interest and made no concessions to paternalistic or humanitarian notions. The petition was composed by the attorney James A. Seddon under Blakey's solicitation. It stated that the oyer and terminer court had assessed Watkins's value at $640, and that Blakey was keen to obtain this sum "as soon as possible to enable him to discharge several pressing executions." Seddon had learned, however, that Blakey would not receive the money until the executive had ruled in the case because if the slave received a full pardon, "the Commonwealth would be under no responsibility to the owner."[79] It was not uncommon for the governor to issue a twelve-month reprieve to a condemned slave before ultimately commuting the sentence to sale and transportation, and, in this light, the primary aim of Seddon's petition appears to have been to hasten the executive decision-making process by obtaining an immediate commutation of Watkins's sentence in order that Blakey might more speedily receive compensation for the loss of his property.

Blakey was not unique in placing financial concerns at the center of a clemency petition. Robert Barker, the guardian of Benjamin A. Harwood, whose slave John Rawlings was sentenced to death for burglary, expressed similar sentiments when he opposed moves by the Commonwealth's attorney and the defense counsel to secure a full pardon for Rawlings. Barker argued that a more appropriate course of action would be to commute the punishment to sale and transportation on the grounds that Rawlings "is undoubtedly a boy of bad character and has been Guilty of several offenses of somewhat similar nature heretofore." Furthermore, Barker indicated that he would not consider Rawlings to be his concern even if a pardon was granted since "the judgment of the Hustings Court operated to divest the property in said Negro from his ward [Harwood] and to vest it in the Commonwealth."[80] This claim implied that, in Barker's opinion, the criminal conviction irreparably severed the bond between master and slave, an assessment that was diametrically opposed to that made by Archibald Govan and that indicates that slaveholders who did not want to see their slaves executed often remained eager to be relieved of the potential difficulties and fears of owning and managing recalcitrant slave criminals. The slave John Rawlings, himself, had a very different agenda that ignored the implications of his status as property. In a remarkable petition that he wrote himself, Rawlings prayed "that he may be pardoned and thus not only released from the awful fate to which he has been sentenced, but also, in the alternative of a commutation of his punishment, released from the unhappy lot of being sent beyond the bounds of Virginia and thus severing all the ties which have made this state and this community his home."[81]

More so than in other southern states, the intervention of the executive was a routine part of the slave punishment process in Virginia. Moreover, the clemency system was highly responsive to the petitions of individual slaveholders and, because of the possibility of commuting death sentences to sale and transportation, it was invariably consistent with these slaveholders' interests as property owners. As at all other stages of slave trial and punishment in Virginia, the demands of the slaveholding elite and the ends of justice were highly compatible because they were not constrained by common-law procedures.

Nevertheless, it is evident from slave pardon petitions that the verdicts of oyer and terminer courts and the interests of slaveholders did not always correspond. Although slaveholders viewed executive clemency as a means to adjust the outcome of slave trials to meet specific ends, the processes of petitioning and pardoning were negotiated by diverse interest groups.[82] Even condemned slaves, who had little agency in the courtroom, could influence the pardoning process either indirectly through their personal relations with whites or more overtly, for example by writing their own pardon petitions or feigning illness. In so doing, slaves challenged the claims of white victims and witnesses and revealed a limitation on white mastery and control.

By the late antebellum era, the tensions between slavery and the enforcement of the criminal law revealed in slave pardon petitions had become acute in Richmond. In particular, sale and transportation was increasingly criticized as an inappropriate punishment for slaves that undermined the crime-control function of the law. One Richmond newspaper editor complained that sale and transportation was no "punishment at all," but "amounts only to a change of master and, when resorted to, the slave undergoes no other punishment than that of being sold by the Governor, instead of his master." Other whites concurred that sale and transportation left convicted slaves "unwhipped of justice" and claimed that "the negroes left behind laugh at the silly operation of the law," as rather than being punished, transported slaves were "better off than they ever were and . . . [had] another chance at robbery or murder."[83] More than this, although transported slaves were legally required to be removed from the United States, it was widely acknowledged that the majority were instead taken to the Deep South and the *Whig* considered it "outrageous . . . that by any Legislative act of ours or the action of our Governor . . . such a pack of house-breakers, burners, murderers and poisoners should be turned loose upon an unsuspecting community."[84]

The urban milieu of late antebellum Richmond provided fertile ground for these complaints because of the importance of judicial processes to slave discipline in the city and the nature of urban white class relations. Editorial commentaries in all of Richmond's major newspapers were critical of the intervention of executive clemency in slave cases. The *Richmond Whig and Public Advertiser* maintained that "it never could have been in the contemplation of the makers of our Constitution, to vest in one man the power to overslaugh all the decisions of the Courts," and argued that death sentences ought to be put into execution "*unless subsequently new and important facts come to light.*"[85] The *Richmond Enquirer* was equally disparaging of a system by which "slaves are indiscriminately executed or transported for the same kind of offenses." The *Enquirer* further maintained that the failure to inflict severe and certain punishment on slave felons undermined slaveholders' authority as well as the morality and happiness of the slaves.[86] Joseph Mayo claimed that there was long-standing popular opposition in Richmond to the sale and transportation of convicted slave felons. In a letter to the *Whig* published in 1852, Mayo wrote that "the citizens of Richmond have felt themselves aggrieved for many years past by the course pursued by the Executive . . . .the Court has performed its duty and condemned the felons to suffer the penalty of the low [*sic*], upon testimony the most irrefragable, and yet they suffered, no punishment; the course has been to sell them thus virtually repealing the law."[87]

Mayo's criticisms of sale and transportation were expressed in the midst of the public debate on the fate of Jordan Hatcher, Richmond's most infamous antebellum slave criminal. Hatcher was a tobacco factory hand who fatally struck his overseer, William Jackson, with an iron poker after Jackson attempted to whip him for the poor quality of his work. After Hatcher was convicted of murder and sentenced to death, a petition containing the signatures of sixty prominent Richmond citizens called upon Governor Johnson to spare Hatcher from the gallows mainly on humanitarian grounds and due to the fact that the fatal blow that killed Jackson "was struck under circumstances tending greatly to aggravate the boy [Hatcher], without premeditation and with no design to kill."[88] This consideration was uppermost in Johnson's reasoning when he remanded Hatcher for sale and transportation. Explaining his decision to the General Assembly, Johnson argued that as "Hatcher was in a state of great excitement and suffering when he struck the blow," the crime was not murder, "but *manslaughter*, without intent to kill," and it would have been treated as such had the defendant been a white man. Finally, "though the *letter of the law* prescribed the *penalty of death*," Johnson believed that it would be, "contrary to the spirit of the laws and of our age, and contrary to *mercy and humanity*," to execute Hatcher.[89]

Slaves condemned to death in Richmond were routinely granted clemency, but the overt insubordination to white authority inherent in Hatcher's crime and the social and sectional tensions of the early 1850s prompted the underlying disquiet with executive intervention in slave sentences to erupt into outright hostility. Johnson's explanation met with widespread condemnation across Virginia that was given visible manifestation when a large crowd gathered outside the Governor's Mansion in Richmond's Capitol Square to show their disapprobation by "groaning and shouting and hissing and cursing."[90] While the petition requesting clemency for Hatcher had been endorsed by many elite Richmonders, including numerous slaveholders, the crowd that protested Johnson's actions was predominantly comprised of young working-class men who were motivated not only by opposition to the commutation but also by the threat that slave labor posed to the employment of white workers.[91] What is more, the danger to slaveholders' interests inherent in this conflict appeared all the greater in the context of increasing white immigration to Richmond, the recent introduction of universal white manhood suffrage in Virginia, growing sectional tensions, and abolitionist activities.[92]

The opposition to slave clemency that was manifested in the Jordan Hatcher case was, in essence, a consequence of the difficulty of reconciling slaveholders' interests as paternalists, masters, and property holders, with the concerns of nonslaveholding white workers and tobacco manufacturers who hired rather than owned most of their enslaved labor force and who demanded that African Americans be held to a stricter form of justice than whites. According to these groups, Johnson's actions implied "that a *negro is as good as a white man*" and undermined "all laws for the protection of the whites against the blacks."[93] While slaveholders endorsed sale and transportation as a means of reconciling control of slave crime with their

Fig. 7. "Richmond, Va. The Governor's Mansion." 1865. Courtesy of Library of Congress, Prints and Photographs online, Selected Civil War Photographs, 1861–1865. <http://hdl.loc.gov/loc.pnp/cwpb.02921>

property interests in slave defendants, many other whites believed that "it would be better to pass a law making the loss fall upon the master who is so unfortunate as to own a felon."[94] Furthermore, as nonslaveholders were all but excluded from participation in slave trials in Virginia by the absence of a jury in courts of oyer and terminer, there was greater potential for conflict between classes of whites over issues of slave justice and punishment than in most other southern states where jury service assured nonslaveholders a prominent role and voice in the regulation of slave crime.[95]

To slaveholders, the sanguinary aspects of the slave penal code were intended to be enforced only in extreme circumstances such as at times of slave rebellion. Despite the sectional tensions of the late antebellum era, as many states were restricting their use of the death penalty and extending due process protections to slaves, and because demand for slave labor in the Southwest was high, there was little support among Richmond slaveholders for the widespread execution of slave convicts. Executive clemency was therefore a necessary corrective to the regular capital sentences passed in courts of oyer and terminer. At the same time, however, the impression that the pardoning power operated in the interests of individual slaveholders was anathema to white solidarity, and it was this that provoked nonslaveholders to contest the slaveholders' extensive discretionary power over the fate of slave defendants. As with other aspects of the judicial system, there was a tension between the efforts of Richmond slaveholders to control the slave population and, at the same time, retain the support of nonslaveholding whites.

Virginia's oyer and terminer court system was responsive to the racial whims of the local community and the property interests of the slaveholding class. This was true of all justice systems in the Old South, but by the Civil War nowhere outside Virginia was the law so subservient to slaveholder influence. Although the absence of due process protections for slaves may at times have compromised slaveholders' interests as property holders, the centrality of the defendant's value as a marketable commodity at every stage of the trial process more than compensated for the threat posed by wrongful convictions. This was evident in the depositions of witnesses, the verdicts and punishments handed down by the court magistrates, and the routine intervention of the executive to commute slave death sentences. Furthermore, by treating slave defendants in an entirely different manner from whites, Virginia's distinctive slave trial system acted as an important counterbalance to urban-industrial developments that were increasing slaves' autonomy and challenging the primacy of the race divide in Richmond.

By the 1850s, however, the foundations of Virginia's system of slave trial and punishment had never been less secure. Attorneys within the state and abolitionists in the North were critical of the absence of due process protections for slave defendants. Moreover, nonslaveholding whites in Richmond resented a system that seemed to respond to the demands of individual slave owners at the expense of the enforcement of the criminal law in the interests of the white population as a whole. On a practical level, sale and transportation—which facilitated the reconciliation of a harsh and summary trial system with the fiscal concerns of the state treasury and the slaveholding class, as well as with the popular reluctance to execute large numbers of slaves—was itself facing insurmountable problems. The international market for transported slaves was moribund, and removing convicted slave criminals to other southern states as a matter of policy, rather than unspoken convenience, was unacceptable. As such, the *Dispatch* wondered if the legislature ought to amend the law so that slaves convicted of "high crimes that did not deserve death" would be confined in the penitentiary for life, "where they would be made useful, and yet kept from mischief and crime."[96] This proposal was also put forward by Governor Henry A. Wise, and in 1858, after several years of popular and political agitation, the legislature replaced transportation with the "employment of Negro convicts on the public works," a punishment that was also endured by free blacks and, within a year, by white penitentiary inmates.[97]

On December 8, 1860, 123 African Americans, free as well as enslaved, who had been sent to the penitentiary "for punishment and transportation" were leased "at fair prices" to contractors on the Covington and Ohio Railroad.[98] The absence of white convicts suggests that there was racial segregation in the labor that prisoners were hired out to perform, but despite this many white Virginians questioned whether hiring out was an appropriate way to punish slave criminals. Similar to the way hiring practices undermined slave discipline in Richmond, labor on the public works also threatened to create a large population of convict slaves, the control of whom was dependent on the relationship between market forces and the penal system. Slave convicts could not be bought or sold, and their status conflicted with the proslavery ideal of paternalistic master-slave relations.

During the Civil War, slave convicts regularly escaped to enemy lines, while fearful whites submitted petitions and threatened mob violence to prevent the employment of enslaved prisoners within their communities.[99] Despite laws that denied slave defendants basic due process rights and resulted in verdicts and punishments that were compatible with slaveholders' concerns as masters and property holders, even in Virginia the regulation of slave crime through law was never an uncontested process.

4

"With these *poor* rogues their *judge* had never dined"

Honor, Law, and the Trial and Punishment of White Criminals

> *Their lot forbade; nor circumscribed alone,*
> *Their grovelling vices, but their joys confined.*
> *To them luxurious banquets were unknown,*
> *With these poor rogues their judge had never dined.*
> —Benjamin Watkins Leigh

While awaiting trial before the United States Circuit Court in Richmond on charges of treason in 1807, Aaron Burr, former vice president of the United States, attended a dinner hosted by one of his defense attorneys, John Wickham. The dinner proved controversial, for also present was Chief Justice John Marshall, who was to be the judge in Burr's trial, as well as several other prominent Richmonders who would serve as jurors in the case. When Burr was subsequently acquitted, the attorney and future United States senator Benjamin Watkins Leigh was unsurprised by the verdict. In a poem that he composed about the case, Leigh commented sardonically that few other defendants in Richmond had such advantageous connections as Burr with the men who sat in judgment upon them.[1]

No one of the political prominence of Aaron Burr stood trial in Richmond in the antebellum era. Local gentlemen, including several newspaper editors, were occasionally arraigned for dueling, and from time to time a wealthy slaveholder was accused of a murder that, invariably, was alleged to have been committed in defense of personal honor. However, the overwhelming majority of white defendants in Richmond were of sufficiently low social status that, were it not for their appearance in court on criminal charges, there would be no extant evidence that they were ever in the city at all. Few were wealthy enough to feature in the records of those who paid personal property tax, while a majority also escaped the attention of the census takers, indicating that they were only ever temporarily resident in the city. These transient participants in Richmond's antebellum history were especially unlikely to be acquainted with the men who judged them in courts of law, but in practice this did not necessarily mean that their fate was any less influenced by extralegal considerations than, in Leigh's estimation, was the acquittal of Aaron Burr.

Class was only one of several factors that shaped the courtroom experiences of white defendants, whether they were tried for misdemeanors in the hustings court or felonies in the circuit court. Not only on the rare occasions that wealthy and powerful men stood trial in Richmond but also in cases involving even the poorest white defendants, the judge and jury mediated judicial processes through diverse extralegal considerations, including their conceptions of a code of honor, racial and gender ideologies, and the nature of the alleged offense.[2]

Throughout the antebellum period, the rule of law was subservient to the community will in Richmond to the extent that the *Richmond Republican* could claim in 1850 that "public sentiment here is practically the law of the land."[3] This statement accords with the view of a lawless Old South that pervades both historical scholarship and the popular imagination. However, like Leigh's assertion of the influence of social class on the administration of criminal justice, the *Republican's* interpretation was simplistic. Although examples of judicial discretion and disregard for rules of evidence appear sporadically in Richmond's late antebellum court records, there was also a growing adherence to due process in criminal trials that was a product not only of evolving American legal culture but also of changing social, economic, and political circumstances in Richmond itself.

When factors such as the race and gender of the victim and the accused did exert a strong influence on verdicts and sentences in late antebellum Richmond, it was invariably in cases of violent crime. In trials for murder, assault, and stabbing, juries at times returned not guilty verdicts that contradicted entirely the evidence presented to the court, and even those defendants who were convicted often received relatively light sentences or were granted clemency by the governor. Richmond trial verdicts and sentences also upheld accepted gender conventions and ideals of patriarchy, female purity, and domesticity. Women were rarely prosecuted for violent crimes, and those who were convicted had usually violated community expectations of appropriate female conduct as well as committing the offense for which they were indicted. Likewise, male defendants were most likely to be convicted when their alleged victim was a woman.

In upholding and reinforcing ideals of female purity and masculine honor and dominance over slaves and white women, the trial verdicts and punishments imposed in cases of violent crime strengthened central elements of the southern social order. Yet, unusually for the Old South, it was crimes against property and prevailing moral standards that dominated the Richmond docket from the 1830s to the 1850s, and in these cases it was more problematic for jurists to sacrifice legal formalism in the interests of serving community norms. There were several reasons for this. First, the impersonal nature of most property crimes mitigated against routine extralegal regulation. Second, property crimes were considered more serious than crimes against the person, both in the courtroom, where the longest average prison sentences were reserved for crimes against property, and in the value system of the community. Finally, in an urban society characterized by transience and anonymity, in which white criminality (especially theft) was increasingly associated with urban class and ethnic divisions, the interests of white egalitarianism required strict adherence to due process. In short, the type of crimes committed by whites in Richmond, coupled with the nature of urban class relations, necessitated that the city's courts exercised less discretion in the trial of white defendants than was common in other parts of the slave states. As with other developments in Richmond's criminal justice system, this concern with legal formalism had unique implications in the context of an urban slaveholding society. Repeatedly, authorities in Richmond discovered that ensuring fair trials for whites compromised the control of the city's slave population.[4] In particular, slave discipline was undermined by the law prohibiting African Americans from testifying against whites in a court of law. The notion that a white defendant might be convicted and potentially imprisoned or even executed on the basis of an African American's testimony was inconceivable in the South, yet this law inevitably enabled many white criminals to escape conviction. What is more, the crimes for which the law had most difficulty in bringing white perpetrators to justice were those most closely associated with slave insubordination, including illegally retailing alcohol, selling and receiving stolen goods, and, most seriously of all, aiding slaves to escape.

As the oyer and terminer system institutionalized violations of common-law due process in slave trials, so another distinctive element of Virginia's judicial structure facilitated and formalized flagrant violations of the rule of law in the prosecution of white defendants charged with the most serious crimes. White men and women indicted by the mayor for felonies were subject to examination by a panel of at least five hustings court magistrates, who decided either to dismiss the case or remand the defendant to face a circuit court grand jury. The examining function of the hustings court was a remnant of the colonial era, when all felony trials were conducted at one of the biannual sessions of the general court in Williamsburg. As attendance at the general court involved great time and expense for all participants in the trial process, especially those in counties far from the state capital, the magistrates of local county and corporation courts were authorized to conduct a preliminary examination in order to ensure that only cases in which there was a strong suspicion of guilt were brought before the grand jury.[5] In 1789, eighteen district courts, each encompassing several counties, were established across Virginia and assumed jurisdiction in felony cases. These courts survived only until 1808, when they were replaced by superior courts of law, which themselves gave way in 1831 to circuit superior courts of law. These courts made criminal trials more of a local affair, but still there were only two court sessions held each year, and the examining role of the county courts consequently remained on the statute books throughout the antebellum period. Even with this system in place, however, in 1860 the *Richmond Dispatch* still bemoaned that prisoners charged with felonies were jailed for an average of three months before standing trial and that this was a cause of overcrowding in the city jail.[6]

Due process was notably absent from hustings court examinations. The duty of the magistrates was to inquire only into the facts and not the law of the case, and the investigation was not constrained by common-law precedent. As such, the accused was not under oath, and it was not necessary for the prosecution to prove its case conclusively, but only to establish the defendant's probable guilt. As a summary hearing held without a jury, therefore, the investigations of the hustings court magistrates provided an opportunity for extralegal factors to influence cases without violating the precepts of the rule of law. Furthermore, as the court was required to hear the case within five to ten days of the indictment being issued, attorneys were often unable to gather all of the available evidence, making the examination's findings far from conclusive.[7]

Contemporary observers noted other aspects of hustings court examinations that undermined the pursuit of justice. An anonymous member of the bar in Louisa County argued that pretrial examinations *"favor the escape of guilt, by harassing and breaking down the Commonwealth's witnesses."* Examinations rarely occurred on the set day, and witnesses were often required to attend court on two or three separate occasions before they were able to present their testimony. According to the attorney from Louisa County, after this negative experience of the legal process, witnesses were likely to look for ways to avoid further involvement in the case. Additionally, the attorney bemoaned that when prosecution witnesses testified before the hustings court, they provided the defense with an opportunity "to learn the strong and weak points" of their evidence.[8]

As well as attorneys, defendants could have cause to oppose the hustings court examination, even though it provided an opportunity to be discharged from further prosecution. Depending on the timing of the case, a defendant found guilty in a hustings court examination might have to wait until a later circuit court session to stand trial than if his case had proceeded straight to the grand jury without delay. For those who could not make bail, this could mean spending several additional months in jail, and it was most likely for this reason that on at least one occasion a prisoner in Richmond waived his right to an appearance before the hustings court magistrates.[9]

Concern with due process in hustings court examinations was often inconsistent, because the court magistrates—the same men who sat in judgment on slaves charged with felonies—were drawn from among the city aldermen and were rarely trained in the law.[10] In 1860, for example, the aldermen included a physician, a grocer, a commission merchant, a hotel owner, a clerk, and a paperhanger.[11] As attorney Jonathan Shook commented in a clemency petition on behalf of one of his white clients in Richmond in the 1850s, jurists' "non acquaintance with Law" meant that "in many cases prejudices take hold of sworn duty and forbid its conscientious exercise." It was not only slaves who suffered legal injustices; as Shook commented to the governor, "we know how many erroneous decisions are rendered and how many unjust verdicts are recorded in all our courts."[12]

Although not always legal experts, hustings court magistrates in Richmond were drawn from the higher echelons of the city's white society. All twelve of the aldermen who served in 1840 were slaveholders, and ten owned at least three slaves, a number that distinguished them from the majority of slaveholders in the city, who owned just a single bondsperson. By contrast, the men who sat on trial juries in Richmond represented more of a cross-section of white society. In 1840, just one in three jurors was a slaveholder, and approximately one-quarter were not even Richmond residents, a finding that is in keeping with other studies that suggest the makeup of petty juries in the antebellum United States was somewhat haphazard and often in contravention of legal regulations.[13]

In total, 780 felony examinations were conducted in the Richmond Hustings Court between 1830 and 1860, and 75 percent of all defendants were sent on to be examined by a circuit court grand jury. Crimes against property accounted for 70 percent of all hustings court felony examinations, and it is notable that the defendants charged in these cases were more likely to be sent on to the circuit court than those accused of violent crimes.[14] This was

Table 4.1: Richmond Hustings Court felony examinations, 1830–1860

Type of offense	Total cases	Sent on for trial Number	Percent
VIOLENT OFFENSES			
Assault	21	16	76.2
Kidnapping	6	5	83.3
Murder	59	40	67.8
Rape	5	5	100.0
Robbery	9	7	77.8
Shooting	20	14	70.0
Stabbing	114	78	68.4
Total	234	165	70.5
PROPERTY OFFENSES			
Arson	8	4	50.0
Breaking and entering	11	11	100.0
Burglary	22	18	81.8
Forgery, counterfeiting, fraud	118	101	85.6
Receiving stolen goods	65	34	52.3
Stealing	292	228	78.1
Total	516	396	76.7
OTHER OFFENSES			
Aiding a slave to abscond	21	19	90.5
Bigamy	2	1	50.0
Circulating an incendiary pamphlet	1	1	100.0
Perjury	6	1	16.7
Total	30	22	73.3
Grand total	780	583	74.7

Source: Richmond Hustings Court Minutes, 1830–60.

in keeping with widespread tolerance of violence throughout the South. In the opinion of the *Republican*, it was unreasonable to expect that men would be punished for offenses "which, in nine cases out of ten, the Judge upon the Bench, every juryman in the panel, and every lawyer at the bar, feels that he would himself commit under the same circumstances."[15] Although the *Republican*'s comments referred specifically to the failure of the courts to enforce the laws against dueling, they resonated in many other cases of violent crime and especially in hustings court examinations in which the social background and lack of legal training of the magistrates gave additional weight to extralegal factors such as honor and commitment to patriarchal values.

Judicial discretion was most often exercised on behalf of defendants drawn from the ranks of the social elite, and this was never more clearly exemplified in Richmond than in the examination of William Myers, his brother, Colonel Samuel S. Myers, and William Burr, who were charged in 1846 with the murder of Dudley Hoyt.[16] Sometime in mid-September 1846, Samuel Myers intercepted a letter from his sister-in-law, Virginia Myers, addressed to Hoyt, a businessman from Massachusetts who had lived in Virginia for thirteen years. The letter confirmed Samuel's suspicions that Virginia and Dudley had been having an affair while Virginia's husband, William Myers, was visiting his home city of Baltimore on business. In fact, Virginia and Dudley had carried on their affair throughout the summer months, passing secret notes through trusted friends and arranging illicit meetings under the cover of respectable social gatherings.

As soon as Samuel learned of the affair, he informed William, who returned to Richmond four days later. Early on the morning of September 28, William and Samuel Myers, accompanied by William Burr, entered Dudley Hoyt's bedroom, which was situated in an office under the Exchange Hotel. Burr presented Hoyt with a paper for his signature, under the terms of which Hoyt was to leave Richmond immediately on pain of death if he ever returned. When Hoyt refused to sign, William Myers shot him in the right side of the head, leaving a wound from which Hoyt died twelve days later.

Following a coroner's investigation, William Myers, Samuel Myers, and William Burr were arrested and charged with murder. On October 12, the mayor conducted a preliminary investigation into the case, and the next day he remanded all three of the accused men in custody to await further examination before the hustings court magistrates, who would determine whether to send the case on for trial. Although the defense attorneys—Robert G. Scott, James Lyons, and Gustavus Myers—were three of the most esteemed figures on the Richmond bar, they did not rest their case only on points of law and evidence but instead played on popular attitudes toward honor and patriarchy. Robert Scott put the defense case passionately and in terms that highlighted what to honorable Virginians were the great limitations of the legal system. Scott argued that Myers had no choice but to exact personal vengeance upon his wife's seducer: "Why, sir, if a man violates your bed what are you to do? Go to the law. Ha! ha! ha! Prosecute him for a misdemeanor! The *law* will let him off with a fine of twenty dollars and a gentle admonition to behave better for the future." In Scott's opinion, Myers's honor would have been compromised had he sought redress through the law, for he would have invited upon himself "the contempt of women" and become a "laughing stock" among men.[17]

When James Lyons addressed the court, he raised a number of points of law, which he claimed demanded that Myers be discharged. First, Lyons questioned the wording of the indictment. He noted that "the accusation is, that *all* killed him," whereas the evidence presented in court showed that William Myers alone had been responsible for Dudley Hoyt's death. Furthermore, Lyons also claimed that "the killing was provoked, justifiable, and in self-defense."[18] This line of defense alluded to the distinction drawn in Virginia criminal law between different degrees of homicide, but it was perhaps more intended to appeal to the personal sympathies of the magistrates, for nowhere did the law state that the killing of an adulterer caught in the act was legally justifiable. What is more, according to a precedent established in the Virginia General Court, neither the mayor nor the hustings court magistrates had the power to decide on the degree of murder in any case. Mayor Lambert was certainly aware that "the stern decree of the law forbids my investigating the justifying circumstances of this case," and on this basis had decided not to dismiss the case himself, but instead to send the accused before the hustings court.[19] However, in contrast to Lambert, and in violation of precedents set in the general court, the hustings court magistrates did assume the right to determine the degree of homicide. After a hearing lasting several days, the magistrates voted by five to two to discharge all three of the defendants, and when the ruling was announced it was greeted *"with rounds of applause from the crowded courtroom."*[20]

In the mid-nineteenth century, men such as William Myers who avenged their sexual dishonor went unpunished in all parts of the United States.[21] In the South, however, such verdicts were particularly significant, for the patriarchal order and honorable sensibilities they upheld were a cornerstone of slave society. To deny the right of a white man to avenge his honor was comparable to denying his mastery as a slaveholder.[22] As such, though the hustings court ruling in the Myers case was unusual in running so entirely contrary to the evidence, the Richmond magistrates also treated leniently white men who committed violent crimes in very different circumstances, and it was not unusual for verdicts that contradicted the evidence to be met with widespread public approval. For example, when Thomas W. Lottier was accused of shooting William P. Cook and discharged without trial, the presiding magistrate was unable to restrain the 150 spectators in the courtroom from applauding and cheering the judgment, even though all were aware that Lottier had indeed fired at Cook.[23] In a similar case, the hustings court magistrates discharged Richard Beazley, a fifty-seven-year-old veteran of the War of 1812, from further prosecution for the murder of William C. Holdsworth. The murder had occurred during a controversy over a horse race in the course of which Beazley had insulted Holdsworth, who had responded by striking his adversary in the face. In retaliation, Beazley had fatally stabbed Holdsworth in his left side. The three magistrates who favored discharging Beazley ruled that the crime was justifiable as it was committed in self-defense. The *Dispatch* also condoned the crime and refrained from condemning the judgment, even as it recognized that there was little doubt that Beazley had acted unlawfully.[24]

Lottier and Beazley, like Myers, were respectable gentlemen, and their social standing contributed to the court's sympathetic opinion of their actions. Lower-class defendants were more likely to be remanded for trial, yet all defendants charged with violent crimes could benefit from jury discretion. When murder defendants were tried in the circuit court, for example, although juries did not return verdicts that were entirely contrary to the evidence, they rarely convicted the accused of the capital crime of murder in the first degree. Between 1849 and 1860, fifteen out of twenty-six whites charged with murder were convicted, but only one of the convicts was deemed by the jury to have killed in circumstances that warranted death. Fourteen others were judged guilty of manslaughter or murder in the second degree and sentenced to between one and eighteen years in the penitentiary.[25]

Writing in 1858, John B. Minor cited three circumstances that could extenuate homicide to manslaughter: first, if there had been reasonable provocation that was "so recent as not to allow time to cool"; second, if the killing had occurred in the course of "mutual combat, suddenly engaged in, in heat of blood, with no difference, at the beginning, in arms"; and, third, if death had occurred while the accused was trying to arrest the deceased on suspicion of committing a felony.[26] These circumstances were interpreted broadly by Richmond juries, which were particularly responsive to defense arguments that claimed that the accused had been provoked or acted "in the heat of blood." For example, Elizabeth Southard, who had struck William Walker a fatal blow with a gridiron, was convicted only of manslaughter, rather than murder, after she explained that she was retaliating after he kicked her in the mouth. Similarly, John Cronin evaded a capital murder conviction for killing his wife by claiming that he had acted when he found her in the water closet with another man.[27]

The only white man to be hanged for murder in late antebellum Richmond was William Totty, who, in 1860, shot his sister-in-law Catherine Thom while she sat eating breakfast in her father's kitchen. It was alleged that Totty had acted after Thom had refused to run away with him, but this was not a crime of passion in the manner of Myers's killing of Dudley Hoyt. Totty could not claim to have acted in the "heat of blood" because Catherine Thom had rejected his advances repeatedly over a three-week period before her death. Furthermore, in contrast to John Cronin's wife, who was

Fig. 8. "The State Penitentiary, Richmond, Va." 1865. Courtesy of Library of Congress, Prints and Photographs online, Civil War Photographs: Anthony-Taylor-Rand-Ordway-Eaton Collection. <http://hdl.loc.gov/loc.pnp/cph.3c05082>

suspected of adultery, Thom's reputation was unsullied at the time of her murder, and the jury consequently could not view Totty's actions with the sympathy that evidently was extended to Cronin. Indeed, Totty was a married man, and for this reason his actions could not be interpreted as defending his honor, rather, they violated his responsibilities to his wife. The only mitigating factors that were raised on Totty's behalf at his trial and in subsequent clemency petitions were that he had been drunk and insane when he committed the murder. Not only did these factors fail to evoke the sympathy of the jury, however, they also did not sway Governor Letcher, who refused to intervene with the judgment of the court.[28]

The hanging of William Totty was an exceptional event, the first execution in Richmond of any convict, either black or white, for eight years. Southern tolerance of violence along with the movement against the death penalty throughout the United States in the post-Revolutionary era help to explain the small number of whites convicted of first-degree murder, yet more importantly, the racial dynamics of southern society must also have influenced jury deliberations in Richmond. At a time when the vast majority of condemned slaves were granted clemency and sold out of the state, it would have been a strange reversal of the racial order had whites regularly been hanged for murder.[29] Again, therefore, features of slave society constrained the administration of criminal justice in cases involving white defendants.

The judicial discretion that shaped violent crime trials was also evident on the sporadic occasions that women appeared before Richmond's criminal courts charged with crimes against person and property. Women were rarely prosecuted in antebellum Richmond, and each case involving a female defendant consequently assumed considerable symbolic importance. When Harriet Hooper was tried for stabbing with intent to kill, for example, her attorney, Robert G. Scott, "remarked that he had, during many years, been practicing his profession, and had defended many criminals, but *never before* had been called to defend a woman charged with felony!"[30] Similar sentiments were expressed in Norfolk, Virginia, when Margaret Douglass was jailed for instructing free blacks to read and write, the *Norfolk Argus* commenting that "it was revolting to the citizens to have a woman imprisoned in our jail."[31] On the rare occasions that women did stand trial, therefore, justices struggled to uphold racialized conceptions of white womanhood that prized domesticity, purity, and subordination to masculine governance, in the face of the reality of female criminal agency.[32]

Between 1830 and 1860, just eighteen women were prosecuted for violent crimes in Richmond, six of whom were indicted in conjunction with at least one male codefendant. In addition, only forty-six women were accused of crimes against property. This meant that women comprised just 4 percent of all whites charged with misdemeanors and felonies against person and property. Although urban-industrial developments, such as rising poverty and an increase in the female workforce, led to more women living outside of patriarchal family units, this did not translate into a rise in rates of female prosecution in Richmond as happened, if only to a limited degree, in northern cities.[33] This sectional distinction may have resulted from a lower rate of female crime in the South, but it also reflected the reluctance of judicial officials at earlier stages of the prosecution process to institute judicial proceedings against women.[34]

In 1860, for example, nine of the ten white women who appeared in the mayor's court charged with stealing were dismissed without prosecution. By contrast, 65 percent of the fifty-seven white men accused of stealing were sent on for further examination and trial.[35] In the same year, only one out of thirty-seven women charged with assault was sent on to the hustings court, in comparison to 25 percent of the nearly two hundred men who appeared before the mayor on the same charge.[36] What is more, many crimes committed by women were not even reported to the mayor. Following a spate of shoplifting incidents involving "females professing to be ladies," the *Dispatch* reported on one case in which a young woman was caught placing several valuable pieces of lace in her pocket by a store clerk but was not turned over

Table 4.2: White Richmond Hustings Court defendants by gender (misdemeanors and felonies), 1830–1860

Type of crime	Male defendants	Female defendants	Female (%)
Murder	48	6	11.1
Stabbing	112	1	0.9
Assault	424	11	2.5
Stealing	519	16	3.0
Receiving stolen goods	126	28	17.6
Forgery	150	2	1.3
Other	188	2	1.1
Total	1,567	66	4.0

Source: Richmond Hustings Court Minutes, 1830–60.

to the police. Had she faced prosecution, the *Dispatch* commented, "the exposure might have deterred others from following in her footsteps."[37] In a similar case, Norbonne E. Sutton initially decided not to report Hannah Sullivan, "a hale, fresh looking, young Irish woman," whom he suspected of receiving goods that had been stolen from his hotel, after she tearfully denied the charge. However, Sutton later reconsidered his decision on discovering that Hannah was married. While Sutton could not conceive of Hannah committing a felony alone, it seems that he suspected that she might have acted under her husband's influence.[38]

The few white women who were prosecuted for violent crimes in Richmond were rarely convicted. Only three out of eleven women indicted for misdemeanor assaults were found guilty in the hustings court, and it is especially notable that none of the other eight women were acquitted by a jury.[39] Instead, in each case the prosecution was abandoned, possibly for lack of evidence or because the attorney for the Commonwealth did not expect to be able to secure a conviction from a jury of men reared in the South's paternalistic culture as adherents to the cult of female domesticity.

Gendered considerations also influenced the fate of the four women who were tried in the Richmond Circuit Court for violent felonies and whose fate is known.[40] Two of these women escaped conviction. The prosecution against Rebecca Chapman, who was charged along with William Hebden with the murder of John Richards, was dropped before the case came to trial, while Virginia Lloyd, who was accused of killing her infant child, was found not guilty. This verdict was in accordance with the hopes of the *Dispatch*, which blamed Lloyd's misfortunes on "her base seducer" and reported the widespread sympathy that had been expressed for Lloyd while she languished in jail awaiting trial.[41] The *Dispatch* was little concerned with the facts of the case; more significant was the preservation of the ideal of white female purity. By shifting responsibility for the child's death from Virginia Lloyd to the man who seduced her, the *Dispatch* denied the reality of female criminal agency.[42]

Despite the example of the Lloyd case, the race and gender of white female defendants was not alone sufficient to secure their acquittal. Class and social status also influenced the fate of the women who stood trial for violent crimes in Richmond. Neither of the two women convicted of violent felonies in the 1850s fitted the ideal of female purity that Virginia Lloyd embodied. In the murder trial of Elizabeth Southard, the prosecution questioned Southard's racial identity and called witnesses who testified that she associated mainly with free African Americans. Meanwhile, in the trial of Harriet Hooper, who was charged with stabbing Elizabeth Mitchell with intent to kill, the testimony showed that both women lived and worked in a brothel.[43]

Even when allegedly disreputable white women were convicted, however, gender conventions mitigated their punishment. The three women found guilty of assault were all fined, and in two cases this was little more than a token gesture on the part of the court. Catherine Chesterton and Martha Drew were fined just one cent and five dollars respectively, and in Chesterton's case, when the victim was a white man, Fabius Hicks, the punishment was perhaps intended to discourage other men from prosecuting white women, an act that contravened southern expectations of honorable and masterful masculine conduct. When Ann Meredith received a more substantial fine of fifty dollars in 1840, it was most likely because she had not appeared at her trial, rather than due to the seriousness of the crime. Harriet Hooper, meanwhile, was sentenced to just three months in jail for stabbing with intent to kill, and Elizabeth Southard served only twelve months for attempted murder. Both of these sentences were less severe than those received by most male defendants in similar circumstances.

Women charged with property crimes were no more likely than men to be acquitted, but in most cases they received more lenient sentences than men convicted of the same offense.[44] The influence of gender on criminal sentences was made explicit in Margaret Douglass's trial in Norfolk, when Judge Baker declared that "under the circumstances of this case if you were of a different sex, I should regard the full punishment of six months imprisonment as entirely just and proper."[45] Similar sentiments influenced the decisions of the Richmond bench. When Elizabeth Bovan was convicted by a circuit court jury of receiving stolen goods, for example, she was sentenced to just one month in jail and two lashes, which were later rescinded by the governor. By contrast, the five men who are known to have been convicted of receiving stolen goods in the 1850s were all sentenced to between one and four years in the penitentiary. Similarly, among the ten women convicted of misdemeanors in the hustings court, only Mary Weaver, who was jailed for three months for stealing, received a custodial sentence of longer than thirty days. Other women, including Eliza Griffin, served as little as one day in jail for crimes including stealing and receiving stolen goods.[46]

Griffin, a Virginia-born seamstress, appeared before the Richmond Hustings Court more often than any other white woman in the antebellum period. On one occasion assuming the name Fanny Ellerson as an alias, Griffin faced three separate charges of stealing between 1845 and 1850 and was convicted each time. At her first trial in 1845, Griffin was sentenced to one month in jail and two lashes. In a clemency petition that prompted the governor to reprieve her from the corporal element of her sentence, it was revealed that Griffin had already spent one month in jail along with her infant child. This child was possibly John Griffin, who was listed among the residents of the poorhouse in the 1850 census along with his two brothers, Thomas, aged two, and Evans, aged two months. If these were Eliza Griffin's children, they may have accounted for the one-day jail sentence that she received in 1849. Had Griffin been imprisoned for any longer, the community might have been burdened with the care of her children, as happened the following year when she was convicted of stealing gold jewelry worth more than $100 and sentenced to the penitentiary. This was an exceptional sentence for a woman, as magistrates were usually reluctant to imprison unmarried mothers when the cost of caring for their dependent children would have to be met by the taxpayer. Perhaps in this case they expected Eliza's husband, James Griffin, to care for the children, but within a month of Eliza's imprisonment, James, too, had been arrested. He was charged with forgery and sentenced to two years in the penitentiary.[47]

Notwithstanding exceptional cases such as those involving Eliza Griffin, trial verdicts and punishments in cases of violent crime, as well as on the rare occasions that women were indicted for serious crimes against person and property, usually reflected and reinforced values of honor, patriarchy, and female purity that prevailed to varying degrees among all classes of southern whites.[48] Southerners were conscious of their distinctive attitude toward law and violence, and this was reflected in the Richmond press, which contrasted the rulings of the city's courts with justice in the northern states. When Dr. John Webster, an experienced and respected professor at Boston Medical College, was sentenced to death for the murder of his colleague Dr. George Parkhurst, the *Republican* condemned the nature of justice administered by "our 'cold Northern brethren.'" Although the *Republican* admitted that Webster's case was "a warning to men of unbridled passions," it argued that the crime did not warrant the death penalty even after Webster had confessed because he had acted under provocation.[49]

The notion that justice was not as "cold" in the South as in the North was indicative of the mitigating influence of community attitudes on law enforcement in the slave states. Yet in Richmond circumstances conspired gradually to discourage discretionary forms of justice. These circumstances included the diversity and transience of large sections of the city's population, the breakdown of traditional personal associations between slaveholders and poor whites, and the fracturing of communities that undermined consensus on issues of crime and punishment. In contrast to more stable and less socially stratified communities, there was a need in Richmond to offset the tendency of the judicial system to target poor and marginal whites through close adherence to an abstract ideal of justice and due process that would affirm the distinction in the treatment of all white defendants from that of slaves and free blacks. Additionally, discretionary justice was discouraged in Richmond by the integration of urban areas into national and international cultural and legal worlds, as well as the demands of the urban business and manufacturing elite, who believed that the law in all its guises, both civil and criminal, had to be certain and rational to free individuals to pursue material gain.[50]

Changing prosecution patterns also encouraged a more complex, rational, and consistent jurisprudence in the urban South. Although southern cities were renowned for fights, brawls, assaults, and murders, prosecutions for morals offenses and property crimes dominated the Richmond docket book. Unlike violent crimes, which to the southern mind were essentially private matters between individuals, crimes against property and the moral order threatened the entire community, and their prosecution had a more overt regulatory dimension in which the state sought to control individual conduct for the good of the whole.[51] As justice in violent crime cases was in large part a matter for the accused and the victim, and because of the widespread tolerance of certain forms of violence in the Old South, judicial discretion supported white hegemony by adhering to extralegal values that were shared by the entire white male community. By contrast, in cases of property crimes and morals offenses, the code of honor was peripheral and could not confer legitimacy on discretionary courtroom proceedings. As such, the courts were required to adhere more consistently to rules of due process in these nonviolent crime cases.

In a perceptive analysis of criminal justice in eighteenth- and nineteenth-century Maryland, the historian James Rice found evidence of the development of a more complex jurisprudence during the antebellum period in the changing conduct of criminal trials and a long-term decline in conviction rates from the colonial era through to the 1830s. Rice attributed these changes in part to the increasing number of defendants who hired defense lawyers. In the colonial and early national periods, most trials lasted for less than an hour, few witnesses were called, cross-examination was rare, common-law rules of evidence were poorly defined and haphazardly interpreted, and the jury often reached its verdict without even leaving the courtroom.[52] From the 1830s, however, this traditional model began to break down in some cases, and a more complex form of adversarial trial emerged.

Unofficial circuit court trial transcripts recorded by the attorney Robert Reid Howison in 1850 and 1851 show that criminal trials in late antebellum Richmond were conducted in an adversarial manner and with considerable concern for due process and legal technicalities.[53] Defense attorneys were involved in all of the trials attended by Howison, and in half of the trials the accused was represented by as many as three attorneys.[54] Lawyers often spent considerable time preparing their arguments. Joseph Jackson, for example, devoted three hours to preparing a defense for Thomas Burgess against charges of rape and "all morning" attempting to construct an argument to secure the acquittal of James H. Smith for embezzlement, despite having "not a point of ground to stand upon."[55]

By the 1850s, Richmond attorneys also routinely subjected witnesses to cross-examination.[56] In the trial of John Fisher for forgery, Howison commented that "the case was earnestly argued, chiefly on the question whether at the time of passing the note the prisoner knew it was counterfeit." Furthermore, rather than deciding their verdict immediately in the courtroom, the jurors who tried Fisher had to be "kept together during the night" and did not conclude their deliberations until eleven o'clock the next morning, when they found Fisher not guilty.[57] In the trial of John Campfield for burglary, meanwhile, the defense attorney John H. Gilmer cited English case precedent to argue successfully that testimony relating to comments made by Campfield immediately after his arrest was inadmissible, as the comments were "made under circumstances which might well be considered as amounting to *moral duress*—admissions made to Capt Wilkinson, who was 'a most imposing looking officer,' and whose very appearance might awe a young prisoner." The ruling of Judge John S. Caskie that Wilkinson's declarations were "clearly inadmissible" was in stark contrast to slave trials in which similar evidence regularly formed a part of the prosecution case.[58]

In the trial of Cornelius Sullivan, who was charged with receiving stolen goods, the defense presented a three-pronged rebuttal of the prosecution's case, arguing that there was no proof that the articles were stolen; that if they were stolen there was no evidence that they were received by the prisoner; and that if they were received by the prisoner, it was not certain that he knew they were stolen. William W. Crump adopted an alternative tactic and commenced the defense of his client Henry B. Allison against charges of theft by objecting to the propriety of the legal process itself. First, Crump argued that the indictment did not adequately describe the property allegedly stolen, and when this motion was overruled, he claimed that Allison "had not been properly examined by an Examining Court according to Law."[59] The court rejected these objections, but similar motions alleging errors on the face of the indictment often met with success. After William P. Adcock was found guilty of embezzlement, for example, he was granted a new trial on the grounds that the stolen goods were "proved to be the property of Ayres & Co., and not of Ward, Ferguson & Barksdale, as laid in the Indictment."[60]

The longest and most complex case recorded by Robert Howison was the murder trial of Samuel Hastings in April 1851: the trial lasted for four days; testimony was heard from forty-one witnesses, and the closing arguments of the prosecution and defense alone consumed almost twelve hours of courtroom time. Hastings was accused of assaulting Robert Childress and striking him a fatal blow on the head with a stick. There was little doubt that Hastings was responsible for the assault, but the prosecution struggled to prove that the blow struck with the stick had caused Childress's death. Although four doctors who had conducted postmortem examinations on Childress testified that the wound to the head inflicted by Hastings was the primary cause of death, the defense countered by depicting Childress as "a man of very intemperate habits" and blamed his death on excessive drinking over a number of years. Rarely was a defense mounted with such vigor in a Richmond trial court: ten doctors were called to give evidence that Childress's death may have been alcohol-related; a number of other witnesses swore that they had seen Childress walking about the city after the assault and prior to his death; and the evidence of the prosecution witnesses was undermined by close cross-examination. When questioned by the defense, Dr. James Bolton was forced to concede that "there is ground on which medical men may doubt" that Hastings's assault had caused Childress's death. Similarly, Caroline Childress, the wife of the deceased, admitted that she had not actually witnessed the assault, and that shortly before the alleged crime her husband had assaulted her and she had him put in jail.[61] When Hastings was found not guilty, the verdict reflected the aspersions that had been cast on Childress's character and the systematic dismantling of the prosecution case.

The most detailed legal arguments were usually made in the circuit court, but concern with the rule of law in cases involving white defendants permeated even the less exalted stages of the judicial process in Richmond. Defense lawyers were often present in mayor's court examinations by the 1830s, and even the most impoverished white defendants accused of minor offenses could obtain legal representation on credit. For example, when Joseph Jackson represented three prisoners and brokered an agreement with a Mr. Ratcliffe to employ them on the fishing shores if the mayor would release them from custody, he agreed to waive his five-dollar fee until the men began working and could afford to pay.[62]

Although mayor's court justice was often swift and summary, two of the three men who served as mayor of Richmond between 1826 and 1865 were former attorneys who at least claimed to apply principles of Anglo-American jurisprudence in their treatment of white defendants. Joseph Tate, who served as mayor from 1826 until his death in May 1839, occasionally noted with evident pride the extent to which due process reigned in his courtroom. When John Grace, charged with felonious stealing, was acquitted, Tate noted in his personal docket book that "the investigation was highly proper."[63] Tate also claimed to be able to distinguish between the "moral" or probable culpability of the accused as might be defined by community consensus, and the more rigorous legal requirements for establishing guilt. In the case of Thomas Locknane, a white man accused of assaulting the tailor Josiah Jones, the prisoner was dismissed from prosecution despite Tate's belief that both the defendant and the complainant in the case were "to a moral tho not legal certainty, petty black-legs."[64]

Mayor Joseph Mayo was equally concerned with due process and in 1860 changed the time at which his court sat so that he could hear cases "before the other Courts commence, thereby giving the lawyers an opportunity of appearing before him, whenever called upon to do so."[65] In 1856, Granville Montelle was examined on a charge of stealing fifteen dollars from Jesse Barnes, and, although such an offense constituted a misdemeanor, Mayo at first sent Montelle on to be examined for felony on the grounds that he had previously served a term in the penitentiary. Later the same day, however, "after taking time to examine the law, the Mayor changed his decision in relation to Granville Montelle . . . and sent him on to be indicted for a misdemeanor at the next Grand Jury term of the Hustings Court."[66] Aside from Virginian legal precedents, the authorities on which Richmond's mayors based their rulings were the same as those consulted by jurists throughout the United States and Great Britain. Hale, Chitty, and Blackstone all influenced mayor's court rulings to greater or lesser degrees.[67]

There is some evidence that rising concern with due process led to declining conviction rates for whites in the mayor's court. It is difficult to determine, however, whether this was a long-term trend or rather a reflection of the background and training of the different mayors. For example, whites were most often judged guilty of assault and stealing by Mayor Lambert, who, in contrast to Mayors Tate and Mayo, had a military rather than a legal background.[68]

In hustings court and circuit court cases, the records reveal a much more significant decline between 1830 and 1860 in the number of indictments that ended in a conviction. This decline was particularly pronounced in property crime cases. Excluding cases in which the defendant pleaded guilty, the number of stealing prosecutions in the hustings court increased more than fivefold between the 1830s and 1850s, from 26 to 134. However, the proportion of defendants who were convicted declined from 73.1 percent to 44 percent. There was a similar decline from 50 percent to 29.4 percent in convictions for receiving stolen goods from the 1830s to the 1850s, even as, again, the total number of cases tried in the hustings court more than doubled to fifty-one. Conviction rates in cases of assault also declined, albeit far more gradually.[69]

That there was such a substantial decline in the rate of convictions for stealing and receiving stolen goods at a time when the number of indictments and the fear of crimes against property was increasing in the wake of growing white immigration and poverty suggests that the courts retained a degree of independence from extralegal influences. It also reflects the great difficulty that the prosecution encountered in acquiring sufficient evidence to secure a conviction. In contrast to violent crimes, which often involved defendants and victims who were acquainted or sometimes even related to each other, few thieves were caught in the act, and as the urban population grew more diverse and transient it became more difficult to trace thieves and burglars. Even in the 1830s, few of the men and women who reported thefts to the police could identify a suspect, partly because four out of every five reported thefts occurred in stores or on business premises and often took place at night when buildings were most likely to be unoccupied.[70]

In contrast to the discretionary judgments in violent crime cases, even elite white men charged with property crimes were held to strict standards of justice. In the case of Samuel Pendleton, who was charged with forgery and counterfeiting, many gentlemen connected to the affair were anxious to

Table 4.3: Change over time in Richmond Hustings Court conviction rates, misdemeanor trials

Type of crime	1830s			1850s			Change in conviction rate
	Total cases[a]	Convictions	Conviction rate (%)	Total cases	Convictions	Conviction rate (%)	
Assault	55	31	56.4	235	113	48.1	-14.3
Receiving stolen goods	20	10	50.0	51	15	29.4	-41.2
Stealing	26	19	73.1	134	59	44.0	-39.8

Source: Richmond Hustings Court Minutes, 1830–60.
[a]Excludes cases in which the defendant pleaded guilty.

protect the honor of the esteemed Pendleton family name, and only one of the several victims chose to press charges. Nevertheless, Samuel's elite acquaintances recognized their limited influence over the prosecution process and courtroom events. While William Myers and other murderers willingly turned themselves over to judicial authorities in expectation of a speedy acquittal, the men connected with Pendleton attempted to remove him from Richmond before the authorities were alerted to his crime.[71]

As Samuel Pendleton struggled to evade arrest and prosecution in the hours and days subsequent to his crime, he received assistance from numerous unlikely sources. First, the exhibitors of a faro bank on whom Pendleton had passed forged checks to repay gambling debts and to whom he had confessed his crime offered him $500 and a horse on which to make his escape, an offer he refused. Second, with the endorsement of Charles Williams, one of the owners of a countinghouse that Pendleton had defrauded, James Gray, who also ran a countinghouse in the city, agreed to cover the value of the forged checks. Police officers were by this time in pursuit of Pendleton, but Benjamin Sheppard, a magistrate in Henrico County, and Egbert Woodford of Goochland County provided him with shelter until Gray could raise sufficient funds to repay the checks.[72] Even when it became evident that Gray could not cover Pendleton's debts, George P. Crump, another of the men who had been defrauded, dissuaded Pendleton from turning himself over to legal authorities and agreed to accept a personal note from Pendleton for the value of the check. Despite having committed a serious criminal offense, Pendleton's word remained his bond within the respectable social circles in which he moved.[73]

That James Gray, Benjamin Sheppard, and other pillars of the local community tried to cover up a case of forgery, repay the fraudulently obtained money, and prevent law officers from catching up with Pendleton is indicative of the tensions between legalism and honor in antebellum Richmond.

However, the efforts of Pendleton's wealthy and powerful benefactors ultimately could not spare him from a fate dictated by the law. Pendleton was arrested, tried, convicted, and sentenced to two years in the penitentiary, a punishment that he served in full after the governor rejected several clemency petitions. In this case of forgery, the judiciary scrupulously upheld the rule of law and in so doing maintained at least the impression that the courts afforded equal treatment to all white defendants irrespective of social status.

The conviction of elite men like Samuel Pendleton served to demonstrate to lower-class whites the evenhandedness of the law.[74] However, Pendleton's was not a unique case that served only a symbolic function. On the contrary, it represented a widespread change in attitudes toward the role of law as a response to crime. As the judicial system assumed a more regulatory rather than private function in antebellum Richmond and the rule of law challenged community consensus as the determining factor in trial verdicts, extrajudicial forms of justice began to attract criticism from commentators who were concerned about their effects on public order and the urban economy. For example, there was much disquiet about the impact of the pardoning process on the efficiency of the judicial system. In 1833, the "Committee of Twenty-Four," set up to examine means of curtailing gambling in Richmond, concluded that "the pardoning power seems to have been used to undermine the certainty of punishment."[75] Just five years later, Mayor Joseph Tate expressed similar sentiments when James Talley became the second gambler convicted in Richmond to be pardoned in the space of a single month. "As far as my experience goes," bemoaned Tate in his personal docket book, "the pardoning power, has operated against all efforts to suppress gaming—see the records."[76] Executive clemency continued to be perceived as a threat to the proper operation of the justice system throughout the antebellum period. In December 1860, the *Dispatch* welcomed the fact that Governor Letcher had exercised the pardoning power sparingly: "Taking it for granted, no doubt, that the Courts and juries, by whom persons are tried, have better opportunities of knowing what punishment they really deserved, the Governor has generally permitted the law to take its course."[77]

Vigilante justice also prompted criticism in Richmond. Although vigilantism was a common response to criminal activity across the slave states, in cities mob violence and lynching could be harmful to business interests. When a free black riverboat man was lynched in St. Louis in 1836, for example, the city's claims to be a civilized place where law and order reigned were undermined, prompting a slump in economic investments. When four black men were charged in the same city with a series of burglaries and murders

Fig. 9. John Letcher, governor of Virginia, 1860–64. Reprinted by permission of the Virginia Military Institute Archives.

five years later, therefore, the authorities took great pains to ensure them a trial in accordance with due process that would help St. Louis develop a law-abiding image.[78]

Civic leaders in Richmond were similarly concerned that the law was permitted to take its course in their city, even in the event of the most heinous crimes and especially when the accused was white. In early June 1857, Thomas Hardy, a white former penitentiary inmate, was arrested and charged with the rape of Laura Bennett, an eight-year-old white girl. At the time of the arrest, Bennett's father attempted to shoot Hardy but was prevented from doing so. Over the next few nights, crowds gathered around the jail where Hardy was held and threatened to exact summary justice. In response, Mayor Mayo called out an entire regiment of the military to surround the jail, a course of action that was approved by the *Dispatch*, which hoped that "for the credit of our city," mob violence would be prevented.[79]

As well as undermining the southern economy, lynching also fueled criticisms of slavery from northerners who perceived extralegal violence as evidence of a corruption and disorder characteristic of the entire South. Especially when abolitionists were the targets of southern mobs, some northerners were pushed toward adopting a more antagonistic view of slavery.[80] It was perhaps with such considerations in mind that in 1858 Mayor Mayo rejected Governor Henry A. Wise's suggestion that he should endorse a proposed vigilance committee that aimed to root out "secret" abolitionist societies in Richmond. Wise depicted the committee as potentially a "lawful, peaceful and protective movement of citizens" that could complement municipal police authority, but Mayo responded forthrightly that vigilantism could never have a lawful purpose.[81]

Richmond never witnessed the extensive rioting that struck northern cities in the 1830s, but vigilante attacks did occur. A crowd of as many as four hundred young men ransacked a number of gambling houses in Richmond in 1834, and in 1853 a group of native Virginians attacked German immigrants. Three years later, a spate of vigilante attacks targeted interracial couples in the city. In the summer of 1856, John McRoberts, a white man, was targeted by vigilantes because of his frequent visits to the home of Jordina Mayo, "a sooty black free negro of bad character."[82] Just a few weeks afterwards, a group of young men in Jefferson Ward, calling themselves the "Rocketts Regulators," publicly announced their intention "to rid Rocketts of all the disgraceful characters, by summary punishment." After their first meeting, the *Dispatch* reported that the men "visited a den in which a Negro woman and a white man lived in most intimate terms, captured the pair and took them to the creek where the man was treated to a ducking and painting and the woman subjected to a scrubbing." Similar punishment was also inflicted on an African American man and a white woman who lived together "at another notorious shanty."[83]

The concern of Richmond vigilantes with interracial crimes in the 1850s reflected the sectional tensions of the era and white southerners' fear of abolitionist activities. However, the formation of the Rocketts Regulators was also indicative of the difficulty of enforcing the laws against interracial crimes. This stemmed throughout the South from statutes that prohibited African Americans from testifying against whites, but it was compounded in Richmond by the importance of legal due process, both as an integral part of the city's response to crime and also as a means of unifying the white community. The historian Jack Williams implicitly recognized the unsuitability of legal processes for dealing with abolitionism and related activities that accounted for more than 90 percent of lynch law cases in South Carolina

Fig. 10. Henry Alexander Wise, governor of Virginia, 1856-60. "Half-length portrait, facing right, arms folded." Ca. 1855. Courtesy of Library of Congress, Prints and Photographs online. <http://hdl.loc.gov/loc.pnp/cph.3b36173>

after 1840. Williams noted that vigilante justice hastened "trial" and punishment, made public examples of criminals that served a deterrent effect, enabled the punishment of individuals who had not committed a specific crime, and kept the general population staunchly antiabolitionist. Formal law could serve none of these functions so effectively.[84]

The Richmond court records reveal that the criminal law struggled to police not only abolitionist activities but also other crimes committed by whites in which slaves were involved as either victims or conspirators. White men and women who assaulted, stabbed, and murdered slaves usually received minimal punishments, and those whose relations with slaves involved the purchase of stolen goods and the illegal sale of liquor were less likely to be convicted than defendants accused of almost any other offense. The failure to convict white defendants of violent slave abuse often served elite interests, as it protected slaveholders' right to punish their slaves almost with impunity and strengthened white solidarity by tacitly endorsing violence against African Americans even when committed by nonslaveholders. In Richmond, however, where so many slaves lived and worked apart from their owners, this endorsement was problematic by the 1850s, as unchecked violent interracial confrontations would threaten both public order and slaveholders' economic investment in enslaved victims. At the same time, far more dangerous to elite interests were crimes in which poor whites, slaves, and free blacks worked together, usually for small economic gains, but sometimes in circumstances that fostered interracial sympathies and occasionally even assisted slaves to runaway.

Abolitionist activities rarely led to criminal prosecutions in Richmond. In 1837, Nathaniel Crenshaw was charged with circulating an incendiary pamphlet and sent on to the circuit court for trial, but his case was unique in the antebellum decades. Abolitionism was seemingly better policed by the community than the courts, but other criminal acts that involved both blacks and whites in either collaboration or confrontation could not be so readily controlled in the city by informal measures, at least in part because they were not so universally abhorred by all sections of white society. The support of nonslaveholding whites for slavery depended in part on their sense of racial superiority, which was compromised, for example, when the law restricted their rights to assault African Americans, as slaveholders could almost with impunity. Furthermore, petty interracial crime, particularly selling liquor to slaves, was an important source of income for many poor whites, and the strict enforcement of the law against this practice could have damaged the already precarious financial circumstances of the many grocers whose premises doubled as grogshops.

From a legal perspective, the prohibition on black testimony against whites served as the most important impediment to the regulation of interracial crimes. This rule was a feature of the criminal law in all of the slave states and was consistent with southern racial ideology that depicted African Americans as inherently untrustworthy. It strengthened white racial supremacy and protected whites from malicious prosecutions instigated by blacks. However, even the Georgia attorney Thomas Cobb recognized that "this universal exclusion of a negro from testifying may, in many supposable cases, operate harshly and to the defeat of justice."[85] Especially in a city such as Richmond, with its extensive and complex networks of interracial associations, the inadmissibility of black testimony against whites was inconsistent with the efficient enforcement of the criminal law in the 1850s. Although Richmond's municipal government enacted ordinances intended to reduce interracial contacts in the late antebellum period, so long as blacks could not testify against whites in court, whites were encouraged to engage in criminal activities with and against slaves and free blacks, safe in the knowledge that if there were no white witnesses to their crimes, they were all but above the law.[86]

Appellate courts throughout the South provided slaves with greater protection from violent abuse in the antebellum period than in the colonial and early national eras.[87] In Virginia, however, there is little evidence that the law was concerned with protecting the person of the slave except to the extent that such protection served slaveholders' interests. Writing the majority opinion in *Commonwealth v. Carver* (1827), which confirmed that whites could be prosecuted under the general mayhem statute for violent crimes against slaves, Judge Brockenbrough reasoned, "It is for the benefit of the master, and consoling to his feelings, that a third person should be restrained under the pains and penalties of felony, from maiming and disabling his slave."[88] According to this ruling, the critical factor in cases of violence against slaves was not the severity of the assault but rather the relationship between the assailant and victim. While the law offered some protection to slaves from third-party violence, therefore, it did not compromise slaveholders' right to inflict any punishment short of death on their human property. In *Commonwealth v. Turner* (1827), the general court held "that a master could not be indicted for the malicious, cruel, and excessive *beating* of his own slave," and as late as 1851 the court had to clarify that it did not follow from this ruling "that a master also was immune from prosecution when an excessive beating resulted in the death of the slave."[89]

There is no record that any slaveholders were charged with excessive violence against their own slaves in antebellum Richmond. However, between 1830 and 1860, fifty-three white defendants, all male, appeared in the hustings court accused of assaulting, maiming, and murdering slaves. In these cases, the discretionary influence of the judge and jury that marked all violent crime trials was enhanced by widespread public acceptance that white violence against slaves was necessary to uphold the southern racial order and maintain slave discipline. This was particularly evident in conviction rates for felonies and in sentencing patterns, both of which varied on account of the victim's race. However, justice was not entirely compromised when whites stood trial for violent crimes against slaves and those charged with minor assault were as likely to be convicted as if their victim had been a white person.

Between 1830 and 1860, twenty-two white defendants in Richmond were examined in the hustings court for felonies that threatened the life and limb of enslaved victims, and fourteen of these men were sent on to the circuit court, a proportion only slightly below the rate at which defendants who had committed violent felonies against other whites were remanded for trial.[90] In the circuit court, however, whites were significantly more likely to be acquitted when their alleged victim was black. The outcome is known in seven of the fourteen circuit court cases in which whites were charged with violence against slaves, and in only one case was the defendant found guilty as charged. In all four cases of stabbing with intent to kill, the defendants walked free from court. George Sharp, Gideon Martin, and James McDonough were found not guilty, and the prosecution against James Gentry was abandoned.[91] Both Joshua Alvis and Erasmus Roper were charged with shooting a slave with intent to kill, and, while Alvis was acquitted, Roper was found guilty, albeit of the less serious charge of malicious shooting. Roper, however, was sentenced to just one day in jail and a fine of five dollars, clear evidence that the court had little interest in protecting slaves from white violence.[92]

The only other white man convicted of a violent felony against a slave in the 1850s was Richard Lambert, who was found guilty of murder in the second degree and sentenced to five years in the penitentiary. Overall, however, the evidence from Richmond is broadly consistent with Arthur Howington's assessment of similar cases in Tennessee, where, at the local level, "Tennesseans proved unwilling to establish and enforce significant safeguards to protect their slaves from violence."[93] This similarity is noteworthy, because at the appellate level the Tennessee Supreme Court was far more prepared than its Virginia counterpart to punish whites for murder and attempted murder of slaves.[94]

When white men were tried for violent crimes that threatened the life of a slave, the judicial system was explicitly protecting the interests of slaveholders as owners of valuable property. However, thirty-one white men in Richmond were prosecuted for less serious assaults on slaves that were classed as misdemeanors. Southern slaveholders sometimes tolerated minor violent attacks on slaves by nonslaveholding whites as a way to give meaning to notions of white supremacy and to reinforce their own authority over the enslaved. In Richmond, however, the courts treated white defendants charged with misdemeanor assaults on slaves in much the same way as those accused of attacking whites. Twenty-one of the misdemeanor defendants were found guilty, a conviction rate of 66 percent, which was higher than when the victim was white.[95] Meanwhile, sentencing patterns were similar irrespective of the victim's race, for even though whites convicted of assaulting slaves were usually ordered to pay a fine and fewer than one-third were jailed, imprisonment was equally rare in cases involving minor acts of violence against whites.[96] These conviction rates and sentencing patterns did not reflect judicial concern for black victims, however, but were more likely due to the fact that relatively few defendants were sent on to the hustings court to stand trial for violent misdemeanors against blacks in the first place. As the mayor sent cases on for trial only when there was substantial evidence tending to prove the guilt of the accused, it is unsurprising and not inconsistent with a judicial system highly responsive to issues of race that whites were regularly convicted in the hustings court for assaulting slaves.

The small number of cases of white violence against slaves that reached the trial courts was also in part a consequence of the prohibition on black testimony. If no white witnesses were willing to give evidence against the accused, an indictment could not be sustained, and most slave assaults came to the attention of the judicial authorities only when a white witness, perhaps the owner of the enslaved victim or a night watchman, took the trouble to make a complaint. Even in the trial courts, however, the restrictions on black testimony enabled some white defendants charged with violent slave abuse to evade conviction. Although witness depositions are not available from any circuit court trials involving white violence against slaves, documented testimony from the hustings court examination of Joshua Alvis, who was charged with shooting a slave with intent to kill, illustrates the difficulties that the courts faced in securing guilty verdicts without black witnesses. The hustings court depositions of prosecution witnesses Nathan Turner and Robert Ralston established that sometime after Alvis had threatened to kill a group of his black neighbors one evening in July 1850, he had fetched a gun from his house and fired a single shot that struck and wounded Thomas, a slave belonging to Frederick Weidmeyer. When the case came before the circuit court, however, Alvis was acquitted. Although both Turner and Ralston had been walking away from the scene of the crime when the shot was fired, their evidence was sufficient to establish the probable degree of guilt required for the hustings court magistrates to send the case on for trial. However, in order to convince a jury to convict Alvis, additional testimony was required, and as the only eyewitnesses to the crime were Alvis's black neighbors, who could not testify, the jury returned a verdict of not guilty.[97]

Beyond issues of law and evidence, the high conviction rate for whites charged with violent misdemeanors against slaves also reflected rising concern with the regulation of interracial encounters between slaves and non-slaveholders in Richmond. With the growth in Richmond's working-class white population, the overcrowding of interracial neighborhoods, and the increasingly harsh economic climate facing newcomers to the city in the mid-nineteenth century, the number of whites prosecuted for violent slave abuse increased. While just five white men appeared in the hustings court charged with violence against a slave in the 1830s, seventeen were prosecuted in the 1840s and thirty-one in the 1850s. Although these figures provide little indication of the incidence of actual white violence against slaves, it is evident that the courts slowly assumed a more prominent role in the regulation of interracial violence.[98] This development was not limited to violent crimes but rather was in keeping with the increasing role of the law in regulating other forms of interracial contact that was also manifested, for example, in a rise in prosecutions of whites for permitting unlawful assemblies of slaves on their property.[99]

Most prosecuted cases of violent slave abuse were a product of the tensions that evolved within Richmond's lower-class community and that were often implicitly predicated on issues of race. When Richard Lambert was arrested, for example, he explained to police officer John Pearce that he had killed the slave Humphrey because "he overcame my sister."[100] Joseph Green, meanwhile, was fined five dollars for striking Peter, a slave, with a stone after he ran over a piece of public ground that was being improved under Green's supervision, and Ezekiel Solomon was arraigned for willfully beating the slave Edward when he came into his store to buy a vest. Solomon claimed that Edward had insulted his sister and knocked him down when he followed him out of the store. The mayor, however, contended that even this provocation did not entitle Solomon to take the law into his own hands, and that he "had no right to pursue the Negro threateningly for sixty feet." While the mayor declined to whip Edward, as he had already suffered a violent beating, Solomon was remanded for trial in the hustings court, a decision with which the *Dispatch* took issue, arguing that in the circumstances, "'binding over' would have been sufficient punishment."[101] In a similar case, Henry Harden was accused of beating Robert Bruce's slave Harry with the butt end of a wagon whip. When two witnesses intervened to protect Harry, who had blood streaming from his head, Harden claimed that Harry had been impudent and deserved the punishment.[102]

The assaults committed by Solomon and Harden were attempts to assert a sense of racial superiority over African Americans and are evidence of interracial tensions among Richmond's lower classes. Other assaults committed on slaves by lower-class whites in antebellum Richmond were motivated by overt racism. In 1845, when Dandridge Hogg asked George Sharpe why he had stabbed the slave Dangerfield, Sharpe replied "that he would kill all of them [slaves]."[103] The sincerity of Sharpe's claim was evident the following year, when he was convicted in the hustings court of assaulting Mary Epperson's slave Nelson, and again in 1857, when he was suspected of stabbing with intent to kill James H. Grant's servant William, although on this occasion a circuit court jury returned a verdict of not guilty.[104]

A further reason for the legal regulation of interracial violence in Richmond was the importance of preserving the public peace in order to create a suitable environment for business and manufacturing and also in accordance with evolving urban bourgeois sentiments. This was illustrated in 1839, when a grand jury charged two white men, John Wise and Richard Ragland, with a brutal assault against a slave. The jury's presentment stated that the assault occurred "near a certain street and common high-way in the said city [Richmond], frequented and used by all the good people of this Commonwealth." Furthermore, "a large concourse and crowd of people were then and there attracted . . . and did . . . witness the said violence and outrage done and committed against the principles and feelings of humanity, the rights of property and the peace and good order of society."[105] While the chastisement of a slave by a nonslaveholding white may have been tolerated in sparsely populated rural areas, it provoked consternation when committed in the heart of Richmond.

In the 1850s, Mayor Mayo made clear his intention to maintain public order even if this meant challenging the right assumed by many poor whites to inflict violent abuse on slaves. When Mayo remanded Henry Harden to appear before a grand jury, for example, he explained that "the streets of Richmond were not proper places for the chastisement of servants . . . [and] it was his duty to preserve the public peace."[106] Unregulated violence on the city streets, even when it was directed against slaves, was at odds with the restrained, rational, and emotionally detached bourgeois sensibilities that infused urban public life. Although slaveholders could inflict more extreme physical tortures on their human chattel in the privacy of the domestic sphere, city residents deemed such practices inappropriate in the public arena and particularly when committed by third parties.[107] Mayo's concern with public order was such that in 1853 he even indicted George Findlay for whipping a six-year-old hired slave boy in his employment. Mayo issued a warrant for Findlay's arrest after the slave was found wandering the streets by a watchman who took him to the cage. When Findlay appeared in court, Mayo stated that although "there was no stronger pro-slavery man in the

Commonwealth than himself . . . he could not recognize the right of a hirer of a slave to treat a boy of this size and age, in the brutal manner in which the lad Claiborne had been treated."[108] A hustings court jury subsequently concurred, finding Findlay guilty of assault and ordering that he pay a fine of ninety-three dollars.[109]

The prosecution of George Findlay was of dubious legality. In *Commonwealth v. Booth* (1824), the Virginia Court of Appeals had ruled that an assault by a slave owner or hirer on his own slave was not in itself unlawful but could become so "by subsequent excess or inhumanity."[110] Although the court did not define what constituted an excessive and inhumane assault on a slave, given the court's judgments in similar cases it is unlikely that any definition would have encompassed an assault that was classed only as a misdemeanor and did not threaten the life or limb of the enslaved victim. Such an interpretation would have been consistent with Judge Dade's 1827 ruling that the law did not "protect the slave against minor injuries from the hand of the master." Mayo himself acknowledged this point six years after the Findlay case during the examination of Mr. R. B. Winston for cruelty to a slave child whom he had hired. After taking some time to consider the legal issues involved, Mayo discharged Winston, citing "similar cases that had been decided by the higher courts of the Commonwealth" to show that the indictment could not be sustained.[111]

The prosecution of poor whites for violent assaults against slaves introduced a class dimension into the meaning of whiteness in antebellum Richmond. While some poor whites claimed that their race entitled them to inflict violent punishment on slaves, the law restricted this right to slaveholders and hirers. If a poor white man was insulted or attacked by a slave, the appropriate legal course of action was to report the matter to the police or to the slave's owner. However, in a society in which it was a matter of honor for individuals to respond personally to verbal and physical insults, this had a divisive impact on the white community. In particular, it tended to emasculate and impugn the honor of nonslaveholding white men who were forced to rely on slaveholders and judicial officers to arbitrate their encounters with slaves.[112] Even though notions of honor were challenged by emerging urban bourgeois norms, in Richmond honor remained central to white masculine identity, and as the intrusion of law into race relations compromised honor, so too it weakened the ideological basis of white supremacy. Indeed, it perhaps did so more in Virginia than elsewhere in the South, for due to the distinct features of the oyer and terminer slave trial system, poor whites could not even pass judgment on slave criminals from the jury box. Here, then, is a further example of Virginia criminal law struggling to promote both slave control *and* white racial solidarity.

Similar conflicts arose in the courts' responses to other types of crime that involved blacks and whites in mutually beneficial partnerships, notably receiving stolen goods and the retail of liquor to slaves. Receiving stolen goods was a crime that invariably involved connections across racial lines. Among white men and women prosecuted for receiving stolen goods as a felony, the identity of the person who sold or provided the goods is known in fifteen cases. Thirteen of these fifteen individuals were African Americans.[113] The relationship between Catherine Houston and Thomas Mosby was typical. Houston was a white woman who kept a "petty Negro groggery on Broad Street," while Mosby was a hired slave who, in December 1852, stole twenty-five pounds of wool from the Virginia Woolen Company, which he sold to Houston in return for drinks and snacks. Appearing before the mayor in January 1853, Mosby was sentenced to thirty-nine lashes for stealing, but when Houston was tried in the hustings court two months later, she was acquitted.[114] Evidence upon which the mayor could convict a slave of stealing was insufficient to convince a jury to return a guilty verdict against the white woman in whose possession the stolen goods were found. Such judgments were common. Overall, just 30 percent of white defendants (27 out of 90) indicted for receiving stolen goods as a misdemeanor were convicted in Richmond's hustings court between 1830 and 1860, and in felony cases the conviction rate was only 18 percent (4 out of 22).[115] By contrast, more than 60 percent of slaves and free blacks (10 out of 16) charged with feloniously receiving stolen goods were found guilty. Although it is unsurprising that African Americans examined in courts of oyer and terminer were found guilty more often than whites tried by a jury for the same crime, rarely was the discrepancy in conviction rates so great.

The inability of the courts to police the trade in stolen goods facilitated slave resistance because the cash profits generated from criminal relationships between slaves and whites could be put to highly subversive ends, including aiding slaves to escape to the free states. Washington Winston, a slave belonging to Mann Valentine Sr., regularly stole from his master's shop and passed at least sixty dollars' worth of property to Nancy Redcross, a free black woman "with whom he was on intimate terms." Along with the stolen property, "letters of a questionable character . . . and books and papers belonging to a secret society" were found at Nancy's house, indicating the close connection between crime and the Underground Railroad.[116] On another occasion, Lewis B. Taylor reported to the police that he was missing more than $600 that he suspected had been stolen by his slave Cyrus, who had run away. It is not known if Cyrus lived with Taylor, but throughout 1840 he worked at Gray's Tobacco Factory and had a pass that permitted him some freedom of movement about the city giving him the opportunity to form connections with whites.[117] Taylor reported the money missing on October 18 and offered a reward of $100 for the return of his slave and the banknotes. The following day, police officers discovered Cyrus and three other slaves on board a vessel at Rocketts wharf, allegedly waiting to sail to the North.[118]

The law against black testimony contributed to the courts' failure to regulate other illegal activities that encouraged and thrived upon interracial associations, including the retailing of ardent spirits without a license. The easy availability of alcohol undermined slave discipline and productivity, and the *Dispatch* believed that if the law against illegal liquor sales could be "rigidly enforced," the value of slave property in Virginia would double.[119] By no means all defendants charged with illegally retailing liquor had made sales to slaves, but illegal grogshops that catered to an interracial clientele were the most likely to attract the attention of judicial authorities. However, prosecutions for selling liquor to slaves could only result when a white person had witnessed the offense and was willing to give evidence in court, and it is possibly for this reason that between 1830 and 1860 there were only eight cases in which it was specifically charged that liquor had been sold to slaves. During the same period, however, the hustings court heard 753 cases of retailing ardent spirits without a license and associated offenses, and it is probable that many of these cases were brought in lieu of charges for selling liquor to slaves, because there was more chance of securing a conviction.

Many of the firms and individuals charged with retailing liquor without a license faced multiple charges. However, although almost 60 percent of defendants were judged guilty on at least one of the counts they faced, plea-bargaining ensured that few were required to pay large fines. Many acted like Williamson Wynne, who pleaded guilty on two counts in return for the prosecution dropping all other charges against him.[120] Almost every conviction of retailing liquor without a license resulted in the accused being sentenced to a thirty-dollar fine, and in the thirty-year period from 1830 to 1860, only three defendants received the more severe punishment of imprisonment. In addition to paying the standard fine, Philip Osiander and Thomas Chinn were both sentenced to six months in jail in 1838, and sixteen years later Barney Litman was jailed for thirty days. Why these individuals received such unusually severe punishments is unclear, but it was possibly because their premises were particularly notorious sites of interracial gatherings. Osiander's grocery was certainly well known to the police. Philip's wife, Rose, had previously been convicted in the mayor's court of permitting an unlawful assembly of African Americans, while Maria Brack, a free black woman who was arrested on separate occasions for drunkenness and streetwalking, claimed to have purchased liquor from the Osianders' shop.[121] Although the cases brought against Philip and Rose Osiander indicate that the police and grand jury took steps to enforce the laws against the sale of liquor to slaves, hustings court magistrates were more often reluctant to impose stiff penalties on white shopkeepers, and even Philip Osiander and Thomas Chinn had their imprisonment remitted on appeal to the governor after they had spent less than two weeks in the city jail.

The clemency petitions submitted on behalf of Osiander and Chinn were endorsed by some of the most prominent men in Richmond, including the attorney for the Commonwealth, police officers, and city aldermen, and they show the conflicting interests that determined responses to the illegal sale of ardent spirits. Osiander and Chinn were depicted in their petitions as hardworking and honest individuals who had not violated the law out of malicious intent but because selling ardent spirits was the only way in which they could generate sufficient profits from their businesses to support themselves and their families. Both men claimed to have abandoned the sale of liquor in the time between their arrest and trial and taken up construction jobs on the James River and Kanawha Canal. Although Osiander's contract to work on the canal had been terminated after his conviction, his petition made plain that he was determined to provide for his family in future by honest means, and also claimed that his wife had already disposed of his entire stock of groceries in preparation to leave the city upon his release from jail. The petition submitted on behalf of Chinn, meanwhile, distinguished him from the "<u>felons</u> and <u>negroes</u>" with whom he was confined in the city jail and who made his "confinement there the most burdensome, wretched and harsh that could be imagined."[122]

The policy of fining poor white men and women who sold liquor without a license represented an attempt to limit the scale of the problem, while recognizing the difficulties and dangers of placing tighter restrictions on poor whites' economic activities. Although the illegal sale of alcohol was a serious threat to slave discipline in Richmond, the law could only have been strictly enforced if there had been a far more extensive and expensive police force in the city. Moreover, had poor white men such as Osiander and Chinn routinely been imprisoned for selling liquor when the act was important to their economic survival, it may have threatened the slaveholders' tenuous racial hegemony by pushing substantial numbers of poor whites closer to a recognition of their mutual interests with slaves and free blacks.

Southern slaveholders recognized that the exclusion of black testimony from white trials compromised the efficiency of the criminal law, but they were willing to tolerate this so long as interracial criminal relationships did not fundamentally threaten their rule. Slave productivity and discipline were undoubtedly undermined by whites who illegally sold liquor, and many slaves were encouraged to pilfer small amounts of their masters' property because they were able to sell it to white men and women. The profits from the trade in stolen goods could assist attempts to escape to the North, but more often slaves put their monetary gains to more mundane uses. As such, the more important role of the law was to protect the legal rights of white defendants in order to bolster white supremacy and reassert the significance of the racial divide in Richmond in the face of the growing frequency and complexity of interracial relations. By upholding all due process protections for poor white defendants and therefore distinguishing the legal treatment of blacks and whites, the courts defused some of the class tensions within white society. The hegemonic function of the law in relation to white Richmonders was based on the fact that although blacks and whites could commit crimes together, associations that formed across the color line counted for little in the courtroom, where they were prosecuted according to distinct judicial processes that reminded the white community of the overriding significance of race.

The law against black testimony had more serious implications for the slaveholders' rule when it resulted in the courts failing to convict and punish whites who aided slaves to escape. Between 1830 and 1860, prosecutions were initiated against fifteen white men for assisting slave runaways, and although only one of six men charged with a misdemeanor was found guilty, all five of the eight men tried for a felony whose fate is known were convicted.[123] However, given Richmond's proximity to the North and the extensive transportation networks that connected the city to the free states by sea and rail, the conviction rate in these cases is less noteworthy than the small number of indictments.[124]

A petition requesting executive clemency for a free black man named William Campbell shows how the law against black testimony contributed to the low number of whites prosecuted for aiding slaves to escape. Campbell was sentenced to a total of $200 in fines and thirty-nine months in the city jail after being convicted on four separate charges of aiding slaves to escape from Richmond. The events that Campbell described in his clemency petition were unusual only in that they were recorded in such detail. Campbell was a native of North Carolina and was employed as a cook on a schooner named the *Chariot*, a vessel that was owned by Edmund M. Smith, a northern man resident in Richmond who traded between Virginia and New York. Soon after Campbell had begun working for Smith, the *Chariot* went to Chickahominy, and, while the ship was in dock, Campbell "was much surprised to find a hack filled with persons of color, (supposed by your petitioner to be slaves) who had been conveyed across the country from Richmond to be received (as appeared by previous understanding) on board, by said vessel." The *Chariot* then sailed to New York, where the ship's captain, Elijah Townsend, received payment from abolitionists for each of the slaves he delivered. In his clemency petition, Campbell claimed that he was immediately aware "that the business in which he had adventured was equally at war with his disposition and his interest," but he was prevented from leaving the ship by the captain and the ship's mate, Alpheus Gifford, who "told him he was bound to remain until his contract had expired."[125]

In February 1834, the *Chariot* spent several days in Richmond moored at Rocketts, where it took on a load of coal. One night during this stay, Gifford boarded the ship accompanied by four slaves bound for the North and a free African American man, who was unknown to Campbell. When Gifford left the ship temporarily, Campbell remained as the only crew member on board. When two night watchmen came along soon afterwards and discovered the fugitive slaves, it was therefore Campbell whom they took into custody.[126]

Campbell was put on trial in the hustings court and pleaded not guilty to the charges against him. He was convicted but continued to protest his innocence. Campbell claimed that as a lowly cook on such a small vessel as the *Chariot*, he could not have aided the slave runaways without the knowledge and assistance of other crew members. Furthermore, Campbell maintained that he valued his own liberty too highly to be "willing to jeopardy it without fee or reward, in the enterprise of emancipating others, whom he had never seen, and in whom he could not be supposed to feel any personal or particular interest." The real culprits, according to Campbell, were the ship's captain and mate, Townsend and Gifford, but although they had been arrested soon after the fugitive slaves were discovered, neither was convicted. Indeed, no charges at all were brought against Gifford, as Campbell could not testify against him on account of his race, and there was no other evidence to prove his involvement in the crime. Townsend was indicted on nine counts of allowing a slave to board his vessel without the permission of his master, but the prosecution abandoned each of these cases before they came to trial. Again, this was most likely due to a lack of evidence. Outside of the courtroom, however, Campbell's accusations carried more weight. A number of white men who had been present at the trial were convinced that Gifford was the guilty party, and on the basis of their arguments Governor Tazewell issued a pardon to Campbell that implicitly acknowledged the failure of the judicial system to convict and punish the real perpetrators of a crime that, more than almost any other, threatened the interests of the slaveholding class.[127]

Urban-industrial development altered the relationship between the criminal law and white society in the South in a number of ways. First, it led to an increase in the rate of serious crime against person and property. Due in part to this change, but also as a result of the breakdown of social bonds of kinship, community, church, and nativity, the courts assumed a more important role in regulating all forms of criminal activity in cities than they did in rural areas. This problem was compounded by the high rate of property crime indictments in Richmond relative to other offenses and in comparison to the rest of the South. In most of these cases, the stolen goods were not of great value, yet collectively property crime was more threatening to the social order of a slave society than violence, which was in many respects an integral and accepted part of southern culture. While verdicts and sentences in violent crime trials were often overtly influenced by extralegal factors such as honor, patriarchy, race, and ideals of white womanhood, trials of defendants charged with property crimes and morals offenses could not be regulated in a similar fashion and consequently were conducted according to a stricter interpretation of rules of legal due process.

In the course of the antebellum period, southern elites regularly subverted common-law ideals in the interests of the slave regime. This was notable at the local level in the trial of slave defendants and measures such as the prohibition on black seamen leaving their ships when docked in southern ports. It was even evident at the national level, for example, when the gag rule silenced abolitionist voices in Congress between 1836 and 1844, and when the Fugitive Slave Act was passed in 1850.[128] These disparate laws and policies aimed to restrict the threat that abolitionists, free African Americans, and slaves themselves posed to the slaveholders' rule. Although they provoked consternation in the North and fueled abolitionist sentiments, the immediate impact of these laws within the South was to stabilize social relations. However, their stabilizing influence was only temporary, and this was not least because it was not only African Americans but also white southerners who acted in ways that compromised slavery. Similar dynamics were also at work at the local level. White Richmonders assaulted slaves, sold them liquor, and purchased goods stolen from slaveholders. These actions violated criminal statutes, yet in Richmond, as throughout the South, attempts to prosecute whites involved in criminal affairs with slaves foundered on the law prohibiting black testimony against whites and the need to maintain white solidarity through a combination of strict adherence to the rule of law and the selective prosecution and punishment of poor white defendants.

It would have been to the slaveholders' great benefit if the courts had admitted black testimony in certain circumstances, and some prominent southerners suggested taking this radical step. In the 1850s, the mayor of Lynchburg, Virginia, proposed that blacks should be permitted to testify against white grogshop owners, and even Thomas Cobb wondered if "it might be well to permit the Negro to testify as to the cruel treatment of himself or his fellows by persons other than his master, when no competent white witness is present to testify as to the transaction." In 1855, a Virginia House delegate proposed permitting "the testimony of negroes against white persons charged with abducting or attempting to abduct slaves from the Commonwealth, when said persons so charged shall be citizens of such states as admit negro testimony in cases in which white persons may be parties."[129] However, most southerners recognized that even the guarded revision of the prohibition on black testimony could not be countenanced, for it would have introduced a glaring division into the legal treatment of whites that would have been felt nowhere more strongly than in Richmond with its large northern- and foreign-born population. Unlike laws that restricted the legal rights of free blacks and slaves, if due legal process had been contravened in cases involving white defendants, it would have compromised southern racial ideology and notions of white supremacy. In an urban society in which class challenged race as the defining feature of the social order, this was unacceptable to the dominant white elite, who recognized that it was incumbent on the law to uphold the primacy of the increasingly fragile racial divide. Southern courts therefore continually struggled to reconcile the dictates of legal due process and the enforcement of the criminal law for the purposes of controlling white crime, with the judicial system's important function as a bulwark of white supremacy and solidarity.

5

The "stigma, of the deepest degradation, was fixed upon the whole race"

Free African Americans and the Criminal Justice System

In his annual address of 1847, Virginia governor William Smith depicted free African Americans as the most criminally inclined class in Virginia, as "moral leper[s]" who occupied an ambiguous space between white citizens and black slaves and corrupted "portions of both races." Examining the penitentiary records, Smith found that free blacks "contribute largely over two fifths of the convicts," a figure out of all proportion to their share of the population. As an advocate of colonization, Smith believed that slavery was the only suitable condition under which African Americans could live in the South and encouraged the removal of free blacks to Liberia. Smith further claimed that the character and lifestyle of African Americans who were not held in bondage was reflected in their criminal tendencies—and vice versa:

> this race is idle, thriftless and unproductive . . . as a general rule they labor only from necessity, content to put up with the most meager supply of their indispensable wants; and not content with their own labor in pursuits of honest industry, they prowl in the dead hour of night and filch the labor of others.[1]

Governor Smith's views resonated strongly with white Richmonders. By 1860, the number of free blacks in the city had declined to 2,576, less than 7 percent of the total population. Thirty years earlier, free African Americans had constituted 12 percent of all Richmonders, yet more than ever on the eve of the Civil War they provoked disproportionate consternation among slaveholders, who feared that the extensive associations between slaves and free blacks in the city threatened slave discipline. Isham Keith warned that in cities free black women led young female slaves to commit crimes "of the deepest die," and that all slaves were made dissatisfied with their condition by the example of free blacks who, as Keith saw it, not being compelled to labor, lived in idleness.[2] Similarly, the *Richmond Dispatch* warned that

Fig. 11. William Smith, governor of Virginia, 1846–49. From *Memoirs of Governor William Smith, of Virginia. His political, military, and personal history*, by John W. Bell (New York, Moss engraving company, 1891). Courtesy of Library of Congress online, American Memory project. <http://hdl.loc.gov/loc.gdc/lhbcb.15643>

"for the good of the negro as well as for the protection of the white man," it would be a "grievous blunder" to grant any privileges to the free colored population that were not enjoyed by slaves.[3] The Richmond Common Council concurred with these sentiments in justifying municipal restrictions on free black conduct: "Occupying an intermediate social relation between the master and slave, they must expect, while they are relieved from many of the restraints of the latter, to be kept subservient to the well being of the former."[4]

In the antebellum period, free African Americans' subservience was maintained by informal community structures, racism that permeated every aspect of southern society, and also the law. Free black criminal laws in Virginia had always been an amalgamation of the forms of trial and punishment for slaves and whites, yet throughout the nineteenth century, and especially after 1830, revisions of the law sought to align free blacks' experience of criminal justice more closely with that of slaves. In an analysis of Virginia's colonial and antebellum statutes and case law, A. Leon Higginbotham Jr. and Greet C. Bosworth have argued that free African Americans were reduced to a legal "no-man's land between slavery and freedom." Moreover, they suggest that repressive legislation supported slaveholder hegemony over free blacks and the submissiveness of the slave population "by preventing blacks from acquiring a 'clear conception of rights' that might empower them to dismantle the slave system."[5]

The formal discrimination that free African Americans encountered in their dealings with the criminal law was greater in Virginia than other southern states, a fact that can be attributed to the large number of free blacks and the instability of slavery in the Upper South.[6] The proximity of the northern free states made Virginia especially susceptible to abolitionist influences and compounded the problem of slave runaways. Furthermore, the hundreds of thousands of slaves who were sold out of Virginia to labor on the plantations of the Deep South and, by the 1850s, further west to Texas and Arkansas attested to the long-term decline in the relative profitability of slavery in the Border South. In this context, the strict legal regulation of the free black population seemed imperative if slave discipline and the racial divide were to be maintained. The rejection of proposals for the abolition of slavery in Virginia in 1831 and the advent of positive good proslavery arguments tended to confirm this impression. As the historian Ira Berlin has argued, "If slavery was the Negro's natural state and freedom somehow was unnatural, then the free Negro was a veritable contradiction in terms, whose very existence challenged every premise in the positive-good argument."[7]

Despite the increasingly restrictive free black laws enacted in antebellum Virginia, some distinctions always remained between the legal rights of the enslaved and free African Americans. Although proslavery advocates and supporters of African colonization schemes depicted free blacks as a burden on the South, profoundly unsuited to freedom, and a threat to the slave regime, individual free African Americans often had white acquaintances who balked at the idea of forced enslavement or colonization, at least so far as these policies might apply to free black men and women whom they knew personally.[8] As late as 1852, the *Dispatch* expressed a favorable opinion of Richmond's free black population and criticized the legal burdens placed upon them: "we have always thought them, in the aggregate, a harmless, peaceable race of people, and we have frequently . . . expressed our dissent from the severe measures taken against them by our Legislature." In part, such sentiments were motivated by economic considerations. With the relative decline of the slave population in the Upper South, demand for free labor in Virginia increased, and many slaveholders believed that free blacks posed less of a threat to their interests than white laborers whose opposition to slavery was all the more dangerous because they had the right to vote.[9] At the same time, whites also feared that the strict enforcement of the laws limiting free blacks' freedom of movement and employment opportunities might compel some to commit crimes or lead them to align their interests more closely with those of slaves.[10] Memories of the slave rebellion planned in 1822 by Denmark Vesey, a free black man in Charleston, South Carolina, reminded whites throughout the South of the threat such alliances could pose.[11]

Free African Americans' experience of the criminal justice system in Richmond was characterized by discrimination, the denial of legal rights, and the capricious infliction of violent punishments. However, as elsewhere in the South, free blacks in Richmond were nevertheless able at times to exploit aspects of their hybrid legal status between slavery and freedom in order to develop a supportive community and social life and challenge the white ideal of black passivity and powerlessness before the law.[12] As defendants, free blacks in the city often turned to white benefactors for protection from the vagaries of the law, but they also employed defense counsel to argue their case, appealed verdicts to higher tribunals, and submitted clemency petitions to the governor. Free black victims, meanwhile, demonstrated a developed legal consciousness and a clear understanding of the rights they were denied in court, selectively seeking the protection of the law and at other times choosing either not to report crimes at all to white legal institutions or turning instead to the African Baptist church courts in search of an alternative standard of justice.

Restrictions on free African Americans' legal rights in Virginia dated to the colonial era, when they were prohibited from holding public office and denied the right to vote. In the late eighteenth century, Revolutionary fervor and Enlightenment ideology temporarily ameliorated the condition of free blacks, but in the 1790s there commenced a continual deterioration in their legal status that persisted until Emancipation. From 1793, free African Americans in Virginia were required to carry at all times a register obtained from the clerk of the city or county in which they resided, and free blacks entering the state could be removed by force. Furthermore, the increase in the free black population that was fueled by the post-Revolutionary surge in manumissions was curtailed in 1806, when a law was passed requiring all newly emancipated slaves to leave Virginia within twelve months or face reenslavement.[13]

Nat Turner's Rebellion in 1831 precipitated an intensification of legal restrictions on the rights and freedoms of free blacks in Virginia, including significant alterations in forms of trial and punishment. New legislation prohibited free African Americans from learning to read and write, owning weapons, participating in public performances and exhibitions, selling goods, and working as barbers. Free black boatmen had to obtain certificates from respectable whites in order to ply their trade, and those who sold agricultural products required a white person to testify that the goods were not stolen. In the courtroom, meanwhile, free blacks charged with noncapital felonies were stripped of the right to trial by jury and made subject to examination in the same summary courts of oyer and terminer as slaves. Similarly, those judged guilty of misdemeanors in the mayor's court could be sentenced to a public whipping instead of the former punishment of a fine or imprisonment.[14] This development assumed particular significance after 1848, when the lash ceased to be imposed as a form of punishment for whites but was retained for free blacks as well as for slaves.

Throughout most of the antebellum period, free blacks convicted of felonies were, like white convicts, sentenced to penitentiary imprisonment, but this apparent racial equality in criminal punishments was always contentious. Whites were uneasy about the effects of racial mixing in the penitentiary, and the notion that inmates would be reformed by their incarceration was at odds with proslavery arguments that African Americans were inherently inclined toward criminal behavior, and that only slavery could regulate their negative and dangerous impact on southern society.[15] For four years in the 1820s, sale into absolute slavery replaced penitentiary imprisonment as the punishment for free black felony convicts, but at a time of widespread support for the American Colonization Society and gradual emancipation, this form of punishment was eventually deemed "incompatible with every principle of morality and justice, and directly repugnant to the just, humane, and liberal policy of Virginia."[16] Amidst the sectional and racial tensions of the late 1850s, however, provision was made in 1858 for free black penitentiary convicts to be leased out to labor on public works, including canals, roads, and bridges. Two years later, the connection between race, slavery, and penality in Virginia criminal law was made explicit once again by the reintroduction of sale into absolute slavery for free black felony convicts.[17] In June 1860, the *Dispatch* reported that Floyd Cousins, convicted of burglary, was the first free African American in Richmond to be enslaved under the

Table 5.1: Free black defendants in Richmond Oyer and Terminer Courts, 1833–1860

	Defendants	Convicted	Convicted of a lesser crime	Pleaded guilty	Total sentenced (%)
VIOLENT OFFENSES					
Assault	6	3	0	0	50.0
Rape	1	0	0	0	0.0
Robbery	1	0	0	0	0.0
Stabbing with intent to kill	25	17	0	0	68.0
Total	33	20	0	0	60.6
PROPERTY OFFENSES					
Arson	3	0	0	0	0.0
Burglary	19	14	2	0	84.2
Forgery, fraud, counterfeiting	5	2	0	0	40.0
Receiving stolen goods	6	4	0	0	66.7
Stealing	63	38	3	4	71.4
Total	96	58	5	4	69.8
OTHER OFFENSES					
Aiding a slave to abscond	13	7	0	0	53.8
Forging a free register	1	0	0	0	0.0
Total	14	7	0	0	50.0
Grand total	143	85	5	4	65.7

Source: Richmond Hustings Court Minutes, 1830–60.

new law. Cousins was sold to a "southern gentleman" for $700 and taken to a cotton field. Before the end of the year, two other free black Richmonders had suffered a similar fate.[18]

To a greater degree than in other southern states, Virginia statute law made race rather than status the determining factor in the trial of free African Americans charged with felonies.[19] Indeed, as defendants in oyer and terminer examinations, free blacks were not only subject to all of the same legal disabilities as slaves, but were also denied the automatic right to legal counsel. Likewise at the local level in Richmond the verdicts of the oyer and terminer court magistrates indicate that the examination process was little influenced by whether the accused was free or enslaved. Between 1833 and 1860 in Richmond, 143 free blacks were tried in courts of oyer and terminer, and 65 percent were found guilty, a higher conviction rate than for slaves. This was in contrast to states such as Tennessee, Georgia, and Louisiana, where free blacks accused of felonies faced trial by jury and were convicted far less frequently than slaves.[20]

When the status of free black defendants did distinguish their treatment in Richmond's courtrooms from that of slaves, it was almost always to their disadvantage. The most important distinction between the examination of slaves and free blacks was the overt impact of the slave's property status on the outcome of slave trials. White property interests often served to protect slaves from the full force of the criminal law in a manner that had no parallel in the examination of free blacks. In cases of burglary, for example, free blacks were convicted far more frequently than slaves, in part because of the financial costs to slaveholders and the state that resulted when enslaved burglars were sentenced to death or sale and transportation.[21]

Similar considerations about the value of slave property influenced the sentencing of free blacks convicted of violent felonies. When free African Americans were convicted of stabbing with intent to kill, the oyer and terminer magistrates reserved the shortest prison terms for those cases in which the victim was also free and black. By contrast, when the victim was enslaved, longer sentences of between two and five years were common. However, although this distinction in sentencing according to the status of the victim was significant, it was always of secondary importance to the victim's race, and free blacks, like slaves, received the most severe sentences when convicted of violent offenses against whites.[22]

The high conviction rates for free African Americans tried in courts of oyer and terminer in Richmond suggest that the legislature's attempts to control free black crime through oppressive trial processes was supported by white magistrates at the local level. However, whites did not universally approve of laws that treated free African Americans as if they were slaves. A small number of attorneys criticized the practice of denying jury trials to free black defendants in felony cases, while, by retaining trial by jury for free blacks charged with capital crimes, Virginia's lawmakers implicitly acknowledged that they did not trust the verdicts of oyer and terminer courts sufficiently to justify the execution of a free person. Thus, the inherent tension between the race and status of free blacks forced Virginia's white elite to endorse a system that was internally inconsistent and underscored the low standards of justice that prevailed in oyer and terminer courts.

Although Virginia enacted distinctive laws to regulate its slave society, the state's legal culture was rooted in the common-law tradition. Similarly, Virginia attorneys were trained in Anglo-American jurisprudence, and consequently some had reservations about free black trial processes. Although free African American defendants were not guaranteed a state-appointed defense counsel, many employed an attorney to argue their case and the courts fully upheld their right to do so. In 1849, for example, magistrates agreed to continue John Binford's oyer and terminer trial for nearly three weeks due to the absence of his counsel.[23] However, the influence that defense lawyers could exert over free black oyer and terminer trials was limited. As in slave cases, attorneys representing free black defendants entered motions challenging elements of the court proceedings that disadvantaged their clients, but these were invariably overruled.[24]

With no route of appeal from the decisions of oyer and terminer magistrates, attorneys' most overt criticisms of the free African American trial system were made in clemency petitions. One vehement critic was John H. Gilmer, who in 1842 represented Richardson D. Smith, a free African American charged with aiding slaves to escape from Richmond to the North. Smith was convicted on two separate charges and sentenced to a total of thirteen years in the penitentiary, of which he had served six before Gilmer first petitioned for his release. Gilmer based his appeal on a highly critical assessment both of the trial process and the severity of Smith's punishment, which he depicted as being in stark contrast to that of Peter Dunivant, a white man who had acted in concert with Smith and faced identical charges, but served just two years in prison. Gilmer's petition was an indictment of the racial divide in Virginia criminal law: "The judgements and informations disclose the fact that both were tried for two offences of precisely the same character and degree. It is not a [illegible] inference, to presume that the free Negro was the victim of prejudice and hasty consideration, while the white man was tried in coolness, found guilty on one indictment and the other dismissed."[25]

The oyer and terminer courts may have served important crime-control functions in Virginia's racially divided slave society, but for Gilmer only trial by jury, "the fairest and surest manner of testing criminal intent of guilt," could serve as a satisfactory arbiter of justice.[26] Perhaps because of the wider implications that Gilmer's arguments held for the administration of black justice in Virginia, Governor William Smith rejected the petition, and the following year his successor, John Buchanan Floyd, was unmoved by a personal appeal for clemency from Richardson Smith that was endorsed by Charles Morgan, the superintendent of the penitentiary. This appeal was based on similar arguments as Gilmer had previously put forward, with Richardson Smith claiming that "the judgment of law as against Dunivant should form a criterion of the justice of the punishment awarded your petitioner."[27]

Richardson Smith was eventually pardoned in 1851 after he had served more than two-thirds of his sentence. The records do not state on what grounds the pardon was granted, but it seems that no new arguments were made in favor of clemency at this time, as the executive papers contain only copies of the earlier clemency appeals submitted by Gilmer and Morgan in 1848 and 1849. Though it is improbable that Governor Floyd concurred with the broader implications for free black trial and punishment that were implicit in Gilmer and Morgan's clemency appeals (and Morgan and Gilmer themselves may not have supported radical reform), his decision to grant a pardon in this case was surely influenced by their arguments since, unlike in slave cases, clemency was rarely extended to free black penitentiary convicts. In the previous twenty years, Virginia governors had released only two other free black Richmonders before the expiration of their penitentiary terms, and on both occasions they did so only on the basis of recommendations by the original trial court.[28]

It is unclear how far attorneys benefited either financially or in terms of their legal reputation when they petitioned for clemency on behalf of free black convicts, but any rewards were surely limited. Nonetheless, many lawyers went to considerable lengths to assist free black prisoners. When Lilburn Pleasants was sentenced to death for burglary in 1833, his elderly mother, Lydia Carter, approached Robert Scott and asked him to petition the governor for a reprieve on the grounds that Pleasants was not a slave for life and was soon to be freed. Although Scott had not represented Pleasants in court, he investigated Lydia Carter's claims. After studying the suit of *Pleasants v. Pleasants*, decided by the court of appeals in May 1799, Scott confirmed that Pleasants was certainly not a slave for life and had quite possibly been born free. On the basis of Scott's investigations, Pleasants's sentence was commuted to penitentiary imprisonment, and in October 1840 he was released following another petition from W. Byrd Chamberlaigne. This second petition noted that despite Scott's earlier efforts, Pleasants had already been held for longer than the maximum sentence that a free African American could receive for burglary, and that if the governor did not intervene, Pleasants would remain in prison for life. Scott's actions were indicative of the bonds of mutual interest that could develop between whites and free blacks and that mitigated the threat of free blacks aligning their interests wholly with the enslaved. Nevertheless, attorneys' efforts in such cases were at odds with the legislature's persistent efforts to restrict free African Americans' legal rights.

Even if motivated only by monetary reward rather than concern for due process and the rights of the accused, attorneys in Richmond were willing to represent free African American defendants even in seemingly trivial mayor's court cases. In so doing, they encountered criticism from white commentators who protested that their actions undermined the repressive crime-control functions of the law. When Eliza Hart, a free woman of color, was charged with assaulting Sophia Maxfield, also a free African American, she was defended by three lawyers. The *Dispatch* reported the scene in court with dismay: "The indefatigable efforts of three lawyers caused the loss of three quarters of an hour of valuable time in the adjudication of this miserable case. The idea of cross-examinations and arguments by counsel in such cases as these, is perfectly ridiculous—and as annoying, time-wasting and provoking as it is rdiiculous [sic]."29

Despite the efforts of her lawyers, Eliza Hart was convicted of assault and sentenced to fifteen lashes and to pay fifty dollars security to keep the peace. By condemning Eliza to the sting of the lash, the court symbolically reasserted her inferior status and reaffirmed the racial order. If the manner in which Eliza had contested the charge against her in court had been inappropriate for an African American defendant, the lashes to which she was sentenced reminded the community of her proper social standing.30 Nonetheless, on hearing the mayor's verdict, Eliza and her counsel did not abandon their case but appealed to the hustings court, which reversed the mayor's ruling and reduced Eliza punishment to five lashes, although the surety she had paid was retained to cover the costs of the appeal.31

Eliza Hart was not the only black defendant to challenge her conviction in the mayor's court. In 1852 alone, five free African Americans attempted to have their sentences rescinded in the hustings court. It is not immediately clear why these particular cases were appealed. None involved exceptional crimes or unusually harsh punishments; in only one case had the defendant been sentenced to thirty-nine lashes, the maximum punishment the court could impose. Although lawyers, who were better versed in the particulars of the appeals process than their clients, may have taken the lead in initiating appeals for financial gain, it is unlikely that they could have acted without any input on the part of free black defendants. The decision of these defendants to appeal their convictions therefore suggests that they believed there was at least a possibility that the court's rulings could be overturned.

The *Dispatch* offered a very different assessment of the appeals process. It did not share black Richmonders' faith that the hustings court would reverse the mayor's decisions in cases involving African American defendants and complained: "These appeals are absolutely of no consequence whatever, and hitherto have proved utterly futile in effecting the reversal of a decision. It is but a postponement of punishment, therefore, to record them. The judgment of the Mayor of the city in these appeal cases has, of course, a legitimate and legal influence upon the subsequent decision of the examining Hustings Court."32 The *Dispatch*'s view reflected the reality that few appeals by free black convicts led to the mayor's verdict being overturned, and a more common outcome was for the original punishment to be increased.33 Nevertheless, two years after the Eliza Hart case, the Virginia Court of Appeals confirmed that "a Negro convicted of a misdemeanor by a justice is entitled to appeal," and if the justice refused to grant an appeal, the higher court was empowered to issue a writ to enforce compliance.[34]

When Virginia's antebellum legislators extended the jurisdiction of oyer and terminer courts to free black felony cases in 1833, they prevented attorneys who represented free black defendants from making arguments based on common-law precedent. However, in pardon petitions and in mayor's court cases where there was greater latitude than in oyer and terminer courts to challenge magistrates' rulings, members of the bar and their free black clients demonstrated a willingness to contest the legislature's drive to deny free black defendants legal protections and subject them to the summary rulings of court magistrates.

In their efforts to challenge the strict enforcement of Virginia's repressive criminal laws, free African Americans in Richmond relied for support not only on attorneys but also on white patrons, neighbors, and acquaintances. White support was most commonly extended to free black men and women who were subject to legal proceedings requiring them to leave Virginia. An illustrative case in Richmond involved John Smith, a free black barber who had traveled to Philadelphia to attend the bedside of his dying aunt only to discover when he arrived that she was already dead and buried. When Smith returned to Richmond, he was in violation of the law prohibiting free blacks from reentering the state. Almost one year later, another free black barber, R. L. West, brought the matter to the attention of legal authorities and Smith was ordered to leave Virginia within ten days or face being sold into slavery. The final outcome of the case is unknown, but Smith's cause attracted the support of sympathetic whites, who commented that he had a reputation "for honesty, industry, integrity, and sobriety that few of his class have ever enjoyed."[35]

The support that white Richmonders showed for John Smith was symptomatic of a wider apathy toward the strict enforcement of Virginia's free black residency laws that persisted even in the particularly hostile racial climate of the 1850s. Between 1830 and 1860, 124 free African Americans in Richmond were charged with being illegal residents, but only 12 were convicted, 9 of whom were sentenced to be sold into slavery and 2 hired out for jail fees.[36] The one other convict, John Brooks, was discharged from custody, which may indicate that, like hundreds of other free African Americans illegally resident in Richmond, he applied to the hustings court for special dispensation to remain in the state.[37]

Most of the free African Americans who obtained permission to remain in Richmond were established members of the community who could depend on white acquaintances to support their case.[38] More concerning to white Richmonders were cases in which free African Americans from other states were found in the city. The hustings court rarely granted permission for non-Virginian free African Americans to remain in Richmond, yet several were found to be temporarily resident in the city at the specific request of white employers.[39] When Samuel Stevenson was arrested as an illegal resident in 1838, he claimed that he was a servant from Baltimore traveling through Virginia with his white master, a Mr. Thompson. It was not illegal for free African Americans born outside Virginia to travel in the state in the company of a white person. However, according to Stevenson's account, fiscal considerations had led him to be separated from his employer; while Thompson was returning to Baltimore via Norfolk, he had decided that Stevenson should travel on the cheaper and slower route through Richmond and Fredericksburg.[40]

In another case in the mid-1830s, Robert Jones, a former Virginia slave who had moved to Philadelphia after he was emancipated, was employed by W. Wallace Cook, also a Philadelphia resident, to look after a horse back in Virginia. Cook recognized the threat to free blacks' civil liberties in Virginia and provided Jones with the names of three white men in Richmond to whom he could turn for "protection and advice," should he require it. Cook also undertook personally "to oppose any power unlawfully applied against him [Jones] even if I should travel from Maine to Georgia." However, Cook was either unaware of, or chose to disregard, the law prohibiting free African Americans from reentering Virginia, an offense for which Robert Jones was arrested and convicted while in Richmond. Cook supported clemency for Jones, although in the petition he submitted to the Virginia executive he attributed all responsibility for the offense to Jones himself. Cook commented that, although Jones may have broken "the <u>letter</u> of the law," he would only have done so unwittingly and in the belief that his actions were "perfectly innocent and proper." Despite Cook's failure to acknowledge his own role in the affair, his relationship with Jones illustrates the potential conflict between white economic interests and Virginia's restrictive free black residency laws.[41]

It was not only when free African Americans were accused of violating the residency laws that they had support from white acquaintances in their engagements with the law.[42] In Richmond, some whites offered support to free blacks convicted of serious criminal offenses against person and property. The actions of the white men who in 1838 petitioned for the early release of Coleman Day, a free black man sentenced to nine years in the penitentiary for the voluntary manslaughter of a slave, provide a remarkable example of a white community taking a long-term interest in the fate of a convicted free black felon. The petitioners all lived in the neighborhood where the crime had been committed, and many were personally acquainted with Coleman Day and had attended his trial. The interest that these men continued to show in Coleman Day's case eight years later is testimony to the strong ties that he had cultivated with his white neighbors.

At the time that the killing took place in 1830, at least four of the nine petitioners were slaveholders, and this suggests that their relationship with Day was likely to have been one of paternalism and deference, in contrast to the more egalitarian relations that could develop between free African Americans and nonslaveholding whites.[43] However, paternalism alone does not adequately characterize the relationship between Coleman Day and the men who petitioned on his behalf, as Day was distinct from the majority of free blacks convicted of violent crimes against slaves in Richmond in that he employed the slave who subsequently became his victim. As a slave hirer, Day was distinguished as a respectable member of the free black community and a man of at least moderate means.

Richmond did not have as distinct a free black elite as Lower South cities such as Charleston and New Orleans, where the color divide between blacks and mulattoes marked an important division in status. However, industrial employment opportunities meant that by 1860 more than two hundred free blacks had purchased town lots.[44] From the perspective of the white community, these lots were potential sites of illegal gatherings of slaves that could facilitate slave resistance and illegal activities such as trade in alcohol and stolen goods. For this reason, as well as because economic success potentially discouraged free blacks from opposing racial slavery in the South, it was in the interests of white neighbors and storekeepers to develop legitimate relationships with free black property owners, particularly those few like Coleman Day who owned and hired slaves.[45]

Unlike Coleman Day, the vast majority of free black prisoners were not drawn from the small stratum of relatively wealthy and successful black Richmonders with ties to white society. Instead, like most white criminals, they were poor and often transient members of the community who had few connections with influential whites.[46] However, sympathetic bonds did at times develop across the color line between free African Americans and whites, and an unusual clemency petition submitted to the governor on behalf of a free African American convict in Richmond suggests the implications this could have for the enforcement of the criminal laws.[47]

In 1855, Andrew James was jailed for three years after being found guilty by a court of oyer and terminer of stealing coins worth twenty-one dollars from Robert Ruffin, also a free African American. Within a week of

Andrew's conviction his mother, Martha James, had sent an affidavit to Governor Johnson attesting to facts that were not revealed at her son's trial and that she claimed showed his innocence. The affidavit was accompanied by a petition signed by nine women and eight men, all white, who asserted that "without hesitation . . . we would place full confidence in her [Martha James's] declarations, whether made generally or under oath." These signatories were not the lawyers, legislators, and wealthy slaveholders who commonly supported appeals for executive intervention.[48] Rather, they were artisans and laborers who most probably knew Martha James well and were suitably qualified to comment on her reputation for truthfulness. Charles Bransford was a wheelwright, Thomas Cousins a laborer, and John Ford a member of the public guard. All three of these men lived on Oregon Hill, and it is likely that Martha James was a member of their local community. Perhaps, like many free black women in Richmond, Martha was a washerwoman who occasionally worked for the Bransford or Cousins families. Free black women who performed such menial domestic tasks for whites had more opportunities to develop personal ties with their occasional employers than free black men, who, particularly when laboring in factories, had a more formally hierarchical relationship with white overseers.[49]

As a washerwoman or domestic servant, Martha's closest acquaintances in the white community would likely have been with women, and this is certainly implied by her petition, which was unusual in containing so many female signatories. Clemency was invariably a masculine business, and women rarely signed petitions. However, in the Andrew James case, women not only signed the petition themselves, but it is also likely that they were instrumental in persuading the eight men to sign too. This is suggested by the fact that all but two of the male petitioners shared a surname with at least one of the women. Five of the seventeen supplicants, three women and two men, were members of the Frawner family and eight further signatures belonged to four couples: Charles and Elizabeth Bransford; Edward and Frances Clarke; Thomas and Charlotte Cousins; and John and Catherine Ford.[50]

As in the case of Coleman Day, the willingness of white men and women to support Martha James's petition indicates a source of tension between the denial of legal rights to free blacks in statute law and the attitudes of whites toward individual free black convicts with whom they were personally acquainted.[51] Even so, it was only on rare occasions that white petitions on behalf of free African Americans were favorably received by Virginia governors, and both Andrew James and Coleman Day were refused clemency.

Even after the introduction of oyer and terminer trials for free African Americans in Virginia in 1833, free blacks charged with crimes carrying the death penalty continued to stand trial in the circuit courts. Although the jury was always composed entirely of white men, circuit court trials did afford free blacks legal protections that they were denied in courts of oyer and terminer, including common-law rules of evidence and the right of appeal. As in other southern states, Virginia's appellate judges at times ruled in favor of free black defendants and overturned convictions.[52] That oyer and terminer examinations were deemed an inappropriate method of establishing guilt and innocence when the life of a free person was at stake was a damning indictment of the quality of justice that most slaves and free blacks received. Nonetheless, even the few free blacks who were tried in the circuit court in Richmond were by no means the beneficiaries of a just and fair trial process.[53]

The extant evidence from Richmond jury trials involving free African American defendants is limited but broadly supports Higginbotham and Jacobs's assessment of antebellum Virginia's two systems of criminal trial: "it is unclear which fate was worse: to be deprived of a jury trial, or to be tried by a panel of angry and hostile jurors."[54] At least six free black defendants were examined for capital felonies in the hustings court between 1833 and 1860, and all were sent on for trial in the circuit court. Three were charged with murder, two with rape, and one with assaulting a white person with intent to kill. Due to the destruction of the circuit court records, only a few details are available about the trials that occurred before 1850. Mayor Tate noted in his docket book in 1837 that Robert Selden, a tobacco factory worker who was charged with the murder of a white man, was sentenced to seven years in the penitentiary.[55] Another of the murder defendants, a weaver named Fleming Winston, appears as a penitentiary inmate in the 1850 census, four years after he murdered Manuel Frayser. Though there is no record of the length of Frayser's sentence, he does not feature in the 1860 census, and, assuming he did not die or escape, he was probably released sometime in the mid-1850s.[56] As both Selden and Winston were convicted but not executed, it is likely that, as was common in murder trials involving white defendants, the jury returned a verdict of guilty of murder in the second-degree.[57]

Far more is known about the two free black men charged with capital felonies in Richmond in the 1850s. The cases of Alexander Burley and Alexander Jackson were both documented in the *Dispatch* and give a decidedly mixed impression of the standard of justice in the trials of free blacks in Virginia. In 1859, Burley was tried for the murder of a white man named Delaware Kersey. Burley and Kersey were both employed as ice cart drivers by Jonathan O. Taylor & Co., and it was reported that they had been friends up to the day of the murder. Although this was a case of murder across racial lines, therefore, Burley and Kersey were in certain respects social equals, and though the trial testimony has not survived, newspaper reports of the mayor's court examination suggest that Burley's race did not greatly affect his fate. On the contrary, it can be speculated that on account of the friendship that had existed between the defendant and the victim, the jury judged Burley's actions as they might have done those of a white man in similar circumstances. The description of the alleged crime given by Thomas E. Ford, who witnessed the whole affair, suggests that Burley was provoked by Kersey, who called him a "d—d son of a b—h" and threatened him with an ice pick. In response, Burley inflicted a single, fatal blow on Kersey with a "heavy dogwood handspike."[58] Although Burley was of mixed race and his counsel admitted to the jury that it was a case of involuntary manslaughter, the white jurors returned a verdict of not guilty, suggesting a degree of empathy with Burley's violent response to the slight against his honor.[59]

The only other free black man tried in the circuit court in late antebellum Richmond whose fate is known was Alexander Jackson, who was charged with the rape of Caroline Swan, a free black woman. Although Jackson was found not guilty, his courtroom experiences show that even the few aspects of the criminal law that were intended to protect the rights of free African Americans could be used for entirely contrary purposes. The month prior to his circuit court appearance, Jackson had been acquitted of the very same charge of rape by a court of oyer and terminer. It was reported that four of the six magistrates who had heard the case in the oyer and terminer court had been in favor of conviction, but without a unanimous judgment the case had to be dismissed. In response, the prosecuting attorney entered a motion for the dismissal to be set aside on the grounds that the court had no jurisdiction to pass final judgment in the case. This motion was sustained, paving the way for a new prosecution in the circuit court.[60]

The legal question at issue in the Jackson case was the right of free blacks to be tried by a circuit court jury when charged with a capital crime. The initial decision to try Jackson in a court of oyer and terminer was erroneous and may have stemmed from confusion surrounding Virginia's rape laws, which were repeatedly amended in the early national and antebellum periods and made no specific reference to cases involving free black women as victims. The most recent revision of the criminal code in 1849 had not mentioned the race of the victim, but stated only that free blacks convicted of raping "a female" were to be punished by "death, or at the discretion of the jury confinement of five to twenty years."[61] The reference to a jury clearly suggests that under this act Jackson should have been tried in the circuit court, and that the prosecution was right to assert that the oyer and terminer court was an inappropriate tribunal. However, the decision to question the court's jurisdiction only after Jackson had been acquitted indicates that the prosecuting attorney was not concerned with Jackson's legal rights. Neither, it seems, were the magistrates in the oyer and terminer court, who in setting aside their judgment contravened one of the few rules governing the oyer and terminer process. As the Virginia Supreme Court of Appeals had confirmed in *Anderson v. Commonwealth* (1835), in the trial of a free African American, the court had "the power to pass final sentence; and one of the incidents to the judgment of such a court, is, that it is not subject to revision."[62] On this rare occasion when the incontestability of oyer and terminer verdicts could have worked in favor of a free black defendant, the court took the illegal step of overruling its initial verdict.

The confusion surrounding the prosecution of Alexander Jackson points to wider problems that were inherent to a judicial system based on binary categories that equated race and status in a society with large numbers of free African Americans and people of mixed racial identity. The division of the criminal laws and trial processes along racial lines was based on the assumption that the racial identity of all participants in the courtroom drama could be positively established. Determining race and status was therefore a prerequisite to the prosecution of any case, yet it was not always a straightforward task, and in numerous cases in Richmond the race of defendants, victims, and witnesses was challenged and contested by defendants, judicial officers, and attorneys.

In Virginia statute law, the lines that distinguished white from black were fixed and immutable. In 1785, the Virginia General Assembly passed a law defining as legally white all persons with up to one-quarter "black blood," and this remained the line of demarcation between blacks and whites throughout the antebellum period.[63] Enforcing this law in practice, however, was never a simple task, and there was not always agreement in the courtroom on issues of racial identity.[64]

According to the Georgia attorney Thomas Cobb, when courts came to assess the status of a defendant, "the black color of the race raise[d] the presumption of slavery."[65] Had this presumption been applicable in all cases it would have greatly enhanced the efficiency of the criminal law to the great benefit of the slaveholding class. However, the southern racial reality did not allow for such a simple equation of skin color with slave or free status. Instead, widespread miscegenation and the presence of free blacks complicated the racial classification of criminal defendants and imbued the process with political significance, since if courts could not accurately determine the race and status of the accused, not only was the practical enforcement of the criminal law constrained, but the ideological basis of the entire southern social order was undermined. As free black convicts could be sold into slavery, it was even possible that an incorrect assessment of a defendant's race could lead to the enslavement of a white citizen.

Although Virginia law theoretically defined black and white in precise terms, it did not make clear how the courts were to assess whether the defendants and witnesses who appeared before them had more or less than one-quarter black blood. Seemingly, the law recognized the difficulty of imposing definitions of racial identity on Virginia's mixed-race population, and concluded that the decision-making process was best conducted at the local level and according to "unspecified" standards.[66] In practice, the courts relied on various types of evidence to determine an individual's race. In the early national period, legal documentation of ancestry provided the most important guide to race, but in the antebellum era, courts turned to emerging theories of racial science, which they believed provided a more precise means of racial classification.[67] At the same time, the courts also began to accept evidence of "racial performance," or how an individual acted and was perceived in the local community. Race as a legal category was therefore based in part on reputation, and being white became dependent on such considerations as whether an individual associated with whites, exercised social and political rights and privileges reserved for whites, and adhered to popular expectations of appropriate white conduct. This central role of whites at the local level in determining an individual's racial identity was given implicit legal sanction by the Virginia General Court in the cases of *Chaney v. Saunders* (1811) and *Dean v. Commonwealth* (1847), yet difficulties remained, not least the fact that there was not always a social consensus on an individual's racial identity for the local courts to reflect.[68] Furthermore, in criminal cases in particular, because the defendant's race could determine the nature of the trial process, the admissibility of evidence, and the type of punishment, the interests of the prosecution and defense with regards to questions of racial identity could conflict, and it was often in the interests of one side or the other to make racial identity a contested issue in the courtroom.

In Richmond, the mayor conducted the first official examination of criminal suspects and was therefore responsible for establishing the race and status of the accused. In the vast majority of cases, the mayor did not hear any testimony about race at all, but determined the race of the defendant and, when appropriate, also of the victim and witnesses, solely on the basis of their physical appearance. Only rarely did the mayor articulate the reasoning behind his assessments of racial identity. For example, when Eliza Loyed accused Joel Williamson of being the father of her illegitimate child, Williamson claimed that Loyed was not competent to make such a charge "she being a free person of color." Mayor Tate, however, dismissed this claim without seeking any legal evidence of Loyed's status. Instead he concluded that she was white as, in his opinion, she had "a clear and transparent skin—the features + hair of a white person—and indignantly rep[udiate]d the sug[gestion] [that she was a mulatto]."[69] Such subjective interpretations of race were always somewhat arbitrary and often inconsistent. When Cynthia Conway appeared before Mayor Tate in 1836, for example, she was examined as the free mulatto daughter of Catherine Conway, a white woman. The following year, however, when both Catherine and Cynthia were charged with keeping a disorderly house, Tate recorded in his personal docket book that both women were white.[70] In another disputable case, the court reporter of the *Richmond Republican* documented the examination of "Mary Hicks, designated in the warrant as a 'free woman of color,' but to our optics a white woman."[71]

In Virginia, the complexity of determining a defendant's racial identity was compounded by an obscure law enacted in 1833 that enabled Native Americans and other persons of mixed ancestry to obtain a certificate from a county court or municipal hustings court declaring them exempt from the legal disabilities endured by free blacks on the grounds that they had "less than one-fourth of negro blood" in their veins. The rationale of this law is perplexing, and the historian Joshua Rothman argues that it "made no sense at all.... Free people who were not black or mulatto should have automatically been exempt from the restrictions—because they would have been white."[72] It is unclear how many individuals tried to obtain certification that they were less than one-quarter black in the 1830s and 1840s, but the *Dispatch* reported a significant increase in the number of cases in the 1850s on account of the more vigilant enforcement of the laws against free blacks changing their county of residence within the Commonwealth and illegally entering Virginia.[73] Not only in residency disputes, however, but also in criminal cases, individuals charged as free blacks sought to evade prosecution by claiming that under the provisions of the 1833 act they were entitled to examination as white persons.

In 1853, Richard Bradly demurred from Mayor Mayo's decision to proceed against him as a free black man on the grounds that he was a member of the Pamunkey tribe of Indians. Bradly's counsel, A. Judson Crane, produced documentary evidence attesting to his client's tribal affiliation and argued that the mayor could not examine Bradly as a free person of color without first establishing that he was at least one-quarter black. However, the mayor contemptuously dismissed this suggestion and ruled that, "the kinky hair and general appearance of the accused was such as to convince him that he was nothing more than a free negro, and he should therefore fine him $1 for being drunk, and commit him to prison as a free negro, without a register."[74] Whether for financial reasons or because they believed they were unlikely to meet with success, Bradly and Crane chose not to appeal the mayor's judgment.

A more complex case arose in 1858 when William Ferguson, a free man of color who had a certificate from the hustings court stating that he was "not a Negro," was examined on a charge of assaulting a free black man. In the course of the examination, John Gregory, Ferguson's attorney, objected to the introduction of three African American witnesses on the grounds that "negroes could only testify against a negro or Indian, and that his client had the certificate of the Hustings Court, declaring that he was not a negro, and did not claim to be an Indian." After taking a few days to examine the law relevant to the case, however, Mayo ruled that

> "mixed bloods" were nothing more nor less, under the law, than free negroes, relieved of the disability of being sold for taxes or county levies, or carrying registers, or from returning to the Commonwealth after visiting a free State, and regulations of that character. He was satisfied that the Legislature had never intended to make white persons of this class, or to create a third class in the State, and until overruled by an appellate tribunal, he should look upon them as free negroes, and treat them as such.[75]

The implication of Mayo's reasoning was that a defendant with any black ancestry would be prosecuted as a free black person, a policy that was in clear violation of the dividing line between black and white of one-quarter black blood that was enshrined in statute law. However, Mayo's actions were not in keeping with his rhetoric, and instead of passing final judgment, as was usual in the examination of free black defendants charged with misdemeanor assault, he instead sent Ferguson before the grand jury for indictment. The grand jury found a true bill, and Ferguson was subsequently tried in the hustings court and sentenced to thirty days imprisonment.[76] There is no evidence that he appealed the mayor's decision, and it is not known whether his claim to be "not a negro" was raised at the trial. Given that Ferguson was convicted, however, it is probable that the three black witnesses were permitted to testify against him and that he was therefore tried as a free black person. If this was indeed the case, Ferguson's trial was unique in the annals of Richmond criminal justice in the late antebellum period. Not only were free African Americans usually denied trial by jury in cases of misdemeanor and noncapital felonies, but the regular punishment imposed upon them for assault was not jail, but a public whipping.[77]

Ferguson's case brings into sharp relief the significance of the mayor's court examination in the overall drama of the criminal justice process. Had Mayo interpreted mixed-blood status differently and prohibited black witnesses from testifying against Ferguson, it is likely that the prosecution's case would have collapsed, and Ferguson would have been discharged without trial. However, according to the *Dispatch,* Mayo was only nominally concerned with Ferguson's procedural rights, and his main interest in sending this case before the hustings court was to enable a higher authority to fix the proper status of free African Americans who had been designated "not negroes," "and thus relieve him of a most perplexing subject."[78]

In felony cases, the summary nature of the oyer and terminer process meant that once the mayor had ruled on whether a black defendant was enslaved or free, there was no legal avenue for the accused to challenge the decision. Even so, a small number of black defendants who were tried as slaves in courts of oyer and terminer did claim to be free. Richmond magistrates were rarely receptive to such claims, but on at least one occasion they did overrule the mayor's assessment of a defendant's status. In 1834, the prosecution dropped its case against Stephen, who had been charged with burglary and indicted as a slave, on the basis that, contrary to the mayor's ruling, Stephen was a free man. Although the oyer and terminer court had jurisdiction over both slaves and free blacks charged with burglary, the defendant's status was significant in this case, as only slaves could be sentenced to death for burglary, while free blacks were subject to penitentiary imprisonment. It is possible that Stephen took advantage of the court's ruling to leave Richmond, as there is no record that he was subsequently tried for the burglary as a free person.[79]

Although Stephen's case illustrates the very direct impact that issues of race and status could have on the efficiency of the justice system in a slave state, his experiences were unusual, and on most occasions magistrates dismissed the claims of defendants who disputed the legal assessment of their status in oyer and terminer courts. Nonetheless, there is evidence to suggest that other defendants challenged the court's classification of their race and status as a tactic to avert prosecution. For example, when Fielding Alexander Edins was charged with stabbing his wife, Fanny Cooper, with intent to kill and prosecuted as a free black man, he moved the court in arrest of judgment, "alleging that he is neither a slave, free negro nor mulatto." This motion was overruled, however, and Edins was convicted and sentenced to the penitentiary. When Robert Tate Wicker, Edins's defense counsel, subsequently submitted a petition for clemency on behalf of his client, he did not mention the claims of disputed racial status that had been thrown out by the court and instead described Edins simply as "a free mulatto."[80] It is ironic that had Edins succeeded in his attempt to kill Fanny Cooper and been charged with the capital crime of murder rather than manslaughter, he would have been entitled to a trial by jury in the circuit court according to common-law rules of due process and could have appealed the court's assessment of his identity.

In contrast to courts of oyer and terminer, when racial identity was contested in the course of a jury trial, rules of due process demanded a more thorough investigation. The prosecution of Elizabeth Southard provides insight into the complexities of determining racial identity in Richmond. Elizabeth stood trial in 1851 charged with the murder of William P. Walker. The prosecution alleged that on the evening of April 12, 1850, William and Elizabeth had been drinking and dancing at the house of Martha Hobson, a mutual acquaintance, and at some point in the evening they had begun to wrestle. When Elizabeth turned to walk away, William "ran after her, and kicked her in the mouth . . . so hard it shook every tooth in her head." In response, Elizabeth picked up a griddle and struck William on the back of the head, knocking him unconscious and inflicting injuries from which he died ten days later.[81] The evidence against Elizabeth left little doubt that she had inflicted the blow that killed William, yet securing her conviction was no simple matter, because at every stage of the prosecution process the judicial authorities failed to agree on whether she was black or white.

When Elizabeth was first examined for murder in the mayor's court, Mayor William Lambert determined that although she had a "somewhat dark complexion," she was, nonetheless, a white woman. When the case came up for further examination in the hustings court, however, the prosecuting attorney claimed that Elizabeth was in fact a mulatto. This was an extremely significant claim, because if it could be proved, then nonwhite witnesses would be eligible to testify against Elizabeth. As African Americans were not permitted to give evidence against white defendants in Virginia, the prosecuting attorney had to establish that Elizabeth had more than one-quarter black blood before he could call his two key witnesses, Martha and Rebecca Hobson, who were both registered as free blacks.[82] Inevitably, the defense objected to this attempt to redefine Elizabeth's racial identity, and the hustings court magistrates, apparently reluctant to decide themselves whether Elizabeth was black or white, ordered that the prosecution be dropped and the case sent back to the mayor's court so that a new indictment could be drawn up. When the mayor investigated Elizabeth for a second time, however, he refused to reconsider his initial assessment of her race and indicted her once more as a white woman. Reporting on these events, the *Republican* commented with some dismay that "the case stands just as it did a month ago! This is queer justice."[83]

As it was not necessary for the prosecution to prove its case conclusively in the hustings court examination but only to establish the probable guilt of the accused, when Elizabeth came before the hustings court for the second time, the prosecuting attorney adopted a new strategy. He chose to avoid the contentious issue of Elizabeth's racial identity by not calling Martha and Rebecca Hobson to the witness stand and instead seeking to establish Elizabeth's *probable* guilt through the testimony of white witnesses alone. Isaiah and John Walker, respectively the brother and cousin of the victim, swore that William Walker had identified Elizabeth as his assailant on a number of occasions in the days before he died. In addition, two medical experts testified that they had examined the deceased and were certain that he had come to his death "by the wound received on his head." Although Elizabeth claimed that this evidence did not establish her probable guilt, the magistrates disagreed and remanded her for trial.[84]

The wheels of justice turned slowly in Richmond, and for the next eleven months Elizabeth languished in the city jail. There is no evidence that the jail itself was segregated, so Elizabeth's race was of little practical significance during her incarceration. Nonetheless, during this time the confusion over her racial identity persisted, for although she had been indicted for trial as a white woman, when the census taker visited the jail in 1850 he recorded that she was a mulatto.[85] In addition to Elizabeth, five other inmates were designated in the census as mulattoes, while four were recorded as black, an indication of the significance that the census enumerators attributed to gradations of skin color in contrast to the bilateral racial categories that legislators worked to establish in law.[86]

When Elizabeth eventually stood trial, the first witnesses called by the prosecution were Martha Hobson and her daughter Rebecca, the two free black women whose racial status had precipitated the collapse of Elizabeth's first hustings court examination. As the only eyewitnesses to the alleged crime, the testimony of these women was critical to the prosecution's case. Although their evidence had not been required to establish Elizabeth's probable guilt in the hustings court, in order to secure a guilty verdict from a circuit court jury, the prosecution needed direct evidence that Elizabeth had inflicted the blow that killed Walker, evidence that only Martha and Rebecca could provide.

As in the hustings court examination, when Martha and Rebecca were called to testify at Elizabeth's trial, the defense protested that they were incompetent witnesses on account of their race, pointing out that they were registered in Henrico County as free mulattoes. In response, the prosecution claimed that Martha and Rebecca had registered as free blacks "merely because they did not wish to be annoyed by questions as to their disabilities and privileges." This argument was based on what appears an unlikely claim: the Hobsons had chosen to register as free blacks even though they were, in actual fact, white. The prosecution additionally claimed the right to question the Hobsons' race on the grounds that the Commonwealth had not been a party when the Hobsons were registered. Consequently, the Commonwealth was "not bound by the action of the County Court." It was this argument that appears to have convinced the presiding judge, John Caskie, to permit the Hobsons to be questioned on their parentage in order to establish whether they were white and if their testimony was consequently admissible.[87] Immediately, therefore, the prosecution's attempts to secure Southard's conviction had become dependent on the judge accepting that racial categories were never fixed or final even when established in a court of law.

Responding to questions from the prosecuting attorney, Martha Hobson gave inconclusive and at times contradictory evidence about her racial identity. It was established that Martha had been born and raised in Little York, Gloucester County, and although she testified that her mother was "generally called an English woman" and her father "was reported to be a white man," she also disclosed that after she was born her mother had lived as the wife of a free black man. Perhaps more significantly, Martha's own husband, although light-skinned, was also "generally thought to be a free man of color," and the couple "associated with colored people in Gloucester." However, it was only when they moved to Richmond that Martha and her husband registered as free blacks, and they did so because they "feared some body might interfere with us." Specifically, Martha and her husband might have feared being mistaken for fugitive slaves in a city where they did not have friends and family to attest to their free status. Had they not registered and their claims to whiteness been challenged, they could also have faced enslavement on the grounds that they were free blacks illegally resident in Virginia.[88] Alternatively, they might have decided to establish formally that theirs was not a mixed-race relationship, in order to ensure they did not fall victim to the vigilante attacks that a number of interracial couples suffered in 1850s Richmond. This raises the intriguing possibility that Martha sacrificed her claims to whiteness and registered as a free black woman in order to safeguard her marriage. In this case, the racial order would appear to have been less stable than Virginia's statute laws implied and slaveholders would have liked to believe.

According to Robert Reid Howison's record of the trial, the court heard no further evidence about Martha's marital status until after it ruled on her racial identity. However, when Martha was later questioned about the events surrounding the alleged murder itself, she revealed under cross-examination that at the time of the crime she had been living as husband and wife with the deceased, William Walker, although she had never married him. It is not certain whether Walker was the same man Martha had previously referred to as her husband, although on balance the evidence suggests he was not. While Martha had referred to her husband as a free black man, the 1850 census recorded that Walker's brothers, John and Isaiah, were white, and both of these men had testified against Elizabeth Southard in the hustings court without their racial status being questioned.[89] What is more, as interracial marriages were illegal in Virginia, Walker's whiteness might explain why he could not marry Martha Hobson after she had registered as a free black woman. Finally, at no point in the record of the case is there any suggestion that Rebecca Hobson was William's child.

The available evidence about Martha's relationship with William Walker supports the impression that in terms of her reputation, as well as her legal status, Martha lived in Richmond as a free black woman. However, Martha's testimony had raised the possibility that her racial ancestry may have satisfied the definition of a white person in Virginia law; if both of Martha's parents were white, as she claimed, then Martha herself could not have been a free black woman. With the prosecution case against Elizabeth Southard resting on Martha's testimony, Judge Caskie decided to investigate the matter further, and he summoned to the witness stand some physicians whom he described as "experts in matters relating to the distinctions between the human races." The first of these "experts" was Dr. R. H. Cabell, who, after examining Martha Hobson, concluded that that she was "a pure Caucasian." He told the court that although "this woman's nose *is* depressed . . . she tells me it has been broken; I find nothing in her hair, or skin or general appearance indicating negro blood." It is ironic that this medical opinion was derived from Martha Hobson's own explanation that her nose had been broken. In effect, Dr. Cabell was giving evidence in the name of science that a woman who was registered in her home county as a free African American had claimed to be white. Evidently the prohibition on black testimony in white trials was not so complete as southern lawmakers supposed.

Although Dr. Cabell's testimony supported Martha's claims that her parents had both been white, it was at odds with the county court records that listed her as a free black woman. Judge Caskie refused to make a ruling on the basis of this contradictory evidence, and the prosecution therefore suggested that the court adopt a new approach to resolving the questions of racial identity raised in the case and address the issue of whether Elizabeth Southard "was as much a negro as the witnesses." The defense objected that it was unfair to question Southard's racial identity, as she had appeared in court expecting to be tried as a white person, but Caskie ruled that this was irrelevant on the grounds that the punishment for murder was the same whether the defendant was black or white.

If the prosecution could prove that Elizabeth Southard was herself a free black woman, Martha and Rebecca Hobson could testify against her irrespective of whether they were black or white. The initial testimony that was presented at this stage did not assess Elizabeth's racial identity in terms of the one-quarter black blood rule but rather *relative* to that of the Hobsons. Dr. Cabell was first recalled to the witness stand and testified that in his opinion Rebecca Hobson had more black blood than Elizabeth Southard, but this view was immediately contradicted by Dr. Haskins, who testified that it was in fact Southard who had more black blood. Haskins based his assessment on Elizabeth's skin and her short hair, which had a "wavy curl" that Haskins believed was distinct from the curl of white women's hair. Although he admitted that Elizabeth's hair might have been cut, Haskins claimed that it had "the appearance of having its natural length."[90]

Even if Cabell and Haskins had been able to substantiate their arguments, their testimony was of dubious legal value. Only if the extent of Elizabeth's black ancestry relative to that of Rebecca Hobson could be related to the one-quarter black blood law would it determine whether Rebecca's testimony was admissible. However, both Cabell and Haskins, as well as two other physicians who were called to testify, expressed serious reservations about their ability to judge on what side of the one-quarter black blood line any individual fell. When cross-examined by the defense, Cabell admitted that although he had testified that Martha Hobson was white he did not think "it would be possible for a physician to say accurately how much negro blood there was in a person; as whether a fourth or more; it would be mere conjecture." When subsequently asked for his opinion on Rebecca Hobson's race, Cabell expressed a reluctance to testify and asked to be excused from the case.[91]

Dr. Haskins concurred with Cabell that it was not possible "for a physician" to determine whether a person had one-fourth black blood, and explained to the court that, "It is rather the province of the *naturalist* than of the physician, to examine these subjects; probably a physician would not have much more skill than any man of general scientific reading." Dr. Albert Sneed, another witness in the case, agreed that a physician might develop "some peculiar knowledge" of racial matters "from his practice among the two races," though even he admitted that it was impossible to tell precisely the ratio of black to white blood in a human body.[92] Clearly racial science, while used in the abstract to support white southerners' arguments in favor of slavery, was far from able to prevent what for the slaveholders was a dangerous blurring of the racial divide when applied to the race of specific individuals in criminal trials.[93]

Once Judge Caskie had concluded his attempt to use scientific evidence to establish the race of Elizabeth, Martha, and Rebecca, he proceeded to summon three further witnesses who had known Elizabeth and her family in Hanover County. These witnesses were asked to comment on the racial standing of the Southard family within the local community, and they provided anecdotal evidence that Elizabeth was most probably white. Isaac Goddin claimed that on one occasion when Elizabeth appeared before the Hanover County Court, it had been determined "that she was a white person." Jacob Holloway and Fleming Harris, meanwhile, both swore that Elizabeth's parents had been regarded as white persons in Hanover County, and Harris also added that he had known Southard's father to muster in the militia, a duty that in antebellum Virginia could only be performed by white men.[94]

After taking a night to consider the case, Judge Caskie declared that the evidence supported what he claimed was his original view that, although Elizabeth had some African blood, it was less than one-quarter, so she could legally be tried as a white person. Martha Hobson was also declared to be a "pure Caucasian" and, therefore, a competent witness, as was her daughter Rebecca. Although Caskie had at first supposed that Rebecca "had much more negro blood than the prisoner," the evidence, as inconclusive as it might appear, had somehow convinced him that she was, in fact, less than one-quarter black.[95] In the course of this remarkable trial, therefore, two women who had previously been legally classified as free blacks had been recast as white. Although Southard was eventually convicted of voluntary manslaughter largely on the basis of Martha Hobson's testimony, the case had revealed significant underlying tensions in Virginia's racial order. Even as Virginia's lawmakers continued to construct statutes to strengthen the divide between the legal rights of blacks and whites, events such as the trial of Elizabeth Southard revealed that in practice race was a far more fluid and contested category than this bilateral system allowed.

Virginia judges never failed to decide whether a defendant or witness was black or white, yet the evidence on which their decisions rested was at times so insubstantial that it highlighted a weakness in southern racial ideology. This weakness was only evident in a small number of criminal cases, and it did not seriously threaten the stability of the southern racial order. However, Elizabeth Southard's trial suggests numerous ways in which the problem of racial classification was exacerbated in urban communities where the population was more ethnically diverse and transient, where poor whites and free blacks mixed most freely, and where the law intervened in everyday life to a far greater extent than in rural areas.

While the Virginia General Court ruled in *Dean v. Commonwealth* that whites at the local level should decide how to handle cases involving people of ambiguous racial origin, in Richmond the dynamics of urban life made this an increasingly impractical proposition. It is notable, for example, that Elizabeth Southard summoned witnesses who had known her in Hanover County to testify to her racial identity. Even though she had lived in Richmond for four or five years by the time of her trial, there was seemingly no one in the local community who could establish to the satisfaction of the law that Elizabeth was white. This might have been because her acquaintances had no knowledge of the race of her parents, or alternatively because she knew only African Americans in the city and they were ineligible to testify to a person's whiteness.

Elizabeth Southard's most important connections in Richmond were with free black men and women who could not testify in court that she was a white woman. As well as Martha and Rebecca Hobson, African Americans with whom Elizabeth socialized in the early 1850s included Robert Smith, with whom she lived as man and wife but could not marry legally on account of his race, and Matilda Finney, who in 1854 was charged with stabbing Elizabeth with intent to kill. The record of Matilda Finney's trial provides clear evidence that even after Judge Caskie determined that Elizabeth was a white woman, her racial identity was far from fixed and, even more remarkably, it lends itself to an interpretation that suggests that Elizabeth's disputed race once again threatened to undermine the enforcement of the law.

As a free black woman charged with a noncapital crime, Matilda Finney stood trial before a panel of magistrates sitting as a court of oyer and terminer. On November 13, 1854, she was convicted and sentenced to two years in the state penitentiary, but in a development that was almost unique in Richmond oyer and terminer cases in the antebellum era, the verdict was subsequently set aside and Finney was granted a new trial. The court did not make explicit its reasons for a retrial, but analysis of the documents in the case reveals two apparent errors on the face of the original indictment that may have influenced the court's decision. In the first place, there is a discrepancy in the trial documents regarding the date of the crime. While the indictment remanding Finney for trial states that the crime was committed on September 27, 1854, the warrant remanding the prosecution witnesses to bail for their appearance in court dates the offense to September 30. Such errors routinely led to the collapse of common-law trials, but there is no evidence that on any other occasion they were so significant in oyer and terminer proceedings.

A more feasible explanation for the retrial is that there was confusion over Elizabeth Southard's racial identity. In the indictment against Finney drawn up by Mayor Joseph Mayo, Elizabeth was referred to as "a negro," but in the course of the trial she deposed that "she is white + her father + mother white, and that she has always been considered a white person." The defense called three white witnesses who broadly endorsed Elizabeth's claims about her racial heritage, but also introduced an element of doubt that may have been sufficient to have the case thrown out. Jacob Holloway, who had provided similar evidence in Elizabeth's murder trial, along with William Day and Richard F. Darracott, testified that Elizabeth's parents had always passed as white in Hanover County, that her father had voted and served in the local militia as a white man, and that both her grandfathers had also been white. However, the witnesses also revealed that it was rumored in Hanover that Southard's grandmothers, who were sisters, both had "a taint of black blood in them."[96]

In contrast to the Elizabeth Southard case, there was no doubt that Matilda Finney was an African American, and as such the issues of racial identity raised in the course of her trial did not have any formal legal ramifications or undermine the prosecution case. However, Elizabeth's race was potentially still of considerable significance, because oyer and terminer courts routinely handed down more severe sentences in cases in which the victim was white.[97] Matilda stood trial for a second time on December 15, 1854. Once again she was convicted, but on this occasion she was sentenced to just one year in the penitentiary, possibly because the magistrates were more convinced than they previously had been that Elizabeth was not a white woman. Although the written record depicts Elizabeth as an African American woman at all stages of the legal proceedings against Matilda, the way in which the magistrates interpreted her racial identity may well have been different at each trial. While this would have constituted an informal revision of Elizabeth's racial status, it would have been entirely consistent with the judicial discretion that shaped the impact of the victim's race on sentencing patterns.

Elizabeth's racial identity was contested both when she was a defendant and a victim in criminal trials, and it is surely not coincidental that in both Elizabeth's own trial and that of Matilda Finney, the other main parties involved were either African Americans or persons of disputed racial identity. It might be speculated that had Elizabeth associated mainly with whites, the court would have presumed that she was white herself, and the matter of her own racial identity may not even have become a legal issue. This possibility is supported by the decision taken by Judge Caskie to consider the racial identity of Elizabeth, Martha, and Rebecca relative to each other rather than against the fixed definitions of black and white established by the one-quarter black blood rule. The prosecution's evidence could not establish conclusively whether any of the three women had more than one-quarter black ancestry, yet it was able to cast sufficient aspersions on Elizabeth's whiteness to place her in a similarly ambiguous racial category as the Hobsons. Although this was not a category recognized in law, and it could not be reconciled with the assumptions of the one-quarter black blood rule, it was compatible with what Richmonders knew about the reality of race in their society. Many people in the city, perhaps most, had both black and white ancestry, but race was as much about class and racial performance as about percentages of black blood. By demonstrating that Elizabeth was part of the same lower-class interracial subculture as Martha and Rebecca Hobson, the prosecution encouraged the court to accept the Hobsons' testimony in spite of any uncertainty about their racial identity.

The urban context complicated questions of racial determination in other ways, not least on account of Richmond's large transient population. Hanover County, Elizabeth's place of birth, lies adjacent to Richmond, and it was therefore relatively easy for Jacob Holloway and the other witnesses who had known Elizabeth's parents to appear in the courtroom. However, had the defendant in this case been one of the thousands of European immigrants who settled in Virginia in the mid-nineteenth century, or one of the northern workers who traveled to Richmond in search of employment, or even a sailor whose ship happened to have docked on the banks of the James River, evidence of her racial origins would have been more obscure.

Elizabeth's gender also contributed to the confusion surrounding her racial identity. While men in Virginia could demonstrate their whiteness in very public ways such as voting, hunting, joining a militia, and displaying mastery over slaves, according to antebellum gender conventions white women were expected to remain outside of the public sphere. As such, women's claims to whiteness based on reputation, as opposed to science or documentary evidence, were most effectively made through their relationships with men and by embodying the ideals of white southern womanhood, most notably domesticity, purity, and subordination to patriarchal governance.[98] Elizabeth Southard violated all of these ideals. The testimony at her trial revealed that she was violent, drank excessively, and, most significant, that she socialized, associated, and slept with free African Americans.

The lives of very few white women in Richmond corresponded with all of the expectations of appropriate female conduct. In particular, large numbers of poor white women were forced to work either to supplement their husband's income or because they had no male relations on whom they could depend for subsistence. Unlike many of their counterparts in rural societies who were more likely to labor within the confines of the household, women in the city commonly had little option but to work for wages. White women in Richmond often worked in factories or as washerwomen, while more than two hundred Irish women toiled as domestic servants, performing duties that were more commonly the preserve of slaves.[99] Even though slavery continued to have a uniquely devastating impact on black women's lives in Richmond, as the city's social and economic development in the antebellum period led to increasing numbers of impoverished and self-reliant white women working outside of the domestic sphere, women's work and family life became a less reliable guide to race.[100]

The trial of Elizabeth Southard shows that in antebellum Virginia racial identities were based on highly subjective evidence that compromised lawmakers' attempts to make the administration of criminal justice correspond to a strict racial divide. It was the irresolvable dilemma of the slaveholding elite that the more they based the criminal law on race in order to support the existing southern social order, the harder it became to enforce the law precisely because the social order did not correspond to a simple racial divide between black and white. Elizabeth's experiences as a mulatto prisoner in 1850, a white defendant in 1851, and a black victim in 1854 were undoubtedly exceptional, yet they illustrate the problems of racial classification and show the numerous ways in which these problems increased as southern society became more diverse and the close community bonds that shaped and regulated rural society were broken down and replaced by institutional legal mechanisms in cities. Urban-industrial growth led to a blurring of the racial divide both literally, as a result of widespread miscegenation, and in consequence of the extensive interracial associations that occurred in the city, particularly among free blacks and poor whites. Immigration and the transient urban population, as well as changing gender roles, and the large numbers of white wage laborers, free blacks, and quasi-free slaves in the city, further complicated the process of determining racial identity in Richmond courts.[101]

The difficulties inherent in determining racial identity complicated the operation of the criminal justice system in Richmond, yet in practice this was of little comfort to free African Americans who suffered under increasingly oppressive criminal laws in the antebellum period. Richmond free blacks adapted to the hostile legal environment in various ways. Some acquiesced in their condition and tried to avoid encounters with the law whenever possible. Others violated the laws with impunity either out of defiance or blind hope that their actions would go undetected. Many simply packed up whatever belongings they had and moved away, though the prospect of leaving enslaved family and friends behind militated against this.[102] Still others, however, continued to assert their few legal rights. As defendants they hired attorneys, appealed court verdicts, submitted clemency petitions, and contested court assessments of their race and status.[103] These actions challenged the white ideal of black legal passivity and demonstrate that despite Virginia's racially discriminatory statutes, free blacks had a conception of their legal rights that they strived to protect.

When free African Americans appeared in criminal courts as victims and complainants, their relationship with the law was more ambivalent than when they were defendants. Black complainants who sought justice in courts dominated by whites were motivated by practical and personal concerns more than abstract considerations about the relationship between race and the justice system. Like white complainants, they wanted the courts to protect their person and property, as well as to regulate disorder and drunkenness within their community.[104] Even on the eve of the Civil War, when the racial discrimination in Virginia criminal law was greater than at any other time in the antebellum era, free African Americans in Richmond accounted for 7 percent of the victims of violent crime who appeared before the mayor, a figure almost identical to their share of Richmond's population at the time.[105] What is more, the vast majority of these cases were internal to the free black community. Free blacks rarely pressed charges against either whites or slaves, and in 1852 as many as 84 percent of assault cases in which the victim was a free black person also involved free blacks as defendants.[106] Free African American women were particularly frequent complainants. In 1852, women were the complainants in twenty-nine out of the forty-nine cases of assault that free African Americans reported to the mayor. This gender division was in stark contrast to that found in assault cases involving white complainants, which in more than three out of four cases were initiated by men.[107]

It is notable that almost 80 percent of female free black complainants made allegations of violence against a free African American man. The inadmissibility of black testimony against whites meant that free black victims of white violence could only make a complaint when there was a white witness to the crime, and even when this was the case, the mayor was usually reluctant to indict the accused. When Richard Bradley was tied up and whipped by Richard Barnes, a white man whom Barnes had allegedly insulted, Barnes's employer, Martin Sweeney, brought the matter to the attention of the mayor. The case was dismissed, however, "the Mayor considering that Barnes had scarcely done the negro justice."[108]

Free African Americans reported property crimes less frequently than they did instances of violence, and when they did the accusations were again usually made against people of their own race.[109] To white men like Governor William Smith, such charges were readily interpreted to support the view that African Americans were prone to violence and theft and that the black community was internally divided and in need of strict white governance. Moreover, black plaintiffs conferred a degree of legitimacy on legal processes, even as the paucity of black prosecutions involving white defendants, and the reliance on white testimony to bring complaints and secure convictions, reaffirmed the extensive limitations on African Americans' use of the law.[110]

Short-term pragmatism and self-interest motivated many black prosecutors in antebellum Richmond, but as Jon-Christian Suggs has shown through an analysis of slave narratives, African American attitudes toward the law in the Old South were not shaped solely by personal interests and acquiescence to white dominance in the courtroom. Instead they were characterized by "a complex welter of hope, cynicism, trust, and clear-eyed, even ironic, understanding."[111] A free black storekeeper who was interviewed in Richmond by a northern reporter in the 1850s encapsulated these attitudes when he complained that if a white man stole goods from his store, he would have "no legal remedy" unless another white man witnessed the offense, and even then "fear of the municipal lash" might restrain him from entering a proper complaint.[112] Many free black victims of crime undoubtedly reached similar conclusions, and few would have taken the decision to prosecute lightly. Yet when free blacks did report offenses to the mayor, they not only submitted to white authority but also simultaneously asserted their right to legal protection and redress and challenged the white ideal of black passivity at law.

Fig. 12. "Richmond, Va. First African Church (Broad Street)." 1865. Courtesy of Library of Congress, Prints and Photographs online, Selected Civil War Photographs, 1861–1865. <http://hdl.loc.gov/loc.pnp/cwpb.02904>

While many free black victims of crime made complaints to the police or the mayor, others sought redress in Richmond's African Baptist churches, which offered an alternative forum in which black victims, enslaved as well as free, could seek a form of justice that many deemed preferable to that found in the white-controlled municipal courts. The minutes of the First African Baptist Church contain frequent references to slaves and free blacks charged with a variety of crimes ranging from intemperance and bigamy to theft, fighting, and murder. These crimes were reported by free black and enslaved victims, and a remarkably formal set of procedural regulations was adhered to in the investigation and examination of church members. By reporting crimes to religious tribunals instead of the mayor's court, free African Americans, as well as slaves, demonstrated that they had internalized many of the legal values that were central to the operation of the municipal and state justice system, such as due process and rules of evidence, but at the same time contested the hegemonic role of the white courts.

Between 1841 and 1860, four African Baptist churches were established in Richmond, and by the eve of the Civil War, 4,600 black Richmonders, or one-third of the city's black population, were Baptist Church members and subject to ecclesiastical discipline. There were significant limitations on the enforcement of African Baptist Church justice, and some slaves and free blacks were skeptical of the extent to which the churches could serve the interests of the black community. Henry "Box" Brown offered a particularly scathing critique following his escape from slavery. Brown argued that whites had permitted the establishment of Richmond's First African Baptist Church as a means of countering the problem of slave runaways by ensuring that slaves had "a strong motive to remain where they were." Furthermore, by continually requiring African American church members to pay additional sums toward the eventual purchase of the church building without ever enabling them to obtain complete ownership of the property, Brown claimed that whites hoped to deprive slaves of the small sums of money that they could earn in the city and that could have been used to finance their escape from bondage.[113]

Henry Brown also maintained that the white pastor of the First African Baptist Church, Robert Ryland, "was a zealous supporter of the slave-holders' cause" and "was not ashamed to invoke the authority of heaven in support of the slave degrading laws."[114] Indeed, many of Richmond's largest slaveholders perceived the African Baptist churches as an important element of slave discipline. James Thomas Jr., a prominent tobacco manufacturer, played a major role in the establishment of the First African Baptist Church, and several of his slaves were church members. Thomas was concerned about his slaves' moral welfare and spiritual advancement and testified against two male slaves who had committed adultery in hearings that led to their exclusion from the church.[115]

The church courts also faced practical problems in their attempts to resolve criminal matters internal to the black community. Slaves and free black men and women who were not members of one of Richmond's four African churches could not seek justice in the ecclesiastical setting, and nor could the churches regulate interracial criminal encounters.[116] Furthermore, even those Baptists who saw in the religious tribunals the potential for a limited form of self-regulation on the part of the black community would have recognized that exclusion from church membership—the sole disciplinary sanction available to the ecclesiastical tribunals—could only be imposed on church members, held little meaning outside of the church community, and could be contradicted by the judgment of a secular court investigating the same case.[117]

Even with these qualifications, however, there is evidence that church discipline played a significant role in the self-regulation of the black community. The church courts functioned very much as an alternative to the municipal criminal justice system; they reflected a distinct value system to that enshrined in statute law, and, in most cases, the church members investigated by ecclesiastical committees were suspected of criminal offences that had not been brought to the attention of white authorities.[118]

In September 1852, Fanny Randall, a free woman, was excluded from the First African Baptist Church for the serious offense of stabbing, but there is no evidence that she was ever examined in the mayor's court on this charge. It is probable that Fanny's victim chose not to report the attack to a magistrate, as it is unlikely that any stabbing would not have been considered serious enough to warrant a criminal investigation. It is also likely that the victim was black as it is improbable that a white victim would have considered reporting an offense to African American church authorities and especially not without also bringing the matter to the attention of the mayor. In all probability, therefore, the Randall case involved a black victim who chose to seek "justice" from the African Baptist Church rather than a secular court of law. A number of factors might have prompted this decision. This particular victim may have been intimidated by the thought of approaching white officers and taking her case through the white court system. Appearing before a committee of church deacons with whom she worshipped on a regular basis was likely a far less daunting prospect than an inquisition conducted by a magistrate. Alternatively, the victim may have believed that the corporal punishment Fanny would likely suffer if found guilty by the mayor was out of proportion to the severity of the crime. It is even possible that Fanny Randall's victim may specifically have wanted her assailant excluded from the church since, in the context of Richmond's black community and Fanny's own religious convictions, this would have been a particularly chastening sanction, more likely than a public whipping to reform Fanny from her violent ways. Implicit in all of these possibilities is the suggestion of an alternative black value system that was not reflected in the provisions of Virginia's criminal laws. Furthermore, although the precise motives that prompted African American victims to invoke religious discipline rather than judicial prosecutions were not recorded in the church minutes, it is clear that African Americans had a choice when deciding how to respond to crime.[119]

The judgments of Richmond's African Baptist churches were not only made in a more congenial context for black appellants and with greater concern for the rights of the accused than was apparent in the white-dominated law courts; they were also frequently based on a different standard of morality and distinct interpretations of crime and justice from those represented in the secular law. When Robert Johnson and John Trice were reported to the church deacons for visiting the circus, for example, they were reprimanded for immoral conduct on the grounds that attending a circus conflicted with the dictates of their religion. It is unclear whether Johnson and Trice were enslaved or free, but, in either case, had they been reported to white authorities, they would have been judged according to the criminal law on the basis of whether they had authority to be at the circus in the form of a pass from their owner or a register of their free status. The moral concerns that were paramount to the church would not have been a consideration in a lay court.[120]

The significant role that the African Baptist churches played in the regulation of Richmond's black community is made evident by comparing the investigations in the African churches with those conducted by the deacons of the white First Baptist Church. In purely numerical terms, fewer cases were brought before the First Baptist Church for adjudication than were handled by the African Baptist churches. In the nine-year period covering November 1851 to November 1860 for which records are available, only twenty-three white church members were investigated for behavior that might have been classed as criminal in a court of law. Eighteen of these cases involved drunkenness or retailing ardent spirits, and only one charge of violent crime and one of stealing were investigated.[121] The deacons of the First African Baptist Church examined a very different selection of criminal offenses than their white counterparts. In 1852 alone, church committees investigated at least twenty-two black Baptists for behavior that the law considered criminal.[122] Fourteen of the twenty-two were charged with violent crimes, six with drunkenness and disorderly conduct, and one each with gambling and theft. Furthermore, although there were no cases of adultery brought before the white First Baptist Church, incidents of marital infidelity were heard by the African Baptist churches on a regular basis.

The contrast between the types of cases investigated by the black and white churches is striking and indicates the unique role of the African churches in shaping black responses to crime in antebellum Richmond and as a force for order and justice within the black community. These were functions, however, that white society did not recognize. On the contrary, whites in Richmond commonly depicted organzed black religion as a root cause of African American criminality and disorder. The *Dispatch*, for example, drew attention to slaves examined in the mayor's court who were church members and claimed that "nearly every negro detected in stealing, is a member of some one of the African Churches."[123] Similarly, Mayor Joseph Tate noted with astonishment in the late 1830s that Edmund Taylor, a slave convicted of stealing, "is or was a Baptist Preacher," while George Washington, another slave thief, "says he has belonged to the Baptist Church for 5 years!"[124]

The African Baptist church deacons tried to ensure the accused a fair hearing independent of external influences and opinions. In operation and form, however, church examinations were greatly influenced by elements of the criminal trial that were fundamental to the operation of secular courts and that were also established practice in white Baptist churches. In the first place, the church established a committee to investigate each case and collect evidence for and against the accused. When the committee reported back to the church deacons with its recommendations, the case was debated and a vote taken. At least seven deacons had to be in attendance to form a quorum over which the pastor or any member of the church committee could preside. The role of the white pastor in church investigations is not entirely clear, but the constitution of the Ebenezer Baptist Church, Richmond's third African Baptist church, established in 1858, suggests that the pastor was not required to be present at disciplinary hearings, and that black deacons could therefore control all aspects of the examinations.[125]

Most church members were proud of their examining system and, much as the high standard of legal oratory displayed by white lawyers was remarked upon in newspapers and trial pamphlets, so the minutes of the First African Baptist Church noted the debating skills of black litigants. Commenting on the case of Peter Kelly, brought before the church on a charge of marrying a woman who had been married before and whose first husband was still alive, it was noted that, "the case was ably argued."[126]

The record of Peter Kelly's case illustrates other elements of the church examination that paralleled the practices of secular trial courts. For example, twenty-seven church deacons decided on the question of Kelly's guilt (Kelly was acquitted 14 to 13), indicating a voting system that compared favorably with the autocratic judgments passed by the mayor on African American defendants. Furthermore, it is also apparent from the Kelly case that an appeals process was in place in the African Baptist churches. In this instance, five deacons appealed against Kelly's acquittal, "the circumstances were again stated—and the arguments briefly recited, whereupon the decision of the church was confirmed by the whole committee."[127] Had Kelly initially been found guilty and excluded from church membership, he too could have appealed the sanction.

Although the African Baptist Church codes represented an alternative value system to that provided by the state criminal law, therefore, it is manifest that slaves and free blacks supported many Anglo-American legal norms.

This was not always the case in rural parts of the South, and particularly not in earlier periods, when African religious beliefs played a more prominent role in the black community's assessment of the guilt or innocence of alleged African American criminals. Throughout the nineteenth-century South, slaves continued to distinguish between "taking" property from their owners and "stealing," while slave preachers and conjurers exercised authority within the slave community according to a value system that diverged from that established in Virginia law.[128] Likewise, in Richmond the meaning of justice could be different for blacks and whites, yet by the late antebellum era and particularly in the urban context, this distinction no longer reflected the influence of an African conception of law and morality. On the contrary, although slaves had distinct attitudes toward, for example, theft from their masters, the manner in which black Richmonders responded to crime in the 1850s is suggestive of the degree to which blacks and whites had shared moral values and similar understandings of justice and the role of legal process. It was because African Americans understood that the legal system did not uphold these notions in cases involving black defendants that many chose not to report crimes at all or turned to alternative remedial forums such as the African Baptist churches.

In late antebellum Richmond, therefore, the relationship between religion and crime control within the black community was very different from that which may have existed in a plantation setting or during the colonial and early national periods. Although it is significant that African Americans relied on the African Baptist churches to examine and punish suspected criminals, their decisions to avoid the white-controlled courts were influenced by the obstacles that they confronted as both accusers and defendants in white courts, as much as by a distinctive African American morality. Like the black victims and defendants who used diverse tactics to assert their limited rights as legal agents in white dominated courtrooms, the investigations conducted by African Baptist churches demonstrated African Americans' understanding and commitment to common law ideals and testified to a black legal consciousness that contested the hegemony of the racist secular judicial system.

By the eve of the Civil War, Virginia legislators had created a judicial system that treated free African Americans in a manner more akin to slaves than free persons. Free black defendants were subject to harsher criminal and penal laws than whites, and in practice in Richmond they were consistently more likely to be convicted than whites for all types of criminal offense. This had disastrous consequences for individual men and women who were torn from their communities, separated from friends and families, forced to leave Virginia, whipped, imprisoned, and sold into slavery. Yet the shift toward more restrictive free black laws never went uncontested, and it was also complicated by structural inconsistencies that legislators could not fully resolve.

Free African Americans resisted the subservient role that the law afforded them in judicial processes. As defendants and complainants, they challenged the white ideal of black passivity and powerlessness before the law. Notably when in the role of victim they demonstrated clear understanding of their limited legal rights by selectively seeking redress through either the mayor's court or the church courts, depending on the circumstances of the crime.

In certain cases, free African Americans could also turn to white Virginians for help in defending themselves from the capriciousness of the legal system. Some white men and women, particularly among the legal fraternity but also on a more sporadic and case-by-case basis among the wider population, refused to endorse the complete eradication of the rights of free people, even if those free people were black. This was for practical, ideological, and personal reasons. The meaning of freedom was such that, irrespective of race, the enslavement of free persons could not be condoned even as a punishment for crime, except in the context of the extreme sectional tensions of the late 1850s. For similar reasons, the death penalty was not imposed on free blacks who had not been afforded a trial by jury and the protection of common law due process.

At a personal level, the support of many Richmonders for free blacks in criminal cases resulted less from faith in legal principles than from the close economic and social ties that developed across the color line in the city. Although there was considerable hostility between poor whites and blacks in Richmond, the urban environment also fostered sympathetic relationships across racial lines. Usually these relationships had little direct impact on specific criminal cases; rather, they contributed to a general current of opinion that could occasionally ameliorate the harsher aspects of the free black laws. In another sense, however, contacts across the color line dramatically altered the course of courtroom proceedings. As Richmond's mixed-race population grew, the dividing line between black and white in the city was blurred in a very literal way. This enabled some individuals classed as free African Americans to deny their racial identity in court and provided the clearest example of the difficulties that could arise in translating race-based statute laws into courtroom practice.

Epilogue

When the Civil War came to Richmond in April 1861, the city's crime problems multiplied. Acts of slave willfulness, disobedience, and resistance increased. In addition to the "crimes" that slaves had perpetrated against person, property, and their status throughout the antebellum period, during the war years Richmond slaves also worked as spies and provided critical information to the Union armies.[1] There was also a rise in white crime during the war, fueled by the economic distress of life on the home front and the presence in the local region of tens of thousands of Confederate troops, which was a boon to those involved in prostitution, gambling, and the sale of liquor. As the war progressed, refugees flooded into Richmond from across the South, and by 1863 the city's population had trebled to more than one hundred thousand. Poverty and food shortages followed, plaguing both blacks and whites, daily serving as a cause of petty crime and, in April 1863, leading to riots instigated by white women after their demands for bread were rejected by the Confederate government.[2]

The response of Richmond's police and courts to slave crime during the war was predictable; Mayor Mayo, who remained in office until the city was occupied by Union troops in April 1865, oversaw repeated increases in police numbers and enforced the city's black codes still more harshly than he had done in the 1850s. However, wartime conditions also prompted greater regulation of the white community. Under the command of J. H. Winder, a former major in the United States Army, it was alleged that the police interfered as never before in the lives of white Richmonders. Even slaveholders who continued to permit self-hire in contravention of the municipal ordinances, were prosecuted more rigorously than before the war.[3] In response to the Bread Riots, Richmond's civic authorities took extreme steps to maintain order among the white population, turning the public guard, so long a defense against slave rebellion in the city, against the rioters. That many of the rioters were white women only exaggerated the extent to which wartime necessity overwhelmed the imperative of reconciling law enforcement with southern racial and gender ideals.

Conflicts on the home front severely weakened the southern war effort, and the failure to regulate crime and disorder was part of the social instability within the Confederacy that contributed to, if it did not cause, the defeat of the South and the abolition of slavery.[4] Long before the first shots were fired on Fort Sumter, however, matters of crime and punishment had exposed tensions within Richmond's urban slave society. Criminal law in the antebellum South was always a tool of the slaveholding elite that was intended to support slavery as a system as well as to control crime. However, the law was a tool over which slaveholders had complete mastery only in the abstract world of the statute books. Irrespective of the extent to which rules of evidence and due process were violated in the course of criminal prosecutions, in practice the outcome and implications of criminal trials were unpredictable and shaped by factors outside the courtroom, as well as by the law itself.

Although prosecutions and fear of crime increased in Richmond during the antebellum decades, most whites in the city believed that the criminal justice system worked well enough. Most importantly, slave defendants were rarely afforded any semblance of due process or rights in the courtroom and consequently were usually found guilty and sentenced to violent punishments. Yet this alone did not mean that the administration of criminal law in all cases helped to support the slave regime. The judicial system mattered in Richmond not only due to the extent that it could be used to control crime but also because of the issues that the city's residents were forced to confront when suspected criminals appeared in court. In part, Richmond's courtrooms were mirrors that reflected problematic aspects of urban slave control and white class relations; they revealed the discontent of the slave population, the mutual class interests of African Americans and poor whites, and the malleability of racial identities. More than this, however, the judicial system itself exacerbated these problems, often at one and the same time as it struggled to maintain the racial divide on which southern slavery was based.

Richmond's courtrooms were always political arenas where ideologies of race and understandings of urban slavery were constructed and contested by slaves, poor whites, and free African Americans, as well as by slaveholders. When John Williams stood trial for the murder of Virginia Winston, the evidence arrayed against him revealed the extent to which urban living eroded slaveholders' ability to regulate slaves' day-to-day activities. When nonslaveholding whites witnessed Charles Cook laboring in chains on the city streets, they were shown that the color of their skin would not always ensure their social superiority over African Americans. Similarly, when they read in the *Richmond Dispatch* about slaves convicted of murder being spared the gallows and instead being sentenced to sale and transportation out of the state, some concluded that the courts and the executive were more concerned with favoring the interests of the slaveholding elite than enforcing laws designed to serve the interests of all white Virginians.

It would be simplistic to describe crime and punishment in antebellum Richmond as representative either of the South or of cities in general. Rather, as in almost all other aspects of its economic, social, and cultural life, so too with regards to criminal justice Richmond was an anomaly. Matters of slavery and race relations shaped profoundly Virginia's criminal laws and also the way in which they were enforced in an urban context. The law's primary function was always to uphold white supremacy and protect property in slaves, as much as it was to control crime. In this regard, Richmonders' experiences of arrests, trials, and punishments were not as unrepresentative of the southern states as the ironworks, tobacco factories, and flour mills that lined the James River and distinguished Richmond from both its rural hinterland and other southern cities that were not so heavily industrialized. Yet developments connected to the processes of urbanization and industrialization meant that the anomalies and weaknesses in Virginia's race-based criminal law were more apparent in the city than anywhere else in the state. In part, this was because social and economic conditions in Richmond made the law a more pervasive presence in the city than in rural Virginia. Because informal methods of crime control were insufficient and sometimes inappropriate for controlling crime in an urban-industrial context, Richmond's magistrates, unlike their rural counterparts, could not avoid the contradictions inherent in Virginia's statutes simply by disregarding law altogether.

More than this, urban social and economic conditions meant that cases arising in Richmond were especially likely to involve those parts of Virginia law based on a division between black and white that in practice were problematic to enforce. A case such as the murder trial of Elizabeth Southard, which revolved around the racial identity of the accused, could have arisen in any county in Virginia, but it was always most likely to occur in Richmond due to the city's diverse and transient population, large free black community, and extensive interracial subculture. For similar reasons, although the laws prohibiting black testimony against whites might lead to white criminals evading conviction anywhere in Virginia, they were most likely to do so in Richmond.

Criminal justice in Richmond warrants comparison not only with rural areas of Virginia but also with other cities in the slave states. Richmond was representative of the urban South in its dependence on formal judicial mechanisms to regulate crime. The anonymity of urban life and the breakdown of traditional community bonds made crime control very different in urban as opposed to rural areas throughout the antebellum United States.

However, there were also important variations in forms of crime control in different urban jurisdictions across the South. These were less the result of variations between cities than a consequence of distinctive state laws. In particular, Virginia's oyer and terminer slave courts, which by the 1850s were unique in the South in denying slaves charged with felonies a trial by jury and that consequently gave slaveholders an unprecedented degree of leverage over courtroom proceedings, meant that far more slaves stood trial in Richmond than in other southern cities.

As Richmond grew as a commercial, industrial, and urban center, it experienced and responded to crime in many ways that were similar to developments in northern cities: property crimes made up an increasing portion of the trial docket; more police officers patrolled the streets; trials became more complex and time consuming; new courts were established; court sessions were held more frequently; and the prison population grew. Neither were disproportionately high rates of black convictions and, in the case of free defendants, prison sentences, unique to Richmond; racial bias was also a feature of northern law enforcement. In Philadelphia, for example, African Americans accounted for one-third of prisoners in 1850 even though they comprised only 5 percent of the city population.[5] However great the similarities in the administration of criminal law, however, in the North patterns of crime and punishment had very different implications than they had in a slave city where a racial divide was the basis of the social order. Northern criminal law was not concerned with upholding notions of white supremacy, at least not overtly. Nor was it especially preoccupied by serving slaveholder property interests, and it was not faced with the legal complexities of dealing with people who were also property. Undoubtedly, other considerations and group interests vied with crime control in shaping how criminal justice was administered in the North, but they did so according to entirely different dynamics than in southern slave societies. In this regard, it would be misleading to overstate the extent to which crime and punishment in Richmond was more similar to northern than southern cities. Irrespective of statistics, the most fundamental distinction in urban crime and punishment was always along sectional lines.

After Emancipation, the law assumed a more pervasive role in policing the African American population throughout the former slave states and particularly in the region's urban areas. As the criminal law existed on the statute books in Virginia, the racial bifurcation that had characterized the antebellum period was eroded. In February 1866, the Virginia legislature repealed those parts of the criminal code that provided separate offenses, trial pro-

Fig. 13. "Richmond, Virginia. Group of Negroes ("Freedmen") by canal" 1865. Courtesy of Library of Congress, Prints and Photographs online, Civil War glass negative collection. <http://hdl.loc.gov/loc.pnp/cwpb.00468>

ceedings, and punishments for African Americans, and enacted legislation that made all Virginians subject to the same trial and penal systems. However, in practice racial discrimination against black defendants and victims of crime persisted. Although the Virginia Supreme Court typically upheld black rights in the few cases on which it ruled, at the local level it was far from certain that African American defendants would receive a fair trial. In a context of continued white dominance of the administration of justice, pervasive fear of black crime, and entrenched social inequality, it is unsurprising that between 1870 and 1901 black convicts constituted 78 percent of all new inmates incarcerated in the Virginia state penitentiary. With black Virginians routinely excluded from jury service, except in cases of black-on-black crime; unable to rely on the law to protect their person and property rigorously; and routinely sentenced more harshly than whites, the criminal justice system remained a bastion of white supremacy through much of the twentieth century.[6]

In addition to the legal system, the fear and reality of mob violence and lynching were widely used to regulate black conduct in the late nineteenth century. As was the case under slavery, from the perspective of African Americans after the Civil War, the division between formal and informal means of crime control was in practice often slight. Like the arbitrary punishments formerly imposed by slaveholders, lynching served in the New South as an extension of the violence and discrimination that transpired in the courtrooms with the sanction of the law.

However, patterns of crime and punishment in the South were no more uniform in the era of Jim Crow than they had been during slavery. Incidents of mob violence and lynching were not as prevalent in postbellum Virginia as they were in the Deep South, and this represents a notable continuity in responses to crime before and after the Civil War, not only in Richmond but also in Virginia more generally. The relative infrequency of lynching in the state after the Civil War may have been in part a consequence of the clear racial divide that had existed in the criminal justice system in the antebellum period and conditioned whites to using law as a means to control black crime.[7] This was in stark contrast to the situation in Deep South states, such as Mississippi, where, historically, there was less distinction between the trial and punishment of blacks and whites and where slaveholders consequently used the law only rarely to control slave crime.[8] To borrow terms coined to characterize race relations in the Reconstruction era, Virginia practiced a *segregated* form of criminal justice in the antebellum period, while in states like Mississippi, African Americans were more often *excluded* from the justice system altogether.[9]

Race remained the determining factor in the administration of criminal justice in Virginia and the rest of the South throughout much of the twentieth century. As during the antebellum era, the judicial system supported white supremacy both at the local level and in federal courts. However, law was also increasingly turned against the southern racial order, notably in appellate cases led by organizations as varied as the National Association for the Advancement of Colored People and the American Communist Party.[10] Since the late 1960s, the overt racial discrimination that once characterized the enforcement of the criminal law has diminished, but the relationship between race and the judicial system in the United States remains complex and controversial and continues to change. The disproportionate rates at which African Americans are imprisoned and executed in the United States today indicate that race remains a salient factor in judicial proceedings even though it has been purged from the statute books. It cannot be taken for granted that a criminal law that upholds principles of justice and racial equality in theory is consistent with those ideals in practice. In the antebellum South, a similar legal reality prevailed, albeit in relation to very different ideals. White legislators could pass any number of laws that discriminated against slaves and free African Americans, supported white supremacy, and guarded the foundations of slave society. However, judges, jurors, attorneys, and police officers faced a constant struggle to ensure that the way in which the criminal law was enforced served these aims in practice. In Richmond, their record of success in this struggle was decidedly mixed.

Appendix A

Hustings Court Misdemeanor Cases, 1830–1860

Table 1: Property offenses

Type of offense	Number of cases	Cases that did not reach trial				Cases tried by jury		
		Guilty plea	Judgment by court	Nolle prosequi	Other	Guilty	Not guilty	Guilty (%)
Arson	2	0	0	0	1	0	1	0.0
Breaking and entering	9	1	0	1	0	6	1	85.7
Damaging property	32	2	0	12	1	11	6	64.7
Forgery, counterfeiting, fraud	33	3	0	21	0	8	1	88.9
Receiving stolen goods	90	2	1	32	7	27	21	56.3
Stealing	251	40	2	60	5	114	30	79.2
Total	417	48	3	126	14	166	60	73.5

Source: Richmond Hustings Court Minutes, 1830–60.

Table 2. Violent offenses

Type of offense	Number of cases	Cases that did not reach trial				Cases tried by jury		
		Guilty plea	Judgment by court	Nolle prosequi	Other	Guilty	Not guilty	Guilty (%)
Assault	415	2	8	163	9	203	30	87.1
Dueling	5	0	0	5	0	0	0	—
Fighting	13	0	0	9	0	3	1	75.0
Robbery	2	0	0	1	0	0	1	0.0
Shooting	5	0	0	0	0	2	3	40.0
Total	440	2	8	178	9	208	35	85.6

Source: Richmond Hustings Court Minutes, 1830–60.

Table 3. Gambling offenses

Type of offense	Number of cases	Cases that did not reach trial				Cases tried by jury		
		Guilty plea	Judgment by court	Nolle prosequi	Other	Guilty	Not guilty	Gui (%)
Cheating at gambling	12	0	0	4	0	3	5	37
Exhibiting gambling	375	2	4	309	24	23	13	63
Gambling	819	63	161	462	7	118	8	93
Total	1,206	65	165	775	31	144	26	84

Source: Richmond Hustings Court Minutes, 1830–60.

Table 4. Slavery/race-related offenses

Type of offense	Number of cases	Cases that did not reach trial				Cases tried by jury		
		Guilty plea	Judgment by court	Nolle prosequi	Other	Guilty	Not guilty	Guil (%)
Helping a slave abscond	30	0	0	16	8	6	0	100
Remaining in the Commonwealth contrary to law	124	2	1	103	4	14	0	100
Permitting a slave to hire himself out	96	18	39	11	9	18	1	94
Permitting an unlawful assembly of slaves or free blacks	48	13	2	14	0	15	4	78
Selling ardent spirits to a slave	4	0	0	0	0	4	0	100
Providing a slave with a free pass	3	0	0	0	1	1	1	50
Bringing a free African American into Virginia	3	0	0	0	0	1	2	33
Other	6	0	0	1	2	3	0	100
Total	314	33	42	145	24	62	8	88

Source: Richmond Hustings Court Minutes, 1830–60.

Table 5. Other offenses

Type of offense	Number of cases	Cases that did not reach trial				Cases tried by jury		
		Guilty plea	Judgment by court	Nolle prosequi	Other	Guilty	Not guilty	Guilty (%)
Keeping a disorderly house	33	0	0	12	1	17	3	85.0
Retailing ardent spirits without a license/ keeping an ordinary without a license	753	61	35	448	15	169	25	87.1
Retailing goods without a license	184	20	12	124	8	18	2	90.0
Improper sexual conduct	17	0	3	2	6	4	2	66.7
Obstructing the course of justice	32	1	3	11	6	7	4	63.6
Causing a public nuisance	25	0	0	15	3	6	1	85.7
Other	83	0	7	34	18	19	5	79.2
Total	1127	82	60	646	57	240	42	85.1

Source: Richmond Hustings Court Minutes, 1830–60.

Appendix B

Richmond Circuit Superior Court Cases, 1852–1860

Table 1: Property offenses

Type of offense	Number of cases	Cases that did not reach trial			Cases tried by jury		
		Guilty plea	Prosecution dropped[a]	Unknown	Guilty	Guilty of lesser crime	Not guilty
Arson	2	0	1	0	1	0	0
Breaking and entering	9	1	0	3	4	1	0
Burglary	8	0	0	0	6	1	1
Forgery, fraud, and counterfeiting	48	2	18	4	14	0	10
Issuing small notes	6	0	6	0	0	0	0
Receiving stolen goods	10	0	4	0	3	0	3
Stealing	88	2	7	17	42	6	14
Total	171	5	36	24	70	8	28

Sources: Richmond Hustings Court Minutes, 1852–60; *Richmond Daily Dispatch*, 1852–60.

Note: These sources were used in the absence of the circuit court records, which were destroyed in 1865. The Richmond Hustings Court Minutes provided details of every case sent on to be heard in the circuit court, while the court reports published in the *Dispatch* recorded the final outcome of each case. Most of the cases listed as "unknown" were probably dropped before coming to court and hence were not mentioned in the press.

[a] Prosecution dropped includes cases in which a nolle prosequi was entered, the grand jury found no true bill, the charge was quashed, or the trial jury was discharged.

Table 2: Violent offenses

Type of offense	Number of cases	Cases that did not reach trial			Cases tried by jury		
		Guilty plea	Prosecution dropped[a]	Unknown	Guilty	Guilty of lesser crime	Not guilty
Assault	14	0	2	7	2	0	3
Kidnapping	1	0	0	0	1	0	0
Murder	21	0	5	1	2	9	4
Rape	3	0	0	0	2	0	1
Robbery	6	0	2	1	1	0	2
Shooting	10	0	0	1	6	1	2
Stabbing	46	0	6	11	15	2	12
Total	101	0	15	21	29	12	24

Sources: Richmond Hustings Court Minutes, 1852–60; *Richmond Daily Dispatch*, 1852–60.
[a]Prosecution dropped includes cases in which a nolle prosequi was entered, the grand jury found no true bill, the charge was quashed, or the trial jury was discharged.

Table 3: Slave-related and other offenses

Type of offense	Number of cases	Cases that did not reach trial			Cases tried by jury		
		Guilty plea	Prosecution dropped[a]	Unknown	Guilty	Guilty of lesser crime	Not guilty
Aiding and abetting a slave to steal	1	0	1	0	0	0	0
Helping a slave abscond	5	0	0	4	1	0	0
Perjury	1	0	0	0	0	0	1
Stealing a slave	1	0	0	0	1	0	0
Total	8	0	1	4	2	0	1

Source: Richmond Hustings Court Minutes, 1852–60; *Richmond Daily Dispatch*, 1852–60.
[a]Prosecution dropped includes cases in which a nolle prosequi was entered, the grand jury found no true bill, the charge was quashed, or the trial jury was discharged.

Notes

Abbreviations

ALUVA   Alderman Library, University of Virginia, Charlottesville.
LVA   Library of Virginia, Richmond.
MCDB   Mayor's Court Docket Book, Valentine Museum, Richmond.
RHCEC   Richmond Hustings Court Ended Causes, Library of Virginia, Richmond.
RHCM   Richmond Hustings Court Minutes, Library of Virginia, Richmond.
VHS   Virginia Historical Society, Richmond.

Preface

1. On antebellum Virginia's race-based criminal laws, see Minor, *A Synopsis of the Law of Crimes and Punishments in Virginia*; Schwarz, *Twice Condemned*; and Guild, *Black Laws of Virginia*. In no other state was the division between black and white trial procedures and punishments drawn so starkly as in Virginia. See Morris, *Southern Slavery and the Law*; Ayers, *Vengeance and Justice*.

Introduction

1. Ellyson, *Ellyson's Business Directory*, 1845, 14–15.
2. On Richmond's economic growth between the Revolution and the Civil War, see Gregg Kimball, *American City, Southern Place*, 15–24; and Goldfield, *Urban Growth in the Age of Sectionalism*.
3. U.S. Census, Richmond City, 1830–60.
4. See, for example, Ayers, *Vengeance and Justice*; Stansell, *City of Women*; and Steinberg, *The Transformation of Criminal Justice*.
5. Studies of urban slavery are extensive. See, for example, Goldin, *Urban Slavery*; Takagi, *Rearing Wolves*; and Wade, *Slavery in the Cities*. The most comprehensive work on slave hiring is Martin, *Divided Mastery*.
6. A powerful argument as to the importance of rural community networks in binding nonslaveholding whites to the slaveholders' cause is made by Fields, "Slavery, Race, and Ideology," 108–11. See also Wyatt-Brown, *Southern Honor*, 370.
7. Gregg Kimball, *American City, Southern Place*; Link, *Roots of Secession*. On white class relations in other antebellum southern cities, see Bellows, *Benevolence among Slaveholders*; and Lockley, *Lines in the Sand*.
8. The development of criminal justice in the southern cities of, respectively, Savannah, Vicksburg, and New Orleans, is discussed in Ayers, *Vengeance and Justice*; Waldrep, *Roots of Disorder*; and Rousey, *Policing the Southern City*. Studies by

Christopher Morris and Crawford, among others, have shown that by the 1850s, as railroads pushed into the southern interior, facilitating trade with coastal seaports and diversifying the economy and population, the rural South was also shaped by the forces of market capitalism. Nevertheless, these processes had a negligible impact on rural forms of criminal justice, which during the antebellum period were increasingly distinct from those in southern cities. See Christopher Morris, *Becoming Southern*, xiv; Crawford, *Ashe County's Civil War*, 38; and Reidy, *From Slavery to Agrarian Capitalism*, 83–86.

9. The real rate of crime in antebellum Richmond cannot be known. The court records provide an indication of the amount and type of criminal activity that occurred in the city, but nothing more. As in all societies, most crimes committed in Richmond went unrecorded, while the cases that did come to the attention of the courts reveal as much about the priorities and efficiency of the judicial system as the true levels and types of crime in the city. See King, *Crime, Justice, and Discretion*, 1.

10. See, for example, Fede, *People without Rights*; and Higginbotham, *Shades of Freedom*. For an argument that southern courts in many cases also aimed to serve the ends of justice, see Nash, "Fairness and Formalism," and "Reason of Slavery." The term "herrenvolk democracy" was influentially used in the context of the antebellum South by the historian George Fredrickson, who argued that, in southern slave society, white social relations were based on "a racially circumscribed affirmation of democracy and equality" (*The Arrogance of Race*, 138–40). See also Wyatt-Brown, *Southern Honor*; and Wayne, "Old South Morality Play," 839–40.

11. Roediger, *The Wages of Whiteness*, 13; Fredrickson, *The Arrogance of Race*, 138–40.

12. Important exceptions are Ayers, *Vengeance and Justice*; Waldrep, *Roots of Disorder*; and Fede, *People without Rights*.

13. Sydnor, "The Southerner and the Laws," 8.

14. Genovese, *Roll, Jordan, Roll*, 25–49, 685; Hindus, *Prison and Plantation*, 1–2; Sydnor, "The Southerner and the Laws"; Wyatt-Brown, "Community, Class, and Snopesian Crime," 174–77; Wayne, "Old South Morality Play," 858.

15. Ayers, *Vengeance and Justice*; Waldrep, *Roots of Disorder*.

16. Kairys, introduction to his *Politics of Law*, 6.

17. James Scott, *Domination and the Arts of Resistance*, 81; Edwards, "Law, Domestic Violence, and the Limits of Patriarchal Authority," 741.

18. Gross, "Beyond Black and White," 655; Block, "Lines of Color, Sex, and Service"; Cole, "Keeping the Peace"; Walter Johnson, "Inconsistency, Contradiction, and Complete Confusion"; Waldrep, *Roots of Disorder*, 37. See also Rice, "Crime and Punishment in Frederick County and Maryland," 354; and Friedman and Percival, *The Roots of Justice*, 13–14.

Chapter 1. Abandoned to "causes of corruption":
Slave Life and Policing in the City

1. Joseph P. Winston was a partner in the firm Nace & Winston, grocers and commission merchants. Reports of the murder identified Philip B. Winston of Hanover County as Joseph's father. This may be the same Philip B. Winston who is listed in Montague's *Richmond Directory and Business Advertiser for 1852* as a deputy sheriff of Henrico County.

2. *Particulars of the Dreadful Tragedy in Richmond*, 5.

3. *Enquirer*, 20 Jul. 1852.

4. *Dispatch*, 21 Jul. 1852.

5. *Whig*, 26 Jul. 1852.

6. *Dispatch*, 26 Jul. 1852.

7. Ibid., 21 Jul. 1852.

8. Ibid., 15 Sept. 1852. On the links between Richmond's black community and Liberia, see Gregg Kimball, *American City, Southern Place*, 143–47.

9. *Dispatch*, 11 Sept. and 23 Oct. 1852.

10. On slave resistance in southern cities, see Takagi, *Rearing Wolves*, 6; Wade, *Slavery in the Cities*, 16–19; Genovese, *The Political Economy of Slavery*, 23; Starobin, *Industrial Slavery*, 115; Stampp, *The Peculiar Institution*, 84; Goldin, *Urban Slavery*; 8–10; Goldfield, *Urban Growth*, 137; and Whitman, *The Price of Freedom*, 163; Fields, *Slavery and Freedom*, 54–55; Ashworth, *Slavery, Capitalism, and Politics*, 92.

11. Historians have devoted much less attention to judicial processes dealing with petty slave crime than to more serious cases, particularly those that came before an appellate court and consequently left far more detailed records. Exceptions are Schafer, "Slaves and Crime"; Wade, *Slavery in the Cities*, 182–95; and Howington, *What Sayeth the Law*, 98–115. Most studies of slavery in the South argue that in rural plantation regions slaves' conduct was regulated informally by their owners or overseers and only in exceptional cases of very serious crime did the law intervene. See, for example, Ayers, *Vengeance and Justice*, 135. For an exception to this rule, see Hindus, "Black Justice under White Law."

12. These records include a docket book kept by Mayor Joseph Tate from 1836 to 1839, as well as reports in the *Dispatch*, which recorded figures of monthly arrests and details of mayor's court cases heard between 1852 and 1860. There is no conclusive evidence that the *Dispatch* recorded every case heard by the mayor, and probably a small number were missed. However, there is every reason to believe that the record of cases in the *Dispatch* is close to comprehensive. The paper reported as a matter of routine even the most trivial offenses that the mayor investigated, and on the rare days when no report of the mayor's court proceedings was published, the *Dispatch* informed its readers that this was because no cases had been heard. MCDB, 1836–39; *Dispatch*, 1852–60.

13. *Particulars of the Dreadful Tragedy in Richmond*, 32–33.

14. Ibid., 36.

15. Berlin and Gutman, "Natives and Immigrants," 1181–82. Historians remain

divided on why the overall urban slave population declined during the antebellum period. For contrasting views, see, for example, Wade, *Slavery in the Cities*, 16–26; Goldin, *Urban Slavery*, 9; and Ashworth, *Slavery, Capitalism, and Politics*, 92.

16. Montague, *Richmond Directory and Business Advertiser for 1850–1851*, 14; Green, "Industrial Transition in the Land of Chattel Slavery," 241.

17. Green, "Black Tobacco Factory Workers," 186–87; Wade, *Slavery in the Cities*, 38–43 and 48–54; Gregg Kimball, *American City, Southern Place*, 27–30; Fogel, Galantine, and Manning, *Without Consent or Contract*, 77; Takagi, *Rearing Wolves*, 78.

18. Takagi, *Rearing Wolves*, 37.

19. *Dispatch*, 27 Oct. 1852.

20. Charles W. Montague to Frances Thruston Hughes, Richmond, 23 Nov. 1845, Montague Family Papers, 1808–1939, VHS. Robert Starobin has argued that industrial slaves were subject to especially harsh treatment as they were not protected by bonds of paternalism (*Industrial Slavery*, 11, 135). The debate over slave hiring, cash payments, and living arrangements persisted in Richmond throughout the 1850s. Municipal ordinances against self-hire and the board system were introduced in 1857 and 1858 but had a limited impact, and the practices continued until emancipation. See Schnittman, "Slavery in Virginia's Urban Tobacco Industry," chap. 6.

21. As Susan Schnittman has argued, "slaves needed bonuses to survive and probably would not work without them. . . . The bonus had come to be seen by slaves as a right rather than a privilege, as a necessity rather than an option subject to the whim of the employer" ("Slavery in Virginia's Urban Tobacco Industry," 222–23, quoted in Ashworth, *Slavery, Capitalism, and Politics*, 110–11 n. 51).

22. *Dispatch*, 23 Dec. 1857.

23. Takagi, *Rearing Wolves*, 79–80. On the sensitivity of urban crime rates in the South to international market forces, see Ayers, *Vengeance and Justice*, 93–94.

24. RHCM, 1830–60

25. "Message II," *Governor's Biennial Messages to the General Assembly of the State of Virginia, December 5, 1859*. For other complaints about slave hiring in 1850s Richmond, see Schnittman, "Slavery in Virginia's Urban Tobacco Industry," 307–9. On John Brown's raid, see John Scott and Robert Scott, *John Brown of Harper's Ferry*.

26. The last fine of fifty dollars for permitting slave self-hire was imposed on Branch Saunders in 1842. See RHCM, 16 Dec. 1842. Although some slaveholders faced multiple charges of permitting slave self-hire, possibly relating to different days on which the offense was committed, none was convicted in more than one case. The fine for permitting slave self-hire was less than whites in Richmond were fined for offenses such as selling goods without a license or gambling.

27. Gregg Kimball, *American City, Southern Place*, xviii.

28. Takagi, *Rearing Wolves*, 87–93; Haunton, "Law and Order in Savannah, 1850–1860," 2.

29. *Dispatch*, 25 Sept. 1857; Cole, "Changes for Mrs. Thornton's Arthur," 373–74.

30. Franklin and Schweninger, *Runaway Slaves*, 125–26.

31. *Dispatch*, 21 and 22 Jul. 1852.

32. Starobin argued that a majority of industrial slave runaways were absent for only a short time before returning voluntarily to their jobs (*Industrial Slavery*, 82). White employers contributed to the problem of runaways in Richmond by hiring slaves who claimed to be free and by failing to check their documents. See *Dispatch*, 16 Mar. 1860.

33. Aptheker, *American Negro Slave Revolts*; Egerton, *Gabriel's Rebellion*; Greenberg, *Nat Turner*; Pearson, *Designs against Charleston*.

34. *Ordinances of the Corporation of the City of Richmond* (1831), 114–17.

35. *Dispatch*, 29 Jul. 1856.

36. RHCM, 13 Nov. 1841.

37. Dr. George Watson to Nancy Watson, Richmond, 13 Sept. 1817, Watson Family Papers, VHS.

38. *Particulars of the Dreadful Tragedy in Richmond*, 32.

39. *Dispatch*, 21 Jul. 1852.

40. In the 1840s, twenty-eight slaves were charged with violent felonies.

41. Trotti, "Murder and the Modern Sensibility," 81–86.

42. RHCM, 1830–50. During the 1850s, only nine slave defendants were recorded as being hired out, a figure that is so low as to suggest that the clerks of the court did not systematically record this information after 1850. Almost all of the eighty-three slaves whose owners were positively identified as non-Richmond residents in the court records were from central Tidewater counties, indicating that they were self hired; that they had been sent to Richmond as part of their regular duties, perhaps to buy or sell goods or run an errand of some kind; or that they had traveled to the city without their owner's consent. Forty-one of the eighty-three slaves were owned by slaveholders in Hanover and Henrico Counties, but slaves with owners in twenty-three other counties were also tried for felonies between 1830 and 1850.

43. RHCM, 1830–50.

44. On free African Americans and Richmond's criminal justice system, see chapter 5 in this volume.

45. *Dispatch*, 1 Oct. 1855 and 4 Mar. 1856.

46. Ibid., 3 Sept., 11 Oct., 3 Dec. 1856; 2 Jan., 24 Sept. 1857. See also O'Brien, "Factory, Church, and Community," 510. Increased police surveillance of slaves in the 1850s occurred throughout the South. See, for example, Lack, "An Urban Slave Community," 259.

47. *Dispatch*, 12 Apr. 1853. Joshua Rothman has claimed that white criminals were especially likely to be dealt with at the watch houses "since whites convicted of misdemeanors were subject primarily to fines, which could easily be collected on the spot if the accused had access to the money." However, when the number of mayor's

court cases is compared with the total number of arrests made in Richmond, it is apparent that slaves were also punished and discharged at the cage. In 1856, a total of 1,051 slaves were arrested in Richmond, but, in the sample year of 1860, just 236 mayor's court slave cases were reported in the *Dispatch*. Only three slaves appeared in the mayor's court in 1860 charged with being without a pass, and just three more were charged with unlawful assembly, suggesting that most slaves accused of these and similar offenses were not examined in the mayor's office. The paucity of slave-pass cases in Mayor Tate's docket book indicates that watch-house examinations of arrested slaves may also have been common in the late 1830s. Rothman, *Notorious in the Neighborhood*, 100.

48. In the three sample years of 1838, 1852, and 1860, a total of only sixteen slaves were examined in the mayor's court for drunkenness.

49. *Dispatch*, 19 Jul. 1853.

50. Wade, *Slavery in the Cities*, 185.

51. Arthur Howington similarly found that justice for slaves charged with trivial offenses in the recorder's court in Memphis, Tennessee, was "informal, swift, and relatively certain." Howington concluded that "the thrust of such proceedings clearly was less to insure justice than it was to control crime by inflicting punishment" (*What Sayeth the Law*, 104, 115).

52. *Dispatch*, 13 Feb. 1852 and 15 Feb. 1853; MCDB, 11 Feb. 1837 and 9 Sept. 1837, 110, 188. On a similar lack of due process in South Carolina, see Hindus, *Prison and Plantation*, 142.

53. MCDB, 6 Oct. 1837, 198.

54. *Dispatch*, 14 Sept. 1852.

55. MCDB, 26 May 1836, 13; *Dispatch*, 15 Jul. 1852.

56. *Dispatch*, 1 May 1860.

57. Howington, *What Sayeth the Law*, 114. In Memphis, the recorder court was the equivalent of Richmond mayor court.

58. MCDB, 1838; *Dispatch*, 1860. It is probable, though unverifiable, that slaves examined at the watch houses were also more likely than whites to be convicted.

59. In 1852, fifty-five out of seventy-three slaves in the mayor court for nonfelonious stealing were sentenced to the maximum punishment of thirty-nine lashes compared to only ten out of sixty-eight in 1838. Figures are not available for 1860 since in that year, although the *Dispatch* specified when slaves were sentenced to corporal punishment, it rarely recorded the precise number of lashes to be inflicted. *Dispatch*, 1852.

60. Mayo's increasing use of watch-house examinations most likely explains why, after 1852, cases of slave-pass violations disappeared from the pages of the *Dispatch*. This casts doubt on the claim of the economist Claudia Goldin that, after 1854, the pass laws were rarely enforced in Richmond (*Urban Slavery*, 48–49).

61. Manarin, *Richmond at War*, 627.

62. *Dispatch*, 3 Sept., 11 Oct., 3 Dec. 1856; 2 Jan., 24 Sept. 1857. See also O'Brien, "Factory, Church, and Community," 510.

63. *Dispatch*, 2 May 1860.

64. In the late 1850s, whites were both arrested *and* appeared before the mayor at a rate of about thirty-eight per one thousand of population. By contrast, slaves were arrested at an average rate of eighty-five per one thousand between 1856 and 1859, but just nineteen per one thousand appeared in court. Approximately half of arrested free blacks were brought before the mayor. *Dispatch*, 1856–60. For additional arrests data see table 1.3.

65. Tripp, *Yankee Town, Southern City*, 20–21.

66. MCDB, 2 May 1836, 1.

67. Ibid., 6 Jun. 1837, 153.

68. *Dispatch*, 22 Jan. 1852.

69. MCDB, 21 May 1838, 270.

70. Ibid., 24 Sept. 1837, 193. See also the protests of Joseph D. James against the arrest of his slave Edmund, MCDB, 14 Sept. 1838, 322.

71. *Dispatch*, 25 Apr. 1853.

72. Ibid., 26 Apr. 1853.

73. MCDB, 30 Mar. 1837 and 13 Mar. 1838, 128, 243.

74. *Dispatch*, 16 Feb. 1858.

75. Sally Hadden cites the comments of the former slave Charles Mitchell, who "remembered that Lynchburg patrols could whip slaves, unlike patrols in the countryside, who had to take the truant country slave to a justice of the peace before the whipping could be administered" (*Slave Patrols*, 40, 61).

76. Flanigan, *The Criminal Law of Slavery and Freedom*, 118.

77. *Dispatch*, 20 Dec. 1859. A.E.K. Nash argued that southern appellate courts insisted on slave defendants' right to counsel "regardless of the master's property interests." There were no such rulings in Virginia, however, as slave cases could not be appealed to the general court ("Fairness and Formalism," 84).

78. Cobb, *An Inquiry into the Law of Negro Slavery*, 268–69. See also Denham, *Rogue's Paradise*, 132.

79. *Dispatch*, 16 Sept. 1852.

80. MCDB, 1 Dec. 1837, 217.

81. *Commonwealth v. Henry Matthews* and *Commonwealth v. James Robinson*, 11 Sept. 1851, RHCM.

82. MCDB, 30 Jun. 1836, 26.

83. Ibid., 30 May 1836, 14.

84. *Dispatch*, 4 Jan. 1853.

85. Ibid., 12 and 14 Mar. 1859.

86. Schnittman, "Slavery in Virginia's Urban Tobacco Industry," 336.

87. Jones, *Born a Child of Freedom*, 35. See also Stampp, *The Peculiar Institution*, 161; Grimstead, *American Mobbing*, 98–99; and Link, *Roots of Secession*, 40–41.

88. Thomas Morris, *Southern Slavery and the Law*, 192.

89. Jones, *Born a Child of Freedom*, 27.

90. On the conflict between paternalism as an ideal and in practice, see Jones,

Born a Child of Freedom, 20; Dusinberre, *Them Dark Days*, 431–36; Tadman, *Speculators and Slaves*, xx; and Christopher Morris, "The Articulation of Two Worlds," 987.

91. This interpretation differs from that of the historian Steven Tripp, who argues in his study of Lynchburg, Virginia, that slaveholders turned to local law enforcement agencies only when slaves rejected their paternalistic overtures (*Yankee Town, Southern City*, 20–21).

92. *Dispatch*, 19 May 1852.

93. Ibid., 29 Jul. 1856.

94. MCDB, 28 Apr. 1838, 259. See also the cases of Julia and George, MCDB, 25 May 1837 and 6 Feb. 1838, 145, 236.

95. Some slaveholders prohibited hirers from inflicting any corporal punishment on their slaves. See Martin, *Divided Mastery*, 132.

96. MCDB, 12 Nov. 1836, 85.

97. By no means were all slaveholders averse to hirers inflicting punishment on their slaves. Elkanah Talley, a slaveholder in Hanover County who hired her slave Nead to Benjamin Brand in Richmond, wrote Brand that "nothing would give me greater satisfaction than for you or aney [sic] other person in town to give him [Nead] a pretty severe correction every time he is caught in Town of a sunday [sic] evening" (Elkanah Talley to Benjamin Brand, Hanover County, 10 Sept. 1809, Benjamin Brand Papers, VHS).

98. *Compiler*, 5 Mar. 1835, in Bernard J. Henley Papers, LVA.

99. Wyatt-Brown, *Southern Honor*, 387.

100. McKivigan, *The Roving Editor*, 31.

101. Jordan, *Black Confederates*, 158.

102. *Dispatch*, 16 Dec. 1856.

Chapter 2. "An evil which demands a speedy remedy": White Criminality in an Urban Slave Society

1. Ashworth, *Slavery, Capitalism, and Politics*, 219–20; *Dispatch*, 14 and 29 Aug. and 2 Sept. 1856.

2. See Steger, "United to Support," 15; Wyatt-Brown, "Community, Class, and Snopesian Crime," 177; and Fronsman, *Common Whites*, 64–65.

3. Waldrep, *Roots of Disorder*, 15–16; Wyatt-Brown, *Southern Honor*, 370. On the importance of local kinship ties in mitigating the impact of the spread of market capitalism in the rural South, see Crawford, *Ashe County's Civil War*, 40; Harris, *Plain Folk and Gentry*, 5; and Wayne, *Death of an Overseer*, 159–60.

4. On the importance of criminal justice in urban areas, see Ayers, *Vengeance and Justice*, chap. 3; and Bodenhamer, "Law and Disorder in the Old South," 113–14.

5. Oakes, *Slavery and Freedom*, 128.

6. Cole, "Keeping the Peace," 156.

7. Barbara Bellows makes similar claims about the dependence of poor white

women on benevolence in antebellum Charleston (*Benevolence among Slaveholders*, 88).

8. Floyd quoted in Schwarz, *Twice Condemned*, 280.

9. Proslavery apologists such as James Henry Hammond, John C. Calhoun, and George Fitzhugh highlighted crime and pauperism in the North as evidence of the superiority of southern slave society. See Freehling, *The Reintegration of American History*, 96–103; Genovese, *The World the Slaveholders Made*, 195–232; and Ashworth, *Slavery, Capitalism, and Politics*, 219–20, 228–46, 281–85. Barbara Bellows distinguished three proslavery positions that commented on the place of white workers in southern slave society. The first argued that "the slave and the workingman could never coexist"; the second posited slavery as a solution to the problem of white poverty; and the third, adopted by Fitzhugh, among others, stated that all wage laborers were, in effect, slaves (*Benevolence among Slaveholders*, 183–84).

10. *Dispatch*, 1852 and 1860. These figures are estimates calculated from the *Dispatch* daily reports of mayor's court cases.

11. This argument is made with reference to the southern temperance movement in Tyrell, "Drink and Temperance," 486.

12. RHCM, 1830–60.

13. Ayers, *Vengeance and Justice*, 90, 115–16, 298 nn. 5 and 6; Waldrep, *Roots of Disorder*, 43; Hindus, "The Contours of Crime and Justice," 218; Bodenhamer, "The Efficiency of Criminal Justice in the Antebellum South," 83; Bolton, *Poor Whites of the Antebellum South*, 59. See also Wyatt-Brown, *Southern Honor*, 367–68.

14. Hindus, "The Contours of Crime and Justice," 218.

15. Steinberg, *The Transformation of Criminal Justice*, 239–40.

16. Bellows, *Benevolence among Slaveholders*, 143.

17. Bodenhamer and Ely, *Ambivalent Legacy*, 4; Wyatt-Brown, *Honor and Slavery*; Bruce, *Violence and Culture*, 239–40; Denham, *Rogue's Paradise*, 12–23.

18. Lane, *Murder in America*, 97.

19. Ayers, *Vengeance and Justice*, 101; Monkkonen, *The Dangerous Class*, 36; Bodenhamer, *The Pursuit of Justice*, 127.

20. This was a common response to white criminality in the South. See Shore, "Making Mississippi Safe for Slavery," 98.

21. On the term *herrenvolk*, see George Fredrickson, *The Black Image in the White Mind*. On proslavery writers who invoked herrenvolk ideas, see Ashworth, *Slavery, Capitalism, and Politics*, 210–28. The terms *working class, lower class, poor*, and *nonslaveholding* whites are used interchangeably in this chapter. These terms are convenient for expressing the idea that the interests of certain groups of white Richmonders were less dependent on the slave regime than those of others, yet it should be recognized that they simplify what were, in reality, complex social divisions within the white community. Slaveholding was not a fixed status. Not only did white men and women buy and sell slaves in response to changing economic fortunes, but widespread slave hiring meant that many who did not own slaves employed slave labor on an occasional basis.

22. Gregg Kimball, *American City, Southern Place*, 58-59.

23. Rachleff, *Black Labor*, 5.

24. Richmond newspapers presented vivid descriptions of crime and immorality in northern cities. See *Dispatch*, 16 Sept. 1856 and 18 Nov. 1859.

25. Ibid., 5 Mar. 1860.

26. *Whig*, 15 Nov. 1842, Bernard J. Henley Papers (Box 5), LVA.

27. Mordecai, *Richmond in By-Gone Days*, 317.

28. Olmsted, *The Slave States*, 46.

29. Ibid., 45.

30. Chesson and Roberts, *Exile in Richmond*, 51 n. 66; Berlin and Gutman, "Natives and Immigrants," 1181; Gregg Kimball, *American City, Southern Place*, 31.

31. Gregg Kimball, *American City, Southern Place*, 32; Berlin and Gutman, "Natives and Immigrants," 1188. Irish immigrants also dominated unskilled labor positions in Vicksburg, Mississippi. Christopher Morris, *Becoming Southern*, 117.

32. For a comparison of the Irish and African American experiences in antebellum cities, see Roediger, *The Wages of Whiteness*, 134.

33. In a study of five southern cities, Dennis Rousey found that northern and foreign-born whites were less likely to own or hire slaves than native southerners who held equivalent wealth. Those foreigners who did enter the slaveholding class tended to own fewer slaves than their southern counterparts ("Friends and Foes of Slavery," 379). See also Gregg Kimball, *American City, Southern Place*, 241. On the importance of the prospect of social mobility in mitigating white class tensions in the South, see Eaton, *The Growth of Southern Civilization*, 174–76.

34. Bellows, *Benevolence among Slaveholders*, 70.

35. Gregg Kimball, *American City, Southern Place*, 167–76, 181. On the Tredegar Ironworks strike of 1847, in which the conflict between slaveholders and white workers was manifested most overtly, see Schechter, "Free and Slave Labor in the Old South," 173; and Dew, *Ironmaker to the Confederacy*, 23–26. Kimball argues that although Joseph Anderson successfully replaced white workers with slaves in 1847, he was later forced to return to white labor and in the 1850s accommodated rather than confronted the white workers' demands.

36. Steger, "United to Support," v, 205. Gregg Kimball has depicted the political and economic accommodation of white workers as a negotiated process in which craftsmen, in particular, used their skills as a bargaining tool to obtain higher wages and secure employment (*American City, Southern Place*, 167).

37. Steger, "United to Support," 197. Numerous historians have argued that racism was central to prohibiting the development of class antagonisms in the antebellum South. See Fredrickson, *The Arrogance of Race*, 140; Bond, *Political Culture in the Nineteenth-Century South*, 8; and Riches, *Industrialization, Paternalism, and Class Conflict*, 27.

38. During the 1840s and 1850s, textile manufacturing and metalworking became occupations almost exclusively reserved for white workers, while tobacco manufacturing became solely a black concern. Green, "Industrial Transition in the Land of

Chattel Slavery," 239–45; Takagi, *Rearing Wolves*, 96–97. See also Barnes, "Southern Artisans," 187; and Lewis, *Coal, Iron, and Slaves*, 231.

39. Else Brown and Gregg Kimball, "Mapping the Terrain of Black Richmond," 302.

40. Sidbury, *Ploughshares into Swords*, 167–68; Egerton, *Gabriel's Rebellion*, 30.

41. Shade, *Democratizing the Old Dominion*, 283.

42. Link, *Roots of Secession*, 15. See also Siegel, "Artisans and Immigrants," 224–25; and Randal Miller, "The Enemy Within," 39–40.

43. Bell, "Regional Identity in the Antebellum South," 9–14.

44. Takagi, *Rearing Wolves*, 33; Steger, "United to Support," 195.

45. Gregg Kimball, *American City, Southern Place*, 181; Rothman, *Notorious in the Neighborhood*, chap. 3. On the threat posed to the southern social order by the confluence of black and white labor experiences, see McDonnell, "Work, Culture, and Society in the Slave South," 126–38.

46. McKivigan, *The Roving Editor*, 34; emphasis in original. Catherine Hopley, an Englishwoman who visited Richmond in the company of a southern family, also commented that Virginians were sensitive about foreigners' attitudes toward slavery. Although curious about Richmond's slave population, Hopley "abstained from asking any questions for fear of appearing too deeply interested in their condition." Quoted in Rousey, "Friends and Foes of Slavery," 282.

47. Rousey, "Friends and Foes of Slavery," 381–82.

48. Lockley, *Lines in the Sand*, xvi.

49. Rutherford, "Commonplace Book," 11 Apr. 1845, VHS.

50. *Dispatch*, 3 Jan. 1856.

51. U.S. Census, Richmond City, 1850 and 1860.

52. Gregg Kimball, *American City, Southern Place*, 179–82; Bellows, *Benevolence among Slaveholders*, 106–7.

53. That many white complainants in mayor's court cases were from poor or lower-class backgrounds is implied by the fact that most did not appear in the census or annual tax records and city directories. Beyond this, there is anecdotal evidence of complainants' class status in newspaper reports and legal documents. See, for example, MCDB, 4 Oct. 1837; *Dispatch*, 22 Nov. 1856; and Howison, *Reports of Criminal Trials*, 39.

54. *Dispatch*, 26 Oct. 1859. On the importance of slave control to the development of southern police forces, see Rousey, *Policing the Southern City*, 13–24; Hadden, *Slave Patrols*, 52–59; and Cei, "Law Enforcement in Richmond," 11–21.

55. Only in 1864 did the council provide for the appointment of a chief of police to command both the night watch and the day police. Manarin, *Richmond at War*, 534–35.

56. Rousey, *Policing the Southern City*, 22–24.

57. Hadden, *Slave Patrols*, 57. Hadden notes that the public guard did help to round up slaves after the city's curfew.

58. *Dispatch*, 23 Aug. 1859.

59. Ibid., 13 Feb. 1852; 17 Sept. 1859; 16 and 29 Aug. 1860.
60. *Ordinances of the Corporation of the City of Richmond* (1831), 15.
61. *Dispatch*, 31 Jul. 1855; 17 Sept. 1859.
62. Ibid., 16 Aug. 1860.
63. Ibid., 25 Feb. 1852; 5 Sept. 1860. The First Watch House was located on Seventeenth Street between Main and Franklin, and the Second Watch House was on Sixth Street between Broad and Marshall.
64. "An Ordinance, to amend the 'Ordinance concerning the Police of the City of Richmond,'" 1831, 11; Monkonnen, "A Disorderly People?" 542.
65. *Dispatch*, 25 Feb. 1852; 5 Sept. 1860.
66. Ibid., 31 May 1854. On the geography of policing in Richmond, see also Rothman, *Notorious in the Neighborhood*, 111–12.
67. *Dispatch*, 6 Mar. 1860.
68. In 1860, all but one of the fifteen aldermen lived within twelve blocks of the Capitol building, and most Richmonders resident in neighborhoods on the outskirts of the city would have faced a long walk to find one of these centrally located law officers. See the list of officers and aldermen in Ferslew, *Second Annual Directory for the City of Richmond*, 39. The concentration of police officers and aldermen in the city center accords with David Goldfield's argument that the "amount of police protection afforded to Virginia's cities seemed to be directly proportionate to the concern of the business community over the safety of their residential and business districts" (*Urban Growth in the Age of Sectionalism*, 146).
69. *Ordinances of the Corporation of the City of Richmond and the Acts of Assembly Relating Thereto* (1831), 110.
70. Mayo, *A Guide to Magistrates*, 16.
71. Minor, *A Synopsis of the Law of Crimes and Punishments in Virginia*, 74–75; emphasis in original.
72. Yngvesson, *Virtuous Citizens, Disruptive Subjects*, 77–78.
73. Introduction to Lazarus-Black and Hirsch, *Contested States*, 6–14.
74. Cole, "Keeping the Peace," 156.
75. This argument is considered in relation to criminal trial courts in Richmond in chapter 4 of this volume.
76. Sally Engle Merry argues that "court hearings serve as critical sites for the creation and imposition of cultural meanings," as they interpret the experiences of people who bring problems there, and, by naming, discussing, and settling these problems, give them new cultural meanings ("Courts as Performances," 36).
77. McCurry, "The Two Faces of Republicanism," 1259.
78. Ibid., 1254.
79. MCDB, 14 May and 4. Oct. 1837; 11 Apr. 1838, 197, 253; *Dispatch*, 1 Feb. 1860.
80. *Dispatch*, 22 Nov. 1856.
81. This interpretation of law and domestic violence is informed by Cole, "Keep-

ing the Peace"; and Edwards, "Law, Domestic Violence, and the Limits of Patriarchal Authority."

82. *Dispatch*, 15 Oct. 1852.

83. Ibid., 10 May 1858; 9 May 1860.

84. Cole, "Keeping the Peace," 157; *Dispatch*, 24 Jan. 1860. On the idea that southern women were constrained from relying on the state to regulate their domestic affairs by notions of honor and patriarchy, see Clinton, *The Plantation Mistress*, 109.

85. Charlotte Cullen to Samuel Taylor, 9 Dec. 1844, Brooke Collection, Huntington Library, San Marino, BR Box 33 (43).

86. For an analysis of women in mid-nineteenth-century America who appealed to civil courts to regulate their domestic relations after attempts at private resolution had failed, see Grossberg, "Battling over Motherhood in Philadelphia," 155–59. On attitudes toward domestic abuse in Richmond, see *Dispatch*, 29 Aug. 1856; 2 Sept. 1859; and 26 Jan. 1860. On the liberalization of divorce law in antebellum Virginia, see Riley, "Legislative Divorce in Virginia, 1803–1850," 51–67.

87. John Cullen to Charlotte Cullen, 2 Nov. 1846, Brooke Collection, Huntington Library, San Marino, BR Box 33 (48).

88. On the restrictive impact of the cult of domesticity on middle-class white women, see Glenn, "Wife-Beating."

89. Details of the mayor's court domestic violence cases involving foreign-born women can be found in the *Dispatch*, 29 Jan., 1 Jun., 20 and 30 Nov. 1852. Information on the nativity of the defendants is in the U.S. Census, Richmond City, 1850. Details of Mrs. Thomas's separation from her husband are in Robert S. Brooke to his wife, Richmond, 16 Feb. 1842, Brooke Family Correspondence, ALUVA. Sharon Block argued that class was as significant as race in determining women's responses to male violence, and that women were likely to have more legal success when their complaint was supported by a strong patriarchal figure. Block, "Lines of Color, Sex, and Service," 156.

90. MCDB, 21 Mar. 1838, 247.

91. Ibid., 11 Aug. 1836, 44.

92. Ibid., 8, 10, 14, 15, 22, 23 Jan. and 1 Feb. 1838, 228–30, 234, 236.

93. *Dispatch*, 14 Jan. 1852–13. Jan. 1853. The one man convicted of assault against his wife between 1830 and 1850 was Edmund M. Smith, who was fined $1,000 in 1845. *Commonwealth v. Edmund M. Smith*, RHCM, 12 Feb. 1845.

94. Cole, "Keeping the Peace," 151.

95. MCDB, 1838; *Dispatch*, 14 Jan. 1852–13 Jan. 1853; 1 Jan. 1860–31 Dec. 1860.

96. In 1853, thirty whites were tried in the hustings court for misdemeanor assaults compared with just ten the previous year and an average of eight per year over the preceding decade. Prosecutions for misdemeanor assault continued to rise during the rest of the 1850s, peaking at thirty-six in both 1859 and 1860. RHCM, 1843–60.

97. In 1860 alone, eighteen women and four men appeared before the mayor accused of keeping a disorderly house or a house of ill-fame. Only one was sent on to

the hustings court. Just three white women were charged with similar offenses in the mayor's court in 1838 and 1852.

98. Rothman, *Notorious in the Neighborhood*, 120–29.

99. *Commonwealth v. Ann Meredith*, Betsey Horton, Mary Weidemeyer, and Amanda Logan. RHCEC, 11–13 Jul. 1837.

100. Elizabeth Cousins was sentenced to thirty days in jail. *Commonwealth v. Elizabeth* Cousins, RHCM, 18 Nov. 1854.

101. In 1860, at least twenty-three women appeared in the mayor's court charged with keeping a disorderly house and keeping a house of ill-fame. Eighteen were convicted and held to a peace warrant or jailed in default of security. RHCM, 1860. On prostitution in 1850s Richmond, see also Barber, "Depraved and Abandoned Women," 158–63.

102. Howison, *Reports of Criminal Trials*, 38–43.

103. Ibid., 1–5.

104. U.S. Census, Richmond City, 1850; Richmond Personal Property Tax Book, 1849–52. Julia Dye only appears in the Richmond tax records in 1850, and there is no record that she ever paid tax in Lynchburg, suggesting that her stay in both cities was short, possibly due to police harassment.

105. There is no evidence that any further action was taken against defendants who did not pay the fine.

106. *Dispatch*, 1 Oct. 1855. The number of whites accused of drunkenness was 131 out of 305 defendants in 1838, 166 out of 553 in 1852, and 226 out of 928 in 1860.

107. *Dispatch*, 30 Jan. 1854.

108. Research on other cities in the northern and southern United States suggests that white defendants' experiences in Richmond Mayor's Court cases were far from exceptional for the mid-nineteenth century. See Howington, *What Sayeth the Law*, 98–115; Steinberg, *The Transformation of Criminal Justice*, 128; and Ferdinand, *Boston's Lower Criminal Courts*, 9–12.

109. Indicative of the fact that most white men convicted of drunkenness in the early 1850s were drawn from the lower orders is the fact that two-thirds were, at least for a short time, jailed in default of the required security.

110. Tolbert, *Constructing Townscapes*, 174.

111. *Dispatch*, 23 Sept. 1852.

112. MCDB, 4 May 1836, 2.

113. MCDB, 26 Aug., 3 Oct., 29 Nov. 1837, 183, 197, 216.

114. Case of John Edgar, John Hughes, James Potter, Enoch Hand, Daniel Green, Joseph Crawford, Executive Papers, box 347, Rejected Claims, 1836.

115. Richmond City Common Council Records, 14 Jul. 1841.

116. *Dispatch*, 23 Aug. 1856. Picking oakum was the tedious task of separating out the strands of old rope. The strands could be sold to shipbuilders for mixing with tar to seal the lining of wooden vessels.

117. See Bellows, *Benevolence among Slaveholders*, 90; Lebsock, *The Free Women of Petersburg*, 242.

118. Richmond City Common Council Records, 29 Mar. 1855. A new poorhouse was eventually built in Richmond in 1860. Henri Garidel, a Confederate refugee in Richmond during the Civil War, was highly complimentary of the appearance of the poorhouse, describing it as "a magnificent building made of northern bricks, 150 feet long with four floors. It is a hospital for poor people. It is truly beautiful." Chesson and Roberts, *Exile in Richmond*, 66. On the parallels between the poorhouse and the city jail in early-nineteenth-century America, see Friedman, *Crime and Punishment in American History*, 101.

119. U.S. Census, Richmond City, 1850 and 1860. Virginians accounted for 69 out of the 84 whites in the poorhouse in 1850, but only 42 of 107 in 1860. During the 1850s, the number of Irish in the poorhouse increased from 7 to 57.

120. The chain gang made its first appearance on the streets of Richmond on 28 August 1856. *Dispatch*, 14, 26, and 29 Aug. 1856.

121. Ibid., 13 Feb. 1857.

122. *Commonwealth v. William Vest*, 9 May 1843; 10 Feb. 1846; 14 Sept. 1850; 13 May 1853; 10 Sept. 1856; Case of William Vest, Executive Papers, Nov. 1856.

123. RHCM, 14 and 15 Aug. 1860. Only two men sentenced to the chain gang by the hustings court were in the city jail at the time of the 1860 census, and neither was a southerner. John Sullivan was an Irishman convicted of stealing, and William Hughes, who was serving a twelve-month sentence for assault, was from New York.

124. Case of William Vest, Executive Papers, Nov. 1856.

125. Cited in Bellows, *Benevolence among Slaveholders*, 109.

126. Although this might suggest that the whipping of whites was more a symbolic than a physical punishment, there was also a widespread belief in the Old South that whites suffered greater pain from the sting of the lash than African Americans. It was therefore considered appropriate that they receive fewer lashes. See Williams, *Vogues in Villainy*, 109.

127. *Commonwealth v. Edward Pepper*, RHCM, 27 Nov. 1835. See also *Commonwealth v. Henry Wilson*, RHCM, 28 Nov. 1835. Between 1832 and 1846, the hustings court sentenced a total of forty white men and two white women to be whipped in addition to serving jail time. Thirty-nine of these convicts were convicted of stealing and three of receiving stolen goods. On punishments for petty larceny, see Tate, *Digest of the Laws of Virginia*, 220.

128. On penal reform in the early national and antebellum eras, see Ayers, *Vengeance and Justice*, 34–72; Meranzes, *Laboratories of Virtue*; and Preyer, "Crime, the Criminal Law, and Reform."

129. Walter Johnson, *Soul by Soul*, 145.

130. Case of John Wade, Executive Papers, box 341, May-Jun. 1835.

131. Case of William McDowell, Executive Papers, Jan. 1842. See also Case of Elizabeth Bovan, Executive Papers, Apr. 1845.

132. *Dispatch*, 9 Aug. 1856; 10 and 13 Feb. 1857.

133. Ibid., 9 and 14 Feb. 1860.

134. Ibid., 9 Feb. 1860. Responses to poverty in Richmond contrasted with those

in rural Virginia, where the poor were more often supported within the community. See Watkinson, "Fit Objects of Charity," 63.

Chapter 3. "The victim of prejudice and hasty consideration": Slave Trials, Clemency, and Punishment

1. *Commonwealth v. Robert*, RHCM, 3 Aug. 1840.

2. The only other witness was William Allison, who testified that Robert was about twenty years old and was to be freed when he reached the age of twenty-five. Although this information had no impact on the trial itself, when the case was reviewed by the governor, Robert's impending emancipation meant that his death sentence was commuted to ten years in the state penitentiary rather than the usual punishment of sale and transportation. *Commonwealth v. Robert*, RHCM, 3 Aug. 1840.

3. "An Act for the more speedy prosecution of slaves committing Capitall Crimes," in Hening, *The Statutes at Large*, 103; Guild, *Black Laws*, 151.

4. Guild, *Black Laws*, 151–59; Schwarz, *Twice Condemned*, 17–29.

5. Guild, *Black Laws*, 160.

6. Schwarz, *Slave Laws*, 74 and chap. 4.

7. Schwarz, "The Transportation of Slaves from Virginia," 217–19; Flanigan, *The Criminal Law of Slavery*, 96.

8. Egerton, *Gabriel's Rebellion*, 81. See also Thomas Morris, *Southern Slavery and the Law*, 218–19. On southerners' faith in the virtue of their legal institutions more generally, see Michael Johnson, "Denmark Vesey"; Roeber, *Faithful Magistrates*, 258; Flanigan, *The Criminal Law of Slavery*, 91; Thomas Morris, *Southern Slavery and the Law*, 219; and Higginbotham and Jacobs, "Law Only as an Enemy," 971–72, 982.

9. On the trial of slaves in Louisiana, see Schafer, "Slaves and Crime," 55–56. On South Carolina, see Henry, *The Police Control of the Slave*, 58.

10. Thomas Morris, *Southern Slavery and the Law*, 218. Historians dispute the reasons for the shift toward greater formalism in slave trials in the nineteenth century. See Fede, *People without Rights*, 159; Nash, "Fairness and Formalism," 76–87; and Watson, "North Carolina Slave Courts," 36.

11. Flanigan, *The Criminal Law of Slavery*, 190.

12. McNair, "Justice Bound," 157.

13. It is notable that there was also a high incidence of slave prosecutions in South Carolina, where, as in Virginia, slaves were denied trial by jury. Hindus, *Prison and Plantation*, 137–39.

14. Byrne, "Slave Crime in Savannah," 359; Waldrep, *Roots of Disorder*, 32. Byrne notes that the total proportion of crimes committed by slaves in Savannah was almost exactly equal to their share of the population. It is particularly notable, therefore, that slaves in Savannah accounted for such a small proportion of defendants charged with the most serious crimes, felonies, for which they were entitled to a trial by jury (59 of 659). In Vicksburg, 1,856 white and 47 nonwhite defendants came before the circuit court between 1817 and 1859.

15. Byrne, "Slave Crime in Savannah," 357. Tim Lockley has argued that "although the standards of justice in the lowcountry were appreciably harsher for African Americans than for white criminals, justices and magistrates often went to some lengths to secure proper convictions" (*Lines in the Sand*, 106).

16. Howington, *What Sayeth the Law*, 215.

17. Ayers, *Vengeance and Justice*, 134. In Richmond courts of oyer and terminer, 63.2 percent of slaves charged with violent felonies were convicted, whereas only 38.2 percent of whites were found guilty following examination by hustings court magistrates and trial in the circuit court. On white trials in Richmond see chapter 4 in this volume.

18. Based on 370 slave cases for which the date of the alleged crime is known. Excluded are approximately thirty cases that ended with no prosecution.

19. Tushnet, *The American Law of Slavery*, 122.

20. Thomas Morris, *Southern Slavery and the Law*, 214. For examples of the impact of common-law due process on the duration of slave prosecutions, see Denham, *Rogue's Paradise*, 132; and Waldrep, *Roots of Disorder*, 52–57.

21. On the importance of slave's property status on trial verdicts even in common-law jurisdictions, see Fede, *People without Rights*, 159; and Higginbotham and Jacobs, "Law Only as an Enemy," 1068.

22. Waldrep, *Roots of Disorder*, 58. See also Harcourt, "Imagery and Adjudication in the Criminal Law," 1207–9; Wren, "Two-Fold Character," 417–31; and Cottrol, "Clashing Traditions," 155.

23. As Higginbotham and Jacobs have argued, the Virginia slave courts "more often than not served as the judicially robed enforcers of a vicious, inhumane system" that reinforced the security of the slave regime, legitimized the exercise of despotic power by white Virginians over all African Americans, and protected slaveholder property interests ("Law Only as an Enemy," 998).

24. See, for example, *Commonwealth v. Moses Campbell and Frederick Banks*, RHCEC, Aug. 1845; *Commonwealth v. George Mercer*, Executive Papers, Mar. 1848; *Commonwealth v. Perry*, RHCEC, Apr. 1854; Case of Matthew, Governor Henry A. Wise Executive Papers, box 18, 9 May 1859.

25. Schwarz, *Twice Condemned*, 215 n. 32.

26. For details of the slaves convicted of murder but spared execution, see cases of *Commonwealth v. Emmanuel*, 15 Nov. 1842; *Commonwealth v. Jordan Hatcher*, 12 Mar. 1852; *Commonwealth v. Lucy*, 16 Sept. 1852; *Commonwealth v. Lucy*, 10 Apr. 1855; and *Commonwealth v. Scott*, 15 Nov. 1859, all in Condemned Blacks Executed or Transported, Records, 1783–1865, LVA. Apart from the four convicted murderers who did not have their sentences commuted by the governor, a fifth slave, Jane Williams, was executed after she pleaded guilty to murder in 1852. See chapter 1 for full details of Jane Williams's case.

27. In this context, the execution of Jane Williams represented unusual treatment for a female defendant. Ariela Gross has argued that white southerners generally

found it easier to imagine black women defendants as incompetent or affected by illness, rather than inherently vicious (*Double Character*, 77).

28. *Commonwealth v. Moses Henry*, RHCM, 26 Jan. 1846.

29. Owens, *This Species of Property*, 158–59.

30. Case of Phillis, Executive Papers, box 412, 7 Jul. 1852; Case of William, Executive Papers, box 413, 28 Oct. 1852; "Record of Court in Jordan Hatcher's Case, Together with the Petition for Commutation of his Sentence," Document 78, House Documents and Annual Report, 1852, LVA.

31. *Commonwealth v. Perry*, RHCEC, Apr. 1854; Case of Scott, Governor Henry A. Wise Executive Papers, box 20, Nov. 1859.

32. Petition of James A. Seddon and H. A. Claiborne, case of Emanuel, Executive Papers, Dec. 1842.

33. Twenty-five out of 107 slave burglary defendants were convicted of larceny.

34. Fifty out of 107 slaves were convicted of burglary compared with 14 out of 19 free African Americans. Overall, slaves charged with burglary were convicted as charged or of the lesser crimes of grand larceny and larceny in 70 percent of cases. Free blacks were found guilty in 85 percent of cases.

35. The two cases in which free black burglary defendants were convicted of a lesser crime were *Commonwealth v. Charles Green*, RHCM, 13 Nov. 1855; and *Commonwealth v. Silas Anderson*, RHCM, 15 May 1860.

36. In the 1850s, three Richmond slaves were charged with stabbing a *white* person with intent to kill. All three were sentenced to sale and transportation. However, several other slaves who also were accused of stabbing white people faced charges that made no explicit reference to the victim race. In such cases, the standard punishment was thirty-nine lashes. This subtle distinction in the wording of criminal charges seems to have reflected differences in the relationship between the victim and the accused. At least two out of the three slaves charged with stabbing a white person with intent to kill had allegedly attacked their overseers. This made their crimes more dangerous acts of resistance to white authority than, for instance, the stabbing of a white stranger, and consequently they warranted more severe punishment.

37. In this section, convictions include only those cases in which the accused was found guilty as charged.

38. This was true, for example, in Tennessee. See Howington, *What Sayeth the Law*, 104.

39. *Commonwealth v. Nancy*, Executive Papers, box 395, 6 Jul. 1849; *Commonwealth v. Lewis*, Governor Henry A. Wise Executive Papers, box 12, 16 Jun. 1858.

40. Although Philip Schwarz suggested that "density of population and structures, fear of fire and the higher probability of dwellings becoming targets" pushed up the rate of convictions in Richmond in the nineteenth century, between 1830 and 1860, just nine out of thirty-three slaves were found guilty of arson, the lowest conviction rate for any type of felonious crime committed by slaves in the city. The conviction rate for slave arson in late antebellum Richmond was similar to that in rural Virginia counties. Between 1785 and 1831, one-third of slave arson defendants

were convicted in Essex, Henry, Southampton, and Spotsylvania Counties. Schwarz, *Twice Condemned*, 211, 299.

41. This sample of forty-three nonmurder slave trials includes all cases in the Hustings Court Ended Causes papers for the years 1830, 1835, 1840, 1845, 1850, and 1855.

42. *Commonwealth v. Daniel*, RHCEC, Jun. 1830.

43. *Commonwealth v. Mary*, RHCEC, Apr. 1845.

44. Stroud, *Sketch of the Laws Relating to Slavery*, 281; emphasis in original.

45. Guild, *Black Laws*, 160. Thomas Morris suggests that the concept of "pregnant circumstances" was most likely based on Blackstone's definition of a "probable presumption" based on circumstances that "'*usually*' attend a fact and should be given 'due weight'" (*Southern Slavery and the Law*, 232–34).

46. Gross, *Double Character*, 152.

47. *Commonwealth v. Moses Campbell and Frederick Banks*, RHCEC, Aug. 1845.

48. Ibid. Transcripts of the testimony of all slaves and free blacks condemned to death or sale and transportation were automatically sent to the governor for his approval. Even if the other witnesses for whom warrants were issued testified against Banks and Campbell, as the executive copy of the transcript does not record their depositions, it can be assumed that the court believed that the evidence of Cook and Jinkins alone was sufficient to justify the guilty verdict.

49. Quite why neither Warwick nor Barksdale testified in the case is unclear, as it was common for the victim of a property crime to be the main prosecution witness.

50. It was rare for any defense testimony to be recorded in oyer and terminer cases, but even in the few cases that it was recorded, the accused did not appear as a witness. In colonial South Carolina, however, slave defendants often gave evidence to the court. See, for example, the trial of John, charged with murdering a slave, discussed in Olwell, *Masters, Slaves, and Subjects*, 84–86.

51. Cobb, *An Inquiry into the Law of Negro Slavery*, 271. See also Thomas Morris, *Southern Slavery and the Law*, 239–46.

52. *Commonwealth v. George Mercer*, Executive Papers, Mar. 1848; *Commonwealth v. Perry*, RHCEC, Apr. 1854.

53. *Dispatch*, 29 Nov. 1853.

54. Thomas Morris, "Slaves and the Rules of Evidence in Criminal Trials," 222.

55. Case of Matthew, Governor Henry A. Wise Executive Papers, box 18, 9 May 1859.

56. A similar argument is made by Michael Johnson, "Denmark Vesey," 942.

57. Between 1830 and 1851, Robert Scott represented fifty-five slave defendants in oyer and terminer cases. Thomas August defended forty-four slaves between 1845 and 1860. RHCM, 1830–60. Christopher Waldrep has argued that in Warren County, Mississippi, where professional judges sat in slave trials, the bench, as well as attorneys, were influenced by a legal culture that respected defendants' rights and

equated due process and formalism with fairness in court (*Roots of Disorder*, 37). See also Friedman, *Crime and Punishment in American History*, 257–58.

58. E. Lee Shepard, "Sketches of the Old Richmond Bar: Robert G. Scott," 47; E. Lee Shepard, "Sketches of the Old Richmond Bar: Thomas P. August," 49.

59. Fifteen of the defendants who pleaded guilty were charged with stealing. The sixteenth was Jane Williams, charged with murder. See *Commonwealth v. Jane Williams*, RHCM, 9 Aug. 1852. Robert Olwell has argued that, in slave trials in colonial South Carolina, the suspect's admission of guilt demonstrated deference and submission, whereas a not guilty plea made the trial a more confrontational "contest between the accused and the law" (*Masters, Slaves, and Subjects*, 88).

60. *Commonwealth v. Elick*, RHCM, 28 Jan. 1831.

61. *Commonwealth v. Fanny*, RHCM 14 and 16 Feb. 1849; Case of Fanny, Executive Papers, box 393, 24 Feb. 1849.

62. *Commonwealth v. Daniel*, RHCM 9 Jun. 1830; *Commonwealth v. Daniel*, RHCEC, 9 Jun. 1830. On hustings court felony examinations, see chapter 4 in this volume.

63. Case of John Watkins, Executive Papers, box 368, 19 Aug. 1841.

64. Case of Emanuel, Executive Papers, 10 Dec. 1842.

65. Case of Scott, Executive Papers, Nov. 1859; Case of John Rawlings, Executive Papers, 2 Dec. 1845.

66. Case of Armistead, Executive Papers, 15 Feb. 1842. A similar tension developed in South Carolina. In 1830, Judge Elihu Bay defended the right of magistrate's courts to bend the law in certain circumstances: "When the dreadful . . . consequences of the insurrection of slaves . . . are taken into consideration, it appears to me that the judges . . . ought to be extremely cautious in interfering with the magistrates and freeholders. . . ." However, criticism of the state's slave trial system mounted during the next three decades, and in the 1850s Governor James H. Adams felt free to criticize the decisions of slave trial courts as "rarely in conformity with justice or humanity." See Hindus, *Prison and Plantation*, 154; and Henry, *The Police Control of the Slave*, 59–60.

67. Condemned Blacks Executed or Transported, Records, 1783–1865, LVA. The fate of one condemned slave, Harry, sentenced to death for burglary in January 1830, is unknown.

68. Schwarz, "The Transportation of Slaves from Virginia," 219; Condemned Blacks Executed or Transported, Records, 1783–1865, LVA; RHCM, 1830–60. The figure of $600 is based on the valuations of twenty-six slaves condemned to death by the Richmond Hustings Court between 1830 and 1860 who were subsequently reprieved for sale and transportation.

69. Walter Johnson, *Soul by Soul*, 29. On the threat of sale and the breakup of slave families as "the most effective long-term mechanism of control," see Jones, *Born a Child of Freedom, Yet a Slave*, 37.

70. Walter Johnson, *Soul by Soul*, 110–11; Gross, *Double Character*, 101.

71. Schwarz, *Slave Laws in Virginia*, 90.

72. Case of George Mercer, Executive Papers, box 390, 2 Mar. 1848.

73. Petition of Fanny, Executive Papers, February 1849. See also Petition of Samuel Ellis and others on behalf of Ellis's slave Lucy, Executive Papers, box 426, Mar.-Jun. 1855.

74. Ariela Gross has noted that in civil cases concerning slave sales, plaintiffs and defendants explained slave behavior in contrasting terms in order to further their own interests in the case. The same was doubtless true of criminal cases and pardon petitions. Had Ruschmer, the slave hirer, recorded his thoughts on Virginia's case, for example, he might have interpreted her actions very differently than did Lucy Govan. See Gross, "Beyond Black and White," 650.

75. Archibald Govan, petition to the Governor and Council of Virginia, n.d.; Sparrow, "Notes Concerning the Case of the Slave Girl Virginia," typescript, VHS.

76. Lucy H. Govan to William M. Waller, 21 Mar. 1843; Sparrow, "Notes Concerning the Case of the Slave Girl Virginia," typescript, VHS.

77. Archibald Govan to William M. Waller, 18 Jun. 1843; Sparrow, "Notes Concerning the Case of the Slave Girl Virginia"; Documents Relating to the Case of the Slave Virginia, Executive Papers, Mar. 1843, transcribed in "Notes Concerning the Case of the Slave Girl Virginia," typescript, VHS.

78. There is substantial evidence that slaves understood legal processes and sought to exploit their legal status as property. Gross, "Beyond Black and White," 661; Suggs, *Whispered Consolations*, 26.

79. Case of John Watkins, Executive Papers, August 1841.

80. Case of John Rawlings, Executive Papers, December 1845.

81. Ibid.

82. Howe, *Punish and Critique*, 68.

83. *Enquirer*, 30 Jul. 1852; *Whig*, 2 Jul. 1852.

84. *Whig*, 2 Jul. 1852.

85. Ibid., 14 May 1852; emphasis in original.

86. *Enquirer*, 30 Jul. 1852.

87. *Whig*, 29 May 1852.

88. Ibid., 11 May 1852.

89. Ibid., 1 Jun. 1852; emphasis in original.

90. Ibid., 14 May 1852.

91. Link, "The Jordan Hatcher Case," 623.

92. Ibid., 627–30. Other interests were also embodied in the public reactions to the Hatcher case. Clemency for Hatcher was opposed by tobacco manufacturers, who feared the breakdown of slave discipline in their factories if the capital sentence of the court were not enforced. The commutation also exposed tensions between East and West Virginians, and provoked a bitter political debate as Whigs attacked the Democratic governor. On the impact of universal manhood suffrage and working-class politics in 1850s Richmond, see Link, *Roots of Secession*, 87; and Shade, *Democratizing the Old Dominion*, 287.

93. *Whig*, 13 and 14 May 1852; emphasis in original.

94. *Dispatch*, 29 May 1852.

95. As Bertram Wyatt-Brown argued, trials by jury "presented the lower orders with the chance to participate" in the operation of the law, thereby reinforcing elite hegemony. The oyer and terminer system did not serve this function. While all of the oyer and terminer magistrates in Richmond in 1840 were slaveholders, in trials by jury held in the same year, just one-third of jurors owned any slaves. Wyatt-Brown, *Southern Honor*, 363. On poor whites' complaints about slaveholders' dominance of the slave trial process in Virginia, see also Lee and Hofstra, "Race, Memory, and the Death of Robert Berkeley," 45. The wealth and political importance of the Richmond magistrates contrasted with the trial by jury of Celia in Missouri, in which only four of the twelve jurors were slaveholders and all were less wealthy than Celia's owner. McLaurin, *Celia, A Slave*, 80.

96. *Dispatch*, 31 Dec. 1857.

97. Ibid., 3 and 10 May 1858; Schwarz, "The Transportation of Slaves from Virginia," 228.

98. Ibid., 8 Dec. 1860. In October 1863, the Virginia General Assembly authorized the governor to hire out any slaves or free African Americans in the penitentiary to work in the state's coal pits. Up to 150 white male convicts could also be hired, but only if they were not required in the penitentiary's workshops. "An ACT to authorize the Governor to hire Free Negro and other Convicts to work in Coal-pits," *Acts of the General Assembly of the State of Virginia*, 1863.

99. Schwarz, *Slave Laws in Virginia*, 114.

Chapter 4. "With these *poor* rogues their *judge* had never dined": Honor, Law, and the Trial and Punishment of White Criminals

1. Dabney, *Richmond*, 72–73.

2. Wyatt-Brown, *Honor and Violence*. The literature on extralegal justice both within and outside the courtroom in the Old South is extensive. See, for example, Cash, *The Mind of the South*, 33, 70; Hindus "The Contours of Crime and Justice," 237; Friedman, *Crime and Punishment*, 180; Waldrep, *The Many Faces of Judge Lynch*; and Grimstead, *American Mobbing*.

3. *Republican*, 5 Jan. 1850.

4. Christopher Waldrep recognized that similar problems resulted when due process infused slave trials. See Waldrep, *Roots of Disorder*, 53. See also Bodenhamer and Ely, *Ambivalent Legacy*, 20; and Ayers, *Vengeance and Justice*, 76.

5. As in slave courts of oyer and terminer, at least five magistrates had to be present to conduct an examination in the hustings court. In contrast to the slave courts, however, a simple majority rather than a unanimous verdict was required to send the prisoner on to the circuit court for trial. See *Hints on Three Defects in the Criminal Laws*, 3; Minor, *A Synopsis of the Law of Crimes and Punishments*, 76; Rankin, *Criminal Trial Proceedings*, 78; and Preyer, "Crime, the Criminal Law, and Reform," 55.

6. On the different courts that held jurisdiction over felony cases in Richmond in the eighteenth and nineteenth centuries, see Peters and Peters, *Courts of the Rich-*

mond Area, 33–35. The complaint about jail overcrowding was made in the *Dispatch*, 2 Apr. 1860. In the same month, the Richmond electorate voted overwhelmingly in favor of the establishment of a new monthly court to try felony cases in the city. See *Dispatch*, 9 Apr. 1860.

7. The functions of the examining court were debated in a number of general court cases. See, in particular, *Commonwealth v. Samuel Myers* (1811), *Commonwealth v. Sorrell* (1786), and *Commonwealth v. Bailey* (1798) in *A Collection of Cases*, 198–200, 253–62. See also Konig, "Dale's Laws," 354–58.

8. *Hints on Three Defects in the Criminal Laws of Virginia*, 3–4; emphasis in original. In March 1860, the *Dispatch* reported that the witnesses in the trial of the "Screamersville rioters" had "been in attendance every term since November last, and it is time that they were relieved from the annoyance of appearing at Court one week in every month" (15 Mar. 1860).

9. See *Commonwealth v. John H. Melton*, RHCM, 13 Oct. 1859.

10. In *Commonwealth v. Samuel Myers*, Judge Nicholas explained that the reason examining courts inquired into only the fact and not the law of the case was that they were composed "of plain men not versed in the nice distinctions of the law." *A Collection of Cases*, 200.

11. Ferslew, *Second Annual Directory for the City of Richmond*, 1860.

12. Case of William Vest, Executive Papers, Nov. 1856; underlining in original.

13. Slaveholding data derived from 1840 Personal Property Tax Records. Residence data on 204 jurors in hustings court misdemeanor cases and circuit court trials held in 1850 and 1851 recorded by Robert Reid Howison drawn from U.S. Census, Richmond City and Henrico County, 1850. Howison, *Reports of Criminal Trials*. On juries, see Bodenhamer, *The Pursuit of Justice*, 83–87; Waldrep, *Roots of Disorder*, 41.

14. Between 1830 and 1860, 165 (70 percent) of 234 violent felony defendants were remanded for trial by the hustings court magistrates in comparison to 396 of 516 (77 percent) of defendants charged with felonious crimes against property.

15. *Republican*, 5 Jan. 1850.

16. Details of the murder and trial are taken from *Letters and Correspondence of Mrs. Virginia Myers*, 3–4; and *An Authenticated Report of the Trial of Myers*, 3–34. Although the hustings court examination increased the potential for judicial discretion to influence the prosecution process, social class also impacted on the administration of justice in trials by jury. See, for example, Schafer, "The Murder of a 'Lewd and Abandoned Woman.'"

17. *An Authenticated Report of the Trial of Myers*, 32; emphasis in original.

18. Ibid., 27.

19. Ibid., 33. See also *A Collection of Cases*, 198–200.

20. *The Letters and Correspondence of Mrs. Virginia Myers*, 3; emphasis in the original.

21. Hartog, "Lawyering Husband's Rights," 67–70; Friedman, *Crime and Punishment*, 221–22.

22. Wyatt-Brown, *Honor and Violence*, 215.
23. *Republican*, 24 Sept. 1849.
24. *Dispatch*, 18 Feb. 1855.
25. *Republican*, 1849–51; *Dispatch*, 1852–60.
26. Minor, *A Synopsis of the Law*, 18.
27. *Commonwealth v. John Cronin*, RHCEC, 10 Oct. 1855; Howison, *Reports of Criminal Trials*, 84.
28. *Commonwealth v. William B. Totty*, Richmond Judges Court, Ended Causes, box 19, 13 Aug. 1860; Case of William B. Totty, Governor John Letcher Executive Papers, box 6, 5 Nov. 1860.
29. Although the hanging of a white man might have encouraged slave insubordination, it does not appear that any attempt was made to prevent slaves from witnessing white hangings. When Reed and Clements were executed for federal crimes in 1852, the *Dispatch* reported that "Full one-half of those present were Negroes," and when Totty was hanged, there were again many African Americans in the crowd. Although the hanging of a white man was a dangerous event for those who feared encouraging black insubordination, this was in part offset by execution rituals that, in their grandeur, solemnity, and displays of troops and militia, reminded the black population of the power of the state apparatus. This was a function also served by more routine militia displays in the city. See Gregg Kimball, *American City, Southern Place*, 7; and Laver, "Rethinking the Social Role of the Militia," 780. *Dispatch*, 24 Apr. 1852; 17 Nov. 1860. On the death penalty in antebellum America, see Masur, *Rites of Execution*.
30. Howison, *Reports of Criminal Trials*, 43.
31. "The Personal Narrative of Mrs. Margaret Douglass," 415.
32. On the role of law in maintaining "the authority of husbands, slave masters, and the state," see Bynum, *Unruly Women*, 11–14. On the cult of female domesticity, see Davis, *Women, Race, and Class*, 12.
33. In all southern states, white women accounted for less than 2 percent of penitentiary inmates. Ayers, *Vengeance and Justice*, 295 n. 57. On female white criminality in northern cities, see Ferdinand, *Boston's Lower Criminal Courts*, 163–72; and Steinberg, *The Transformation of Criminal Justice*, 43.
34. Laura F. Edwards has argued that "Antebellum gender conventions blinded court officials to the possibility that a white woman could participate in a brutal murder," and the evidence from Richmond suggests that official responses to less serious violent crimes and also to property offenses were influenced by similar gendered assumptions. Edwards, "Law, Domestic Violence, and the Limits of Patriarchal Authority," 733.
35. *Dispatch*, 1860. These figures include both felonies and misdemeanors. The treatment of women suspected of crime in Richmond was similar to that of women in antebellum Charleston. Between 1857 and 1859, only 20 percent of females named in grand jury bills were tried for any crime in comparison with more than 40 percent of males. Hindus, "The Contours of Crime and Justice," 231.

36. *Dispatch*, 1860.

37. When the *Dispatch* reported an incident of swindling committed by a "genteel looking young lady," it warned that "the "Fair cloak" has been very successful, and will continue to be so until some of them are exposed." *Dispatch*, 3 May 1855 and 28 Jan. 1860.

38. Howison, *Reports of Criminal Trials*, 17.

39. By comparison, 207 out of 431 white men (48 percent) charged with misdemeanor assault were found guilty, and a further 28 entered a guilty plea. RHCM, 1830–60.

40. The outcome of the trials of two other women is unknown. One woman charged with a violent felony was discharged by the hustings court magistrates without trial.

41. *Dispatch*, 13 Oct. 1857.

42. On the denial of agency to female criminals, see Vivien Miller, *Crime, Sexual Violence, and Clemency*, 243.

43. On female character and criminal justice, see Hobson, "A Murder in the Moral and Religious City of Boston," 9–21; and Halttunen, "Domestic Differences."

44. Eight out of sixteen women charged with property crime felonies and examined in the hustings court were sent on for trial. In three of the five trials for which the outcome is known, the defendant was convicted. The other two cases, against Eliza Doyle for stealing and Mary Hardaman for receiving stolen goods, were dropped by the prosecution. *Commonwealth v. Eliza Doyle*, RHCM, 14 Jan. 1860, and *Commonwealth v. Mary Hardaman*, RHCM, 24 May 1860.

45. "The Personal Narrative of Mrs. Margaret Douglass," 422–23.

46. *Commonwealth v. Eliza Griffin*, RHCM, 15 May 1849; *Commonwealth v. Isabella Rix*, RHCM, 21 Jul. 1858; *Commonwealth v. Charlotte Griffith*, RHCM, 15 Dec. 1858.

47. *Commonwealth v. Eliza Griffin*, RHCM, 13 Aug. 1845, 12 Feb. 1850; *Republican*, 24 Apr. and 5 Nov. 1850; Bynum, *Unruly Women*, 110.

48. Link, *Roots of Secession*, 69.

49. *Republican*, 6 May 1850.

50. Bodenhamer, *Fair Trial Rights of the Accused*, 52.

51. Hindus, *Prison and Plantation*, 96.

52. Rice, "The Criminal Trial before and after the Lawyers," 458–62. See also Friedman and Percival, *The Roots of Justice*, 160.

53. Defense attorneys were present in all thirteen of the circuit court cases that Robert Reid Howison recorded in 1850 and 1851. Rice found that as early as the period 1818 to 1825 in Frederick County, Maryland, 92.1 percent of felony defendants were represented by attorneys ("The Criminal Trial," 457).

54. Howison, *Reports of Criminal Trials*, 1, 6, 13, 20, 30, 38, 44. This assessment of the role of lawyers in Richmond trials contrasts with Jack Williams's assertion that in antebellum South Carolina successful lawyers depended more on a thorough

understanding of local pride and custom and moving oratory than on legal reasoning or case precedent. Williams, *Vogues in Villainy*, 92.

55. Joseph Jackson Jr. Almanac and Diary, 11 Mar. and 26 Apr. 1847.

56. In property crime felony cases, there was an increase in the number of witnesses called by the prosecution from an average of 2.6 per case in the 1830s to 3.9 in the 1850s. Statistics collated from RHCEC, 1830, 1835, 1850, and 1855.

57. Howison, *Reports of Criminal Trials*, 5.

58. Ibid., 11. In 1853, the court of appeals "decided that any confessions of prisoners, made to an officer while in custody, if brought about by any questions asked him as to his participation in the crime, shall not be given in the evidence against him, as it is a fair presumption that any statement thus made, is given either under the fear of punishment or the hope of leniency or reward." Mayor Mayo advised the Richmond police of this ruling "and directed them in future to govern their conduct by it." *Dispatch*, 29 Nov. 1853.

59. Howison, *Reports of Criminal Trials*, 17, 21.

60. Ibid., 36.

61. Ibid., 44–73.

62. Joseph Jackson Jr., Almanac and Diary, 2 Mar. 1847. However, not all whites were represented even in felony trials. See, for example, Case of John M. Thornton, Governor Henry A. Wise Executive Papers, box 8, 22 Jun. 1857.

63. MCDB, 2 May, 3 Jun. 1837, p. 138. See also *An Authenticated Report of the Trial of Myers*, 25.

64. MCDB, 25 Jul. 1837, 174.

65. *Dispatch*, 24 Mar. 1860.

66. Ibid., 18 Feb. 1856.

67. *An Authenticated Report of the Trial of Myers*, 25. See also the case of Bacon Tait, MCDB, 20 Jun. 1836, 22; Howison, *Reports of Criminal Trials*, 74–75.

68. In the mayor's court, the conviction rate for whites charged with assault was 69 percent in 1838 (Tate), 82 percent in 1852 (Lambert), and 62 percent in 1860 (Mayo). In stealing cases, the conviction rate was 64 percent in 1838, 68 percent in 1852, and 57 percent in 1860.

69. Much of the decline in the ratio of indictments to guilty verdicts in Richmond was due to a substantial increase in the number of cases in which the prosecution entered a nolle prosequi. Between 1830 and 1849, the prosecution was abandoned in just 10 percent of stealing cases, but in the next ten years this figure trebled, possibly in response to increasingly strict standards of evidence. The decline in the conviction rate for cases that came to trial was less marked, but still notable. Between the 1830s and the 1850s the rate of conviction in stealing trials fell from 86 percent to 73 percent and in assault cases the decline was from 91 percent to 81 percent.

70. *Daybook of the Richmond Police Guard*, 1 Jan. 1834–25 Feb. 1844.

71. Case of Samuel S. Pendleton, Executive Papers, box 343, Rejected Claims, 1835.

72. Ibid.

73. Bertram Wyatt-Brown argues that in cash- and credit-poor economies, indebtedness "was a means to cement long-standing social connections," and that "it would not do to turn down a friend's request for a loan." Although late antebellum Richmond was by no means a cash-poor economy, it seems that similar ideas of noblesse oblige meant that Crump had no hesitation in accepting Pendleton's bond. Wyatt-Brown, *Honor and Violence*, 137.

74. On the hegemonic function of criminal punishment, see Hay, "Property, Authority and the Criminal Law," in *Albion's Fatal Tree*.

75. "Report of the Superintendent of the Penitentiary," *Journal and Documents of the House of Delegates*, 1835; *Report of the Committee of Twenty-Four*, 19. On gambling in Richmond, see also *Report of the Minority of the Committee of Twenty-Four* and *Controversy between "Erskine" and "W. M."*

76. MCDB, 25 May 1838, 272.

77. *Dispatch*, 8 Dec. 1860. These criticisms support Friedman's argument that in a republican society it was expected that justice would be based on clear and definitive legal codes rather than on the "grace and favor" of magistrates, jurors, and the executive, which seemed reminiscent of a monarchical system (*Crime and Punishment*, 63–65).

78. Seematter, "Trials and Confessions," 38–39.

79. *Dispatch*, 11, 12, 15, and 16 Jun. 1857.

80. Waldrep, *The Many Faces of Judge Lynch*, 27, 39, 45.

81. *Dispatch*, 30 Jun. 1858.

82. On the gambling riots of 1834, see *Report of the Committee of Twenty-Four*. On the interracial attacks, see *Dispatch*, 5 Jun. 1856; and Rothman, *Notorious in the Neighborhood*, 127–28.

83. *Dispatch*, 28 Jun. 1856, Bernard J. Henley Papers, LVA.

84. Williams, *Vogues in Villainy*, 120.

85. Cobb, *An Inquiry into the Law of Negro Slavery*, 233.

86. Chief Justice Drewry Ottley of St. Vincent noted that, because of the prohibition on slave testimony against whites, "the difficulty of legally establishing facts is so great, that White [sic] men are in a manner put beyond the reach of the law." As a result, in the 1820s, slaves who could show that they were Christians and who understood the significance of an oath were permitted to testify against whites in the West Indies. Thomas Morris, *Southern Slavery and the Law*, 229.

87. For interpretations of this development that respectively stress southern judges' concern with due process and the humanity of the slave and slaveholders' self-interest, see Nash, "A More Equitable Past?" 233–38; and Fede, "Legitimized Violent Slave Abuse," 150.

88. Higginbotham and Jacobs, "Law Only as an Enemy," 1048, 1054.

89. Throughout the colonial and early national periods, the law provided slaves with little legal protection from slaveholder violence. An act passed in 1669 allowed a master to kill his slaves with impunity on the assumption that "it cannot be presumed that prepensed malice (which alone makes murther a felony) should induce

any man to destroy his owne estate [*sic*]." Changes in the law occurred during the eighteenth century. From 1723, whites could be prosecuted for the "wilful, malicious, or designed killing of a slave," but it was not until 1788 that whites could be punished for slave manslaughter. Higginbotham, and Jacobs, "Law Only as an Enemy," 1034.

90. Twelve white men were charged with stabbing a slave with intent to kill, four with shooting with intent to kill, and five with murder.

91. *Dispatch*, 17 Apr. 1852, 12 Apr. 1856, 13 Oct. 1857, 13 Apr. 1858.

92. *Republican*, 6 May and 2 Nov. 1850; *Commonwealth v. Erasmus H. Roper*, 13 Dec. 1849; *Commonwealth v. Joshua Alvis*, RHCEC, 13 Aug. 1850.

93. Howington, *What Sayeth the Law*, 96.

94. Nash argued that the Tennessee court found in slaves' favor more consistently than any other southern court ("A More Equitable Past," 213).

95. The conviction rate in white-on-white assault cases was 48 percent (168 out of 348).

96. Six of nineteen white defendants convicted in the hustings court of assaulting slaves were jailed for between ten days and twelve months. All nineteen of the convicts were fined between one cent and $150, but in all but three cases the fine was less than $100, and in eleven cases it was $25 or less. RHCM, 1830–60.

97. *Commonwealth v. Joshua Alvis*, RHCEC, 13 Aug. 1850.

98. Tim Lockley found a similar increase in prosecutions of whites for violence toward slaves in Lowcountry Georgia and argued that "it was precisely the nonslaveholders' slaveless status that ensured that their violence toward bondspeople would be prosecuted." (*Lines in the Sand*, 101–4). It is also possible that slaveholders were less likely to be prosecuted as they better understood what represented acceptable treatment of another's slave. Following his escape from slavery, Henry "Box" Brown recalled an instance when his wife's owner, Joseph Colquitt, "seemed wishful to whip me . . . but, as I did not belong to him, he was deprived of the pleasure." (*Narrative of the Life of Henry Box Brown*, 45).

99. Between 1830 and 1840, just ten whites were charged with offenses relating to the unlawful assembly of slaves. In the 1850s, however, forty-three such cases were heard in the hustings court.

100. *Commonwealth v. Richard Lambert*, RHCEC, 13 Mar. 1855.

101. *Dispatch*, 17 and 18 May 1853. The case against Solomon ended without a prosecution.

102. *Dispatch*, 18 Oct. 1853.

103. *Commonwealth v. George Sharpe*, RHCEC, 14 Nov. 1845.

104. Ibid., RHCEC, 14 Sept. 1846; *Dispatch*, 14 Oct. 1857. Sharpe was also charged with a misdemeanor assault on a slave in 1848, but the prosecution was dropped before the case came to trial. *Commonwealth v. George Sharpe*, RHCM, 11 May 1848.

105. *Commonwealth v. John Wise and Richard W. Ragland*, RHCEC, 12 Mar. 1839.

106. *Dispatch*, 18 Oct. 1853.

107. Frederick Douglass claimed that southern towns were pervaded by a "general

sense of decency" that did "much to check and prevent . . . atrocious cruelty . . . and . . . dark crimes . . . openly perpetrated on the plantation." Wade, *Slavery in the Cities*, 95.

108. *Dispatch*, 3 May 1853.

109. *Commonwealth v. George Fenley* [Findlay], RHCM, 13 Aug. 1853.

110. Thomas Morris, *Southern Slavery and the Law*, 188.

111. Ibid., 189; *Dispatch*, 20 Oct. 1858.

112. Throughout the South, however, slaveholders were concerned by unregulated white violence against their slaves. Hadden, *Slave Patrols*, 70, 89; Wyatt-Brown, *Southern Honor*, 391.

113. The identity of the thief from whom the stolen goods were allegedly purchased is known in fifteen of the twenty-nine felony cases that were sent on to the circuit court for trial. In thirteen of these cases, the thief was either a slave or a free African American. Three of the four white men accused of receiving stolen goods in 1852 were listed in the city directory as grocers.

114. *Dispatch*, 26 Jan. 1853; *Commonwealth v. Catherine Houston*, RHCM, 17 Mar. 1853.

115. The outcome is known of twenty-two cases of feloniously receiving stolen goods heard in the hustings court between 1850 and April 1860. Ten of these defendants were sent on for trial in the circuit court, of whom four were convicted. RHCM, 1850–60; and *Dispatch*, 1852–60.

116. Gregg Kimball, *American City, Southern Place*, 122.

117. On hired and self-hired slaves as runaways, see Franklin and Schweninger, *Runaway Slaves*, 137–45.

118. Cyrus was convicted and sentenced to thirty-nine lashes. A free black man named William Macklin was charged with two counts of aiding slaves to abscond, but both cases were dropped before coming to trial. *Daybook of the Richmond Police Guard*, 18 Oct. 1840; RHCM, 26 Oct. and 14 Dec. 1840.

119. *Dispatch*, 29 Jul. 1856.

120. *Commonwealth v. Williamson Wynne*, 28 May. 1831.

121. All of these cases were settled in the mayor's court. On Rose Osiander, see also Rothman, *Notorious in the Neighborhood*, 107.

122. Cases of Philip F. Osiander and Thomas Chinn, Executive Papers, box 354, 19 and 21 Apr. 1838.

123. RHCM, 1830–60; *Dispatch*, 1852–60.

124. The most famous slave to escape from Richmond in this manner was Henry Box Brown. See Brown, *Narrative of the Life of Henry Box Brown*.

125. Case of William Campbell, Executive Papers, box 343, 14 Dec. 1835.

126. *Daybook of the Richmond Police Guard*, 20–21 Feb. 1834.

127. The only white man to appear in the hustings court records in connection with this affair was Edmund Smith, the owner of the *Chariot*, who was indicted on eight counts of aiding slaves to abscond. Although charged with misdemeanors, Smith's fate is unknown as he obtained writs of certiorari to have the case sent on to

the circuit court, and the records of this court have not survived. Elijah Townsend was indicted on nine counts of allowing a slave to board his vessel without the permission of his master, but the prosecution was dropped in each of these cases. RHCM, 28 Feb., 1 Mar., 30 Apr., 30 May and 22 Aug. 1834; Case of William Campbell, Executive Papers, box 343, 14 Dec. 1835.

128. On the Negro Seaman's Acts, see Bodenhamer and Ely, *Ambivalent Legacy*, 5.

129. Tripp, *Yankee Town, Southern City*, 80; Cobb, *An Inquiry into the Law of Negro Slavery*, 233; Schwarz, *Slave Laws in Virginia*, 139.

Chapter 5. The "stigma, of the deepest degradation, was fixed upon the whole race": Free African Americans and the Criminal Justice System

1. Governor's Message, 7 Dec. 1846, Virginia General Assembly, House Journals, etc. 1846/47, LVA, Richmond.

2. Loose document written by Isham Keith, Keith Family Papers, 1862, VHS, Richmond.

3. *Dispatch*, 12 Mar. 1858.

4. Richmond City Council Minutes, 2 Mar. 1858, LVA.

5. Higginbotham and Bosworth, "Rather Than the Free," 21–23. See also Higginbotham and Jacobs, "Law Only as an Enemy," 975; and Bogger, *Free Blacks in Norfolk*, 156. Bogger has claimed that "the free blacks of the 1850s were so disillusioned with the legal process that when they struck against injustice, they did so outside the law" in ways that were indicative of despair and hopelessness.

6. Flanigan, *The Criminal Law of Slavery*, 190.

7. Berlin, *Slaves without Masters*, 368.

8. Ashworth, *Slavery, Capitalism, and Politics*, 201; Berlin, *Slaves without Masters*, 362.

9. Berlin, *Slaves without Masters*, 327; Fields, *Slavery and Freedom*, 88; Stevenson, *Life in Black and White*, 274. See also Phillips, *Freedom's Port*, 183. The needs of the local economy ensured that blacks continued to drive drays, wagons, and carts in Richmond despite laws prohibiting these practices. Sheldon, "Black-White Relations in Richmond," 41.

10. Nash, "A More Equitable Past?" 232.

11. Berlin, *Slaves without Masters*, 318, 327. See also Michael Johnson and James Roark, *Black Masters*, 42.

12. On free African Americans in the South, see Gregg Kimball, *American City, Southern Place*, 125; Stevenson, *Life in Black and White*, 267; Powers, *Black Charlestonians*, 61; Phillips, *Freedom's Port*, 185; and Whitman, *The Price of Freedom*, 163.

13. Stevenson, *Life in Black and White*, 264.

14. Higginbotham and Bosworth, "Rather Than the Free," 24–29; Stevenson, *Life in Black and White*, 275–90. The nature of the trial process for free African Americans charged with misdemeanors was often quite arbitrary. Joseph Mayo believed that the mayor "may, in his discretion, either try the [free black] offender or recognize

him to answer as in the case of a white person." Mayo, *A Guide to Magistrates*, 16. See also Sidbury, *Ploughshares into Swords*, 217.

15. On early nineteenth-century ideas concerning the reformative capacity of penitentiary imprisonment, see Meranzes, *Laboratories of Virtue*.

16. See Governor's Message, 7 Dec. 1846, and Governor's Message, 1847, *House Documents and Annual Reports*, 1847, LVA. On white attitudes toward imprisoning free blacks in Virginia, see Berlin, *Slaves without Masters*, 323; and *Annual Report of the Board of Directors of the Penitentiary Institution*, 1852. On support for the American Colonization Society in Virginia, see Shade, *Democratizing the Old Dominion*, 194.

17. In 1853 and 1858, the Virginia legislature debated the forcible expulsion of free African Americans from the state on pain of enslavement. Berlin, *Slaves without Masters*, 363, 371.

18. Free African Americans were sold into limited terms of servitude throughout the South for unpaid fines and jail fees, but rarely were they subject to "absolute" enslavement as in Virginia. Berlin, *Slaves without Masters*, 334; Schwarz, "The Transportation of Slaves from Virginia," 218. On the Cousins case, see *Dispatch*, 13 Jun. 1860.

19. Although free blacks were nowhere tried by their African American peers or permitted to give testimony against whites, only in Virginia were they denied trial by jury when charged with felonies. Conversely, however, Virginia was also unusual in using penitentiary imprisonment to punish free blacks. See Ayers, *Vengeance and Justice*, 61. On the development of the penitentiary in Virginia, see Preyer, "Crime, the Criminal Law, and Reform," 76–79. On free black punishments in other southern states, see Rice, "This Province, So Meanly and Thinly Inhabited"; Franklin, *The Free Negro in North Carolina*, 86–91; and Michael Johnson and James Roark, *Black Masters*, 47.

20. Howington, *What Sayeth the Law*, 241; McNair, "Justice Bound"; Hepler, "Color, Crime, and the City," 110–11, 116.

21. See chapter 3 in this volume.

22. For example, both James Hamblin and Matilda Finney were incarcerated for one year for stabbing free blacks. By contrast, John Binford, a shoemaker, and William Dungey were sentenced to seven and ten years respectively for stabbing white men. See *Commonwealth v. James Hamblin*, RHCM, 13 Nov. 1851; *Commonwealth v. Matilda Finney*, RHCM, 15 Dec. 1854; *Commonwealth v. John Binford*, RHCM, 12 Apr. 1849; and *Commonwealth v. William Dungey*, RHCM, 21 Sept. 1840.

23. *Commonwealth v. John Binford*, RHCM, 12 Apr. 1849.

24. See, for example, *Commonwealth v. Elizabeth Mildridge Harris*, RHCM, 28 Jun. 1833; *Commonwealth v. James Smith*, RHCM, 15 Oct. 1849; *Commonwealth v. Floyd Cousins*, RHCM, 15 May 1860.

25. John H. Gilmer to Governor William Smith, 6 Apr. 1848, *Commonwealth v. Richardson D. Smith*, Executive Papers, box 396, Rejected Claims, 1849; underlining in the original.

26. John H. Gilmer to Governor William Smith, 6 Apr. 1848.

27. C. S. Morgan to Governor John Floyd, 19 Jan. 1849; Richardson D. Smith to Governor John Floyd, 7 Feb. 1849; *Commonwealth v. Richardson D. Smith*, Executive Papers, box 396, Rejected Claims, 1849, LVA.

28. Mary Nicholson was released after serving five years of a twelve-year sentence for infanticide. Fielding Alexander Edins was jailed for five years for stabbing with intent to kill, but the court recommended that he be released after six months because of the circumstances in which the stabbing was committed. *Commonwealth v. Mary Nicholson* (alias Mary Scott), RHCM, 31 Nov. 1831 and Case of Mary Nicholson, Executive Journals of the Secretary of the Commonwealth, 2 Aug. 1837; *Commonwealth v. Fielding Alexander Edins*, RHCM, 16 Dec. 1840.

29. *Dispatch*, 30 Sept. 1852.

30. Wade, *Slavery in the Cities*, 186.

31. *Dispatch*, 14 Oct. 1852.

32. Ibid., 25 Mar. 1853.

33. Benjamin Rix's sentence of seventy-four lashes to be administered over three separate days was increased by twenty-four lashes after a failed appeal. Alexander Jackson's sentence of twenty lashes for a misdemeanor was increased to thirty-nine lashes. *Dispatch*, 12 May and 13 July 1853.

34. Morris ex parte, 1854 in Catterall, *Judicial Cases Concerning American Slavery*, 1: 230.

35. *Dispatch*, 12 Oct. 1854.

36. Eighty percent of illegal residency prosecutions were dropped before coming to court. RHCM, 1830–60.

37. When submitted by Richmond residents, 60 percent of such petitions were successful in the antebellum era. See Green, "Black Tobacco Factory Workers," 195. The large number of cases that were dropped also suggests that the threat of sale into slavery caused many defendants to leave Richmond before their scheduled appearance in court. RHCM, 1830–60.

38. On white support for free blacks charged with illegal residency, see Bogger, *Free Blacks in Norfolk*, 101; and Stevenson, *Life in Black and White*, 269.

39. The hustings court approved less than 14 percent of petitions for residency in Richmond made by free blacks from outside the city. Green, "Black Tobacco Factory Workers," 195.

40. Case of Samuel Stevenson, Executive Papers, Rejected Claims, 1838. Mayor Tate did not believe Stevenson's story, and the petition was rejected. Nevertheless, the case illustrates the potential clash between white economic interests and Virginia's restrictive free black laws.

41. Case of Robert Jones, Executive Papers, May-June 1835.

42. Loren Schweninger has argued that whites provided "'protection' to individual free blacks whom they deemed especially industrious," while Thomas Bogger has claimed that whites protected reputable free blacks threatened with the loss of their liberty in order to reinforce paternalistic ties between the leaders of white society and

"unoffending free blacks." Schweninger, "Prosperous Blacks in the South," 46; Bogger, *Free Blacks in Norfolk*, 101. See also Berlin, *Slaves without Masters*, 339–40.

43. Richmond Personal Property Tax Book, 1830. The slaveholders who petitioned each owned between two and twelve slaves.

44. Bogger, *Free Blacks in Norfolk*, 60.

45. See Powers, *Black Charlestonians*, 50, 57–59, 72.

46. On the free black elite in the antebellum South, see Schweninger, "Prosperous Blacks," 31–46; Michael Johnson and James Roark, *Black Masters*; and Bynum, *Unruly Women*, 27, 78–79.

47. On sympathetic interracial relationships, see Rothman, *Notorious in the Neighborhood*, 6; and Lockley, *Lines in the Sand*, 56.

48. Convicts often drew attention to the high social status of the men and women who supported their petitions. See, for example, Case of John H. Richardson, Executive Papers, July 1842; Case of Granville Winston, Executive Papers, Rejected Claims, 1842; Case of William H. Oney, Executive Papers, Nov. 1853.

49. Stevenson, *Life in Black and White*, 263.

50. Case of Andrew James, Executive Papers, box 427, 19 Jun. 1855.

51. Case of Coleman Day, Executive Papers, box 356, Rejected Claims, 1838.

52. See, for example, *Attoo v. the Commonwealth*; *Commonwealth v. Fields*; *Commonwealth v. Watts*; *Day v. Commonwealth*, in Catterall, *Judicial Cases Concerning American Slavery*, 1: 169, 175–76, 210. On appellate rulings in trials of blacks in the Old South, see Nash, "Reason of Slavery," 7–218.

53. Daniel Flanigan has argued that "the Virginia judiciary would not formulate special rules in accordance with blacks' inferior position in society" (*The Criminal Law of Slavery*, 134).

54. Higginbotham and Jacobs, "Law Only as an Enemy," 992.

55. MCDB, 22 Feb. 1837, 115.

56. There is no record that Winston was pardoned during the 1850s. *Commonwealth v. Winston*, RHCM, 8 Jun. 1846. Lists of penitentiary inmates are contained in U.S. Census, Richmond City, 1850 and 1860.

57. Many murder defendants were convicted of manslaughter, but this does not appear to have been the case with Winston; the census takers specifically recorded that he was imprisoned for murder.

58. *Dispatch*, 15 Sept. 1858.

59. *Semi-Weekly Enquirer*, 18 Oct. 1859. Even slave defendants charged with the most serious crimes sometimes received a sympathetic hearing from white jurors if they had acted in defense of their honor. See, for example, Joshua Rothman's discussion of the case of Manuel, a slave in King George County, Virginia, who murdered a white man who had sexual relations with his (Manuel's) wife (*Notorious in the Neighborhood*, 149). See also Lockley, "The Strange Case of George Flyming," 250.

60. *Dispatch*, 10 Sept. and 17 Oct. 1856; RHCM, 9, 10, and 20 Sept. 1856.

61. During the first third of the nineteenth century, free blacks could not be executed for rape in Virginia. In 1796, the state legislature had abolished the death pen-

alty for all crimes committed by free persons except murder in the first degree. The revised criminal code of 1819 specifically provided penitentiary imprisonment as the punishment for all free persons convicted of rape, including free African Americans. In 1823, however, an act was passed that clouded the situation considerably by making the attempted rape of a white woman by a slave or a free black person a capital crime. It appears, therefore, that until a further revision of the law in 1837, free blacks could be executed for attempted rape, but if their attempts had proved successful, they could only be imprisoned. Even the 1837 legislation did not make clear how Jackson should have been tried, as it mandated the death penalty only for the rape or attempted rape of a white woman and made no reference to free black rape victims. Guild, *Black Laws*, 161–65.

62. *Anderson v. Commonwealth*, 4 Leigh 505, Catterall, *Judicial Cases Concerning American Slavery*, 1: 177–78.

63. Although the precise fraction of black blood that defined a person as a mulatto varied, similar laws were enacted in most southern states in the antebellum period. Only in Delaware, Georgia, and South Carolina was a different system established. In these three states, race was defined in terms of observation, reputation, appearance, and performance. Gross, "Litigating Whiteness," 109–88, 111–12; Michael Johnson and James Roark, *Black Masters*, 55.

64. Gross, "Litigating Whiteness," 112.

65. Thomas Morris, *Southern Slavery and the Law*, 21.

66. This argument is discussed at greater length in Rothman, *Notorious in the Neighborhood*, 209–10.

67. See for example, the North Carolina case of *State v. Jacobs* (1859), in which the court ruled that "the effect of the intermixture of the blood of the different races of people is surely a matter of science, and may be learned by observation and study. . . . Any person of ordinary intelligence, who for a sufficient length of time, will devote his attention to the subject, will be able to discover, with almost unerring certainty, the adulteration of the Caucasian with the Negro or Indian blood." Quoted in Johnston, *Race Relations in Virginia*, 197.

68. Gross, "Litigating Whiteness," 111; Rothman, *Notorious in the Neighborhood*, 218–20.

69. MCDB, 15 Nov. 1836.

70. Ibid., 10 Jun. 1836 and 30 Mar. 1837, quoted in Rothman, *Notorious in the Neighborhood*, 175.

71. *Republican*, 8 Jun. 1850.

72. Rothman, *Notorious in the Neighborhood*, 211.

73. *Dispatch*, 14 Sept. 1853.

74. Ibid., 1 Dec. 1853.

75. Ibid., 25 Aug. and 1 Sept. 1858.

76. In contrast to the fate that the hustings court prescribed for Ferguson, there is no evidence that free blacks who were convicted of assault in the mayor's court were sentenced to imprisonment. In 1852, the mayor convicted thirty-eight free blacks of

assault, all of whom were either whipped or bound over to keep the peace. In 1860, the mayor adjudged fourteen free blacks guilty of assault. Thirteen were sentenced to the lash, and one gave security to keep the peace. *Dispatch*, 14 Jan. 1852–13 Jan. 1853 and 1 Jan.–1 Dec. 1860.

77. The only other free black defendants who were tried for misdemeanors in the hustings court after 1833 were Margaret Dunlop and William Campbell. Dunlop was accused of arson and discharged as the jury was divided, while Campbell was convicted on four counts of aiding a slave to abscond. It is unclear why the mayor sent these cases for trial, for as misdemeanors they were not capital offenses when committed by whites. There is also no evidence that either Dunlop or Campbell claimed to be "not Negroes." As both cases occurred within eighteen months of the enactment in Virginia of new laws abolishing jury trials for free blacks in all but capital felony cases, it is likely that simple judicial error was responsible for the mistaken form of prosecution. See *Commonwealth v. Margaret Dunlop*, RHCM, 19 Jul. 1833; Case of William Campbell, Executive Papers, box 343, 14 Dec. 1835, and *Commonwealth v. William Campbell*, RHCM, 28 Feb. and 1 Mar. 1833. At least one other free person of color who was officially "not a negro" was remanded to appear before the grand jury charged with a misdemeanor, but the case never came to trial. In 1858, the *Dispatch* reported that Agnes Cosby was to appear at the next session of the hustings court to answer the charge that she beat her free black husband. The hustings court minutes do not contain a record of Cosby's case, however, and it is therefore probable that the grand jury did not find a true bill, possibly because of the defendant's mixed race status. *Dispatch*, 2 Sept. 1858.

78. *Dispatch*, 2 Sept. 1858.

79. *Commonwealth v. Elick*, RHCM, 28 Jan. 1831, *Commonwealth v. Stephen*, RHCM, 25 Oct. 1834.

80. *Commonwealth v. Fielding Alexander Edins*, RHCM, 16 and 19 Dec. 1840; Case of Fielding Alexander Edins, Executive Papers, 29 Jan. 1842.

81. Howison, *Reports of Criminal Trials*, 76, 84.

82. Cobb, *An Inquiry into the Law of Negro Slavery*, 226. In the 1850s, Louisiana allowed free blacks to testify against white defendants, though their social standing could be taken into account when evaluating their testimony. Hepler, "Color, Crime, and the City," 162.

83. *Republican*, 13 Jun. 1850.

84. *Commonwealth v. Elizabeth Southard*, RHCEC, 20 Jul. 1850.

85. U.S. Census, Richmond City, 1850.

86. Rothman counted sixty-one different ways that the skin color of runaway slaves was reported to the Richmond police in the 1830s and 1840s (*Notorious in the Neighborhood*, 204).

87. Howison, *Reports of Criminal Trials*, 78.

88. On the increasingly strict enforcement of the 1806 residency law in the 1850s see Green, "Black Tobacco Factory Workers," 195–96.

89. U.S. Census, Richmond City, 1850.

90. Howison, *Reports of Criminal Trials*, 79.

91. Ibid., 79–80.

92. Ibid., 80.

93. In her analysis of cases of racial determination appealed to southern state supreme courts, Ariela Gross concluded that, even at the end of the antebellum period, science was not the "dominant racial discourse" in southern trials ("Litigating Whiteness," 179).

94. Gregg Kimball, *American City, Southern Place*, 184.

95. Howison, *Reports of Criminal Trials*, 82–83.

96. *Commonwealth v. Matilda Finney*, RHCEC 13 Nov. and 15 Dec. 1854.

97. For example, see *Commonwealth v. James Hamblin*, RHCM, 13 Nov. 1851; *Commonwealth v. John Binford*, RHCM, 12 Apr. 1849; and *Commonwealth v. William Dungey*, RHCM, 21 Sept. 1840.

98. On hunting and constructions of masculinity in the Old South, see Proctor, *Bathed in Blood*, 21. On gender and expectations of appropriate female conduct, see Bynum, *Unruly Women*, 7, 110. On gender and constructions of racial identity, see Walter Johnson, "The Slave Trader," 37–38.

99. Gregg Kimball, *American City, Southern Place*, 32.

100. Sidbury discusses black and white gender conventions in early national Richmond in *Ploughshares into Swords*, 221–23, 249.

101. For an alternative interpretation suggesting that the prospect of white slavery did not threaten southern slaveholders, see Wilson and Wilson, "White Slavery," 18.

102. Free African Americans who left Richmond headed to all parts of the United States from Philadelphia to Ohio and as far afield as California. The records of the First African Baptist Church document that sixty-nine free church members left Richmond in the 1840s and a further two hundred in the 1850s. Gregg Kimball, *American City, Southern Place*, 128–29.

103. *Dispatch*, 2, 9, and 12 Mar. 1858.

104. For a similar assessment of free black complainants in Maryland, see Rice, "Crime and Punishment in Frederick County," 441.

105. In 1860, free African Americans accounted for 21 out of the 284 victims of violent crime in mayor's court cases whose race and status was recorded in the *Dispatch*. *Dispatch*, 1 Jan.–31 Dec. 1860.

106. In 1838, there were just two mayor's court cases in which free blacks appeared as victims of assault by whites and both were sustained by evidence from white men. In 1852, the *Dispatch* recorded only five cases of whites assaulting free blacks, and one of these was dismissed despite being brought by a white man.

107. *Dispatch*, 14 Jan. 1852–13 Jan. 1853.

108. Ibid., 22 Jun. 1852. In the final three decades of the antebellum period, just seventeen cases of violent crime committed by whites against free blacks were considered sufficiently serious to be sent on to the hustings court. RHCM, 1830–60.

109. Between 1830 and 1860, only eight free African Americans appear in the

hustings court records as victims of property crime in cases involving white defendants. RHCM, 1830–60.

110. Rice, "Crime and Punishment in Frederick County," 441. In his study of race and crime in New Orleans, Mark Hepler claimed that whites all but encouraged African Americans to employ the legal system in their disputes with each other as this impeded the cohesiveness of the black community ("Color, Crime, and the City," 116).

111. Suggs, *Whispered Consolations*, 26.

112. McKivigan, *The Roving Editor*, 29.

113. Brown, *Narrative of the Life of Henry Box Brown*, 40.

114. Ibid., 41.

115. Other major slaveholders were also involved in church affairs. James Grant served as an officer of the African Baptist Church and sponsored the membership of many of his slaves, as did Thomas and Samuel Hardgrove. John Enders and Poiteaux Robinson regularly "involved themselves in sponsoring, excluding, and restoring church memberships of slaves they owned or hired." Schnittman, "Slavery in Virginia's Urban Tobacco Industry," 71–79.

116. This was one of the few negative consequences for African Americans of Richmond's segregated Baptist churches. Betty Wood has argued that black members of interracial Baptist and Methodist churches sought an equality of respect and the right to protection from any form of abuse, verbal or physical, perpetrated against them by any other of their fellow church members, black or white. Indeed, until the early nineteenth century, black testimony was admissible against whites in Virginia church courts. Wood, "For Their Satisfaction or Redress," 110, 114–15.

117. Only when Jane and John Williams were charged with the murders of Virginia Winston and her daughter did the First African Baptist Church pass judgment on an offense that was also brought to the attention of white authorities. Both slaves were excluded from the church. Minutes of the First African Baptist Church, 18 Jul. 1852, LVA.

118. See Tyler-McGraw and Kimball, *In Bondage and Freedom*, 36.

119. Minutes of the First African Baptist Church, 5 Sept. 1852, LVA.

120. Ibid., 3 Mar. 1844, LVA.

121. Other offenses that were examined included unchristian conduct and swearing.

122. Seventeen of these church members were slaves, and five were free African Americans.

123. *Dispatch*, 3 Sept. 1858.

124. MCDB, 6 Feb. and 21 Sept. 1838, 236, 326.

125. Minutes of the Ebenezer Baptist Church, 18 July 1858, LVA.

126. Minutes of the First African Baptist Church, Jan. 1842, LVA.

127. Ibid., Jan. 1842.

128. Schwarz, *Slave Laws in Virginia*, 33.

Epilogue

1. Takagi, *Rearing Wolves*, 132–42.
2. Gregg Kimball, *American City, Southern Place*, 249–50.
3. William Kimball, *Starve or Fall*, 42–43.
4. It is far beyond the scope of this study to examine why the Confederacy lost the Civil War. However, the case of crime and punishment in Richmond supports an interpretation that affords some importance to factors on the home front. For a contrary argument see Gallagher, *Confederate War*.
5. Du Bois, *The Philadelphia Negro*, 239. See also Slaughter, *Bloody Dawn*, 39.
6. Pincus, *Virginia Supreme Court*, 19-26, 122; Rabinowitz, *Race Relations*, 31–60; Kennedy, *Race, Crime, and the Law*, 312-16. See also Oshinsky, *Worse Than Slavery*.
7. Brundage explains the lower rate of lynching in the postbellum Border South in terms of the region's economy (*Lynching in the New South*, 141–56).
8. Waldrep, "Substituting Law for the Lash," 1426–27.
9. Rabinowitz argues that there was a transition in southern race relations from the *exclusion* of African Americans from public buildings and institutions during the antebellum era to the establishment of segregated facilities after the Civil War (*Race Relations*, 331–32).
10. Rise, "Race, Rape, and Radicalism," 461–90; Klarman, "The Racial Origins of Modern Criminal Procedure"; Higginbotham, *Shades of Freedom*, 137–68.

Bibliography

Manuscripts and Archival Sources

ARCHIVES RESEARCH SERVICES, LIBRARY OF VIRGINIA, RICHMOND

Condemned Blacks Executed or Transported. Records, 1783–1865.
Ebenezer African Baptist Church, Richmond City. Minute Book, 1858–72.
Executive Journals of the Secretary of the Commonwealth, 1832–60.
Executive Papers: Letters Received, Pardon Papers, 1833–60.
First African Baptist Church, Richmond City. Minute Book, 1841–59.
First Baptist Church, Richmond City. Minute Book, 1851–60.
Henley, Bernard J. Papers, 1917–89.
House Documents and Annual Reports, 1830–60.
Richmond City Council Minutes, 1830–60.
Richmond City Hustings Court, Ended Causes, 1830–60.
Richmond City Hustings Court, Minutes, 1830–60.
Richmond City Personal Property Tax Registers, 1830–60.
Richmond City Records of Criminal Charges.
Sheppard, Ludwell William. Diary, 1853–54.
U.S. Census, Richmond City, 1830–60.
Whitlock, Philip. Recollections, 1843–1913.

VIRGINIA HISTORICAL SOCIETY, RICHMOND

Keith Family Papers, 1710–1865.
Letter (2 June 1836, University of Virginia) of William Garland Pendleton (1788–1839) to Charles Stephen Morgan.
Montague Family Papers, 1808–1939.
Richmond City Sergeant Papers, 1841–51.
Rutherford, John Coles. Common Place Book, 1844–49.
Society for the Prevention of the Absconding and Abduction of Slaves (Richmond, Va.). Minutes, 1833–49.
Sparrow, Caroline Lambert. "Notes Concerning the Case of the Slave Girl Virginia Who Was Tried before the Hustings Court of Richmond, Virginia, in February and March 1843 for Setting Fire to and Burning a Dwelling by William B. Rushmer and Belonging to Thomas Cowles and Sterling I. Crump." Typescript.
Watson Family Papers, 1771–1934.
Wise, Obadiah J. Papers.

VALENTINE MUSEUM, RICHMOND

Richmond Mayor's Court Docket Book, 1836–39.

SPECIAL COLLECTIONS DEPARTMENT, UNIVERSITY OF VIRGINIA LIBRARY, CHARLOTTESVILLE

Brooke Family Correspondence.
Jackson, Joseph, Jr. Diary, January 1–June 30, 1847.
Daybook of the Richmond Police Guard, 1834–43.

HUNTINGTON LIBRARY, SAN MARINO, CALIFORNIA

Brock, Robert. Collection.

RARE BOOK, MANUSCRIPT, AND SPECIAL COLLECTIONS LIBRARY, DUKE UNIVERSITY, DURHAM, NORTH CAROLINA

Robinson, Conway. Papers, 1830–33.

Newspapers

Richmond Daily Dispatch, 1852–61.
Richmond Enquirer, 1833–61.
Richmond Republican, 1849–51.
Richmond Whig and Public Advertiser (semiweekly), 1845–49.

Published Primary Sources

Acts of Assembly relating to the city of Richmond, and ordinances of the Common Council, subsequent to January 1831. Collected and printed by order of the Common Council. Richmond, 1831.
Acts of the General Assembly of the State of Virginia, Passed at Called Session, 1863, in the Eighty-Eighth Year of the Commonwealth. Richmond, 1863. http://docsouth.unc.edu/imls/vasess63/vasess63.html.
Acts of the General Assembly of Virginia. Richmond, 1851.
Annual Report of the Board of Directors of the Penitentiary Institution. Richmond, 1852.
The Annual Report of the Richmond Society for the Promotion of Temperance. Richmond, 1832.
An Authenticated report of the trial of Myers and others, for the the Murder of Dudley Marvin Hoyt. With the able and eloquent speeches of counsel, and "the letters" in full, with explanatory notes, which furnish a clear and complete history of the case.... Drawn up by the Editor of the "Richmond Southern Standard." New York, 1846.
Brown, Henry. *Narrative of the Life of Henry Box Brown: Written by Himself.* New York: Oxford University Press, 2002.

Catterall, Helen, ed. *Judicial Cases Concerning American Slavery and the Negro*. Vol. 1. New York: Negro Universities Press, 1968.

The Charters and Ordinances of the City of Richmond with the Declaration of Rights and Constitution of Virginia. Richmond, 1859.

Chesson, Michael B., and Leslie J. Roberts, eds. *Exile in Richmond: The Confederate Journal of Henri Garidel*. Charlottesville: University Press of Virginia, 2001.

Cobb, Thomas R. R. *An Inquiry into the Law of Negro Slavery in the United States of America*. Athens: University of Georgia Press, 1999.

A Collection of Cases decided by the General Court of Virginia, Chiefly relating to the Penal Laws of the Commonwealth. Commencing in the year 1789, and ending in 1814. Copied from the Records of Said Court, with Explanatory Notes, by Judges Brockenbrough and Holmes. Philadelphia, 1815.

Controversy between "Erskine" and "W. M." on the Practicability of Suppressing Gambling. Richmond, 1862.

Duke, Maurice, and Daniel P. Jordan. *A Richmond Reader, 1733–1983*. Chapel Hill: University of North Carolina Press, 1983.

Ellyson, H. K. *Ellyson's Business Directory, and Almanac, for the Year 1845*. Richmond, 1845.

Ferslew, W. Eugene. *First Annual Directory for the City of Richmond, to Which is Added a Business Directory for 1859*. Richmond, 1859.

———. *Second Annual Directory for the City of Richmond, to Which is Added a Business Directory for 1860*. Richmond, 1860.

The First Annual Report of the Richmond Society for the Promotion of Temperance. Richmond, 1830.

Flournoy, H. W., ed. *Calendar of Virginia State Papers and Other Manuscripts from January 1, 1836 to April 15, 1869 Preserved in the Capitol at Richmond*. Vol. 11. Richmond, 1893; reprint, New York, 1968.

Governor's Biennial Messages to the General Assembly of the State of Virginia, December 5, 1859. Richmond, 1859.

Guild, June Purcell. *Black Laws of Virginia: A Summary of the Legislative Acts of Virginia Concerning Negroes from Earliest Times to the Present*. Richmond: Whittet and Shepperson, 1936.

Hening, William Waller, ed. *The Statutes at Large; being a Collection of all the Laws of Virginia, from the First Session of the Legislature, in the year 1619*. 13 vols. Richmond, 1809–23.

Hints on Three Defects in the Criminal Laws of Virginia. Louisa, Va.: [a Member of the Bar], 1845.

Howison, Robert Reid. *Reports of Criminal Trials in the Circuit, State and United States Courts, Held in Richmond, Virginia*. Richmond, 1851.

The Letters and Correspondence of Mrs. Virginia Myers, (Which Have Never Before Been Published or Even Read in Court,) to Dudley Marvin Hoyt, who was Murdered At Richmond, Sept. 28th, 1846, By William R. Myers, and Two Others. Together with a denial of the truth of Mrs. Myers' Letter of Explanation of November

Last, from Alta Vista. Likewise added A Short Biography of D.M. Hoyt by a Relative of the Deceased. Philadelphia, 1847.

Manarin, Louis, ed. *Richmond at War: The Minutes of the City Council, 1861–1865.* Chapel Hill: University of North Carolina Press, 1966.

Mayo, Joseph. *A Guide to Magistrates: With Practical Forms for the Discharge of their Duties out of Court to which are added precedents for the use of Prosecutors, Sheriffs, Coroners, Constables, Escheators, Clerks, &c. Adapted to the new code of Virginia.* Richmond, 1850.

McKivigan, John R. ed. *The Roving Editor, or Talks with Slaves in the Southern States, By James Redpath.* University Park: Pennsylvania State University Press, 1996.

Minor, John B. *A Synopsis of the Law of Crimes and Punishments in Virginia.* Philadelphia, 1858.

Montague, William L. *Montague's Richmond Directory and Business Advertiser for 1850–1851.* Richmond, 1851.

———. *Montague's Richmond Directory and Business Advertiser for 1852.* Richmond, 1852.

Mordecai, Samuel. *Richmond in By-Gone Days: Being Reminiscences of an Old Citizen.* Richmond, 1856.

Olmsted, Frederick Law. *The Slave States.* New York: Capricorn, 1959.

Ordinances of the Corporation of the City of Richmond and the Acts of Assembly Relating Thereto. Richmond, 1831.

Ordinances passed by the Council of the city of Richmond, since the year 1839. Published by authority of the Council. Richmond, 1847.

Particulars of the Dreadful Tragedy in Richmond on the morning of the 19th July, 1852: Being a Full Account of the Awful Murder of the Winston Family. . . . Richmond, 1852.

"The Personal Narrative of Mrs. Margaret Douglass, a Southern Woman, who was Imprisoned for One Month in the Common Jail of Norfolk, under the Laws of Virginia, for the Crime of Teaching Free Colored Children to Read." In *Slave Rebels, Abolitionists, and Southern Courts: The Pamphlet Literature,* edited by Paul Finkelman. Ser. 4, vol. 2. New York: Garland, 1988.

Report of the Committee of Twenty-Four, Appointed at a Meeting of the Citizens of Richmond, Held the 28th day of October, 1833, for the purpose of devising means to suppress the Vice of Gambling in this City. Richmond, 1833.

Report of the Joint Committee on the Penitentiary. Richmond, 1839.

Report of the Minority of the Committee of Twenty-Four on the Subject of Gambling in the City of Richmond. Richmond, 1833.

Revised Code of the Laws of Virginia. Richmond, 1849.

Stroud, George M. *Sketch of the Laws Relating to Slavery in the Several States of the United States of America.* Philadelphia, 1827.

Tate, Joseph. *Digest of the Laws of Virginia, which are of a Permanent Character and General Operation; Illustrated by Judicial Decisions: to which is added, An Index of the Names of the Cases in the Virginia Reporters*. Richmond: Smith and Palmer, 1841.

Published Secondary Sources

Aguirre, Carlos. "Working the System: Black Slaves and the Courts in Lima, Peru, 1821–1854." In *Crossing Boundaries: Comparative History of Black People in Diaspora*, edited by Darlene Clark Hine and Jacqueline A. McLeod. Bloomington: Indiana University Press, 1999.

Aptheker, Herbert. *American Negro Slave Revolts*. New York: International, 1990.

Ashworth, John. *Slavery, Capitalism, and Politics in the Antebellum Republic*. Cambridge: Cambridge University Press, 1995.

Ayers, Edward L. *Vengeance and Justice: Crime and Punishment in the Nineteenth-Century American South*. Oxford: Oxford University Press, 1984.

Barber, E. Susan. "Depraved and Abandoned Women: Prostitution in Richmond, Virginia, across the Civil War." In *Neither Lady nor Slave: Working Women of the Old South*, edited by Susanna Delfino and Michele Gillespie, 155–73. Chapel Hill: University of North Carolina Press, 2002.

Bardaglio, Peter. "Rape and the Law in the Old South: 'Calculated to Excite Indignation in Every Heart.'" *Journal of Southern History* 60 (1994): 749–72.

Barnes, L. Diane. "Southern Artisans, Organization, and the Rise of a Market Economy in Antebellum Petersburg." *Virginia Magazine of History and Biography* 107 (1999): 159–88.

Beattie, James. *Policing and Punishment in London, 1660–1750*. Oxford: Oxford University Press, 2001.

Bell, Michael Everette. "Regional Identity in the Antebellum South: How German Immigrants Became 'Good' Charlestonians." *South Carolina Historical Magazine* 100 (1999): 9–28.

Bellows, Barbara L. *Benevolence among Slaveholders: Assisting the Poor in Charleston 1670–1860*. Baton Rouge: Louisiana State University Press, 1993.

Bender, Thomas, ed. *The Antislavery Debate: Capitalism and Abolitionism as a Problem in Historical Interpretation*. Oxford: University of California Press, 1992.

Benton, Orville Vernon, and Robert C. McMath, eds. *Class, Conflict, and Consensus: Antebellum Southern Community Studies*. Westport, Ct.: Greenwood Press, 1982.

Berlin, Ira. *Many Thousands Gone: The First Two Centuries of Slavery in North America*. Cambridge: Harvard University Press, 1998.

———. *Slaves without Masters: The Free Negro in the Antebellum South*. New York: Pantheon, 1974.

Berlin, Ira, and Herbert G. Gutman. "Natives and Immigrants, Free Men and Slaves: Urban Workingmen in the Antebellum American South." *American Historical Review* 88 (1983): 1175–200.

Berry, Thomas S. "The Rise of Flour Milling in Richmond." *Virginia Magazine of History and Biography* 78 (1970): 387–408.

Blassingame, John W. *The Slave Community: Plantation Life in the Antebellum South*. New York: Oxford University Press, 1972.

Block, Sharon. "Lines of Color, Sex, and Service: Comparative Sexual Coercion in Early America." In *Sex, Love, Race, and Crossing Boundaries in North American History*, edited by Martha Hodes. New York: New York University Press, 1999.

Bloomberg, Thomas G., and Karol Lucken. *American Penology: A History of Control*. New York: de Gruyter, 2000.

Bodenhamer, David J. "The Efficiency of Criminal Justice in the Antbellum South." *Criminal Justice History* 3 (1982): 81–95.

———. *Fair Trial Rights of the Accused in American History*. New York: Oxford University Press, 1992.

———. "Law and Disorder in the Old South: The Situation in Georgia, 1830–1860." In *From the Old South to the New: Essays on the Transitional South*, edited by Walter J. Fraser Jr. and Winfred B. Moore Jr. Westport, Ct.: Greenwood Press, 1981.

———. *The Pursuit of Justice: Crime and Law in Antebellum Indiana*. New York: Garland, 1986.

Bodenhamer, David J., and J. W. Ely, eds. *Ambivalent Legacy: A Legal History of the Old South*. Jackson: University Press of Mississippi, 1984.

Bogger, Thomas L. *Free Blacks in Norfolk, Virginia, 1790–1860: The Darker Side of Freedom*. Charlottesville: University Press of Virginia, 1997.

Bolton, Charles C. *Poor Whites of the Antebellum South: Tenants and Laborers in Central North Carolina and Northeast Mississippi*. Durham: Duke University Press, 1994.

Bolton, Charles C., and Scott P. Culclasure, eds. *The Confessions of Edward Isham: A Poor White Life of the Old South*. Athens: University of Georgia Press, 1998.

Bond, Bradley G. *Political Culture in the Nineteenth-Century South: Mississippi, 1830–1900*. Baton Rouge: Louisiana State University Press, 1995.

Brown, Else Barkley, and Gregg D. Kimball. "Mapping the Terrain of Black Richmond." *Journal of Urban History* 21 (1995): 296–346.

Brown, Richard Maxwell. *Strain of Violence: Historical Studies of American Violence and Vigilantism*. New York: Oxford University Press, 1975.

Bruce, Dickson D. *Violence and Culture in the Antebellum South*. Austin: University of Texas Press, 1979.

Brundage, William F. *Lynching in the New South: Georgia and Virginia, 1880–1930*. Urbana: University of Illinois Press, 1993.

Bynum, Victoria E. *Unruly Women: The Politics of Social and Sexual Control in the Old South*. Chapel Hill: University of North Carolina Press, 1992.

Byrne, William A. "Slave Crime in Savannah, Georgia." *Journal of Negro History* 79 (1994): 352–62.

Cash, W. J. *The Mind of the South*. New York: Knopf, 1941.

Cashin, Edward J., and Glenn T. Eskew, eds. *Paternalism in a Southern City: Race,*

Religion, and Gender in Augusta, Georgia. Athens: University of Georgia Press, 2001.

Cei, Louis Bernard. "Law Enforcement in Richmond: A History of Police-Community Relations, 1737–1974." Ph.D. diss., Florida State University, 1975.

Click, Patricia. *The Spirit of the Times: Amusements in Nineteenth-Century Baltimore, Norfolk, and Richmond*. Charlottesville: University Press of Virginia, 1989.

Clinton, Catherine. *The Plantation Mistress: Woman's World in the Old South*. New York: Pantheon, 1982.

Cohen, Patricia Cline. *The Murder of Helen Jewett*. New York: Vintage, 1999.

Cole, Stephanie. "Changes for Mrs. Thornton's Arthur: Patterns of Domestic Service in Washington, DC, 1800–1835." *Social Science History* 15 (1991): 367–79.

———. "Keeping the Peace: Domestic Assault and Private Prosecution in Antebellum Baltimore." In *Over the Threshold: Intimate Violence in Early America*, edited by Christine Daniels and Michael V. Kennedy. New York: Routledge, 1999.

Cottrol, Robert J. "Clashing Traditions: Civil Law and Common Law and the American Culture of Slave Governance." *Slavery and Abolition* 19 (1998): 150–57.

Crawford, Martin. *Ashe County's Civil War: Community and Society in the Appalachian South*. Charlottesville: University Press of Virginia, 2001.

Culclasure, Scott P. "'I Have Killed a Damned Dog': Murder by a Poor White in the Antebellum South." In *The Confessions of Edward Isham: A Poor White Life of the Old South*, edited by Charles C. Bolton and Scott P. Culclasure. Athens: University of Georgia Press, 1998.

Dabney, Virginius. *Richmond: The Story of a City*. New York: Doubleday, 1976.

Denham, James M. *"A Rogue's Paradise": Crime and Punishment in Antebellum Florida, 1821–1861*. Tuscaloosa: University of Alabama Press, 1997.

Dew, Charles B. *Ironmaker to the Confederacy: Joseph Anderson and the Tredegar Ironworks*. New Haven: Yale University Press, 1966.

Deyle, Steven. *Carry Me Back: The Domestic Slave Trade in American Life*. New York: Oxford University Press, 2005.

Du Bois, W.E.B. *The Philadelphia Negro: A Social Study*. Philadelphia: University of Pennsylvania Press, 1996.

Dusinberre, William. *Them Dark Days: Slavery in the American Rice Swamps*. New York: Oxford University Press, 1996.

Eaton, Clement. *The Growth of Southern Civilization, 1790–1860*. New York: Harper and Row, 1961.

Edwards, Laura F. "Law, Domestic Violence, and the Limits of Patriarchal Authority in the Antebellum South." *Journal of Southern History* 65 (1999): 733–70.

Egerton, Douglas R. *Gabriel's Rebellion: The Virginia Slave Conspiracies of 1800 and 1802*. Chapel Hill: University of North Carolina Press, 1993.

Ernst, William Joel, III. "Urban Leaders and Social Change: The Urbanization Process in Richmond, Virginia, 1840–1880." Ph.D. diss., University of Virginia, 1978.

Fede, Andrew. "Legitimized Violent Slave Abuse in the American South, 1619–1865." *American Journal of Legal History* 29 (1985): 93–150.

―――. *People without Rights: An Interpretation of the Fundamentals of the Law of Slavery in the U.S. South.* New York: Garland, 1992.
Femia, Joseph V. *Gramsci's Political Thought: Hegemony, Consciousness and the Revolutionary Process.* Oxford: Clarendon Press, 1981.
Ferdinand, Theodore. *Boston's Lower Criminal Courts.* London: Associated University Press, 1992.
Fields, Barbara Jeanne. *Slavery and Freedom on the Middle Ground: Maryland during the Nineteenth Century.* New Haven: Yale University Press, 1985.
―――. "Slavery, Race, and Ideology in the United States of America." *New Left Review* 181 (1990): 95-118.
Finkelman, Paul. Dred Scott v. Sandford: *A Brief History with Documents.* Boston: Bedford, 1997.
Flanigan, Daniel. *The Criminal Law of Slavery and Freedom, 1800-1868.* New York: Garland, 1987.
Fogel, Robert W., Ralph A. Galantine, and Richard L. Manning, eds. *Without Consent or Contract: The Rise and Fall of American Slavery: Evidence and Methods.* London: Norton, 1992.
Foucault, Michel. *Discipline and Punish: The Birth of the Prison.* London: Allen Lane, 1977.
Fox-Genovese, Elizabeth, and Eugene D. Genovese. *Fruits of Merchant Capital: Slavery and Bourgeois Property in the Rise and Expansion of Capitalism.* Oxford: Oxford University Press, 1983.
Franklin, John Hope. *The Free Negro in North Carolina: 1790-1860.* New York: Russell and Russell, 1967.
Franklin, John Hope, and Loren Schweninger. *Runaway Slaves: Rebels on the Plantation.* New York: Oxford University Press, 1999.
Frederickson, George M. *The Arrogance of Race: Historical Perspectives on Slavery, Racism, and Social Inequality.* Hanover, N.H.: Wesleyan University Press, 1988.
―――. *The Black Image in the White Mind: The Debate on Afro-American Character and Destiny, 1817-1914.* New York: Harper and Row, 1971.
Freehling, William W. *The Reintegration of American History: Slavery and the Civil War.* New York: Oxford University Press, 1994.
Friedman, Lawrence M. *Crime and Punishment in American History.* New York: Basic, 1993.
Friedman, Lawrence M., and Robert V. Percival. *The Roots of Justice: Crime and Punishment in Alameda County, California 1870-1910.* Chapel Hill: University of North Carolina Press, 1981.
Fronsman, Bill C. *Common Whites: Class and Culture in Antebellum North Carolina.* Lexington: University Press of Kentucky, 1992.
Gallagher, Gary W. *The Confederate War: How Popular Will, Nationalism, and Military Strategy Could Not Stave Off Defeat.* Cambridge: Harvard University Press, 1999.

Genovese, Eugene D. *The Political Economy of Slavery: Studies in the Economy and Society of the Slave South*. New York: Vintage, 1967.

———. *Roll, Jordan, Roll: The World the Slaves Made*. New York: Vintage, 1974.

———. *The World the Slaveholders Made: Two Essays in Interpretation*. New York: Vintage, 1969.

Glenn, Myra C. "Wife-Beating: The Darker Side of Victorian Domesticity." *Canadian Review of American Studies* 1 (1984): 17–33.

Goldfield, David R. *Region, Race, and Cities: Interpreting the Urban South*. Baton Rouge: Louisiana State University Press, 1997.

———. *Urban Growth in the Age of Sectionalism: Virginia, 1847–1861*. Baton Rouge: Louisiana State University Press, 1977.

Goldin, Claudia Dale. *Urban Slavery in the American South: A Quantitative Analysis*. Chicago: University of Chicago Press, 1976.

Green, Rodney D. "Black Tobacco Factory Workers and Social Conflict in Antebellum Richmond: Were Slavery and Urban Industry Really Compatible?" *Slavery and Abolition* 8 (1987): 183–203.

———. "Industrial Transition in the Land of Chattel Slavery: Richmond, Virginia, 1820–60." *International Journal of Urban and Regional Research* 8 (1984): 238–53.

Greenberg, Kenneth S. *Honor and Slavery: Lies, Duels, Noses, Masks, Dressing as a Woman, Gifts, Strangers, Humanitarianism, Death, Slave Rebellions, the Proslavery Argument, Baseball, Hunting, and Gambling in the Old South*. Princeton: Princeton University Press, 1996.

———. *Nat Turner: A Slave Rebellion in History and Memory*. New York: Oxford University Press, 2003.

Grimstead, David. *American Mobbing, 1828–1861: Toward Civil War*. New York: Oxford University Press, 1998.

Gross, Ariela J. "Beyond Black and White: Cultural Approaches to Race and Slavery." *Columbia Law Review* 101 (2001): 640–89.

———. *Double Character: Slavery and Mastery in the Antebellum Southern Courtroom*. Oxford: Princeton University Press, 2000.

———. "Litigating Whiteness: Trials of Racial Determination in the Nineteenth-Century South." *Yale Law Journal* 108 (1998): 109–88.

———. "Pandora's Box: Slave Character on Trial in the Antebellum Deep South." *Yale Journal of Law and the Humanities* 7 (1995): 267–316.

Grossberg, Michael. "Battling over Motherhood in Philadelphia: A Study of Antebellum American Trial Courts as Arenas of Conflict." In *Contested States: Law, Hegemony, and Resistance*, edited by Mindie Lazarus-Black and Susan F. Hirsch. London: Routledge, 1994.

———. "Social History Update: "Fighting Faiths" and the Challenges of Legal History." *Journal of Social History* 25 (1991): 191–201.

Guha, Ranajit, ed. *A Subaltern Studies Reader 1986–1995*. Minneapolis: University of Minnesota Press, 1997.

Hadden, Sally E. *Slave Patrols: Law and Violence in Virginia and the Carolinas.* Cambridge: Harvard University Press, 2001.

Hahn, Steven. *The Roots of Southern Populism: Yeoman Farmers and the Transformation of the Georgia Upcountry, 1850–1890.* New York: Oxford University Press, 1983.

Halttunen, Karen. "'"Domestic Differences": Competing Narratives of Womanhood in the Murder Trial of Lucretia Chapman." In *The Culture of Sentiment: Race, Gender, and Sentimentality in Nineteenth-Century America*, edited by Shirley Samuel, 43–57. Oxford: Oxford University Press, 1992.

Harcourt, Bernard E. "Imagery and Adjudication in the Criminal Law: The Relationship between Images of Criminal Defendants and Ideologies of Criminal Law in Southern Antebellum and Modern Appellate Decisions." *Brooklyn Law Review* 61 (1995): 1165–246.

Harris, J. William. *Plain Folk and Gentry in a Slave Society: White Liberty and Black Slavery in Augusta's Hinterlands.* Baton Rouge: Louisiana State University Press, 1998.

Hartog, Hendrik. "Lawyering Husband's Rights, and 'the Unwritten Law' in Nineteenth-Century America." *Journal of American History* 84 (1997): 67–96.

Haunton, Richard H. "Law and Order in Savannah, 1850–1860." *Georgia Historical Quarterly* 56 (1972): 1–24.

Hay, Douglas, Peter Linebaugh, John G. Rule, E. P. Thompson, and Cal Winslow. *Albion's Fatal Tree: Crime and Society in Eighteenth-Century England.* New York: Pantheon, 1975.

Haynes, Douglas, and Gyan Prakash, eds. *Contesting Power: Resistance and Everyday Social Relations in South Asia.* Delhi: Oxford University Press, 1999.

Henry, Howell M. *The Police Control of the Slave in South Carolina.* New York: Negro Universities Press, 1968.

Hepler, Mark. "Color, Crime and the City." Ph.D. diss., Rice University, 1972.

Herrup, Cynthia. *The Common Peace: Participation and the Criminal Law in Seventeenth-Century England.* Cambridge: Cambridge University Press, 1987.

Higginbotham, A. Leon, Jr. *Shades of Freedom: Racial Politics and Presumptions of the American Legal Process.* New York: Oxford University Press, 1996.

Higginbotham, A. Leon, Jr., and Greet C. Bosworth, "'Rather Than the Free': Free Blacks in Colonial and Antebellum Virginia." *Harvard Civil Rights–Civil Liberties Law Review* 26 (1991): 17–66.

Higginbotham, A. Leon, Jr., and Anne F. Jacobs. "The 'Law Only as an Enemy': The Legitimization of Racial Powerlessness through the Colonial and antebellum Criminal Laws of Virginia." *North Carolina Law Review* 70 (1992): 969–1070.

Hindus, Michael S. "Black Justice under White Law: Criminal Prosecutions of Blacks in Antebellum South Carolina." *Journal of American History* 63 (1976): 575–99.

———. "The Contours of Crime and Justice in Massachusetts and South Carolina, 1767–1878." *American Journal of Legal History* 21 (1977): 212–37.

———. *Prison and Plantation: Crime, Justice, and Authority in Massachusetts and South Carolina, 1767–1878*. Chapel Hill: University of North Carolina Press, 1980.

Hindus, Michael S., and Douglas Lamar Jones. "Quantitative Method or Quantum Meruit? Tactics for Early American Legal History." *Historical Methods* 13 (1980): 63–74.

Hobson, Barbara. "A Murder in the Moral and Religious City of Boston." *Boston Bar Journal* 22 (1978): 9–21.

Hodes, Martha, ed. *Sex, Love, Race, and Crossing Boundaries in North American History*. New York: New York University Press, 1999.

Holloway, Thomas H. *Policing Rio de Janeiro*. Stanford: Stanford University Press, 1993.

Howe, Adrian. *Punish and Critique: Towards a Feminist Analysis of Penality*. New York: Routledge, 1994.

Howington, Arthur F. *What Sayeth the Law: The Treatment of Slave and Free Blacks in the State and Local Courts of Tennessee*. New York: Garland, 1986.

Jordan, Ervin L. *Black Confederates and Afro-Yankees in Civil War Virginia*. Charlottesville: University Press of Virginia, 1995.

Johnson, David. *Policing the Urban Underworld: The Impact of Crime in the Development of the American Police, 1800–1887*. Philadelphia: Temple University Press, 1979.

Johnson, Michael P. "Denmark Vesey and His Co-Conspirators." *William and Mary Quarterly* 58 (2001): 915–76.

Johnson, Michael P., and James L. Roark. *Black Masters: A Free Family of Color in the Old South*. New York: Norton, 1984.

Johnson, Walter. "Inconsistency, Contradiction, and Complete Confusion: The Everyday Life of the Law of Slavery." *Law and Social Inquiry* 22 (1997): 405–33.

———. "The Slave Trader, the White Slave, and the Politics of Racial Determination in the 1850s." *Journal of American History* 87 (2000): 13–38.

———. *Soul by Soul: Life inside the Antebellum Slave Market*. Cambridge: Harvard University Press, 1999.

Johnston, James Hugo. *Race Relations in Virginia and Miscegenation in the South: 1776–1860*. Amherst: University of Massachusetts Press, 1970.

Jones, Norrece T., Jr. *Born a Child of Freedom, Yet a Slave: Mechanisms of Control and Strategies of Resistance in Antebellum South Carolina*. Hanover, N.H.: University Press of New England, 1990.

Jordan, Ervin L. *Black Confederates and Afro-Yankees in Civil War Virginia*. Charlottesville: University Press of Virginia, 1995.

Kairys, David., ed. *The Politics of Law: A Progressive Critique*. New York: Pantheon, 1990.

Kaplan, Michael. "New York City Tavern Violence and the Creation of a Working-Class Male Identity." *Journal of the Early Republic* 15 (1995): 592–616.

Kennedy, Randall. *Race, Crime, and the Law*. New York: Random House, 1998.
Kimball, Gregg D. *American City, Southern Place: A Cultural History of Antebellum Richmond*. Athens: University of Georgia Press, 2000.
Kimball, William J. *Starve or Fall: Richmond and Its People 1861–1865*. Michigan: University Microfilms International, 1976.
King, Peter. *Crime, Justice, and Discretion in England 1740–1820*. Oxford: Oxford University Press, 2000.
Klarman, Michael J. "The Racial Origins of Modern Criminal Procedure." *Michigan Law Review* 991, no. 1 (2000). http://papers.ssrn.com/sol3/papers.cfm?abstract_id=206428.
Konig, David Thomas. "'Dale's Laws' and the Non-Common Law Origins of Criminal Justice in Virginia." *American Journal of Legal History* 26 (1982): 354–75.
Lack, Paul D. "An Urban Slave Community: Little Rock, 1831–1862." *Arkansas Historical Quarterly* 41 (1982): 258–87.
Lane, Roger. *Murder in America: A History*. Columbus: Ohio State University Press, 1997.
———. *Policing the City: Boston 1822–1885*. Cambridge: Harvard University Press, 1967.
Laver, Harry S. "Rethinking the Social Role of the Militia: Community-Building in Antebellum Kentucky." *Journal of Southern History* 68 (2002): 777–816.
Lazarus-Black, Mindie, and Susan F. Hirsch, eds. *Contested States: Law, Hegemony, and Resistance*. London: Routledge, 1994.
Lebsock, Suzanne. *The Free Women of Petersburg: Status and Culture in a Southern Town, 1784–1860*. New York: Norton, 1984.
———. *A Murder in Virginia: Southern Justice on Trial*. New York: Norton, 2003.
Lee, Deborah A., and Warren R. Hofstra, "Race, Memory, and the Death of Robert Berkeley: 'A Murder of . . . Horrible and Savage Barbarity.'" *Journal of Southern History* 65 (1999): 41–76.
Lewis, Ronald L. *Coal, Iron, and Slaves: Industrial Slavery in Maryland and Virginia, 1715–1865*. Westport, Ct.: Greenwood Press, 1979.
Link, William A. "The Jordan Hatcher Case: Politics and 'A Spirit of Insubordination' in Antebellum Virginia." *Journal of Southern History* 64 (1998): 615–48.
———. *Roots of Secession: Slavery and Politics in Antebellum Virginia*. Chapel Hill: University of North Carolina Press, 2003.
Litwack, Leon F. "The Federal Government and the Free Negro, 1790–1860." *Journal of Negro History* 43 (1958): 261–78.
Lockley, Timothy J. *Lines in the Sand: Race and Class in Lowcountry Georgia, 1750–1860*. Athens: University of Georgia Press, 2001.
———. "The Strange Case of George Flyming: Justice and Gender in Antebellum Savannah." *Georgia Historical Quarterly* 84 (2000): 230–53.
Martin, Jonathan D. *Divided Mastery: Slave Hiring in the American South*. Cambridge: Harvard University Press, 2004.

Masur, Louis P. *Rites of Execution: Capital Punishment and the Transformation of American Culture, 1776–1865*. New York: Oxford University Press, 1989.

McCurry, Stephanie. "The Two Faces of Republicanism: Gender and Proslavery Politics in Antebellum South Carolina." *Journal of American History* 78 (1992): 1245–64.

McDonnell, Lawrence T. "Work, Culture, and Society in the Slave South, 1790-1861." In *Black and White Cultural Interaction in the Antebellum South*, edited by Ted Ownby. Jackson: University Press of Mississippi, 1993.

McLaurin, Melton A. *Celia, a Slave*. Athens: University of Georgia Press, 1991.

McNair, Glenn M. "Justice Bound: Aframericans, Crime, and Criminal Justice in Georgia, 1751–1865." Ph.D. diss., Emory University, 2001.

Meranzes, Michael. *Laboratories of Virtue: Punishment, Revolution, and Authority in Philadelphia, 1760–1835*. Chapel Hill: University of North Carolina Press, 1996.

Merry, Sally Engle. "Courts as Performances: Domestic Violence Hearing in a Hawai'i Family Court." In *Contested States: Law, Hegemony, and Resistance*, edited by Mindie Lazarus-Black and Susan F. Hirsch. London: Routledge, 1994.

Miller, Randal M. "The Enemy Within: Some Effects of Foreign Immigrants on Antebellum Southern Cities." *Southern Studies* 24 (1985): 30–53.

Miller, Vivien M. L. *Crime, Sexual Violence and Clemency: Florida's Pardon Board and Penal System in the Progressive Era*. Gainesville: University Press of Florida, 2000.

Miller, Wilbur R. *Cops and Bobbies: Police Authority in New York and London, 1830–1870*. Chicago: University of Chicago Press, 1977.

Monkkonen, Eric H. *The Dangerous Class: Crime and Poverty in Columbus, Ohio, 1860–1885*. Cambridge: Harvard University Press, 1975.

———. "A Disorderly People? Urban Order in the Nineteenth and Twentieth Centuries." *Journal of American History* 68 (1981): 539–59.

Morgan, Gwenda. *The Hegemony of the Law: Richmond County, Virginia, 1692–1776*. New York: Garland, 1989.

Morris, Christopher. "The Articulation of Two Worlds: The Master-Slave Relationship Reconsidered." *Journal of American History* 85 (1998): 982–1007.

———. *Becoming Southern: The Evolution of a Way of Life, Warren County and Vicksburg, Mississippi, 1770–1860*. Oxford: Oxford University Press, 1995.

Morris, Thomas D. "Slaves and the Rules of Evidence in Criminal Trials." In *Slavery and the Law*, edited by Paul Finkelman. Madison, Wisc.: Madison House, 1997.

———. *Southern Slavery and the Law, 1619–1860*. Chapel Hill: University of North Carolina Press, 1996.

Nash, A. E. Keir. "Fairness and Formalism in the Trials of Blacks in the State Supreme Courts of the Old South." *Virginia Law Review* 56 (1970): 64–100.

———. "A More Equitable Past? Southern Supreme Courts and the Protection of the Antebellum Negro." *North Carolina Law Review* 48 (Fall 1970): 197–241.

———. "Reason of Slavery: Understanding the Judicial Role in the Peculiar Institution." *Vanderbilt Law Review* 32 (1979): 7–218.
Oakes, James. *Slavery and Freedom: An Interpretation of the Old South*. New York: Knopf, 1990.
O'Brien, John T. "Factory, Church, and Community: Blacks in Antebellum Richmond." *Journal of Southern History* 44 (1978): 509–36.
Olwell, Robert. *Masters, Slaves, and Subjects: The Culture of Power in the South Carolina Low Country*. London: Cornell University Press, 1998.
Oshinsky, David M. *"Worse Than Slavery": Parchman Farm and the Ordeal of Jim Crow Justice*. New York: Free Press, 1996.
Owens, Leslie Howard. *This Species of Property: Slave Life and Culture in the Old South*. New York: Oxford University Press, 1976.
Pearson, Edward A., ed. *Designs against Charleston: The Trial Record of the Denmark Vesey Slave Conspiracy of 1822*. Chapel Hill: University of North Carolina Press, 1999.
Peters, John O., and Margaret T. Peters. *Courts of the Richmond Area: A Primer*. Richmond: Bar Association of the City of Richmond, 1969.
Pincus, Samuel N. *The Virginia Supreme Court, Blacks and the Law: 1870-1902*. New York and London: Garland, 1990.
Phillips, Christopher. *Freedom's Port: The African American Community of Baltimore, 1790–1860*. Urbana: University of Illinois Press, 1997.
Powers, Bernard E., Jr. *Black Charlestonians: A Social History, 1822–1885*. Fayetteville: University of Arkansas Press, 1994.
Preyer, Kathryn. "Crime, the Criminal Law and Reform in Post-Revolutionary Virginia." *Law and History Review* 1 (1983): 53–85.
Proctor, Nicolas W. *Bathed in Blood: Hunting and Mastery in the Old South*. Charlottesville: University Press of Virginia, 2002.
Quist, John W. *Restless Visionaries: The Social Roots of Antebellum Reform in Alabama and Michigan*. Baton Rouge: Louisiana State University Press, 1998.
Rabinowitz, Howard N. *Race Relations in the Urban South, 1865–1890*. Athens: University of Georgia Press, 1996.
Rachleff, P. *Black Labor in Richmond, Virginia, 1865–1890*. Urbana: University of Illinois Press, 1989.
Rankin, Hugh F. *Criminal Trial Proceedings in the General Court of Colonial Virginia*. Charlottesville: University Press of Virginia, 1965.
Reed, Mark Alan. "Thieving Times: Criminals, Victims, and the Judicial System in Richmond, Virginia, 1868–1872." M.A. thesis, University of Virginia, 1985.
Reidy, Joseph P. *From Slavery to Agrarian Capitalism in the Cotton Plantation South: Central Georgia, 1800–1880*. Chapel Hill: University of North Carolina Press, 1992.
Rice, James D. "Crime and Punishment in Frederick County and Maryland, 1748–1837: A Study in Culture, Society, and Law." Ph.D. diss., University of Maryland, 1994.

———. "The Criminal Trial before and after the Lawyers: Authority, Law, and Culture in Maryland Jury Trials, 1681–1837." *American Journal of Legal History* 40 (1996): 455–75.

———. "'This Province, So Meanly and Thinly Inhabited': Punishing Maryland's Criminals, 1681–1850." *Journal of the Early Republic* (1999): 15–42.

Richards, Leonard L. *"Gentlemen of Property and Standing" Anti-Abolition Mobs in Jacksonian America*. Oxford: Oxford University Press, 1970.

Riches, W.T.M. *Industrialization, Paternalism and Class Conflict: White Workers in Antebellum Southern Industry, 1830–1860*. Coleraine: University of Ulster, 1987.

Riley, Glenda. "Legislative Divorce in Virginia, 1803–1850." *Journal of the Early Republic* 11 (1991): 51–67.

Rise, Eric W. "Race, Rape, and Radicalism: The Case of the Martinsville 7, 1949-1951." *Journal of Southern History* 58 (1992): 461-490.

Roeber, A. G. *Faithful Magistrates and Republican Lawyers: Creators of Virginia Legal Culture, 1680–1810*. Chapel Hill: University of North Carolina Press, 1981.

Roediger, David R. *The Wages of Whiteness: Race and the Making of the American Working Class*. London: Verso, 1991.

Rothman, Joshua D. *Notorious in the Neighborhood: Sex and Families across the Color Line in Virginia, 1787–1861*. Chapel Hill: University of North Carolina Press, 2003.

Rousey, Dennis C. "Friends and Foes of Slavery: Foreigners and Northerners in the Old South." *Journal of Social History* 35 (2001): 373–96.

———. *Policing the Southern City: New Orleans, 1805–1889*. Baton Rouge: Louisiana State University Press, 1996.

Saunders, Robert M. "Crime and Punishment in Early National America: Richmond, Virginia, 1784–1820." *Virginia Magazine of History and Biography* 86 (1978): 33–44.

Schafer, Judith Kelleher. "The Murder of a 'Lewd and Abandoned Woman': *State of Louisiana v. Abraham Parker*." *American Journal of Legal History* 44 (2000): 19–39.

———. "Slaves and Crime: New Orleans, 1846–1860." In *Local Matters: Race Crime and Justice in the Nineteenth-Century South*, edited by Christopher Waldrep and Donald G. Nieman. Athens: University of Georgia Press, 2001.

Schecter, Patricia A. "Free and Slave Labor in the Old South: The Tredegar Ironworkers' Strike of 1847." *Labor History* 35 (1994): 165–86.

Schneider, John C. *Detroit and the Problem of Order, 1830–1880: A Geography of Crime, Riot, and Policing*. Lincoln: University of Nebraska Press, 1980.

Schnittman, Suzanne Gehring. "Slavery in Virginia's Urban Tobacco Industry, 1840–1860." Ph.D. diss., University of Rochester, 1987.

Schwarz, Philip J. *Slave Laws in Virginia*. Athens: University of Georgia Press, 1996.

———. "The Transportation of Slaves from Virginia, 1801–1865." *Slavery and Abolition* 7 (1986): 215–40.

———. *Twice Condemned: Slaves and the Criminal Laws of Virginia, 1705–1865.* Baton Rouge: Louisiana State University Press, 1988.

Schweninger, Loren. "Prosperous Blacks in the South, 1790–1880." *American Historical Review* 95 (1990): 31–56.

Scott, James. *Domination and the Arts of Resistance: Hidden Transcripts.* New Haven: Yale University Press, 1990.

Scott, John Anthony, and Robert Alan Scott. *John Brown of Harper's Ferry.* New York: Facts on File, 1988.

Seematter, Mary E. "Trials and Confessions: Race and Justice in Antebellum St. Louis." *Gateway Heritage* (1991): 36–47.

Shade, William G. *Democratizing the Old Dominion: Virginia and the Second Party System, 1824–1861.* Charlottesville: University Press of Virginia, 1996.

Sheldon, Marianne P. B. "Black-White Relations in Richmond, Virginia, 1782–1820." *Journal of Southern History* 45 (1979): 27–44.

———. "Richmond, Virginia: The Town and Henrico County to 1720." Ph.D. diss., University of Michigan, 1975.

Shepard, Alexander, and Philip Withington, eds. *Communities in Early Modern England: Networks, Place, Rhetoric.* Manchester: Manchester University Press, 2000.

Shepard, E. Lee. "Sketches of the Old Richmond Bar: Robert G. Scott." *Richmond Quarterly* 5 (1982): 46–50.

———. "Sketches of the Old Richmond Bar: Thomas P. August." *Richmond Quarterly* 6 (1984): 48–51.

Shoemaker, Robert B. *Prosecution and Punishment: Petty Crime and the Law in London and Rural Middlesex, c. 1660–1725.* Cambridge: Cambridge University Press, 1991.

Shore, Lawrence. "Making Mississippi Safe for Slavery: The Insurrectionary Panic of 1835." In *Class, Conflict, and Consensus: Antebellum Southern Community Studies*, edited by Orville Vernon Benton and Robert C. McMath, 96–127. Westport, Ct.: Greenwood Press, 1982.

Sidbury, James. *Ploughshares into Swords: Race, Rebellion, and Identity in Gabriel's Virginia, 1730–1810.* Cambridge: Cambridge University Press, 1997.

Siegel, Fred. "Artisans and Immigrants in the Politics of Late Antebellum Georgia." *Civil War History* 27 (1981): 21–30.

Slaughter, Thomas P. *Bloody Dawn: The Christiana Riot and Racial Violence in the Antebellum North.* New York: Oxford University Press, 1991.

Stampp, Kenneth M. *The Peculiar Institution: Negro Slavery in the American South.* London: Eyre and Spottiswoode, 1964.

Stansell, Christine.*City of Women: Sex and Class in New York, 1789-1860.* Urbana: University of Illinois Press, 1987.

Starobin, Robert S. *Industrial Slavery in the Old South.* New York: Oxford University Press, 1970.

Steger, Werner H. "'United to Support, But Not Combined to Injure': Free Workers

and Immigrants in Richmond, Virginia, during the Era of Sectionalism, 1847–1865." Ph.D. diss., George Washington University, 1999.
Steinberg, Allen. *The Transformation of Criminal Justice: Philadelphia, 1800–1880*. Chapel Hill: University of North Carolina Press, 1989.
Stevenson, Brenda E. *Life in Black and White: Family and Community in the Slave South*. New York: Oxford University Press, 1996.
Suggs, Jon-Christian. *Whispered Consolations: Law and Narrative in African American Life*. Ann Arbor: University of Michigan Press, 1999.
Sydnor, Charles S. "The Southerner and the Laws." *Journal of Southern History* 6 (1940): 3–23.
Tadman, Michael. *Speculators and Slaves: Masters, Traders, and Slaves in the Old South*. Madison: University of Wisconsin Press, 1996.
Takagi, Midori. *"Rearing Wolves to Our Own Destruction": Slavery in Richmond, Virginia, 1782–1865*. Charlottesville: University Press of Virginia, 1999.
Tise, Larry E. *Proslavery: A History of the Defense of Slavery in America, 1701–1840*. Athens: University of Georgia Press, 1987.
Tolbert, Lisa C. *Constructing Townscapes: Space and Society in Antebellum Tennessee*. Chapel Hill: University of North Carolina Press, 1999.
Tripp, Stephen. *Yankee Town, Southern City: Race and Class Relations in Civil War Lynchburg*. New York: New York University Press, 1997.
Trotti, Michael Ayers. "Murder and the Modern Sensibility: Sensationalism and Cultural Change in Richmond, Virginia, from the Victorian Era to the Age of Ragtime." Ph.D. diss., University of North Carolina at Chapel Hill, 1999.
Tushnet, Mark V. *The American Law of Slavery 1810–1860*. Princeton: Princeton University Press, 1981.
Tyler-McGraw, Marie, and Gregg D. Kimball. *In Bondage and Freedom: Antebellum Black Life in Richmond, Virginia*. Richmond: Valentine Museum, 1988.
Tyrell, Ian R. "Drink and Temperance in the Antebellum South: An Overview and Interpretation." *Journal of Southern History* 48 (1982): 485–510.
Wade, Richard C. *Slavery in the Cities: The South, 1820–1860*. London: Oxford University Press, 1964.
Waldrep, Christopher. *The Many Faces of Judge Lynch: Extralegal Violence and Punishment in America*. New York: Palgrave Macmillan, 2002.
———. *Roots of Disorder: Race and Criminal Justice in the American South, 1817–1880*. Urbana: University of Illinois Press, 1998.
Waldrep, Christopher, and Donald G. Nieman, eds. *Local Matters. Race Crime and Justice in the Nineteenth-Century South*. Athens: University of Georgia Press, 2001.
Watson, Alan D. "North Carolina Slave Courts, 1715–1785." *North Carolina Historical Review* 60 (1983): 24–36.
Wayne, Michael. *Death of an Overseer: Reopening a Murder Investigation from the Plantation South*. New York: Oxford University Press, 2001.

———. "An Old South Morality Play: Reconsidering the Social Underpinnings of the Proslavery Ideology." *Journal of American History* 77, no. 3 (1990): 838–63.

Whitman, T. Stephen. *The Price of Freedom: Slavery and Manumission in Baltimore and Early National Maryland.* New York: Routledge, 2000.

Williams, Jack Kenny. *Vogues in Villainy: Crime and Retribution in Ante-Bellum South Carolina.* Columbia: University of South Carolina Press, 1959.

Wilson, Carol, and Calvin D. Wilson. "White Slavery: An American Paradox." *Slavery and Abolition* 19 (1998): 1–19.

Wood, Betty. "'For Their Satisfaction or Redress': African Americans and Church Discipline in the Early South." In *The Devil's Lane: Sex and Race in the Early South*, edited by Catherine Clinton and Michele Gillespie, 109–21. London: Oxford University Press, 1997.

Wren, J. Thomas. "A "Two-Fold Character": The Slave as Person and Property in Virginia Court Cases, 1800–1860." *Southern Studies* 37 (1985): 417–31.

Wyatt-Brown, Bertram. "Community, Class, and Snopesian Crime: Local Justice in the Old South." In *Class, Conflict, and Consensus: Antebellum Southern Community Studies*, edited by Orville Vernon Benton and Robert C. McMath, 173–206. Westport, Ct.: Greenwood Press, 1982.

———. *Honor and Violence in the Old South.* New York: Oxford University Press, 1986.

———. *Southern Honor: Ethics and Behavior in the Old South.* New York: Oxford University Press, 1982.

Yngvesson, Barbara. *Virtuous Citizens, Disruptive Subjects: Order and Complaint in a New England Court.* New York: Routledge, 1993.

Young, Jeffrey R. *Domesticating Slavery: The Master Class in Georgia and South Carolina, 1670–1837.* Chapel Hill: University of North Carolina Press, 1999.

Index

Abolitionism: and interracial relations, 50; and morals offenses, declining prosecutions of, 45; and runaway slaves, 31, 143, 148; and slave trials, 77, 106; and vigilantism, 130–32; and white crime, regulation of, 3, 39, 64, 144. *See also* John Brown's Raid
Abram, a slave, 30
Act, extending the jurisdiction of the Magistrates of the City of Richmond, and for other purposes (1819), 55
Act, for the more Speedy Prosecution of Slaves Committing Capital Offenses (1692), 77
Adcock, William P., 124
Aiding a slave to abscond: and black testimony, 8, 110, 142; and free African Americans, 153, 227n118, 233n77; and stolen goods, 139; and white defendants, 227n127
Aldermen, 22, 55, 94, 112, 141, 210n68
Alexander, a slave, 36
Allison, Henry B., 124
Allison, William, 76
Alvis, Joshua, 134, 135
American Colonization Society, 150. *See also* Colonization
Anderson v. Commonwealth (Va.), 162
Anderson, a slave, 36–37
Anderson, Albert, a slave, 32
Andrews, John, 68
Ann, a slave, 96
Ann, a slave of John C. Brockenham, 31
Anna, a slave, 11, 19
Anthony, a slave, 16
Armistead, a slave, 97–98
Arson, 43, 82, 88, 95, 99, 216n40, 233n77
Assault: committed by slaves, 82, 86–88; domestic violence, 59–60, 63–64, 211n93; examination and trial of whites, 56–57, 109, 124–26, 211n96, 223n39, 224nn68,69, 226nn95,96; free African Americans and, 154–55, 160, 165–66, 177–78, 232n76, 234n106; punishment of whites for, 67–69, 71, 73; slaves and, 12, 26–27, 34, 36; whites and, 41, 45, 46, 52, 122; violent slave abuse by whites, 131–38, 144; white women and, 118–20
Attorneys: criticisms of, 32, 155; and declining conviction rates, 123–26; and due process, 7; and free African Americans, 152–54; and Mayor's Court slave defendants, 32–33
August, Thomas, 94, 217n57

Baker, Amelia J., 59
Banks, Frederick, 91–92
Barnes, Richard, 178
Batley, Daniel, a slave, 25
Beazley, Richard, 115
Bellentine, Maria, 31
Bennett, Laura, 129
Billy, a slave of J. W. Ditrell, 33
Billy, a slave of Thomas Massie, 30
Binford, John, 152
Black Codes. *See* Municipal ordinances
Black testimony: in slave trials, 90–91; prohibited against white defendants, 8, 110, 132–33, 135, 140; and runaway slaves, 142; proposals to permit against white defendants, 145. *See also* Southard, Elizabeth
Blakey, Henry, 96, 101
Boaz, Daniel, 30
Botts, John Minor, 50
Bovan, Elizabeth, 120
Brack, Maria, 141
Bradly, Richard, 164–65
Bransford, Charles, 159
Breeden, James, 30
Brockenbrough, John W., 133

Brockenham, John, 31
Brooks, John, 156
Brown, Henry "Box," a slave, 180
Brown, James, 33
Brown, John. *See* John Brown's Raid
Brown, William, 93–94
Bullifin, Martha, 68–69
Burgess, Thomas, 123
Burglary: as capital slave crime, 85–86, 101; free African Americans and, 150, 152, 154, 166; slave trials and, 76, 82, 88–89, 91–93, 95, 96–97, 216nn33,34; white defendants, 123
Burley, Alexander, 160–61
Burr, Aaron, 108
Burr, William, 114

Cabell, Dr. R. H., 170–71
Campbell, Moses, 91–92
Campbell, William, 142–44, 233n77
Campfield, John, 123
Carter, Lydia, 154
Caskie, John S., 123, 169–73, 175
Chain gang, 7, 41, 69–72, 213nn120,123
Chamberlaigne, W. Byrd, 154
Chaney v. Saunders, 163
Chapman, Rebecca, 119
Charleston, S.C.: compared with Richmond, 1, 46, 222n35; free African American population, 158; opposition to a work house in, 72; and slave rebellion, 19, 149
Chenery, James G., 33
Chesterton, Catherine, 120
Childress, Robert, 124–25
Childrey, Thomas and Lavinia, 60
Chinn, Thomas, 140–41
Claiborne, a slave, 138
Claiborne, H. A., 96
Class: and domestic violence, 60–62; and drunk and disorderly conduct, 68; prosecution of white defendants and, 108–9, 113, 115–16; and racial identity, 176. *See also* Interracial lower class community; White class relations; White crime
Clemency. *See* Executive clemency
Cobb, Thomas: on attorneys in capital slave trials, 32; and black testimony against white defendants, 132, 145; on race and slavery, 162; on slave confessions, 93
Colonization, 146. *See also* American Colonization Society; Liberia
Committee of Twenty-Four. *See* Gambling
Commonwealth v. Booth (Va.), 138
Commonwealth v. Carver (Va.), 133
Commonwealth v. Turner (Va.), 133
Conway, Catherine and Cynthia, 164
Cook, Charles: and chain gang, 41, 42–43, 187
Cook, George, 92
Cook, William P., 115
Cook, W. Wallace, 157
Cooper, Fanny, 166–67
Cosby, Agnes, 233n77
Counterfeiting. *See* Forgery
Cousins, Floyd, 150–51
Cousins, Thomas, 159
Crenshaw, Nathaniel, 132
Crew, Mr., 36
Criminal trials. *See* Oyer and terminer courts; Richmond Circuit Court; Richmond Hustings Court
Crime. *See* Property crime; Violent crime; *specific types of crime*
Cronin, John, 116
Crump, George P., 127
Crump, William W., 124
Cullen, John and Charlotte, 61–62
Cyrus, a slave, 140

Dangerfield, a slave, 137
Daniel, a slave, 89–90, 95
Darracott, Richard F., 174
Day, Coleman, 157–58
Day, William, 174
Dean v. Commonwealth (Va.), 163, 173
Dickens, Charles, 48
Dill, Mr., 30
Ditrell, J. W., 33
Domestic violence: and chain gang, 41, 68; elite responses to, 60–62; and honor, 116; Mayor's Court cases, 59–60, 62–64; and slaves, 83, 84
Douglass, Margaret, 118, 120
Drew, Martha, 120

Drunk and disorderly conduct: and Baptist churches, 182; chain gang as punishment for, 41; free African Americans and, 165, 177; prosecution rates, 45, 212n106; regulation of, in Mayor's Court, 56, 64, 67–68; slaves and, 12, 20, 22–23, 28–29, 85, 204n48; and white poverty and class relations, 7, 43, 52, 58, 75, 212n109
Dueling, 42, 108, 113
Dunivant, Peter, 153
Dunlop, Margaret, 233n77
Dye, Julia, 66–67, 212n104

Ebenezer Baptist Church, 183
Edins, Fielding Alexander, 166–67
Edward, names of slaves, 25, 136
Elick, a slave, 95
Ellis, Thomas H., 98–99
Emanuel, a slave, 85, 96
Enders, John, 11, 235n115
Evans, Thomas J., 96
Executive clemency: criticisms of, 103, 128; mentioned, 142; slaves and, 76, 96–97, 98, 102–3, 106. *See also* Sale and transportation

Fanny, a slave of John Morris, 95, 99
Ferguson, William, 165–66
Fighting, 12, 30, 46, 179
Findlay, George, 137–38
Finney, Matilda, 173–75
First African Baptist Church, 8, 10, 15; criminal investigations, 179–84
First Presbyterian Church, 14–15
Fisher, John, 66, 123
Floyd, John Buchanan, governor of Virginia: clemency and, 153; on crime and poverty in Virginia, 43–44
Ford, John, 159
Forgery, 44, 121, 123, 126–28
Francis, a slave, 25–26
Franklin, Jesse, 37
Frayser, Manuel, 160
Free African Americans: arrest rates, 22; and attorneys, 152–55; as complainants, 8; Hustings Court misdemeanor trials, 165–66, 233n77; jury trials, 9, 160–62;

and law, 2–3, 5, 8, 147–50, 161; oyer and terminer trials, 85–87, 151; poor whites, relations with, 1, 120; punishment of, 41, 151; in Richmond, 1, 15, 146; and runaway slaves, 31, 143; and slavery, 2; white attitudes toward, 47, 146; and white patrons, 156–60. *See also* Colonization; Racial identity; Sale into absolute slavery; and *specific types of crime*

Gambling: Committee of Twenty-Four report on, 128; and First African Baptist Church, 182; and Pendleton case, 127; slaves and, 12, 37; and vigilante attacks, 130; white prosecution rates, 45
Gender: and judicial response to Bread Riots, 186; and free African American complainants, 177–78; and notions of criminality, 11, 109, 222n34; and racial identity, 175–76; and slave murder defendants, 82–84. *See also* Domestic violence; White women
German, a slave, 30
German immigrants. *See* Immigration
Gifford, Alpheus, 143
Gilmer, John H., 123, 153–54
Goddin, Isaac, 30–31, 172
Govan, Archibald, 100–101
Govan, Lucy, 99–100
Governor of Virginia: *See* Executive clemency; *names of individual governors*
Grace, John, 125
Grand jury, 54, 55, 69, 137, 141; cases of disputed racial identity, 165, 233n77; and Hustings Court examinations, 110–11, 112; on tobacco slaves, 20
Granger, Thomas, 30–31
Gray, James, 127
Green, James, 20
Green, Joseph, 136
Gregory, John, 165
Griffin, James and Eliza, 121

Hammond, James Henry, 41
Hanging: slaves, 11, 76, 82, 85, 96, 97; whites, 116–17, 222n29. *See also* Punishment
Harden, Henry, 13

Hardy, Thomas, 129
Harris, Fleming, 172
Harry, a slave of Robert Bruce, 136
Hart, Eliza, 154–55
Haskins, Dr., 171
Hastings, Samuel, 124
Hatcher, Jordan, a slave, 83, 103–4, 219n92
Hebden, William, 119
Henrico County, Va., 54, 127, 169, 203n42
Hicks, Fabius, 120
Hicks, Mary, 164
Hobson, Martha and Rebecca, 167–73, 175
Hogg, Dandridge, 137
Holdsworth, William C., 115
Holloway, Jacob, 172, 174, 175
Honor: and crime control, 42, 47, 58, 120, 121–22, 127, 211n84; and free African Americans, 161; and judicial discretion, 7, 109, 113, 115, 231n59; and law, 114, 138; and murder, 108, 117; and slavery, 35, 91
Hooper, Harriet, 66, 118, 120
Houston, Catherine, 139
Howison, Robert Reid, 123, 124, 170
Hoyt, Dudley, 114–15, 116
Hughes, Frances, 16
Humphrey, a slave, 136
Hustings Court. *See* Richmond Hustings Court; Richmond Hustings Court felony examinations

Immigration: attacked by vigilantes, 130; and crime, 47, 51, 65, 71, 75, 126; and domestic violence, 62; and imprisonment, 51–52; and racial identity, 175, 176; and slavery, 49–52, 104; and white social divisions, 42, 48, 49. *See also* White class relations
Infanticide, 83–84
Interracial crime: African Baptist churches and, 180; aiding slaves to escape, 142; receiving stolen goods, 139–40; and vigilantism, 8, 130; violence, 132, 137
Interracial lower class community: and black testimony, 133; and racial identity, 9, 175–76, 188; and urban slavery, 16, 18, 136; and white supremacy, 49, 52

Interracial sexual relationships, 45, 65, 130, 133, 169–70
Irish immigrants. *See* Immigration
Isaac, a slave, 85, 96

Jackson, Alexander, 160–62
Jackson, Jane, 59
Jackson, Joseph, 123, 125
Jackson, Patsy, 59
Jackson, William, murder of, 103
Jacobs, Harriet, a slave, 25
Jail, Richmond City: and immigrants, 51–52; and labor on public works, 71; mentioned, 12; overcrowding, 111; and poverty, 7; proposed reform of, 68–69; and slaves, 100
James, Andrew, 158–59
James, Clinton, 31
James, Fleming, 33
James, Martha, 159
Jim, a slave, 37
Jinkins, Burwell, Captain of the Night Watch: and confession of George Mercer, 93; runaway slave searches, 31; testimony against Banks and Campbell, 91–92; Winston murders, 10
John Brown's Raid, 17–18
Johnson, Joseph, governor of Virginia, 159; and Jordan Hatcher case, 103–4
Johnson, Robert, 181–82
Jones, Charles Colcock, 37
Jones, Josiah, 125
Jones, Robert, 157
Jurors, 112, 220n95

Keith, Isham, 146
Kelly, Peter, 183
Kersey, Delaware, 160–61

Lambert, Richard, 134, 136
Lambert, William: and assault convictions, 224n68; determines racial identity, 167; domestic violence cases, 64; and Mayor's Court slave defendants, 27, 30; Mayor's Court white defendants, 126; murder investigations, 115
Larceny. *See* Stealing

Law: and free African Americans; 2–3, 5, 8, 147–50, 161; historiography of, 4–5; in post–Civil War Virginia, 189–92; and race, xi, 3; and slaves, 12, 37, 77–79, 106–7; and urbanization, 2–3; and whites, 42–43, 57, 74–75, 109–10, 145. *See also* Oyer and terminer courts; Richmond Circuit Court; Richmond Hustings Court; Richmond Mayor's Court; Punishment; Rural South; Urban slavery; White class relations
Lee, A. S., 26
Leigh, Benjamin Watkins, 108
Letcher, John, governor of Virginia, 117
Lew, Edward Van, 33
Liberia, 11, 146. *See also* American Colonization Society; Colonization
Litman, Barney, 140
Lloyd, Virginia, 119–20
Locknane, Thomas, 125
Lottier, Thomas W., 115
Louisa County, Va., 46, 111
Loyed, Eliza, 163–64
Lucy, a slave of Charles Colcock Jones, 37
Lyons, James: Charlotte Cullen case, 61; *State v. Daniel*, 89–90, 95; trial of John Williams, 11; William Myers case, 114–15
Lyons, Rebecca and Emanuel, 63

Manigault, Louis, 34
Manslaughter: and free African American defendants, 157, 161, 167, 172, 231n57; and killing of slaves, 226n89; and slave defendants, 82–83, 96, 104; and white defendants, 116
Martin, Gideon, 134
Mary, a slave, 90
Massachusetts, 46, 114
Massie, Thomas, 30
Mathew, a slave of Robert Ford, 93–94
Mathews, Henry, a slave, 33
Maxfield, Sophia, 154
Mayo, Jordina, 130
Mayo, Joseph: and assault convictions, 224n68; and chain gang, 41, 68; city ordinances, strict enforcement of, 6, 27, 28; during Civil War, 186; as Commonwealth's Attorney, 28, 76; and due process, 125; early life and career, 27; on examination of free African Americans, 228n14; and policing, 31, 54, 64, 224n58; and prostitution, 65; and racial identity, 166, 174; reputation of among African Americans, 38; on sale and transportation, 103; slave examinations, 22–23, 26; vigilantism, opposition to, 129–30; and violent slave abuse, 137–38; white petty crime and poverty, regulation of, 64, 68
Mayor's Court. *See* Richmond Mayor's Court
McDonough, James, 134
McRoberts, John, 130
Memphis Recorder's Court, 26
Mercer, George, a slave: clemency appeal, 98; confession of, 93
Meredith, Ann, 120
Miller, Zacharia, 11
Minor, John B., 56, 57, 116
Mitchell, Elizabeth, 66, 120
Montague, Charles, 16
Montelle, Granville, 125
Moore, Reverend T. V.: urban slavery, criticisms of, 14, 15, 20
Mordecai, Samuel, 48
Morris, John W., 99
Mosby, Thomas, 139
Municipal Ordinances, 3, 51, 53; in Civil War, 186; enforcement of in 1850s, 27, 38, 39; and free black employment, 52; and interracial relations, 133; and race, xi; and slavery, 6, 17, 19, 30, 37, 202n20; and whites, 55
Murder: comparison of northern and southern states, 43, 121; and slave clemency, 103–4; slaves, trials of, 82–86, 88–89, 90, 96, 215n26; Southard, Elizabeth, trial of, 170–71, 174; free African Americans, trials of, 160, 167, 179, 188; white men, trials of, 108, 109, 114–17, 124, 134, 226n90; white women, trials of, 66, 119, 120; Winston family, 11, 15, 20, 179
Myers, Gustavus A., 76, 114
Myers, Samuel S., 114
Myers, Virginia, 114
Myers, William, 113–15, 116, 127

Nat Turner's Rebellion, 150
Nelson, a slave, 137
New York, 48, 49, 53, 68, 143
Night watch: expansion of, 53–55; and slaves, 12, 14, 30–31, 135, 143. *See also* Richmond police
Norfolk Argus, 118
Northern states: crime, attitudes toward, 121–22; crime and prosecution patterns compared with South/Richmond, 43–44, 46–48, 189; female crime, 118; southern lynching, views on, 130

Olmsted, Frederick Law, 48–49
Osiander, Philip and Rose, 140–41
Owen, James, a slave, 26
Oyer and terminer courts: black testimony in, 91; comparison with slave trials outside Virginia, 79–80; defense attorneys in, 94–95, 156, 217n57; due process in, 79, 80–81, 87–88, 95–96, 97, 174; free African American defendants, 9, 150–53, 158, 159–60, 161–62, 166, 173; hired slaves in, 43; and nonslaveholding whites, 7, 104–6, 138–39, 220n95; origins and regulations of, 77, 79; pregnant circumstances, 91; slave confessions, 11, 92–94, 217n50; slave conviction rates, 80, 82–83, 85, 87–88, 215n17; slave defendants, 11, 26; slaveholders' property interests and, 7, 78, 81, 90, 98

Page, Archy, a slave, 25
Parkhurst, George, 121
Pass laws, 22, 27, 28, 30–31, 182, 203–4n47, 204n60
Paternalism: and free African Americans, 158, 230n42; and nonslaveholding whites, 7, 104–6, 138–39, 220n95; and the Mayor's Court, 38–39; and urbanization, 2; and white women, 119
Pearce, John, 136
Pendleton, Samuel, 126–28
Perjury, 25
Perry, a slave, 84
Peter, a slave, 136
Philadelphia, 27, 46, 156, 157, 189

Pitt, James and Lockley, 63
Pleasants, Lilburn, 154
Pleasants v. Pleasants (Va.), 154
Policing. *See* Richmond police
Poorhouse, 42, 53, 70, 73–75, 121, 213n118. *See also* Work house
Pritchard, James and Virginia, 63
Property crime: and chain gang, 71; conviction rates, 126; prosecution rates, 20–21, 44–47, 144, 189; reported by free African Americans, 178; and rule of law, 110, 122, 126–28; and white defendants, 55, 112. *See also* Slave crime; White crime; White women; *specific types of property crime*
Prostitution: in Civil War, 186; white women and, 43, 45, 56, 64–67, 68
Public Guard, 53, 159, 186, 209n57
Punishment: racial differences in, xi. *See also* Assault; Chain gang; Free African Americans; Hanging; Jail, Richmond City; Richmond Hustings Court; Richmond Mayor's Court; Whipping

Racial identity: determined by mayor, 163–66; laws defining, 162–63; in oyer and terminer cases, 166–67. *See also* Southard, Elizabeth
Ralph, a slave, 25
Ralston, Robert, 135
Randall, Fanny, 181
Rape, 123, 129, 160–61, 231n61
Rawlings, John, a slave: clemency appeal of, 96–97, 101–2
Receiving stolen goods: conviction rates, 126, 227n115; and gender, 120–21; and interracial crime, 8, 110, 139, 227n113; slave crime, 25; and whites, 44, 123–24, 213n127
Redcross, Nancy, 139
Redpath, James, 51
Remaining in the Commonwealth contrary to law, 156–57, 230n36
Retailing ardent spirits, 45, 140, 182
Reuben, a slave, 25
Richards, John, 119
Richmond: in Civil War, 186–87; compared with northern cities, 48, 189; compared

with other southern cities, xii; economic growth, 1, 15; and law, 2–3, 5–9, 188; population, 1, 15, 49; racial identity in, 175–76. *See also* Immigration; Northern states; Rocketts; Slaves; Urban slavery; White class relations

Richmond Bread Riots, 186

Richmond Circuit Court, 66, 77, 109, 110; abolitionists and, 132; conviction rates, 126, 215n17, 227n115; delay in holding trials, 95, 112; due process, 123, 223n53; free African Americans, trials of, 160–62, 167, 168; murder trials, 116; violent slave abuse cases, 134–35, 137; white women, trials of, 119, 120

Richmond Common (City) Council, 7, 12, 17, 19, 27, 53, 69, 93, 147, 209n55

Richmond Daily Dispatch, 31, 33, 35, 38, 160, 187; on the city jail, 111; condones white violence, 116; on executive clemency, 128; on free African Americans, 146, 148, 150, 154–55, 164; on judicial slave control, 23, 32, 34, 36, 89, 107; Mayor's Court proceedings, as record of, 201n12, 203–4n47, 204nn59,60; on mob violence, 129–30; on racial identity cases, 166; on Richmond police, 54–55; on slave crime, 11, 17, 20, 29, 39; on slave crime and religion, 182; on slavery and white crime, 140; on white crime and punishment, 41, 59, 67–70, 74, 136; on white female crime, 118–20

Richmond Enquirer, 51, 103

Richmond Hustings Court: appeals to from Mayor's Court rulings, 33, 155; conviction rates, decline in, 126; free African Americans remaining in Virginia contrary to law, 156–57, 230n39; grand jury, 20; misdemeanor trials, 66, 109, 139, 143, 211n96, 213n127, 233n77; and racial identity, 164–70; white convicts, punishment of, 41, 70, 72, 141, 226n96; white defendants, 44–45, 55, 64, 65, 118, 125, 134–37, 138, 140; white female defendants, 119, 121. *See also* Oyer and terminer courts; Richmond Hustings Court felony examinations

Richmond Hustings Court felony examinations: criticisms of, 111–12; discretionary judgments, 113–16, 221n16; due process in, 95; free African American defendants, 160; origins, operation, and purpose of, 110–11, 220n5; outcome of cases, 112–13, 134–36, 221n14, 223n44, 227n115

Richmond Mayor's Court: African Baptist church and, 179, 181, 182, 185; appeals from, 33, 155–56; defense attorneys in, 32, 125, 154; due process, 125–26; free African American defendants, 161, 166, 167, 232n76, 234n105; and gender issues, 58–59, 65, 66, 118, 211–12n97, 212n101; immigrants, 62; location of, 12; press reports of, 201n12, 203–4n47; slave conviction rates compared with whites, 26–27; slave defendants, 12, 21–23, 204n48; slave examinations, 24–26, 28, 92; slave punishments, 24, 27, 32, 36–40; slaveholders' attitudes toward, 34, 38, 40; white conviction rates, 224n68; white defendants, 7, 41, 45, 55–57, 58, 64, 66, 67, 75, 141, 150, 209n53. *See also* Watch house examinations; Lambert, William; Mayo, Joseph; and Tate, Joseph

Richmond police: arrest rates, 22, 29–30; during Civil War, 186; and free African Americans, 179; growth of, 3, 12, 53–54, 64, 130, 189, 205n55; and master-slave relationship, 9, 38; morale of, 69; rural police compared with, 55; and slaves, 28–29, 31, 37, 85, 92, 138, 140; slaveholders' criticisms of, 30–31; violence against, 54; and white crime, 7, 42–43, 65, 66, 75, 119, 126, 140–41. *See also* Night watch

Richmond Republican, 51, 109, 113, 121–22, 164, 168

Richmond Whig, 103

Roach, Merriweather, 60

Robbery, 103

Robert, a slave, 25

Robert, a slave of Mr. Slater, 30

Robert, a slave of William Allison, 76

Robinson, James, a slave, 33

Robinson, Windham, governor of Virginia: on imprisonment of northern mariners, 69

Rocketts, 48, 59, 60, 130, 143

Rocketts Regulators, 130
Roper, Erasmus, 134
Ruffin, Chief Justice Thomas, 34, 35
Rural South, compared with Richmond: law, 5, 42, 188; policing, 55; slavery, 2, 19
Rutherford, John Coles, 51
Ryland, Reverend Robert: confession of Jane Williams, 10; criticized by Henry "Box" Brown, 180; sermon on the Winston family murders, 15

Sale and transportation, 82, 83, 85, 96–98; criticisms of, 102–3, 104; governor and, 78, 101; replaced by labor on public works, 107; slaveholders' support for, 105–6
Sale into absolute slavery, 72, 86; in 1820s, 150; and free African American residency laws, 156, 230n37; and racial identity, 163; white opposition to, 185; outside Virginia, 229n18
Savannah, Ga.: compared with Richmond, 46, 80, 214n14; policing, 53
Schuricht, Herrmann, 51
Scott, a slave, 84
Scott, Robert G.: as defense attorney for slaves, 89–90, 94, 217n57; on female defendants, 118; and *Pleasants v. Pleasants*, 154; and William Myers case, 114
Screamersville, 54
Seal, Thomas, 60
Seddon, James, 96, 101
Selden, Robert, 160
Sharp, George, 134, 137
Shenandoah County, Virginia, 46
Sheppard, Benjamin, 127
Shook, Jonathan, 71–72, 75, 112
Shooting with intent to kill, 115, 134–35, 226n90
Slave hiring: in Civil War, 186; and crime, 16, 21–22, 25, 139, 203n42; domestic servants, 18; and free African Americans, 158; and murder, 83; and slave control, 2, 16–18, 20, 203n32; and slave punishment, 36–37, 99, 104, 107, 137–38, 206n97; and slaveholders, 17–18, 33; tobacco factories and, 15–17, 20, 140; and white class relations, 207n21

Slaveholders: and African Baptist Church, 180, 235n115; and criminal law, 2–7, 9, 187, 189; criminal prosecutions of, 108, 115; and free African Americans, 146, 148–49, 158; and judicial/police control of slaves, 30–33, 35–36, 39, 53; as magistrates, 112, 220n95; and nonslaveholding whites, 42, 50, 52, 122, 141, 208n35; and personal reputation, 33–34; and prohibition on black testimony, 142, 144–45; and racial identity, 172; and slave control, 12–14, 29; and slave self-hire, 18; and violent slave abuse, 132–34, 137–38, 225n89, 226n98. *See also* Oyer and terminer courts; Paternalism; Slave hiring; Urban slavery; White class relations
Slave patrols, 34
Slave trials. *See* Oyer and terminer courts; and *specific types of crime*
Slaves: and African Baptist Church, 15, 179–80, 182–83; attitudes toward crime, 184; arrest rates, 22; in Civil War, 186; as domestic servants, 18; and law, 12, 37; living arrangements, 16–17, 202n20; occupations of, in Richmond, 1; prosecution rates, 20–21, 80–81; in rural Virginia, 2; runaways, 19, 31, 38; in tobacco factories, 15–17, 20. *See also* Oyer and terminer courts; Richmond Mayor's Court; Slave crime; Slave hiring; Urban slavery; *specific types of crime*
Smith, Edmund M., 142
Smith, James H., 123
Smith, John, 156
Smith, Richardson D., 153
Smith, Robert, 173
Smith, Tamer, a slave, 25
Smith, William, governor of Virginia, 146, 153, 178
Snead, Dr. Albert, 172
Solomon, Ezekiel, 136
Southard, Elizabeth: contested racial identity of, 120, 167, 169–73, 174–76, 188; gender issues and, 116, 120; Matilda Finney case and, 173–74
St. Louis, 1, 128–29
Stabbing: free African Americans and, 152,

166, 173, 181, 229n22, 230n28; slave trials, 86, 88, 216n36; white on black, 134, 137, 226n90; whites and, 66, 109, 118, 120
State v. Mann (N.C.), 34
Stealing: free African Americans and, 139, 158, 182–83; slave attitudes toward, 184; slave crime and, 21, 25–26, 27, 36; and slave examinations and trials, 82, 85–88, 204n59, 216n34, 218n59; whites and, 44, 52, 71, 72, 125–26, 213n127, 224nn68,69; white women and, 118, 121
Stephen, a black defendant, 166
Stevenson, Samuel, 157
Sullivan, Cornelius, 123
Sullivan, Hannah, 119
Sullivan, Mary, 59
Sullivan, William, 60
Sunrise courts. *See* Watch house examinations
Susan, a slave, 36
Sutton, Norbonne E., 119
Swan, Harrison, 31

Talley, James, 128
Tate, Joseph: assault conviction rates, 224n68; on clemency and gambling, 128; determines racial identity, 164; docket book of, 201n12; domestic violence cases, 63; drunk and disorderly cases, 67, 69; due process and legal background of, 125; Mayor's Court slave cases, 25, 33, 37; on religion and slave crime, 182–83; search warrants, 31; slave pass violations and, 27
Taylor, Edmund, a slave, 182–83
Taylor, Lewis B., 139–40
Taylor, Samuel, 61
Tazewell, Littleton W., governor of Virginia, 143
Tennessee Supreme Court, 134
Thom, Catherine, 116
Thomas, a slave, 135
Thomas, James, Jr., 180
Thompson, Mr., 157
Tobacco manufacturers: defend slaves' independent living, 16–17; oppose clemency for Jordan Hatcher, 104, 219n92; and slaves, 11, 15–16, 39, 180

Totty, William, 116–17
Townsend, Elijah, 143
Townsend, John, 41
Traiman, Nancy, 59
Trespass, 31
Trevilian, Colonel John M., 34
Trice, John, 181–82
Turner, Nathan, 135

Underground Railroad, 31, 139. *See also* Free African Americans; Slaves
Unlawful assembly, 22, 23, 28, 141, 203–4n47, 226n99
Urban slavery: decline of, outside Richmond, 1, 14; compared with rural slavery, 2, 19, 35; and resistance/crime, 11–12, 14, 17, 20–22; and law, 12, 14, 29, 37, 187; and immigration, 49; and white crime and punishment, 57–58. *See also* Slave hiring; Slaves; *names of individual slaves*

Vandervall, Samuel, and chain gang, 41
Vesey, Denmark, 149
Vest, William, 71–72
Vicksburg, Miss., 46, 80, 214n14. *See also* Warren County, Miss.
Vigilantism, 8, 128–31
Violent crime: free African American victims of, 177; and judicial discretion, 113, 115–16, 126, 144; prosecution rates, 20–21, 44–47; and white Mayor's Court defendants, 56. *See also* Gender; Honor; White women; *specific types of violent crime*
Virginia, a slave, 99–101
Virginia General Court, 111, 115, 133, 163, 173, 205n77
Virginia Penal Code (1849), 85, 96, 161

Walker, Isaiah and John, 168
Walker, William P., 116, 167–68, 170
Warren County, Miss., 46, 217n57. *See also* Vicksburg, Miss.
Washington, George, a slave, 183
Watch house examinations, 23–24, 28–29
Watkins, John, a slave, 96, 101
Watson, Dr. George, 20

Weaver, Mary, 121
Webster, John, 121–22
Weidmeyer, Frederick, 135
West, R. L., 156
Whipping: free African Americans, 166, 181; slaves, 12, 19, 24, 30, 36, 42, 82, 85, 88, 137, 150, 205n75; whites, 72–73, 213n126. *See also* Punishment; Richmond Mayor's Court
White, Thomas, 66
White class relations: and assaults on slaves, 134–35, 137–39; and law, 3, 42–43; and liquor offenses, 141; and politics, 50, 51; and racial solidarity, 53; and rule of law, 110, 122, 128, 132; and slave clemency, 103–5; and slavery, 2, 49–52; in southern cities, 42, 46–47; urbanization and, 2. *See also* Immigration
White crime: associated with poverty, 7, 47, 68; judicial discretion and, 110; prosecution patterns, 44; Richmond compared with other jurisdictions, 46–47; and urban slavery, 58. *See also* Honor; Property crime; Violent crime; White women; *specific types of crime*
White women: and Bread Riots, 186; as complainants and victims, 7, 43, 58–59; prosecution of, 7, 118–20, 223n44; and poverty, 176; and punishment, 69–70, 118, 120–21, 222n33. *See also* Domestic violence; Gender; *specific types of crime*

Wicker, Robert Tate, 167
William, a slave, 31
Williams, Charles, 126
Williams, Jane, 12; confession of, 10–11, 215n26, 218n59; and female criminality, 215n27; and urban slavery, 14, 39–40
Williams, John, 12; and African Baptist Church, 235n117; and urban slavery, 14, 20, 39–40, 187; and Winston murders, 10–11
Williamson, Joel, 164
Willis, Maria, 59
Winder, J. H., 186
Winney, a slave, 25
Winston, Fleming, 160
Winston, Joseph, 10–11, 18
Winston, R. B., 138
Winston, Virginia, 20, 187; murder of, 10–11; funeral of, 14, 15
Winston, Washington, a slave, 139
Wise, Henry A., governor of Virginia: on John Brown's Raid and urban slavery, 17–18; opposition to sale and transportation, 107; proposes vigilance committee, 130
Work house, 68–70. *See also* Poorhouse
Wortham, James, 20
Wyatt-Brown, Bertram, 4, 41, 220n95, 225n73
Wynne, Williamson, 140

Yngvesson, Barbara, 57

James Campbell is a lecturer in American history at the University of Leicester.

New Perspectives on the History of the South
Edited by John David Smith, Charles H. Stone Distinguished Professor of American History at the University of North Carolina at Charlotte

"In the Country of the Enemy": The Civil War Reports of a Massachusetts Corporal, edited by William C. Harris (1999)
The Wild East: A Biography of the Great Smoky Mountains, by Margaret L. Brown (2000; first paperback edition, 2001)
Crime, Sexual Violence, and Clemency: Florida's Pardon Board and Penal System in the Progressive Era, by Vivien M. L. Miller (2000)
The New South's New Frontier: A Social History of Economic Development in Southwestern North Carolina, by Stephen Wallace Taylor (2001)
Redefining the Color Line: Black Activism in Little Rock, Arkansas, 1940–1970, by John A. Kirk (2002)
The Southern Dream of a Caribbean Empire, 1854–1861, by Robert E. May (2002)
Forging a Common Bond: Labor and Environmental Activism during the BASF Lockout, by Timothy J. Minchin (2003)
Dixie's Daughters: The United Daughters of the Confederacy and the Preservation of Confederate Culture, by Karen L. Cox (2003)
The Other War of 1812: The Patriot War and the American Invasion of Spanish East Florida, by James G. Cusick (2003)
"Lives Full of Struggle and Triumph": Southern Women, Their Institutions, and Their Communities, edited by Bruce L. Clayton and John A. Salmond (2003)
German-Speaking Officers in the United States Colored Troops, 1863–1867, by Martin W. Öfele (2004)
Southern Struggles: The Southern Labor Movement and the Civil Rights Struggle, by John A. Salmond (2004)
Radio and the Struggle for Civil Rights in the South, by Brian Ward (2004; first paperback edition, 2006)
Luther P. Jackson and a Life for Civil Rights, by Michael Dennis (2004)
Southern Ladies, New Women: Race, Region, and Clubwomen in South Carolina, 1890–1930, by Joan Marie Johnson (2004)
Fighting Against the Odds: A Concise History of Southern Labor Since World War II, by Timothy J. Minchin (2004; first paperback edition, 2006)
"Don't Sleep With Stevens!": The J. P. Stevens Campaign and the Struggle to Organize the South, 1963–1980, by Timothy J. Minchin (2005)
"The Ticket to Freedom": The NAACP and the Struggle for Black Political Integration, by Manfred Berg (2005; first paperback edition, 2007)
"War Governor of the South": North Carolina's Zeb Vance in the Confederacy, by Joe A. Mobley (2005)
Planters' Progress: Modernizing Confederate Georgia, by Chad Morgan (2005)
The Officers of the CSS Shenandoah, by Angus Curry (2006)
The Rosenwald Schools of the American South, by Mary S. Hoffschwelle (2006)
Honor in Command: Lt. Freeman S. Bowley's Civil War Service in the 30th United States Colored Infantry, edited by Keith Wilson (2006)
A Black Congressman in the Age of Jim Crow: South Carolina's George Washington Murray, by John F. Marszalek (2006)
The Spirit and the Shotgun: Armed Resistance and the Struggle for Civil Rights, by Simon Wendt (2007; first paperback edition, 2010)
Making a New South: Race, Leadership, and Community after the Civil War, edited by Paul A. Cimbala and Barton C. Shaw (2007)

From Rights to Economics: The Ongoing Struggle for Black Equality in the U.S. South, by Timothy J. Minchin (2008)

Slavery on Trial: Race, Class, and Criminal Justice in Antebellum Richmond, Virginia, by James M. Campbell (2008; first paperback edition, 2010)

Welfare and Charity in the Antebellum South, by Timothy James Lockley (2008; first paperback edition, 2009)

T. Thomas Fortune the Afro-American Agitator: A Collection of Writings, 1880–1928, by Shawn Leigh Alexander (2008; first paperback edition, 2010)

Francis Butler Simkins: A Life, by James S. Humphreys (2008)

Black Manhood and Community Building in North Carolina, 1900–1930, by Angela Hornsby-Gutting (2009; first paperback edition, 2010)

Counterfeit Gentlemen: Manhood and Humor in the Old South, by John Mayfield (2009; first paperback edition 2010)

The Southern Mind under Union Rule: The Diary of James Rumley, Beaufort, North Carolina, 1862–1865, edited by Judkin Browning (2009)

The Quarters and the Fields: Slave Families in the Non-Cotton South, by Damian Alan Pargas (2010)

The Door of Hope: Republican Presidents and the First Southern Strategy, 1877-1933, by Edward O. Frantz (2011)

Painting Dixie Red: When, Where, Why, And How The South Became Republican, edited by Glenn Feldman (2011)

After Freedom Summer: How Race Realigned Mississippi Politics, 1965–1986, by Chris Danielson (2011)

Dreams and Nightmares: Martin Luther King Jr., Malcolm X, and the Struggle for Black Equality in America, by Britta W. Nelson (2012)

www.ingramcontent.com/pod-product-compliance
Lightning Source LLC
Chambersburg PA
CBHW032019230426
43671CB00005B/141